Managing
Team Centricity in
Modern Organizations

A volume in
Research in Human Resource Management
Dianna L. Stone and James H. Dulebohn, *Series Editors*

Research in Human Resource Management

Dianna L. Stone and James H. Dulebohn, *Series Editors*

Managing Team Centricity in Modern Organizations

edited by

Brian Murray
University of Dallas

James H. Dulebohn
Michigan State University

Dianna L. Stone
Universities of New Mexico, Albany, and Virginia Tech

INFORMATION AGE PUBLISHING, INC.
Charlotte, NC • www.infoagepub.com

Library of Congress Cataloging-in-Publication Data

A CIP record for this book is available from the Library of Congress
http://www.loc.gov

ISBN: 979-8-88730-024-5 (Paperback)
       979-8-88730-025-2 (Hardcover)
       979-8-88730-026-9 (E-Book)

Printed in the United States of America

CONTENTS

PART III

WORK FLEXIBILITY AND THE TEAM

PART IV

VIRTUAL TEAM ELECTRONIC COMMUNICATION AND DIVERSITY

CHAPTER 1

NEW DIRECTIONS FOR RESEARCH ON THE MANAGEMENT OF TEAMS

Brian Murray
University of Dallas

James H. Dulebohn
Michigan State University

Dianna L. Stone
Universities of New Mexico, Albany, and Virginia Tech

ABSTRACT

This volume of *Research in Human Resource Management* showcases nine papers that examine the future of team research and management through the lenses of systems thinking; machine learning and data science; drivers of team performance; the changing nature of flexible, remote, and virtual work and its impact on teams; and the implications for diverse members of virtual teams. This introduction to the volume provides both an orientation to the chapters and an assessment of the connections among them and to the

Managing Team Centricity in Modern Organizations, pages 1–13
Copyright © 2022 by Information Age Publishing
www.infoagepub.com
All rights of reproduction in any form reserved.

existing team literature. We conclude that the future of team research must incorporate a systems or network perspective, studies that model and test dynamic variables and relationships that evolve over time or across contexts, research conducted at the task level, and examinations of the evolving nature and outcomes of remote, flexible, and virtual work across a diverse workforce.

Teamwork is undoubtedly an important characteristic of the contemporary workplace that offers significant management challenges. In Deloitte's 2019 Global Human Capital Trends survey, 31% of respondents reported that *most* or *almost all* work was done in teams and 65% reported that some work was done by cross-functional teams even though the organization was a hierarchical, functional structure (Schwartz et al., 2019). In the same survey, 74% of respondents whose organizations conducted work at least partially in cross-functional teams reported that performance improved when they shifted to teams, with 35% of respondents indicating a significant performance improvement. Hand in hand with the performance improvements, however, have been important challenges for managing the team centric organization. Schwartz et al. (2019) reported that in the Deloitte survey "only 6 percent [of respondents] rated themselves very effective at managing cross-functional teams" (para. 5). Based on subsequent evidence, Deloitte research analysts predicted that an emerging trend for teams is the growth of self-managed teams that will challenge organizations to foster involvement in creating the design of the work, to build a climate of respect, fairness, and belonging, to incorporate team member engagement measures for team effectiveness, and to provide decision-making authority and autonomy (Hiipakka, 2021).

In addition to the typical challenges of managing teams, organizations have faced a more immediate challenge, with the impact of COVID-19, of managing them virtually. Virtual teams introduce issues regarding how to collaborate using technology, monitor team progress and performance, maintain relationship characteristics including trust and empowerment, and ensure team member well-being (Deloitte, 2020). The COVID-19 virtual shift also uncovered a concern for diversity and inclusion efforts in organizations. Immediate virtualization due to remote-work requirements led to confusion and loss of clarity for teams; issues of personal life disclosure for LBGTQIA+, women, and minority team members; access limitations; and demands arising from workspace and homelife characteristics (Dolan et al., 2020).

Just as team management has become a dominant concern in organizations, teams and work groups have grown into a topic of research commanding significant attention. Published research on teams and work groups extends back almost a hundred years and has concentrated on individuals both within and compared to teams, team characteristics and dynamics, team structures and systems, and team tasks and outcomes (Mathieu, Hollenbeck, et al., 2017, Mathieu, Wolfson, & Park, 2018). Additionally, contemporary research has focused on virtual teams (Dulebohn & Hoch, 2017), the impact of remote work (e.g., van der Lippe & Lippenyi, 2019), the methods of team research (Delice et al., 2019), and the dynamics of diversity and inclusion in work groups (Chung et al., 2020; Shore et al., 2011; Shore & Chung, 2021).

Looking to the future, prominent scholars have prioritized directions for team research based on gaps found in the literature as well as factors limiting the identification and pursuit of new directions. Mathieu and colleagues (Mathieu, Hollenbeck, et al., 2017; Mathieu, Wolfson, & Park, 2018; Mathieu et al., 2019) called for advancements in team research models and methodologies beyond the static input-process-output (IPO) model that is common in team research. They prioritized the incorporation of temporal issues and the development of network approaches. Mathieu and colleagues also presented an argument for greater attention to task characteristics, teams within multilevel dynamic systems, team composition and diversity, and team emergent states.

Dulebohn and Hoch (2017) organized research on virtual teams in the IPO framework. They presented existing and potential research streams that add information and communication technology, team member diversity, and team virtuality to the predominant variables in team studies. They also summarized a set of articles that offered conceptual development to advance virtual team research and with them prioritized research topics including communication in virtual teams, team leadership approaches and shared leadership, the interaction of culture and team virtuality, the interaction of core team dimensions and virtuality, and shared mental models within virtual teams.

Shore and colleagues (2011) reviewed diversity literature and developed a model of inclusion to guide research on work groups. They called for an examination of fairness, belongingness, and uniqueness as aspects of inclusion, inclusion climate in work groups, the theoretical development of mediating mechanisms linking inclusion to outcomes, and inclusion-driven outcomes such as creativity. Though their work has been in print for over a decade, the issues of fairness and belongingness continue to be important team topics among the emerging trends in team management (see previous reference to Hiipakka, 2021). Likewise, the contemporary issues in diversity research continue to include the need for research on the complexity of diversity, a broadening of the effects that are studied, greater emphasis and depth of study on mediating mechanisms, and the contextual generalizability of diversity models (Roberson, 2019).

The present volume of Research in Human Resource Management addresses the trends in team management and important research gaps in four areas. First, we present two chapters on the science of teams that consider reframing how we think about teams in a complex systems perspective and machine learning. Second, we introduce three chapters that examine how engagement, feedback, and situated expertise relate to team outcomes. Third, we provide two chapters that examine outcomes related to flexibility in work design for team members taking into account leadership and team member shared norms for availability. Fourth, we offer two chapters addressing virtual communication technology and diversity.

THE SCIENCE OF TEAMS

The IPO framework for conceptualizing and ordering relevant team characteristics and outcomes as well as the mediating and moderating variables that influence the relationships between inputs and outcomes has served team research extremely well. There is a well-established body of knowledge and evidence about teams, team leadership, and team member characteristics as well as their relationship to performance, team, and team member outcomes. It likely will continue to serve the field well as contextual factors and other variables are studied as moderators to the IPO paths that connect its components. However, Mathieu et al. (Mathieu, Hollenbeck, et al., 2017; Mathieu, Wolfson, & Park, 2018; Mathieu et al., 2019) highlighted the weaknesses of relying solely on an IPO perspective, and there is well-founded concern that an overreliance on it may limit future advancements in team research. In the present volume, Strauss and Grand (Chapter 2) and Rosopa (Chapter 3) tackle this issue by offering an alternate perspective for conceptualization and an analytic approach for inductive research, respectively, that promise to be paradigmatic shifts in how researchers look at team dynamics and the direction they take for modeling and analysis.

Strauss and Grand (Chapter 2) address the challenge posed by Mathieu et al. (Mathieu, Hollenbeck, et al., 2017; Mathieu, Wolfson, & Park, 2018; Mathieu et al., 2019) to move beyond the IPO framework for conceptualizing and studying team dynamics by introducing readers to systems concepts. They orient readers to important characteristics distinguishing open, dynamical, and agent-based systems. They also contrast systems thinking to IPO and multilevel theory to demonstrate how conceptualization of team dynamics differs and yields new insight to what is a variable, process, or mechanism. They demonstrate that IPO and multilevel theory focus on patterns of covariance. This focus yields an understanding of the strength and direction of relationships among variables on average between teams; however, the authors conclude that the IPO framework does not inform the underlying generative mechanisms for observed covariations. In contrast, they explain that systems thinking is grounded in the actors and their actions versus a statistical covariation, that its designation of variables as independent, dependent, or mediating, or at specific levels is more fluid and less specific, and that its processes are represented as mechanisms rather than variables. By their comparative exposition of the popular IPO framework to systems thinking, Strauss and Grand achieve their objective of raising systems awareness, demonstrating it as a conceptualizing framework, and pointing to new paths for team research.

Like Strauss and Grand, Rosopa (Chapter 3) challenges the prevailing framework and methods for conceptualizing and studying teams. He presents data science, and more specifically machine learning, as a basis for inductive research into team variables and dynamics. He frames his discussion in the complex nature of the quantity and sources of data about teams alongside the dynamic and sequential aspects of it. He proposes that commonly used statistical methods cannot adequately address these data characteristics. As a solution he proposes a machine learning approach. Rosopa orients the reader to data science and its inductive aspects in contrast to strictly deductive analytic approaches. He then presents the basic machine learning algorithms as supervised learning, unsupervised learning, and semi-supervised learning. He explains and demonstrates with examples the connections between supervised learning and neural networks and between unsupervised learning and principal components analysis. Through the examples he establishes the relevance and promise of machine learning for inductive research on teams and the examination of complex nonlinear dynamic patterns within team research data.

ENHANCING TEAM PERFORMANCE

The outcomes attributed to team characteristics and processes are many and varied including team-level variables such as productivity, efficiency, work quality, and creativity as well as member-level variables such as individual work performance, helping behaviors, absences, attitudes, and turnover intentions (Mathieu, Hollenbeck, et al., 2017). The potential drivers of these outcomes have been likewise numerous and included concerns for leadership styles, task design, team member characteristics, and collective team characteristics. Moving beyond the existing research, the emerging industry trends point to a need to better understand the design and behaviors of self-managed teams; the development of climates for respect, fairness, and belongingness; the role of engagement, and the provision of decision-making and autonomy in order to manage performance outcomes (see previous reference Hiipakka, 2021). In the present volume, authors explore and expand on these concerns: Dickey et al. (Chapter 4) focus on team engagement as the lynch pin connecting team performance management and team leader behaviors with team performance outcomes, Mockevičiūtė et al. (Chapter 5) direct attention to the driving role of feedback in affecting team performance, and Austin (Chapter 6) draws on transactive memory systems to demonstrate how awareness of available expertise and team member actions for engaging expertise within and across team boundaries influences team effectiveness.

Dickey et al. (Chapter 4) offer three important contributions to advancing team research by developing a model of team performance built on team engagement. First, drawing from prior research, they highlight the distinctive characteristics of team engagement (Costa et al., 2012, 2014a, 2014b; Costa et al., 2017; Sharma & Bhatnagar, 2017) and propose the connection to team performance (Rahmadani et al., 2020). Second, they integrate the work of Hackman (1987) and Aguinis (2019) to present a multiphase model of performance management that they relate to team engagement. Third, they explain the role of team leadership in the performance management and engagement linkage. Transcending the bounds of their individual chapter, Dickey and colleagues' (Chapter 4) dynamic, multistage, process model reinforces the need for systems thinking (Strauss & Grand, Chapter 2) when conceptualizing and planning future team research. They expose the complexity of the interaction of full-range leadership components with the several sequenced phases of performance management and the challenges of representing them as singular constructs.

Mockevičiūtė et al. (Chapter 5) continue the conversation of performance management by digging deeply into the topic of feedback and its effect on team performance. Just as we have indicated that remote work and virtualization have changed where, when, and how teams operate as well as how team members and leaders communicate and share information, the authors recognize that the changing nature of work provides contextual elements that either are not recognized or are emerging in contemporary team research. They conducted a systematic review of contextual influences on the feedback-performance relationship and recommended avenues for future research grounded in a multilevel and spillover theory perspective. From their review, they constructed a mediated model of the feedback-performance relationship including intra-team mechanisms such as team and individual characteristics and top management team potency. They also summarized the influence of other-team performance and organizational and environmental characteristics. They expanded their model with avenues for future research by mapping the potential influence of several inter-team characteristics such as feedback exchange, conflict, and trust as well as extra-team factors including societal influences.

Austin (Chapter 6) shares Mockevičiūtė et al.'s contention that a useful future path for team research lies in the exchange between team members and extra-team environments. Austin presents an inductive, qualitative study of transactive memory systems from which he derives a set of propositions about situated expertise and the engagement of extra-team expertise sources. Though the preponderance of team research about transactive memory systems, the identification of expertise, and the engagement of expertise is at the within-team level, Austin found that a higher impact of transactive memory system interventions existed when team members extended the principles of expertise identification and help-seeking to non-team members. Building on existing transactive memory theory, he laid out paths for future research to study team member awareness of the locations of extra-team expertise and the quality of extra-team expertise use. Of particular note is Austin's identification of the task level for analysis and its potential for informing how team boundaries are made more fluid to encourage greater extra-team expertise sharing. His call to direct attention to the task mirrors Mathieu, Hollenbeck, et al. (2017) more general call for attention to the task level for team research. Austin's presentation of transactive memory systems and his study's results are particularly relevant in today's emerging cross-functional team environment where team members are selected due to functional knowledge and reinforce the importance of considering networks and systems that Strauss and Grand (Chapter 2) emphasized.

WORK FLEXIBILITY AND THE TEAM

In contrast to the notion of the shared experiences of team members and homogeneity of work context among them, a growing phenomenon in contemporary workplaces is the customization of individuals' work into flexible work arrangements either through idiosyncratic deals (i-deals) or by job crafting. An i-deal is a negotiated agreement between an employee and supervisor that allows non-regular considerations for when, where, or how work is done in order to better fit work with the particular needs or wants of the employee. These agreements extend beyond general work policies and may or may not be available to other employees (Rousseau et al., 2006; Liao et al., 2016). Job elements that are commonly addressed by i-deals may include flexibility in workplace (flex-space) or time (flex-time), opportunities for professional development, workload reduction, job design, and financial incentives (Liao et al., 2016). Job crafting is similar to i-deals, except that the employee creates job differences without the express permission or input from the supervisor (Wrzesniewski & Dutton, 2001), and they are developed to improve the social aspects of the work and use of the employees' knowledge, skills, and abilities and to reduce stress (Hornung et al., 2014). Job crafting has been shown to relate to engagement and job performance (Lazauskaite-Zabielske & Ziedelis, 2021), and both job crafting and i-deals have been shown to positively relate to job performance, affective commitment, and intention to stay (Rofcanin et al., 2016).

The idea of job crafting has been translated to the team level. Team job crafting is a collaborative effort among team members to affect the resources, demands, and design of work to improve team processes and outcomes. It has been shown to relate positively to both engagement and team performance (Makikangas et al., 2016; Tims et al., 2013). As such, it is a promising area for team research to inform self-managed teams, autonomy, and decision-making. Especially in a virtually distanced environment between management and teams and in the face of idiosyncratic contextual factors across remote teams, between-team differences in job crafting may be particularly important for explaining team performance.

Two chapters in this volume directly address the impact of customized work arrangements. Baumgärtner and Hartner-Tiefenthaler (Chapter 7) tackle the autonomy paradox at the intersection of individual team member work flexibility and shared expectations among team members for work availability. Liao (Chapter 8) tests the impact of team member i-deals on team performance with specific reference to the role of the servant leader supervising the team.

Baumgärtner and Hartner-Tiefenthaler (Chapter 7) set the stage for understanding flexible work arrangements in a team context by recognizing the inevitability and importance of time and place flexibility in today's work environment and more specifically in answer to COVID-19 work restrictions. However, they explain that uncoordinated exercise of flexibility among team members leads to uncertainty about availability for teamwork and interaction which subsequently drives the emergence of collective norms about availability. The authors posit that those norms err toward constant availability, which has negative implications for disengagement, respite, and recovery from work. They propose interaction scripts to define commonly held expectations about availability, while recognizing implications for justice perceptions and the creation of shared mental models. They contribute to the practice of team management and shaping availability norms by describing a process of clarifying expectations, defining a reflexivity process, and implementing scripts.

On the surface, Liao (Chapter 8) takes a decidedly different perspective on customized work arrangements. In general, his arguments and data analysis suggest that more is better. He hypothesizes and demonstrates that a higher overall level of i-deals within a team is related to team potency and performance. However, his arguments and findings are presented within the context of servant leadership behaviors exhibited by the supervisor. He explains the complementarity of the servant leadership style for enacting a systematic i-deals program among team members by identifying core characteristics of the servant leader. These characteristics include attentiveness to the needs, desires, and goals of the individual, a desire to benefit stakeholders including employees, and an intention to foster the overall effectiveness of the team while minimizing intra-team conflicts among members.

Arguably, the servant leader is the complement to the collaborative interaction script development and reflexivity processes proposed by Baumgärtner and Hartner-Tiefenthaler (Chapter 7). The former is appropriate to i-deal circumstances because the supervisor is a leading player in each negotiation and has the ability to coordinate across all customized arrangements; alternately, the latter works for job crafting situations because they are driven by the employees themselves without direction from a single leader. As a pair, these two chapters inform future team research efforts by bringing clarity to why and how the competing notions of i-deals and job crafting might work differently but achieve similar outcomes depending on context.

VIRTUAL TEAM ELECTRONIC COMMUNICATION AND DIVERSITY

The growth in geographically distributed team members as well as the move to remote and flexible work arrangements due to COVID-19 has expanded the role of electronic communication as the primary collaborating mechanism for many teams. Team researchers have established that virtual electronic communication can be a component of effective team commitment, cohesion, decision and action quality, and innovation (Gressgård, 2011; Maznevski & Chudoba, 2000). However, the use of electronic communication for one common activity, virtual meetings, raises concerns for its impact on interaction and outcomes based on gender (Dhawan et al., 2021).

In the present volume, we present two chapters that address the emerging issue of electronic communication and its implications for members of diverse groups. Canedo et al. (Chapter 9) present the use and type of electronic communication technology as a moderator of the link between diversity (i.e., variation in demographic characteristics of group members) and factors influenced by diversity (e.g., prejudice, stereotyping, status differences). This moderated relationship is positioned as a driver of virtual team processes (e.g., communication, cooperation, conflict) and ultimately team outcomes (e.g., performance, creative, team member satisfaction). Bommer and Schmidtke (Chapter 10) address the question of differences in communication behaviors in face-to-face versus virtual meeting formats as well as provide empirical evidence regarding whether there is a positive or negative behavioral difference for females.

Linking diversity to work outcomes is challenging because conceptual development and empirical evidence point to both positive and negative hypotheses as well as supporting, refuting, and nonsignificant statistical results (Hass, 2010; Roberson, 2019). Canedo, Stone, and Lukaszewski

(Chapter 9) adopt the perspective that diversity introduces challenges to team communication and coordination that are heightened in the virtual context. They review the research on diversity in virtual teams and derive an interaction model of electronic communication use in virtual teams with diversity. From their conceptual development, they offer propositions regarding the favorability of outcomes due to text-based communication technology relative to visual and auditory technology, the intervening effects on stereotyping, positive interpersonal relations, perceived status differences, diverse members' participation in virtual activities, and cross-cultural communication and conflict, and the resulting outcomes for intra-team cooperation, cohesion, conflict resolution, and communication effectiveness. Building on their review of existing research and model development, the authors offer a four-prong strategy for mitigating negative effects of virtuality for diverse teams including cross-cultural and diversity training, technology training, team-based reward systems, and team building efforts.

Bommer and Schmidtke (Chapter 10) also recognize the lack of clarity in the available evidence regarding diversity impacts on work outcomes, especially related to issues of virtual communication. They present an empirical assessment of whether the move to videoconferencing for virtual teams "levels the playing field" or heightens the problems for female team members. They conducted an assessment center comparative study of women versus men in face-to-face versus virtual meeting contexts. They measured agentic and communal behaviors and participant activity level to test for gender and modality differences.

Bommer and Schmidtke's results identified behavioral differences due to modality, but reinforced the generalizability of prior findings on gender differences in meetings. Their data provided evidence to support that videoconferencing was associated with fewer communication activities than face-to-face meetings including both fewer agentic and communal behaviors and men were associated with a greater number of participation behaviors than women including both agentic and communal behaviors. Their data did not provide evidence, however, that the videoconferencing versus face-to-face modality impacted the behaviors of men differently than women. The lack of a significant interaction effect pointed toward an inconclusive or non-effect for gender differences in the move from in-person to virtual teams relative to meeting technology. The authors proposed several avenues for future research: (a) exploration of the relationship between member behaviors and team and individual outcomes; (b) contextual determinants of "appropriate" behaviors relative to virtual versus in-person team meetings; (c) extension of the present research to include race, ethnicity, and social status; (d) the impact of technical specifications on videoconferencing effects, such as lighting, camera angle, and video quality; (e) exploration of team composition homogeneity, heterogeneity, and forms of heterogeneity; and (f) extension of past research on face-to-face meetings to the virtual context to explore the dynamic nature of effects from initial meetings for new teams to on-going meetings for mature teams.

WHERE DO WE GO FROM HERE?

The authors and their work presented in this volume advance contemporary thinking on the management of teams, provide evidence to address some existing questions, and offer avenues for future research. Perhaps most instructive are the common threads across the chapters that tie back to existing research and studies in the team literature. From these commonalities, we suggest that the future of team research needs to prioritize (a) research from a systems or network perspective; (b) research that models and tests dynamic variables and relationships that evolve over time or across contexts; (c) research focused on the task level; and (d) research that examines the evolving nature and outcomes of remote, flexible, and virtual work for a diverse workforce.

REFERENCES

Aguinis, H. (2019). *Performance management* (4th ed.). Chicago Business Press.

Chung, B. G., Ehrhart, K. H., Shore, L. M., Randel, A. E., Dean, M. A., & Kedharnath, U. (2020). Work group inclusion: Test of a scale and model. *Group & Organization Management, 45*(1), 75–102. https://doi.org/10.1177/1059601119839858

Costa, P. L., Passos, A. M., & Bakker, A. B. (2012). *Teamwork engagement: Considering team dynamics for engagement* (Working Papers Series 2 12-06). ISCTE-IUL, Business Research Unit (BRU-IUL).

Costa, P. L., Passos, A. M., & Bakker, A. B. (2014a). Teamwork engagement: A model of emergence. *Journal of Occupational & Organizational Psychology, 87*(2), 414–436. https://doi.org/10.1111/joop.12057

Costa, P. L., Passos, A. M., & Bakker, A. B. (2014b). Empirical validation of the teamwork engagement construct. *Journal of Personnel Psychology, 13*(1), 34–45. https://doi.org/10.1027/1866-5888/a000102

Costa, P. L., Passos, A. M., Bakker, A. B., Romana, R., & Ferrão, C. (2017). Interactions in engaged work teams: A qualitative study. *Team Performance Management: An International Journal, 23*(5/6), 206–226. https://doi.org/10.1108/TPM-12-2016-0054

Delice, F., Rousseau, M., & Feitosa, J. (2019). Advancing teams research: What, when, and how to measure team dynamics over time. *Frontiers in Psychology, 10*, 1324. https://doi.org/10.3389/fpsyg.2019.01324

Deloitte. (2020, March). Leading virtual teams. *Human Capital.* https://www2.deloitte.com/content/dam/Deloitte/global/Documents/About-Deloitte/gx-leading-virtual-teams-guide-march-2020.pdf

Dhawan, N., Carnes, M., Byars-Winston, A., & Duma, N. (2021). Videoconferencing etiquette: Promoting gender equity during virtual meetings. *Journal of Women's Health, 30*(4), 460–465. https://doi.org/10.1089/jwh.2020.8881

Dolan, K., Hunt, V., Prince, S., & Sancier-Sultan, S. (2020, May 19). Diversity still matters. *McKinsey Quarterly.* https://www.mckinsey.com/featured-insights/ diversity-and-inclusion/diversity-still-matters

Dulebohn, J. H. & Hoch, J. E. (2017). Virtual teams in organizations. *Human Resource Management Review, 27,* 569–574. http://dx.doi.org/10.1016/j.hrmr.2016 .12.004

Gressgård, L. J. (2011). Virtual team collaboration and innovation in organizations. *Team Performance Management, 17*(1/2), 102–119. https://doi.org/10.1108/ 13527591111114738

Haas, H. (2010). How can we explain mixed effects of diversity on team performance? A review with emphasis on context. *Equality, Diversity and Inclusion: An International Journal, 29*(5), 458–490. https://doi.org/10.1108/02610151011052771

Hackman, J. (1987). The design of work teams. In J. L. Lorsch (Ed.), *Handbook of organizational behavior* (pp. 315–342). Prentice Hall.

Hiipakka, J. (2021, January 21). *Predictions 2021: Teams.* Deloitte. https://www2 .deloitte.com/us/en/blog/human-capital-blog/2021/predictions-teams .html

Hornung, S., Rousseau, D. M., Weigl, M., Muller, A., & Glaser, J. (2014). Redesigning work through idiosyncratic deals. *European Journal of Work and Organizational Psychology, 23*(4), 608–626. https://doi.org/10.1080/1359432X.2012.740171

Lazauskaite-Zabielske, J., & Ziedelis, A. (2021). Who benefits from time-spatial job crafting? The role of boundary characteristics in the relationship between time-spatial job crafting, engagement, and performance. *Baltic Journal of Management, 16*(1), 1–19. https://doi.org/10.1108/BJM-07-2020-0236

Liao, C., Wayne, S. J., & Rousseau, D. M. (2016). Idiosyncratic deals in contemporary organizations: A qualitative and meta-analytic review. *Journal of Organizational Behavior, 37,* S9–S29. https://doi.org/10.1002/job.1959

Makikangas, A., Aunola, K., Seppala, P., & Hakanen, J. (2016). Work engagement-team performance relationship: Shared job crafting as a moderator. *Journal of Occupational and Organizational Psychology, 89,* 772–790. https://doi .org/10.1111/joop.12154

Mathieu, J. E., Gallagher, P. T., Domingo, M. A., & Klock, E. A. (2019). Embracing complexity: Reviewing the past decade of team effectiveness research. *Annual Review of Organizational Psychology and Organizational Behavior, 6,* 17–46. https://doi.org/10.1146/annurev-orgpsych-012218-015106

Mathieu, J. E., Hollenbeck, J. R., van Knippenberg, D., & Ilgen, D. R. (2017). A century of work teams in the Journal of Applied Psychology. *Journal of Applied Psychology, 102*(3), 452–467. https://doi.org/10.1037/apl0000128.supp

Mathieu, J. E., Wolfson, M. A., & Park, S. (2018). The evolution of work team research since Hawthorne. *American Psychologist, 73*(4), 308–321. https://doi .org/10.1037/amp0000255.supp

Maznevski, M. L., & Chudoba, K. M. (2000). Bridging space over time: Global virtual team dynamics and effectiveness. *Organization Science, 11*(5), 473–492. https://doi.org/10.1287/orsc.11.5.473.15200

Rahmadani, V. G., Schaufeli, W. B., Stouten, J., Zhang, Z., & Zulkarain, Z. (2020). Engaging leadership and its implication for work engagement and job outcomes at the individual and team level: A multi-level longitudinal study. *International Journal of Environmental Research and Public Health, 17,* 776–797. https://doi.org/10.3390/ijerph17030776

Roberson, Q. M. (2019). Diversity in the workplace: A review, synthesis, and future research agenda. *Annual Review of Organizational Psychology and Organizational Behavior, 6,* 69–88. https://doi.org/10.1146/annurev-orgpsych-012218-015243

Rofcanin, Y., Berber, A., Koch, S., & Sevinc, L. (2016). Job crafting and i-deals: A study testing the nomological network of proactive behaviors. *The International Journal of Human Resource Management, 27*(22), 2695–2726. https://doi .org/10.1080-09585192.2015.1091370

Rousseau, D. M., Ho, V. T., & Greenberg, J. (2006). I-deals: Idiosyncratic terms in employment relationships. *Academy of Management Review, 31*(4), 977–994. https://www.jstor.org/stable/20159261

Schwartz, J., Roy, I., Hauptmann, M., & Van Durme, Y. (2019). Organizational performance: It's a team sport. 2019 Global Human Capital Trends. *Deloitte Insights.* https://www2.deloitte.com/us/en/insights/focus/human-capital-trends/2019/team-based-organization.html

Sharma, A., & Bhatnagar, J. (2017). Emergence of team engagement under time pressure: Role of team leader and team climate. *Team Performance Management, 23*(3), 171–185. https://doi.org/10.1108/TPM-06-2016-0031

Shore, L. M., & Chung, B. G. (2021). Inclusive leadership: How leaders sustain or discourage work group inclusion. *Group & Organization Management, 1* (online access). https://doi.org/10.1177/1059601121999580

Shore, L. M., Randel, A. E., Chung, B. G., Dean, M. A., Holcombe Ehrhart, K., & Singh, G. (2011). Inclusion and diversity in work groups: A review and model for future research. *Journal of Management, 37*(4), 1262–1289. https://doi.org/10.1177/0149206310385943

Tims, M., Bakker, A. B., & Rhenen, W. V. (2013). Job crafting at the team and individual level: Implications for work engagement and performance. *Group & Organization Management, 38*(4), 427–454. https://doi.org/10.1177/10596011 13492421

van der Lipper, T. & Lippenyi, Z. (2019). Co-workers working from home and individual and team performance. New Technology, *Work and Employment, 35*(1), 60–79. https://doi.org/10.1111/ntwe.12153

Wrzesniewski, A., & Dutton, J. E. (2001). Crafting a job: Revisioning employees as active crafters of their work. *Academy of Management Review, 26*(2), 179–201. https://doi.org/10.2307/259118

.

PART I

THE SCIENCE OF TEAMS

CHAPTER 2

APPLYING SYSTEMS SCIENCE TO ADVANCE RESEARCH ON TEAM PHENOMENA

Joshua A. Strauss
University of Maryland

James A. Grand
University of Maryland

ABSTRACT

The recognition of teams as complex dynamic systems was a hallmark and among the earliest considerations of research on team functioning. However, the popularization of conceptual heuristics such as the input-process-outcome (IPO) framework and the accessibility of methodological, analytical, and meta-theoretical principles from multilevel theory (MLT) have disconnected contemporary theory and empirical research from this foundational perspective. Thus, the primary motivation for the present paper is to facilitate and stimulate future research on team phenomena that embraces systems thinking. To do so, we describe key concepts, terminology, and ideas from specific branches of the systems sciences—namely open systems theory, dynamical systems, and agent-based systems—that have direct relevance for

Managing Team Centricity in Modern Organizations, pages 17–51
Copyright © 2022 by Information Age Publishing
www.infoagepub.com
17

researching team phenomena as complex systems. Additionally, a comparison between two example models of team performance that are rooted in an IPO + MLT versus a systems-oriented perspective is offered to highlight the difference in foci, applications, and inferences these approaches offer. The paper concludes with a summary of key advantages as well as potential obstacles for reintroducing systems thinking back into team science.

As the nature of work has continued progressing towards more complex tasks and operational environments, teams have increasingly become the primary unit of work for organizations (Bersin et al., 2017; Mathieu et al., 2019). Teams are also relied upon to carry out many of society's most vital functions, such as performing medical procedures, conducting humanitarian operations, and advancing scientific breakthroughs (Kozlowksi & Ilgen, 2006). Understanding how to support, maintain, and facilitate high performing teams thus represents an area of critical importance. In recognition of this significance, the past 40 years of organizational science has witnessed an exponential increase in the amount of published research on work-team functioning (Mathieu et al., 2017).

In taking stock of the progress that has been made in our understanding of teams and team performance over this time span, it is informative to consider how the organizational sciences have tended to conceptualize teams and their functioning. For example, several taxonomies for classifying team properties have been proposed, such as characteristics of groups versus teams (e.g., membership, boundary permeability, entitativity; Forsyth, 2013), the types of actions teams engage in to facilitate taskwork (e.g., transition, action, and interpersonal processes; Marks et al., 2001), and differences in the context and nature of work performed by teams (e.g., action teams, decision-making teams; McGrath, 1984; Sundstrom et al., 1990). Beyond these classification schemes though, one of the earliest and foundational characterizations of teams is the recognition that they operate as *complex dynamic systems* (Allport, 1924; Lewin, 1943; Parsons, 1937; Sherif et al., 1955). That is, teams are collections of unique yet interdependent individuals who engage in behaviors and interactions with one another in a commonly experienced environment to satisfy personal goals and collectively recognized demands. Through these exchanges, unique social structures (e.g., norms, roles, cultures), affective and cognitive perceptions (e.g., trust, knowledge, cohesion), and patterns of behavior can manifest that both describe and shape how teams and their members function and perform (Arrow et al., 2000; Cronin et al., 2011; Katz & Kahn, 1978; Kozlowski & Klein, 2000; McGrath, 1991; Weick, 1979).

Given the historical precedent and widely acknowledged view of teams as complex systems, it is surprising that so little conceptual and empirical work has accumulated on teams in the social and organizational sciences in line with this foundational perspective. A recurrent theme in contemporary reviews of the literature is the modal treatment of theories, methods, and empirics directed towards teams as static, holistic, and often anthropomorphized entities (e.g., teams "possess" personality, cognitive ability, trust, etc.; Crawford & LePine, 2013; Cronin et al., 2011; Humphrey & Aime, 2014; Kozlowski et al., 2013; Mathieu et al., 2019; Waller et al., 2016). In other words, teams have most commonly been described in ways that reify them as aggregated, homogenized, and undifferentiated "wholes" rather than rich, interactive, and dynamic systems.

A consequence of viewing "teams as wholes" versus "teams as systems" is that the former tends to promote theory, measurement, and analytic techniques that focus almost exclusively on the extent to which attributes, perceptions, behaviors, and so forth are consensually shared among team members and the extent to which that shared content correlates with other similarly formulated team-level variables at the population level (e.g., teams with higher shared perceptions of team cohesion exhibit stronger correlations with team performance on average; Dansereau et al., 1999; Klein et al., 1994; Kozlowski et al., 2013). Besides failing to capture the inherent dynamics of the team system, this focus generally neglects examinations of *how*, *why*, and *what* teams do to function effectively that could provide actionable guidance for facilitating team performance (McGrath & Tschan, 2007). We do not wish to imply that the past 4 decades of research on teams has been unfruitful or unproductive. On the contrary, the field has identified many useful constructs and accumulated valuable knowledge about teams, and we suspect that team science will continue to observe incremental improvements in understanding under the current paradigm (e.g., Mathieu et al., 2017; Waller et al., 2016). However, we posit that there is considerable potential for advancing team science by more purposefully incorporating and embracing teams as complex systems.

The primary goal of this paper is thus to provide a primer on systems thinking for the teams researcher and its utility for advancing theory and research. We first describe several key concepts and terminology from the broader domain of systems science and their relevance for representing team phenomena. Next, we highlight critical differences in the foci, applications, and inferences that can be advanced from adopting a systems approach to team functioning relative to those afforded by contemporary approaches by contrasting two example models of team performance from both perspectives. We then conclude with a summary of the strengths and likely challenges of incorporating the systems-based approach for conceptualizing and researching team phenomena.

CURRENT PARADIGM FOR STUDYING TEAMS
IN THE ORGANIZATIONAL SCIENCES

Before elaborating on a systems-oriented perspective to teams research, it is useful to describe the prevailing paradigm for studying teams in the social and organizational sciences. Contemporary theory and research have arguably been most significantly shaped by two seminal perspectives: (a) the input-process-outcome (IPO) framework of team functioning (McGrath, 1964) and its derivatives (e.g., the input-mediator-outcome-input (IMOI) framework; e.g., Ilgen et al., 2005; Mathieu et al., 2008) and (b) the "meta-theoretical" principles of multilevel theory (MLT; e.g., Kozlowski & Klein, 2000).

The IPO framework has provided a useful and widely adopted heuristic for discussing factors related to team effectiveness. *Inputs* in the IPO framework refer to the attributes of members (e.g., knowledge, skills, abilities, dispositions), the team (e.g., norms, roles), and the organization/environment (e.g., resources, time demands) that constitute a team's operational conditions. *Processes* are generally described as team members' actions that facilitate task accomplishment and produce characteristic patterns of social interaction and structure (e.g., trust, climates, cohesion). Lastly, *outcomes* are the cumulative results of teams' efforts and most commonly refer to performance-related outputs and affective/perceptual reactions (e.g., satisfaction, commitment). Although the IPO framework was never intended to reflect a theory or model of team functioning (McGrath, 1984), the causal chain it implies—in which a team's inputs impact its processes which impact its outcomes—has shaped how researchers have described, studied, analyzed, and drawn inferences about teams for over half a century.

In contrast to the IPO framework's specific focus on team functioning, MLT represents a broad collection of philosophies and methodological recommendations for considering phenomena involving collective entities (e.g., teams, multi-team systems, organizations). A fundamental tenet of MLT is that an organizational system can be characterized as a hierarchy of nested levels in which lower-level units (e.g., individuals) reside within higher-level units (e.g., teams). Two important consequents of this premise have strongly impacted the study of teams in the organizational sciences. First, substantively meaningful constructs can be conceptualized and operationalized at different levels of analysis (e.g., commitment represented as either/both an individual-level construct and a team-level construct). This proposition has inspired multiple decades of work devoted to developing conceptual frameworks, definitions, measurement approaches, and statistical indicators that capture constructs at different levels of analysis (e.g., Chan, 1998; Krasikova & LeBreton, 2019). Second, constructs residing at different levels of analysis can influence each other. This proposition has encouraged the development of elaborate conceptual models spanning multiple organizational levels and which attempt to capture how factors at the same and different levels of analysis relate to one another (e.g., individual-level attitudes and team-level cohesion simultaneously influence individual-level commitment). Efforts to test predictions from these conceptual models have also spurred the development of improved statistical models suitable for handling nested data structures (e.g., random coefficient modeling, Gonzalez-Roma & Hernandez, 2017; multilevel structural equations modeling, Preacher et al., 2010). In short, MLT provided organizational scientists with a valuable paradigm and readily understood standards for presenting theory, designing research, and analyzing data relevant to teams and their functioning.

In conjunction, the IPO framework and principles derived from MLT have engendered an approach to describing and modeling teams in a manner consistent with what Macy and Willer (2002) describe as "factor thinking." In factor thinking, efforts to explain and develop an understanding of team phenomena are pursued through the identification of *consistent covariation* between two (or more) variables (Bechtel & Richardson, 1993; Smith & Conrey, 2007). Thus, a factor-thinking researcher who seeks to understand team performance would pursue this goal by identifying potential predictor variables (i.e., inputs such as team cognitive ability or team cohesion, or processes such as communication or coordination), quantifying those variables at the team level (e.g., using statistical indices to determine whether members' ability scores and ratings of cohesion can be aggregated, creating a score for a team's overall communication quality), and then examining whether those sets of factors reliably and regularly covary with team performance. Both the IPO framework—with its emphasis on classifying variables relevant to team functioning as inputs, processes, or outcomes and establishing the intervening mediating chain—and MLT—with its emphasis on defining aggregate constructs and exploring within- and cross-level relationships—readily equip the factor-thinking teams researcher with an accessible and potent toolkit for developing conceptual models and conducting empirical research.

Although factor thinking affords several strengths for describing and studying teams, an "actor thinking" approach represents an alternative perspective less commonly embraced by the organizational sciences but which is well suited for representing teams as complex systems (Macy & Willer, 2002). In actor thinking, efforts to explain and develop understanding of phenomena are pursued through the identification of *generative mechanisms* that characterize how one (or more) ongoing processes unfold and lead to recognizable patterns (Bechtel & Richardson, 1993; Smith & Conrey, 2007). Thus, an actor-thinking researcher who seeks to understand team performance might pursue this goal by examining how, when, and why individual members in a team engage in different activities (e.g., individuals possess multiple goals which they seek to accomplish), influence one another (e.g., task demands and individuals' unique goal pursuits create opportunities for interaction over time), and form relationships that lead to specific patterns/outcomes relevant to team performance (e.g., team members self-organize into smaller interconnected subgroups to accomplish taskwork). Through explicating and exploring these mechanisms and how they play out over time, the actor-thinking researcher seeks to describe how team performance emerges from the things that members *do* and how changes to those processes influence team outcomes, experiences, and trajectories under specific circumstances (Kozlowski et al., 2013). Actor thinking is thus directly aligned with the thesis of teams as complex dynamic systems in which collective phenomena (i.e., team performance, cohesion, conflict, trust, etc.) are conceived as continually unfolding consequences of the interactions within and between elements of a system (i.e., individuals and their actions).

We submit that factor thinking is the de facto and modal paradigm through which teams are considered in the contemporary organizational sciences. This perspective has been bolstered by decades of conceptual, methodological, and statistical work that have ingrained factor thinking into the cultural milieu of teams research. To reiterate, factor thinking can and does play a valuable role in summarizing basic predictions and aggregate descriptions of teams and their performance; it need not be completely abandoned. However, we believe that advancing the state of team science on topics such as team performance will require efforts to embrace and explicitly study teams in a manner more consistent with actor thinking. One of the challenges in shifting the teams research paradigm from factor to actor thinking is that many of the concepts, methods, and techniques of the latter are unfamiliar and rooted in the diffuse and disjointed domain of systems science (e.g., Epstein, 1999; Gorman et al., 2017; von Bertalanffy, 1972). In the following sections, we thus direct attention to key concepts from these areas that we believe are valuable for teams researchers interested in adopting a more actor- and systems-oriented view of team functioning.

SYSTEMS CONCEPTS FOR THE TEAM SCIENTIST

A *system* can most generally be described as a collection of independent yet interconnected and interacting *elements* (von Bertalanffy, 1972). Like teams, systems are defined with respect to their boundaries that may vary across space (e.g., physical location of members, location of team members in a workflow network), time (e.g., changes in membership or responsibilities), and purpose (e.g., shifts in team and member goals). Systems are also commonly characterized as being embedded within an *environment* whose conditions (e.g., resources, task demands, policies) can influence and be influenced by the actions/outputs of the system and its elements. Given the breadth of applications and the interdisciplinary nature of systems science in general, several different philosophies, models, and methodological conventions exist for discussing and studying systems (social or otherwise). Although these varying perspectives share the common goal of characterizing systems as defined previously, they often draw attention to and emphasize different aspects of system functioning in their interpretations and explanations. For purposes of the present discussion, we limit our focus to three branches of systems that are particularly relevant for advancing more systems-oriented treatments of team phenomena—open systems, dynamical systems, and agent-based systems.

Open Systems

The consideration of teams and organizations as *open systems* is among the earliest and most widely recognized systems perspectives in the social and organizational sciences (e.g., Katz & Kahn, 1978; Kozlowski & Klein, 2000; Mathieu et al., 2008; Parsons, 1937; von Bertalanffy, 1972). An open system is one in which material and energy can enter and leave through exchanges between the system and its environment (von Bertalanffy, 1950). For example, teams use available equipment and information, (i.e., materials) in conjunction with the capabilities of their members to make products, services, and decisions that are subsequently distributed both within and outside the team to secure new resources. Further, teams transform these materials by continually drawing from and maintaining the affective/motivational, cognitive, and behavioral efforts of members (i.e., energy). Open systems are commonly contrasted against *closed systems* in which there is no net change in material or energy with the surrounding environment. By way of metaphor, an insulated and vacuum-sealed water bottle is a closed system as it is designed to keep its contents at the same level and temperature by preventing energy (e.g., heat) and material (e.g., water) from escaping or entering. In contrast, a cup with no lid is an open system as it is completely exposed to the environment and its contents can be influenced by the surroundings (e.g., water molecules can evaporate into the air, new substances can fall into the cup, heat is exchanged between the cup's contents and the surrounding air/surfaces). In this sense, a closed system is construed as completely isolated from its environment, whereas an open system is separate from, yet in constant exchange with, its environment.

In nature—and social systems in particular—there are few perfectly closed systems. Consequently, the significance of recognizing and treating teams as open systems is important for at least two reasons. First, the open systems view of teams emphasizes the critical importance of integrating a team's environment into explanatory accounts of team functioning. Team's environments can be conceptualized in numerous ways and according to several facets (e.g., Meyer et al., 2019; Ostroff, 2019), including the physical environment, the task environment, and the sociocultural environment. Each of these embedding contexts reflects unique environmental facets with which teams and their members exchange material and energy. Environments also contain resources and demands that can facilitate or constrain (respectively) team functioning by placing differential value on certain member attributes, actions, and their distribution within a team (Guzzo & Shea, 1992; Mathieu et al., 2008). For example, the presence of stormy weather versus clear skies affects the criticality of attention, alertness, and communication among members in an air traffic control team to effectively carry out its tasks.

Second, an implied condition of all open systems is that they are in "perpetual motion"; that is, they engage in near continuous exchanges of material and energy with their environment. Notably, this is true even in situations where an open system is said to be "at rest" or equilibrium. Consider again the example of the sealed bottle versus the open cup. It is possible for both systems to achieve an equilibrium temperature wherein the heat of their contents does not change. However, the way in which these equilibria are reached and how they react to subsequent exchanges differs. In the closed system of the sealed bottle, an equilibrium temperature is attained once the heat contained in the air and liquid molecules trapped in the container has been equally distributed. Furthermore, this temperature will remain constant once reached unless new material/energy is added or removed from this system, at which point a qualitatively new equilibrium point should emerge (e.g., adding hot water to the bottle will raise the internal temperature of the contents to a new stable level). In contrast, the constant exchange between the open cup and its surrounding environment means that one would need to near *continuously* heat the contents of the cup to maintain its temperature at a given level. An open system can only maintain an equilibrium by continuing to import new material or energy from the environment. One can thus think of teams and their members as needing to continually generate effort—which necessitates a steady supply of support in the form of materials (equipment, information, etc.) and energy (motivational sources, capabilities, etc.)—to maintain a steady level of functioning (Katz & Kahn, 1978; von Bertalanffy, 1972).

An open system that has achieved this degree of homeostasis (i.e., rate of material/energy entering equals the rate at which material/energy is leaving) is said to be in a *stable or steady state* (von Bertalanffy, 1950). An important takeaway from the recognition of steady states in an open system is that, unlike in closed systems, it can be difficult to infer whether changes to the material/energy of an open system produce a demonstrable change if only the system's outcomes are observed. For example, adding heat to the open cup may not raise the internal temperature of its contents if the rate at which heat dissipates from the cup also simultaneously increases. However, such changes should be evident in *how* the system is operating over time. Extending this insight to teams, changing the resources, capabilities, efforts, composition, and so forth of a team may or may not influence its observable performance if the interactions, roles, behaviors, exchanges, and so forth carried out by members adapt accordingly. Such *equifinality* (i.e., potential for any single state/outcome in a system to be achieved through different initial conditions and different processes) is common in open systems and yet another reason why focusing on how and what teams do (i.e., actor thinking) is critical for understanding team phenomena.

Dynamical Systems

In many respects, dynamical systems theory attempts to provide an overarching methodology, set of tools, and analytical frameworks for representing the behavior characterized by open systems theory (cf. Thelen & Smith, 1994). Although some in the organizational sciences have equated the application of dynamical systems theory to teams with analyzing the trajectory of team-level constructs over time (e.g., autoregressive/dual change score models of team cohesion; Cronin et al., 2011; Matusik et al., 2019), the foundations of dynamical systems theory are broader and encompass efforts to capture *global* system features/patterns and their implications for understanding *local* occurrences. In the context of dynamical systems theory, local and global refer to whether the primary explanatory lens for a phenomenon is oriented towards a system's elements or the system itself, respectively (Gorman et al., 2017). For example, a local account for team cognition might focus on the extent to which similarity and overlap among the content of individual members' knowledge exists and the individual-level processes involved in producing convergence of those outcomes (e.g., how individuals' attention, memory, and information interpretation processes operate; Dionne et al., 2010; Grand et al., 2016). In contrast, a global account of team cognition might focus on identifying sequences of behavior that occur while teams interact and the extent to which those sequences represent generalizable, stable, and predictable patterns indicative of how teams learn (e.g., identifying and categorizing sequences of communication as indicative of different team learning functions; Cooke et al., 2013; Gorman, et al., 2009; Kennedy & McComb, 2014). This latter example is consistent with the dynamical systems approach to understanding team behavior as it seeks to describe and quantify a more "macro" system-level pattern of behavior rather than elaborate the more "micro" actions/processes carried out by specific individuals within that system.

A common technique for representing and summarizing the sorts of change dynamics represented in the dynamical systems perspective is through feedback loops (or multiple interlocking feedback loops). A *feedback loop* describes a recursive relationship among system variables in which it is possible for a variable to influence itself over time either directly or indirectly through its effect on other intervening variables (Sterman, 2000). A notable implication of representing a system's dynamics through feedback loops is that distinctions between inputs and outputs become blurred. The circular influence structure inherent in a feedback loop means that any factor, process, or event involved in the cycle can be conceptualized as both an input and an output depending on when it is considered in the sequence of events (Cronin et al., 2011).

For example, Mathieu et al. (2015) describe an empirical study in which they examined the reciprocal relationship between team cohesion and team performance over time. In their data, team cohesion served as an input to performance at time t, but an output impacted by team performance at time $t+1$. The authors observed that increases in team cohesion were associated with increases in team performance, which were subsequently related to increases in team cohesion. This form of recursion exemplifies a *positive or self-reinforcing feedback loop* in which a reciprocal positive relationship exists between two variables in a system (e.g., higher cohesion at time $t \rightarrow$ higher performance at time $t+1$; higher performance at time $t+1 \rightarrow$ higher cohesion at time $t+2$). Positive feedback loops have the potential to compound over time and thus produce explosive patterns of exponential growth or collapse. Alternatively, a *negative or self-limiting feedback loop* is one in which changes in one variable restrict or attenuate changes in another variable over time. For example, DeShon et al. (2004) suggest that individuals working in teams regulate their efforts around accomplishing both individual- (i.e., "I need to type up my daily report") and team-level (i.e., "Our team needs to deliver the final product by the deadline") goals. However, in cases where these goals conflict or cannot be accomplished simultaneously, directing efforts towards one goal comes at the cost of effort and achievement relevant to the other goal that must be corrected through future actions (e.g., higher effort towards individual goal at time $t \rightarrow$ lower performance on team goal at time $t+1$; lower performance on team goal at time $t+1 \rightarrow$ reduced effort towards individual goal at time $t+2$). Negative feedback loops result in asymptotic patterns in which changes in the implicated system variables eventually reach an equilibrium. Assuming unlimited time and resources, the feedback loops described by DeShon et al. (2004) would (eventually) result in team members exerting effort towards individual and team goals such that the effort directed towards each goal proceeds at a rate equivalent to its respective desired level of achievement.

Of note, the sorts of change dynamics previously depicted can only occur if certain concepts/factors in a system are *dynamic variables* (sometimes referred to as *stocks*, Sterman, 2000). A dynamic variable is one that can maintain its state over time and thus operate as though it has a "memory" of its current state when changing over time (Vancouver & Weinhardt, 2012; Weinhardt & Vancouver, 2012). From this perspective, team cohesion would be considered a dynamic variable as it likely does not exist only at a single time point; it is presumed to exist over and through time such that its level can accumulate or dissipate from moment-to-moment as team members interact or events unfold. Recognizing that certain variables/constructs persist and ebb-and-flow in a near continuous fashion is critical to the conceptualization of teams as complex dynamic systems.

The example feedback loops presented previously were relatively simple and involved only two reciprocally related variables. However, a feedback loop may be comprised of several intervening elements. For example, Rudolph and Repenning (2002) offer a dynamical systems representation for how "performance disasters" might occur in teams (i.e., team becomes so overwhelmed with tasks that it effectively collapses). In their theory, the number of tasks a team must complete is represented as a dynamic variable such that tasks can continuously accumulate over time and are resolved at a rate equal to the team's capabilities. The authors propose that when faced with a quota of tasks, teams formulate a perception for how quickly those demands can be resolved (number of tasks remaining → perceived resolution rate). This perceived resolution rate subsequently contributes to a team's stress level (perceived resolution → stress), conceptualized as the ratio of a team's perceived resolution rate to its typical resolution rate (e.g., perceiving that more needs to be done than can typically be accomplished increases stress). Lastly, stress is proposed to exhibit a nonlinear relationship with how many tasks a team resolves in a given time period such that increased stress improves performance up to a point after which it results in increasingly worse performance (stress → number of tasks remaining).

This (moderately) more complex feedback loop highlights some additional points of interest with respect to representing team phenomena from the perspective of dynamical systems. First, the passage of time is an essential and explicit feature of dynamical systems theories as it permits the transmission of influence among variables/concepts within a feedback loop(s). However, this transmission process need not occur instantaneously and therefore provides a unique way in which substantive concepts or environmental conditions can be incorporated into the representation of team dynamics. For example, including a delay between the arrival of new tasks and when a team becomes aware of those tasks in Rudolph and

Repenning's (2002) theory could be used to represent the effect of team situational awareness or the transparency of environmental task demands. Second, dynamical systems representations can incorporate multiple interlocking feedback loops that permit a researcher to explore the combinatorial and opponent processes that commonly exist within real team systems. Although not immediately obvious, Rudolph and Repenning's (2002) theory is comprised of two interlocking feedback loops: (a) a negative/self-limiting feedback loop for when the effects of stress on performance are beneficial (i.e., increased stress → better performance rate → ability to keep up with accumulating tasks) and (b) a positive/self-reinforcing feedback loop for when the effects of stress performance are harmful (i.e., increased stress → poorer performance rate → inability to keep up with accumulating tasks). Lastly, the existence of different and/or different combinations of feedback loops allows researchers to represent and examine the conditions that may give rise to several characteristic types of dynamic patterns. Most notably, dynamical systems theory is particularly well-suited for representing tipping points and periodic/oscillating patterns of system behavior.

Two final concepts gleaned from the dynamical systems perspective that have proven useful for characterizing team dynamics are attractors and perturbations. An *attractor* represents a "state of being" towards which a system evolves over time (Gorman et al., 2017; Nowak et al., 2005). Although there are formal methods for mathematically representing attractors and the "push–pull" they exert on systems, an intuitive characterization of an attractor is that it reflects a point at which a system has converged on a predictable and repeated set of actions, behaviors, and processes given its current conditions. Consistent with the previously discussed notion of steady states, a system and its elements within the domain of influence of an attractor are not necessarily inert. Rather, it means that the sequence of behaviors and interactions within and among system elements and the strength and pattern of cyclical relations among a system's variables have stabilized, such as when a team has settled into a predictable routine for how its members engage in problem-solving and exchange information.

However, this seemingly stable system behavior may change if conditions change. A *perturbation* represents a "shock" or external disturbance to a system. If sufficiently disruptive, a perturbation may knock a system away from its current attractor state, forcing it to reorganize to enter its previous attractor again or potentially sending it towards a new attractor. Thus, if a change in team membership occurs in which several members turnover and are replaced by new members, the previous sequence of interactions which characterized a team's communication patterns may change (either suddenly or incrementally) as members establish new preferences and expectations for how to interact. Over time, the team may settle back into the communication structure it used prior to the perturbation or it may transition into an entirely new way of communicating and interacting. Consequently, scientists that apply dynamical systems theories to team phenomena often study and purposefully leverage perturbations in a team's environment to identify potential attractors that may exist in a team system and the extent to which teams that reside in different attractors function effectively.

Agent-Based Systems

In contrast to the dynamical systems perspectives, the agent-based system perspective focuses on explicating how local interactions among specific entities within a collective give rise to more global distributions, patterns, and trajectories produced by a system (Bechtel & Richardson, 1993; Epstein, 1999; Smith & Conrey, 2007). Nevertheless, many of the same concepts (e.g., dynamic variables, feedback loops, perturbations) central to the dynamical systems perspective are represented and captured within the agent-based system perspective as well. However, the explicit focus of agent-based systems on how local occurrences/events give rise to global system properties raises some additional key concepts.

The three most fundamental concepts of agent-based system descriptions are agents, environments, and rules (Wilensky & Rand, 2015). *Agents* are the elementary components/entities of a system that are capable of acting, reacting, or otherwise behaving (e.g., individuals within a team). Agents are described as possessing *attributes* whose levels may be static (e.g., race, sex, personality) or dynamic over time (e.g., perceptions, goals, motivation). In theories rooted in agent-based systems, it is common to consider agents as possessing several attributes simultaneously and to describe the overall "profile" of attribute levels within an agent at any moment in time as the agent's *state*. Consequently, inferences about element- and system-level outcomes from the agent-based perspective often involve interpretations of agent states rather than (or in addition to) aggregate correlations among singular attributes/factors (e.g., which combination of attributes within and between team members contribute to more rapid team cohesion). The initial configuration and subsequent changes in the level and/or distribution of attributes across agents in a system are also typically of interest in agent-based system theories and research (Kozlowski et al., 2013). In this sense, agent attributes both establish the initial conditions of a system as well as provide a continual and recursive source of influence whose effects may change over time.

The second fundamental component of agent-based systems, *environments*, holds a similar connotation as depicted by the previous systems perspectives and characterizes the context in which agents are embedded and interact. However, explications of phenomena from an agent-based system perspective frequently entail efforts to precisely characterize and define specific features of an environment and how they constrain and shape the behaviors/interactions in which agents can engage. Perhaps the most significant such environmental feature in the context of team systems is interdependence. Broadly construed, *interdependence* describes how and/or the extent to which conditions, actors, and/or actions are coupled with (and therefore mutually influenced by) other variables, actors, and/or actions in a system (Weick, 1979). For example, a team task that exhibits a sequential form of interdependence will strongly dictate the order in which the activities and goal-relevant behaviors of individual members are performed (e.g., an emergency medical team needs to establish a patient's airway before directing attention to other bodily injuries; Van de Ven et al., 1976). The structure imposed by this workflow interdependence can subsequently affect how members' social relationships, perceptions, and expectations form by restricting when, which, and how members interact with one another. Relatedly, the environment can also determine how individual contributions to performance are combined to constitute collective system performance (e.g., team sales equal the sum of individuals' sales; speed of a rowing team is determined by the slowest member; Steiner, 1972). This form of behavioral interdependence can impact how individuals in a team allocate resources, coordinate and organize behaviors, and respond to environmental changes.

The final foundational component of agent-based systems are rules. *Rules* are intended to describe the actions, procedures, and/or mechanisms that individual agents and/or environments enact in response to specific events or conditions (Wilensky & Rand, 2015). Intuitively, the rules specified in an agent-based system elaborate "instructions" that elements of the system "follow" when faced with particular stimuli. In team applications, such rules are analogous to team processes in that they reflect which, when, and to what end individual members engage in behaviors related to task accomplishment (Marks et al., 2001; McGrath, 1964, 1984). The focus on explicating rules that characterize why and how a system's elements behave is unique to the agent-based system approach. For example, the description of the positive feedback loop between team cohesion and team performance described by Mathieu et al. (2015) conveys how these properties are expected to mutually unfold over time. However, this relationship does not convey what members in these teams are *doing* that would cause these variables to be related and produce a mutually reciprocal pattern. A set of rules such as "members help those they like" and "members like those who perform well" provides one possible generative account for this system-level relationship, but there are likely other rules or rule-combinations capable of producing a positive feedback loop between team cohesion and performance. Thus, a critical purpose of explicating rules in an agent-based system is to provide a transparent description of the potential generative mechanisms within a system that enables research to explore how particular patterns of system behavior can arise and be influenced.

Building upon this latter point, an axiom commonly advanced in the broader systems science literature is that "the whole [i.e., a system] is often more than the sum of its parts" (e.g., von Bertalanffy, 1972, p. 407). Although this mantra is referenced in relation to several different aspects of system behavior, it most generally reflects that a system and its outcomes usually cannot be well understood by only examining its constituent elements in isolation. Instead, understanding system phenomena requires understanding how collective outcomes emerge from the unique actions, relations, and interdependencies among lower-level entities. *Emergence* describes the process through which novel and coherent properties, structures, and patterns arise within a system due to the actions and interactions of the system's constituent elements (Corning, 2002; Goldstein, 1999). Research in the organizational teams literature is replete with examinations of *emergent constructs/states* that reflect discernable "signatures" of stable/emerged behavioral routines, perceptions, and relations (e.g., team performance, team cohesion, team efficacy, team trust, team climates; Kozlowski & Ilgen, 2006; Marks et al., 2001). However, attempting to understand or predict system behavior by focusing only on their emerged properties while ignoring the underlying processes of emergence is akin to trying to infer the plot of a movie by looking only at a single still frame from the film. Consequently, the agent-based systems perspective emphasizes that adequately understanding and impacting emergent system-level properties necessitates explicating the agents, environment, and rules of a system. Through repeated enactment of rules by agents in an environment, unique system characteristics (e.g., team cognition, team norms, team cultures) are created from the "bottom–up." These emergent properties can also subsequently influence behavior and interaction in a more "top–down" manner, thus reflecting the reciprocal "micro ↔ macro relationship" commonly attributed to complex dynamic systems (Page, 2018).

TEAM PHENOMENA FROM AN IPO + MLT VERSUS SYSTEMS-ORIENTED PERSPECTIVE

Although the foci of the open systems, dynamical systems, and agent-based systems perspectives suggest different implications for how one might pursue research, they collectively offer an important foundation upon which to begin developing a more dynamic and actor-oriented view of teams. In the remainder of the paper, we attempt to directly highlight the unique value that this perspective holds for team science by considering how the explication of a specific team phenomena—team performance—might be approached from the conventional IPO + MLT paradigm versus a more systems-oriented approach. To do so, we present and discuss the characteristic features of two models that a researcher might propose to account for team performance. One model is consistent with contemporary treatments of team phenomena, whereas the other adopts a systems-based perspective.

Importantly, the purpose of this discussion is not to develop, articulate, promote, or justify the conceptual rationale of either team performance model. Although we have attempted to make the example models logical and uncontroversial with respect to the team performance literature, the concepts and relations they include are largely irrelevant. Neither representation is intended to advance an account of team performance we advocate be tested or developed in future research per se. Rather, the goal is to highlight how the foci, considerations, rationale, and philosophies underlying the representation of team phenomena (and the accompanying methodologies, inferences, and generalizations they afford) differ when approached from the IPO + MLT (i.e., factor thinking) perspective versus a systems-oriented (i.e., actor thinking) perspective. We begin by considering an example model from the more familiar IPO + MLT perspective followed by an example model grounded in a systems-oriented perspective. We then conclude with a summary of some of the strengths and considerations for integrating systems-oriented thinking to advancing team science research.

Factor Thinking: An IPO + MLT Team Performance Model

Model Description

Figure 2.1 presents a visual summary of an example model of team performance that might be advanced by a researcher approaching team performance from the IPO + MLT perspective. The model depicts a causal/mediating chain of variables that move unidirectionally from input to process to outcome. The structural relationships reflected in the model suggest that team-level ability and extraversion are expected to be positively associated with team-level task coordination and task communication (respectively). In turn, task coordination and task communication are expected to share positive relationships with team performance and team efficacy. Additionally, the model posits that task complexity moderates the relationship between team ability and task coordination such that the impact of team ability on task coordination is magnified when task environments are complex. Team cohesion is also proposed to be positively related to the level of observed task communication. At the individual level, a single relationship is posited that suggests a member's ability will be positively related to their self-efficacy perceptions. Lastly, the model indicates that the team ability,

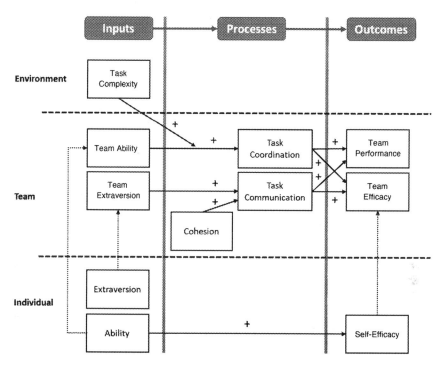

Figure 2.1 Example team performance model consistent with a factor-thinking/ IPO+MLT perspective.

team extraversion, and team efficacy variables are aggregate constructs of their individual-level counterparts.

Characteristic Features

The exemplar model in Figure 2.1 highlights several salient features common to models rooted in the IPO + MLT paradigm. First, the model contains multiple constructs specified at different levels of analysis (e.g., individual, team, environment). This conceptual structure is intended to convey that certain variables reside or are only interpretable at a particular level of aggregation within a nested hierarchical system. For example, cohesion is specified as a team-level construct in Figure 2.1 because it is a property of and is only meaningful for describing teams. Cohesion thus has no meaning or direct interpretation for describing either individual team members or the environment.

Second, the arrows connecting different constructs in Figure 2.1 are generally intended to reflect the expectation that the antecedent variable will account for some proportion of observed variance in the consequent variable. Thus, the lateral connections from the team-level input variables to the team-level process variables in Figure 2.1 indicate that the observed level/amount of the former are presumed to covary with the observed level/amount of the latter (and similarly so for the connection between process and outcome variables). In this manner, the structure of the IPO framework shares a strong resemblance with the logic of statistical mediation in which the goal is to convey which variables are associated with (and presumably cause) variation in other constructs. Furthermore, these relationships are commonly conceptualized and described in terms of the simple linear direction of the proposed association (e.g., higher team ability leads to better team coordination which leads to better team performance; Ilgen et al., 2005; Mathieu et al., 2008).

In addition to these feed-forward causal paths, there are two other noteworthy relationships reflected in Figure 2.1 that draw inspiration from the tenets of MLT (Kozlowski & Klein, 2000). The first are *top–down/cross-level relationships* which involve either the direct or moderating effect of a variable situated at a higher-level of analysis on a variable situated at a lower level of analysis. In Figure 2.1 for example, task complexity (a higher-level environmental input factor) is shown as moderating the relationship between team ability and coordination (a lower-level team input and process variable, respectively). The logic of such top-down relationships is that the higher-level factor in some way "creates" or imposes demands, conditions, and so forth that impact how lower-level units function and thus should account for some proportion of the observed variance in lower-level variables. The second type of relationship exemplified in Figure 2.1 are *bottom–up/ emergent aggregations*. These relationships are also cross-level in that the variables of interest are positioned at different levels of the hierarchical system; however, the causal direction is reversed such that the lower-level variable is proposed to compose a higher-level variable. For models rooted in the IPO + MLT paradigm, such bottom–up relationships are generally restricted to characterizing that a construct situated at a lower-level manifests as a functionally similar construct at a higher level of analysis. For instance, Figure 2.1 depicts a causal arrow from extraversion at the individual to the team level to indicate that team extraversion is a function of individual members' extraversion. However, no causal path can exist between individual-level extraversion and, say, communication at the team-level to represent how a member's extraversion might influence communication within the team. Of note, this restriction is more a statistical limitation of the analytical techniques most commonly used to evaluate factor-based models (Preacher et al., 2010) rather than the inability to conceptually explicate or empirically document the impact of a lower-level unit on a collective system (e.g., Kozlowski et al,. 2013; Weingart et al., 2010).[1] This point will be briefly revisited in the discussion on systems-oriented models of team phenomena.

A final notable feature of IPO + MLT models is that their modeled constructs and relationships are typically conceptualized as stable, time-independent, and oriented towards inferences between rather than within teams. Consistent with their roots in the factor-thinking philosophy (in which the goal is to examine patterns of covariance among variables), IPO + MLT models of team phenomena seldom acknowledge or attempt to represent that (a) many variables of interest to teams researchers are dynamic, cumulative, and/or emergent (Kozlowski et al., 2013; Vancouver & Weinhardt, 2012; Weingart et al., 2010, Weinhardt & Vancouver, 2012); nor (b) the relationships proposed to exist on average and between teams may not generalize to the dynamic relationships that exist within teams (e.g., Fisher et al., 2018; Molenaar, 2004). With respect to the first consideration and as noted previously in the discussion on dynamic variables, a variable such as team cohesion is unlikely to be a static or time-independent concept. As an aggregate representation of members' experiences, perceptions, and so forth, it is more akin to a persistent variable that can change over time rather than a static variable whose level is time-invariant.[2] Taken from this perspective, the significance of the second highlighted limitation of the IPO + MLT paradigm can be better appreciated—observing a team's "average" cohesion at a single time point (or even aggregated over a few time points) provides little to no information about how the construct functions or operates within teams.

To elaborate this latter point, Figure 2.2 demonstrates how the correlation between team cohesion and communication that is proposed to exist in Figure 2.1 may differ if conceptualized between-team (i.e., measured at a single random time point or averaged over time) versus within-team (i.e., over time). A researcher considering this relationship from the IPO + MLT perspective would typically state that, on average, teams whose members are attracted to one another are expected to exhibit more/richer task communication. This is implicitly reflected in the structural arrow between cohesion and communication shown in Figure 2.1 and the nature of this covariation is summarized by the larger black-outlined oval in Figure 2.2. However, a researcher adopting a more dynamic perspective might reason that as team members develop familiarity with one another and their task requirements over time, cohesion may increase while the need for task communication decreases. From this perspective, although teams could differ from one another on their overall levels of cohesion and communication, the association between these variables within-team may be *negative* over time (e.g., gray-outlined ovals in Figure 2.2). Note that both interpretations can be "empirically correct" in that they can simultaneously exist in the same observable data. However, only the latter within-team consideration acknowledges or provides insight into how these variables *play out over time* for a given team.

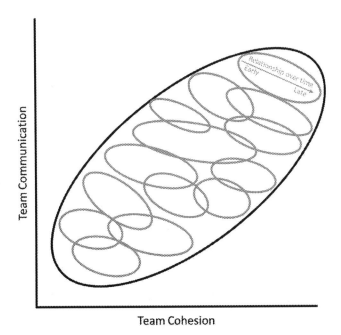

Figure 2.2 Demonstration of the potential for differences in the correlation between team cohesion and task communication when considered within- versus between-teams. *Note:* The larger, black-outlined oval represents a between-team relationship between team cohesion and task communication calculated by assessing teams' data on both variables either at a single time point or averaged over time. The smaller, gray-outlined ovals represent the within-team relationship between team cohesion and task communication observed for several teams based on observations of both variables over time. The annotation in the figure indicates that the within-team relationships are negative because the relationship between team cohesion and team communication decreases from earlier to later measurement periods.

In other words, the emphasis on between-team thinking commonly reflected in the representation of team phenomena from the IPO + MLT perspective generally fails to consider (or, as in the present example, may promote inferences completely opposite to) how variables and concepts of interest relate to team functioning (Cronin et al., 2009). There is, of course, nothing which inherently prevents the factor-thinking paradigm from adopting a more longitudinally oriented or within-team perspective. However, it is important to note that examining the relationship between team-level constructs over time provides little insight into the actions, events, or generative mechanisms responsible for producing a longitudinal pattern. Consequently, observing and analyzing within-team relationships over time still falls short of fully embracing teams as complex systems.

Summary

The example team performance model depicted in Figure 2.1 provides an illustrative demonstration of the basic logic and affordances of conceptualizing team phenomena from the IPO + MLT perspective. Owing to its grounding in the philosophy of factor-thinking research (Macy & Willer, 2002), the models and accounts generated under this paradigm are generally directed towards describing expected patterns of covariance among aggregate team-level variables. In so doing, the IPO + MLT approach to teams research implicitly equates explanatory accounts of team phenomena with the extent to which variance in focal team-level outcomes are accounted for by other team-level variables (typically assessed at a single time point). An important and related consequent of this recognition is that the understanding/knowledge of team functioning advanced within this paradigm may only be appropriate for characterizing the strength and direction of relationships that exist on average between teams. The rationale for why and/or the extent to which relationships among important team factors/ variables also hold within teams is seldom described or pursued. Lastly, models rooted in the IPO + MLT paradigm do not formally explicate or describe the underlying generative mechanisms and dynamics proposed to account for, or give rise to, observed between- and within-team patterns of covariation. However, this focus is central to the actor- and systems-oriented approach to conceptualizing teams to which we now direct attention.

Actor Thinking: A Systems-Oriented Team Performance Model

Model Description

Figure 2.3 visualizes an example team performance model consistent with a more systems-oriented perspective. In contrast to the IPO + MLT model of Figure 2.1, the directional arrows and set of concepts shown in Panel A of Figure 2.3 depict *what* and *how* a team member does, chooses, and/or produces (i.e., process mechanisms) to carry out performance-relevant actions in service of a team's task. Stated differently, Figure 2.3a summarizes a "blueprint" or "script" that an individual team member is proposed to follow, and which describes what happens as they work towards accomplishing team performance goals. Panel B of Figure 2.3 highlights that *each* member of the team (i.e., the five circles labeled Members A–E) is proposed to act in accordance with this same script. The lines connecting members in Figure 2.3b further characterize the potential of the actions/outputs of one member to impact the actions/outputs (i.e., exhibit

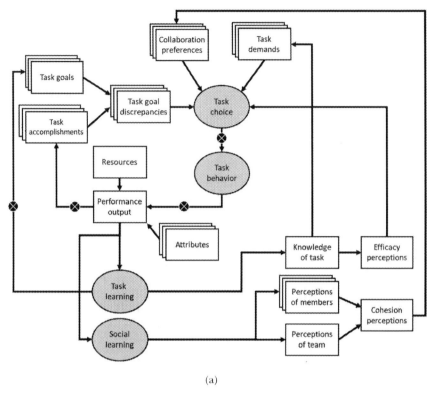

(a)

Figure 2.3 Representation of the generative mechanisms (a) and system-level view (b) of example team performance model consistent with an actor-thinking/systems-oriented perspective. *Note:* In panel (a), shaded gray circles reflect process mechanisms, stacked boxes reflect that the construct is represented by a vector of values rather than a single value, and black circles with a cross reflect where the actions/outputs of a team member can be impacted by the actions/outputs of other team members (e.g., the task choice of Member A can impact the task behaviors of Member B). In panel (b), each member is shown as adhering to the same generative mechanism model depicted in panel (a), with the solid lines connecting members reflecting the potential for interdependence among the actions/outputs of team members.

interdependence with) other members as they engage in performance behaviors relevant to accomplishing the overall team task.[3]

The core set of generative process mechanisms for the exemplar team performance model are depicted in Figure 2.3a. The model "begins" with a member contrasting its understanding of the team's task goals to be completed against the current state of accomplishment on those goals. This action results in the realization/awareness of goal discrepancies indicating

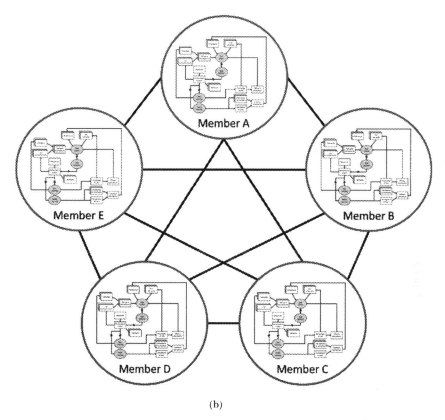

(b)

Figure 2.3 (cont.) Representation of the generative mechanisms (a) and system-level view (b) of example team performance model consistent with an actor-thinking/systems-oriented perspective. *Note:* In panel (a), shaded gray circles reflect process mechanisms, stacked boxes reflect that the construct is represented by a vector of values rather than a single value, and black circles with a cross reflect where the actions/outputs of a team member can be impacted by the actions/outputs of other team members (e.g., the task choice of Member A can impact the task behaviors of Member B). In panel (b), each member is shown as adhering to the same generative mechanism model depicted in panel (a), with the solid lines connecting members reflecting the potential for interdependence among the actions/outputs of team members.

which tasks still require completion. Next, the individual is posited to choose a task goal on which to focus effort. The arrows leading into the task choice mechanism indicate that this decision is a function of several considerations: (a) the previously computed task goal discrepancies, (b) the individual's preferences for collaborating with other members, (c) the individual's understanding of the demands required to complete each task goal, and (d) the individual's overall self-efficacy. Once this choice is made, the individual directs behavior towards accomplishing the selected goal. As indicated in Figure 2.3a, the nature of this behavioral expression can be influenced by the task choices of other team members (e.g., if both Member A and Member B elect to work on the same task, the amount of effort directed towards the task may be altered or a different behavioral action performed compared to if only one of these members had chosen to work on the task). This behavioral expression subsequently results in the realization of output that can be operationally defined with respect to task performance (e.g., progress is made on a client report, a widget is produced). Additionally, this model also posits that the degree to which performance output is accrued is affected by the resources available to perform the task as well as the attributes of the individual(s) performing the task (e.g., knowledge, skills, abilities).

The output of this task-relevant performance event is proposed to feed into three subsequent processes for the individual team member. The first involves updating the status of the team's task accomplishments based on the performance outputs generated across all members of the team (cf. Figure 2.3b). The second process depicted in Figure 2.3a is task learning. This process is intended to reflect that an individual may develop expertise or task-specific understanding because of their performance efforts that can inform (a) the state of task goals and (b) the demands/requirements for completing a given task. Additionally, the acquisition of task knowledge is posited to affect an individual's perceptions of their self-efficacy. Of note, all three of these consequents are proposed to influence subsequent task choices. The final process depicted in Figure 2.3a is labeled social learning and is intended to reflect that an individual may develop perceptions of affinity towards their team and other team members through their performance experiences. These affinities form the basis of an individual's cohesion perceptions, which subsequently impact future preferences for collaboration and potentially future task choice decisions. Following these processes, the entire cycle "begins" anew and continues until the team's task goals are completed.

Characteristic Features

The example team performance model summarized in Figure 2.3 illustrates several unique features of team phenomena conceptualized from a systems-oriented perspective. A first characteristic—and perhaps the most striking in comparison with the IPO + MLT models such as that shown in Figure 2.1—is that the systems-oriented perspective focuses on identifying and elaborating core concepts and mechanisms relevant to team phenomena from the perspective of the actors and their actions rather than statistical covariation. In this respect, the representation shown in Figure 2.3 may be more aptly described as a model of team "perform*ing*" rather than a model of team "perform*ance*." Though the model can be used to discuss and/or conceptualize what contributes to team performance, its primary purpose is not to convey the antecedents, moderators, mediators, and so forth of this outcome per se. Rather, the model attempts to explicate how and why team performance as a dynamic construct emerges from the behaviors, perceptions, decisions, and interactions of individuals in the team. To facilitate such formulations, it is often helpful to initially approach the development of an actor-oriented/systems-based model by considering how one might "tell the story" about how a phenomenon of interest is proposed to unfold. This strategy encourages the teams researcher to begin thinking through questions that focus more directly on the critical elements of the team as a system, such as . . .

- Who are the relevant actors? What attributes/characteristics do actors possess which are important to their affective, behavioral, and cognitive responses?
- What exists in the actor's external/operational environment? Which and how do different forces, resources, constraints, and so forth in the external/operational environment influence when, which, and why actors may interact, change, and/or react?
- How, where, when, and why might actors interact with other actors and their environment? What actions are the actors able or likely to do in response?
- What are the states in which actors and/or environmental properties can exist over time? Which of these qualities are dynamic versus static over time and why?

Although these questions appear abstract in the absence of any context, their resolution typically becomes more tractable as they are applied to a particular team phenomenon. For instance, the example model in Figure 2.3 and the verbal description of its operation provided previously were generated by attempting to reason through these questions in relation to a generic team performance scenario. In sum, a characteristic feature of models rooted in the systems-oriented perspective is their attention towards which, how, and why the concepts and mechanisms of interest are proposed to emerge and interface with other concepts and mechanisms over time, as opposed to only considering the covariation between sets of static, aggregate, and "already emerged" collective variables.

A second noteworthy characteristic of systems-oriented team models concerns the representation of key variables/concepts important to the explanation for the phenomenon. Compared to IPO + MLT models, there is generally less consideration of whether to categorize variables as input, process, or outcomes or how to ascribe those variables to specific levels of analysis. One reason for this is the variables represented in systems-oriented models often span or fail to adequately fit neatly into such classifications. For example, Figure 2.3 suggests that an individual's cohesion perceptions serve as an *input* to collaboration preferences, exist and operate within a social learning *process*, and are an *outcome* of an individual's affinity towards their other team members and the team. Furthermore, cohesion perceptions are technically situated as an "individual-level" construct in this model because those beliefs are represented as residing with the individual/actor that produces them. However, and as alluded to by Figure 2.3b, cohesion could be operationalized as a collective (i.e., team-level) property by aggregating members' cohesion perceptions together if desired.

In addition, the variables represented in systems-oriented models often allow for—or in some cases necessitate—a broader array of operationalizations that can encourage researchers to think about phenomena through new or alternative lenses. The consideration of variables as dynamic, cumulative, and emerging previously discussed as neglected by IPO + MLT models is fundamental to actor-thinking/systems-oriented representations (Kozlowski et al., 2013; Weinhardt & Vancouver, 2012). Furthermore, the conceptualization of variables as dyadic and/or in the context of relational networks is far more common in systems-oriented models. For example, Figure 2.3 suggests that cohesion is a function of both dyadic/relational perceptions among members (i.e., members' affinities towards each other member) as well as more "gestalt" and/or aggregate perceptions of the team writ large. Explicitly incorporating both representations of cohesion into the same model of team functioning thus encourages future research to consider how and why different patterns of affinity could emerge across both operationalizations and the manner by which they may uniquely or jointly affect member and team outputs.

On a related note, it may seem unusual that the team performance model shown in Figure 2.3 does not contain any variable labeled team performance. However, the model has several concepts that could be used to conceptualize team performance in unique yet complementary ways. For instance, the performance output variable shown in Figure 2.3 reflects the amount and/or quality of output produced by a member for a given task at a given time point. Thus, the total performance output generated across all members and tasks at a given time point offers one method for operationalizing team performance. A different representation might rely on task goal discrepancies as this concept captures which, how many, and how much of a team's goals remain to be accomplished. Using this variable, team performance could be conceptualized as the rate of discrepancy reduction within and/or across task goals. Additional ways of conceptualizing team performance in Figure 2.3 could likely be derived. Although the potential to define a single construct in multiple ways may seem undesirable from the perspective of parsimonious explanation, it acknowledges the reality that many psychological and team-relevant variables are complex constructs that can manifest in different yet informative ways. For example, organizational scholars have long discussed the challenges with developing a straightforward and generalizable definition of performance, highlighting that it can entail different operational definitions (e.g., performance as behavior/action versus outcome/production), foci (task versus contextual performance), and time frames (short-term versus long-term; e.g., Sonnentag & Frese, 2012). The fundamental thrust of the actor-thinking and systems-oriented philosophy to explicate *how* teams function thus recognizes and affords the opportunity to explore the complexities and multifaceted nature of the core variables and constructs involved in team phenomena.

A final distinguishing feature of systems-oriented models is that they attempt to represent team processes as *mechanisms* rather than *variables*. For example, task coordination and task communication are presented as process variables in the IPO + MLT model shown in Figure 2.1, but would typically be conceptualized as things that a team can do "more/less of" or "better/worse at." In contrast, task choice, task behavior, task learning, and social learning are presented as process mechanisms in the systems-oriented model of Figure 2.3. In a fully articulated model (which the example model described in this section is not) these process mechanisms would be precisely specified in a manner that describes *how, what, and when* actions occur.

For this reason, many systems-oriented models are constructed using *computational modeling techniques* rather than through narrative description alone. Although a detailed explanation of these techniques is beyond the scope of the present paper, a computational model is a formal and algorithmic description of how a set of processes are proposed to occur and unfold over time (for general and accessible introductions to computational modeling that are oriented towards organizational scholars, see Davis et al., 2007; Harrison et al., 2007; Vancouver & Weinhardt, 2012; or Weinhardt & Vancouver, 2012). The formalism of a computational model derives from the use of declarative logic (e.g., IF $[X \geq \lambda]$, THEN $[Y = 1]$, ELSE $[Y = 0]$), and/or mathematical equations (e.g., $Y_t = 1 / 1 + e^{-\lambda*(X_t - X_{t-1})}$) to convey how the core concepts and variables of a system are proposed to change. The algorithmic nature of a computational model derives from declaring the order and sequence in which actions/events are proposed to unfold over time and/or in response to other actions/events which may occur in the system. These elements of a computational model's specification may be informed by theory, logic, or established through empirical observation. In either case, the end goal is to develop a transparent, precise, and descriptive account of how a system is proposed to operate. Further, most contemporary computational models are translated into computer code and used to conduct simulations and "virtual experiments" that allow one to examine how the proposed set of mechanisms operate under different conditions. This enables the researcher to identify/verify predicted patterns, evaluate the plausibility of potential system outcomes, and design or test "interventions" for influencing system behavior (for examples related to team phenomena in the organizational sciences, see Coen, 2006; Flache & Mäs, 2008; or Grand et al., 2016). Thus, the specification of processes as mechanisms rather than variables in systems-oriented models affords the means for team scientists to precisely describe, explore, and probe how teams function in ways that can promote practical and actionable recommendations for achieving desired team and member outcomes (e.g., McGrath & Tschan, 2007).

Summary

Despite not being a fully developed or articulated model of team performance, Figure 2.3 offers a useful stimulus for summarizing the characteristic features and underlying philosophy of actor-thinking and the systems-oriented perspective for representing team phenomena. The fundamental orientation of accounts generated within this paradigm are directed towards explicating the activities, events, and interactions that occur within a team system as well as how these processes unfold over time through individual members and their environment. In so doing, the actor-thinking approach promotes conceptualizations and considerations of team phenomena that are targeted towards uncovering and defining core concepts and generative mechanisms of team phenomena that are capable of and/or responsible for producing the emergent patterns, relationships, and properties observed in teams. This focus also permits the potential to generate inferences, predictions, and explanations that are relevant to both between- and within-team generalizations. Lastly, the development of actor-thinking and more systems-oriented models are enhanced through formal model building and evaluation techniques (i.e., computational modeling and simulation). These tools afford researchers the capacity to probe the logic and specification of models, explore multiple and alternative conceptualizations of key variables and outcomes, and develop transparent and precise accounts of generative mechanisms.

CONCLUSION

Teams and their functioning have long been discussed as operating in a manner consistent with complex dynamic systems (e.g., Allport, 1924; Arrow et al., 2000; Lewin, 1943; Parsons, 1937). However, this conceptualization is seldom reflected in the contemporary theory, methodology, and empirical research on teams in the social, organizational, and managerial sciences. We contend that one cause of this mismatch is that many of the fundamental tenets, ideas, tools, and orientations embodied by systems science are unfamiliar and/or their significance greatly undervalued by team scientists (Epstein, 1999; Gorman et al., 2017). The goal of this paper was to introduce several key concepts across the diffuse and eclectic domains of systems science and demonstrate their application for conceptualizing and researching team phenomena. Additionally, key features of models developed within the currently predominant factor-thinking paradigm (which draws heavily from the IPO framework of team functioning, (McGrath, 1964), and the meta-theoretical and methodological recommendations of MLT (Kozlowski & Klein, 2000), and those rooted in an alternative actor-thinking paradigm (which draws heavily from the principles of complex, dynamic, and adaptive systems (von Bertalanffy, 1972), were summarized to highlight the unique differences and foci these approaches hold for considering collective phenomena (Macy & Willer, 2002).

We contend that the perspective advanced by adopting a more systems-oriented approach holds significant promise for advancing the state of team science. Most significantly, this approach draws attention towards explicating *how* teams function, interact, and exert/experience influence from their environments by considering *what, when,* and *why* team members "do" when working within teams (Kozlowski et al., 2013). The identification and specification of these generative mechanisms affords team researchers the potential to more precisely explicate and directly explore how the dynamic patterns and emergent properties of teams unfold as well as how those properties are produced and thus can be impacted (Epstein, 1999).

Lest one conclude that the actor-thinking and systems-oriented perspective is a panacea for team science, there are some noteworthy challenges and likely obstacles with adopting this approach that are worth recognizing. The inherent complexities of considering both the intra- and inter-individual dynamics that occur within teams means that more systems-oriented models can easily become complicated, cumbersome, and onerous to comprehend if not appropriately restricted. Additionally, the temporal scale for many team phenomena is both poorly understood and likely to differ across constructs, contexts, and member configurations. Consequently, although actor-based and systems-oriented models can be developed and readily used to propose potential trends, trajectories, and/or patterns of team outcomes, predicting the actual or required durations for such developments to occur is difficult. Additionally, and as alluded to when describing the features of the example model in Figure 2.3, most representations of team functioning rooted in this perspective must be translated into formal quantitative/computational models to fully articulate and examine how they operate (e.g., Cronin et al., 2009). We do not believe this a limitation of the actor-thinking and system-oriented approach per se; on the contrary, the development of more precise, transparent, and rigorous theory would be a boon for team science (Cronin et al., 2011; Kozlowski et al., 2013). However, it does entail a skill set (i.e., computer modeling/programming, expressing propositional statements in formal logic and mathematical equations) for which many social and organizational scientists do not receive training. Nevertheless, the potential of embracing a more dynamic and actor-oriented view on teams far outweigh these potential obstacles. Through attempting to realign team science with its origins in systems thinking, we believe the discipline can be propelled into a vibrant and impactful future.

ACKNOWLEDGMENTS

We gratefully acknowledge the U.S. Army Research Institute for the Behavioral and Social Sciences (ARI; W911NF-14-1-0026) and the Defense Medical Research and Development Program JPC-1 (DMRDP; W81XWH-18-1-0089) for funding that supported the preparation of this paper. Any opinions, findings, conclusions, and recommendations expressed are those of the authors and do not necessarily reflect the views of ARI or DMRDP.

NOTES

1. As an aside, this recognition offers a compelling example of how the analytical/statistical models implemented by the factor-thinking/IPO + MLT researcher have strongly influenced the development of theories and models of team phenomena.
2. To the extent a team's cohesion was stable or unchanging over time, it would still be most appropriate to conceptualize the variable as existing in a steady state such that it is continuously "sustained" by the perceptions of individuals' momentary perceptions.
3. Figure 2.3b presents all members as interconnected and therefore interdependent with one another. However, such a fully connected configuration is not required. For example, a team in which members fulfill specific roles may result in some members being highly connected with others whereas some members exhibit less interdependence (e.g., Humphrey, et al., 2009). Furthermore, the interdependencies among members may be fixed or variable, such as when particular tasks require different subsets of members to collaborate at different points in time to accomplish. To simplify our discussion of the exemplar model in this section, we do not consider these possibilities or their potential generative mechanisms in the text, but simply acknowledge that interdependence networks need not be static or uniform across members in a team.

REFERENCES

Allport, F. H., (1924). The group fallacy in relation to social science. *Journal of Abnormal and Social Psychology, 19*, 60–73. https://doi.org/10.1037/h0065675

Arrow, H., McGrath, J. E., & Berdahl, J. L. (2000). *Small groups as complex systems: Formation, coordination, development, and adaptation.* SAGE Publications. http://dx.doi.org/10.4135/9781452204666

Bechtel, W., & Richardson, R. C. (1993). *Discovering complexity: Decomposition and localization as strategies in scientific research.* Princeton University Press.

Bersin, J., McDowell, T., Rahnema, A., & Van Durme, Y. (2017). *The organization of the future: Arriving now. 2017 Global Human Capital Trends.* Deloitte Insights. https://www2.deloitte.com/us/en/insights/focus/human-capital-trends/2017/organization-of-the-future.html

Chan, D. (1998). Functional relations among constructs in the same content domain at different levels of analysis: A typology of composition models. *Journal of Applied Psychology, 83*, 234–246. https://doi.org/10.1037/0021-9010.83.2.234

Coen, C. A. (2006). Seeking the comparative advantage: The dynamics of individual cooperation in single vs. multiple-team environments. *Organizational Behavior and Human Decision Processes, 100*, 145–159. https://doi.org/10.1016/j.obhdp.2006.02.005

Cooke, N. J., Gorman, J. C., Myers, C. W., & Duran, J. L. (2013). Interactive team cognition. *Cognitive Science, 37*, 255–285. https://doi.org/10.1111/cogs.12009

Corning, P. A. (2002). The re-emergence of "emergence": A venerable concept in search of a theory. *Complexity, 7*, 18–30. https://doi.org/10.1002/cplx.10043

Crawford, E. R., & LePine, J. A. (2013). A configural theory of team processes: Accounting for the structure of taskwork and teamwork. *Academy of Management Review, 38*(1), 32–48. https://doi.org/10.5465/amr.2011.0206

Cronin, M. A., Gonzalez, C., & Sterman, J. D. (2009). Why don't well-educated adults understand accumulation? A challenge to researchers, educators, and citizens. *Organizational Behavior and Human Decision Processes, 108*, 116–130. https://doi.org/10.1016/j.obhdp.2008.03.003

Cronin, M. A., Weingart, L. R., & Todorova, G. (2011). Dynamics in groups: Are we there yet? *Academy of Management Annals, 5*(1), 571–612. https://doi.org/10.1080/19416520.2011.590297

Dansereau, F., Yammarino, F. J., & Kohles, J. C. (1999). Multiple levels of analysis from a longitudinal perspective: Some implications for theory building. *Academy of Management Review, 24*(2), 346–357. https://doi.org/10.2307/259086

Davis, J. P., Eisenhardt, K. M., & Bingham, C. B. (2007). Developing theory through simulation methods. *Academy of Management Review, 32*, 480–499. https://doi.org/10.5465/amr.2007.24351453

DeShon, R. P., Kozlowski, S. W. J., Schmidt, A. M., Milner, K. R., & Wiechmann, D. (2004). A multiple-goal, multilevel model of feedback effects on the regulation of individual and team performance. *Journal of Applied Psychology, 89*, 1035–1056. https://doi.org/10.1037/0021-9010.89.6.1035

Dionne, S. D., Sayama, H., Hao, C., & Bush, B. J. (2010). The role of leadership in shared mental model convergence and team performance improvement: An agent-based computational model. *The Leadership Quarterly, 21*, 1035–1049. https://doi.org/10.1016/j.leaqua.2010.10.007

Epstein, J. M. (1999). Agent-based computational models and generative social science. *Complexity, 4*(5), 41–60. https://doi.org/10.1002/(SICI)1099-0526 (199905/06)4:5<41::AID-CPLX9>3.0.CO;2-F

Fisher, A. J., Medaglia, J. D., & Jeronimus, B. F. (2018). Lack of group-to-individual generalizability is a threat to human subjects research. *Proceedings of the National Academy of Sciences, 115*, E6106–E6115. https://doi.org/10.1073/pnas .1711978115

Flache, A., & Mäs, M. (2008). Why do faultlines matter? A computational model of how strong demographic faultlines undermine team cohesion. *Simulation Modelling Practice and Theory, 16*(2), 175–191. https://doi.org/10.1016/j.simpat .2007.11.020

Forsyth, D. R. (2013). *Group dynamics* (6th ed.). Cengage Learning.

Goldstein, J. (1999). Emergence as a construct: History and issues. *Emergence, 1*(1), 49–72. https://doi.org/10.1207/s15327000em0101_4

González-Romá, V., & Hernández, A. (2017). Multilevel modeling: Research-based lessons for substantive researchers. *Annual Review of Organizational Psychology and Organizational Behavior, 4*, 183–210. https://doi.org/10.1146/annurev -orgpsych-041015-062407

Gorman, J. C., Cooke, N. J., Amazeen, P. L., Hessler, E. E., & Rowe, L. (2009). *Automatic tagging of macrocognitive collaborative processes through communication analysis* (Technical Report for Office of Naval Research Grant N00014-05-1-0625). Office of Naval Research.

Gorman, J. C., Dunbar, T. A., Grimm, D., & Gipson, C. L. (2017). Understanding and modeling teams as dynamical systems. *Frontiers in Psychology, 8*, 1053. https://doi.org/10.3389/fpsyg.2017.01053

Grand, J. A., Braun, M. T., Kuljanin, G., Kozlowski, S. W. J., & Chao, G. T. (2016). The dynamics of team cognition: A process-oriented theory of knowledge emergence in teams. *The Journal of Applied Psychology, 101*(10), 1353–1385. https://doi.org/10.1037/apl0000136

Guzzo, R. A., & Shea, G. P. (1992). Group performance and intergroup relations in organizations. In M. D. Dunnette & L. M. Hough (Eds.), *Handbook of industrial and organizational psychology* (pp. 269–313). Consulting Psychologists Press.

Harrison, J. R., Lin, Z., Carroll, G. R., & Carley, K. M. (2007). Simulation modeling in organizational and management research. *Academy of Management Review, 32*, 1229–1245. https://doi.org/10.5465/amr.2007.26586485

Humphrey, S. E., & Aime, F. (2014). Team microdynamics: Toward an organizing approach to teamwork. *Academy of Management Annals, 8*(1), 443–503. https://doi.org/10.1080/19416520.2014.904140

Humphrey, S. E., Morgeson, F. P., & Mannor, M. J. (2009). Developing a theory of the strategic core of teams: A role composition model of team performance. *Journal of Applied Psychology, 94*(1), 48–61. https://doi.org/10.1037/a0012997

Ilgen, D. R., Hollenbeck, J. R., Johnson, M., & Jundt, D. (2005). Teams in organizations: From input-process-output models to IMOI models. *Annual Review of Psychology, 56*, 517–543. https://doi.org/10.1146/annurev.psych.56 .091103.070250

Katz, D., & Kahn, R. L. (1978). *The social psychology of organizations* (2nd ed.). Wiley. https://doi.org/10.1093/sf/57.4.1413

Kennedy, D. M., & McComb, S. A. (2014). When teams shift among processes: Insights from simulation and optimization. *Journal of Applied Psychology, 99*(5), 784–815. https://doi.org/10.1037/a0037339

Klein, K. J., Dansereau, F., & Hall, R. J. (1994). Levels issues in theory development, data collection, and analysis. *Academy of Management Review, 19*(2), 195–229. https://doi.org/10.5465/AMR.1994.9410210745

Kozlowski, S. W. J., Chao, G. T., Grand, J. A., Braun, M. T., & Kuljanin, G. (2013). Advancing multilevel research design: Capturing the dynamics of emergence. *Organizational research methods, 16*(4), 581–615. https://doi.org/10.1177/1094428113493119

Kozlowski, S. W. J., & Ilgen, D. R. (2006). Enhancing the effectiveness of work groups and teams. *Psychological Science in the Public Interest, 7*(3), 77–124. https://doi.org/10.1111/j.1529-1006.2006.00030.x

Kozlowski, S. W. J., & Klein, K. J. (2000). A multilevel approach to theory and research in organizations: Contextual, temporal, and emergent processes. In K. J. Klein & S. W. J. Kozlowski (Eds.), *Multilevel theory, research, and methods in organizations: Foundations, extensions, and new directions* (pp. 3–90). Jossey-Bass.

Krasikova, D. V., & LeBreton, J. M. (2019). Multilevel measurement: Agreement, reliability, and nonindependence. In S. E. Humphrey & J. M. LeBreton (Eds.), *The handbook of multilevel theory, measurement, and analysis* (pp. 279–304). American Psychological Association. https://doi.org/10.1037/0000115-013

Lewin, K. (1943). Defining the "field at a given time." *Psychological Review, 50*(3), 292–310. https://doi.org/10.1037/h0062738

Macy, M. W., & Willer, R. (2002). From factors to actors: Computational sociology and agent-based modeling. *Annual Review of Sociology, 28,* 143–166. https://doi.org/10.1146/annurev.soc.28.110601.141117

Marks, M. A., Mathieu, J. E., & Zaccaro, S. J. (2001). A temporally based framework and taxonomy of team processes. *Academy of Management Review, 26*(3), 356–376. https://doi.org/10.2307/259182

Mathieu, J. E., Gallagher, P. T., Domingo, M. A., & Klock, E. A. (2019). Embracing complexity: Reviewing the past decade of team effectiveness research. *Annual Review of Organizational Psychology and Organizational Behavior, 6,* 17–46. https://doi.org/10.1146/annurev-orgpsych-012218-015106

Mathieu, J. E., Hollenbeck, J. R., van Knippenberg, D., & Ilgen, D. R. (2017). A century of work teams in the Journal of Applied Psychology. *The Journal of Applied Psychology, 102*(3), 452–467. https://doi.org/10.1037/apl0000128

Mathieu, J. E., Kukenberger, M. R., D'innocenzo, L., & Reilly, G. (2015). Modeling reciprocal team cohesion-performance relationships, as impacted by shared leadership and members' competence. *Journal of Applied Psychology, 100*(3), 713–734. https://doi.org/10.1037/a0038898

Mathieu, J., Maynard, M. T., Rapp, T., & Gilson, L. (2008). Team effectiveness 1997–2007: A review of recent advancements and a glimpse into the future. *Journal of Management, 34*(3), 410–476. https://doi.org/10.1177/0149206308316061

Matusik, J. G., Hollenbeck, J. R., Matta, F. K., & Oh, J. K. (2019). Dynamic systems theory and dual change score models: Seeing teams through the lens of developmental psychology. *Academy of Management Journal, 62*(6), 1760–1788. https://doi.org/10.5465/amj.2017.1358

McGrath, J. E. (1964). *Social psychology: A brief introduction.* Holt, Rinehart, & Winston.

McGrath, J. E. (1984). *Groups: Interaction and performance* (Vol. 14). Prentice-Hall.

McGrath, J. E. (1991). Time, interaction, and performance (TIP): A theory of groups. *Small Group Research, 22*(2), 147–174. https://doi.org/10.1177/1046 496491222001

McGrath, J. E., & Tschan, F. (2007). Temporal matters in the study of work groups in organizations. *The Psychologist-Manager Journal, 10*(1), 3–12. https://doi .org/10.1080/10887150709336609

Meyer, R. D., England, K., Kelly, E. D., Helbling, A., Li, M., & Outten, D. (2019). Ask not what the study of context can do for you: Ask what you can do for the study of context. In S. E. Humphrey & J. M. LeBreton (Eds.), *The handbook of multilevel theory, measurement, and analysis* (pp. 67–88). American Psychological Association. https://doi.org/10.1037/0000115-004

Molenaar, P. C. M. (2004). A manifesto on psychology as idiographic science: Bringing the person back into scientific psychology, this time forever. *Measurement, 2,* 201–218. https://doi.org/10.1207/s15366359mea0204_1

Nowak, A., Vallacher, R. R., & Zochowski, M. (2005). The emergence of personality: Dynamic foundations of individual variation. *Developmental Review, 25,* 351–385. https://doi.org/10.1016/j.dr.2005.10.004

Ostroff, C. (2019). Contextualizing context in organizational research. In S. E. Humphrey & J. M. LeBreton (Eds.), *The handbook of multilevel theory, measurement, and analysis* (pp. 39–65). American Psychological Association. https:// doi.org/10.1037/0000115-003

Page, S. E. (2018). *The model thinker.* Basic Books. https://doi.org/10.1111/risa .13388

Parsons, T. (1937). *The structure of social action.* McGraw-Hill. https://doi.org/10 .1007/978-3-658-13213-2_30

Preacher, K. J., Zyphur, M. J., & Zhang, Z. (2010). A general multilevel SEM framework for assessing multilevel mediation. *Psychological Methods, 15*(3), 209–233. https://doi.org/10.1037/a0020141

Rudolph, J. W., & Repenning, N. P. (2002). Disaster dynamics: Understanding the role of quantity in organizational collapse. *Administrative Science Quarterly, 47*(1), 1–30. https://doi.org/10.2307/3094889

Sherif, M., White, B. J., & Harvey, O. J. (1955). Status in experimentally produced groups. *American Journal of Sociology, 60*(4), 370–379. https://doi.org/10 .1086/221569

Smith, E. R., & Conrey, F. R. (2007). Agent-based modeling: A new approach for theory building in social psychology. *Personality and Social Psychology Review, 11*(1), 87–104. https://doi.org/10.1177/1088868306294789

Sonnentag, S., & Frese, M. (2012). Dynamic performance. In S. W. J. Kozlowski (Ed.), *The Oxford handbook of organizational psychology* (Vol. 1, pp. 548–575). Oxford University Press. https://doi.org/10.1093/oxfordhb/9780199928309.001.0001

Steiner, I. D. (1972). *Group process and productivity.* Academic Press.

Sterman, J. D. (2000). *Business dynamics.* Irwin/McGraw-Hill.

Sundstrom, E., De Meuse, K. P., & Futrell, D. (1990). Work teams: Applications and effectiveness. *American Psychologist, 45*(2), 120–133. https://doi.org/10.1037/0003-066X.45.2.120

Thelen, E., & Smith, L. B. (1994). *A dynamic systems approach to the development of cognition and action.* MIT Press. https://doi.org/doi:10.1016/S1364-6613(03)00156-6

Vancouver, J. B., & Weinhardt, J. M. (2012). Modeling the mind and the milieu: Computational modeling for micro-level organizational researchers. *Organizational Research Methods, 15*(4), 602–623. https://doi.org/10.1177/1094428112449655

Van de Ven, A. H., Delbecq, A. L., & Koenig, R., Jr. (1976). Determinants of coordination modes within organizations. *American Sociological Review, 41*(2), 322–338. https://doi.org/10.2307/2094477

Von Bertalanffy, L. (1950). The theory of open systems in physics and biology. *Science. 111*(2872), 23–29. https://doi.org/10.1126/science.111.2872.23

Von Bertalanffy, L. (1972). The history and status of general systems theory. *Academy of Management Journal, 15*(4), 407–426. https://www.jstor.org/stable/255139

Waller, M. J., Okhuysen, G. A., & Saghafian, M. (2016). Conceptualizing emergent states: A strategy to advance the study of group dynamics. *Academy of Management Annals, 10*(1), 561–598. https://doi.org/10.1080/19416520.2016.1120958

Weick, K. E. (1979). *The social psychology of organizing* (2nd ed.). McGraw-Hill. https://doi.org/10.3917/mana.182.0189

Weingart, L. R., Todorova, G., & Cronin, M. A. (2010). Task conflict, problem-solving, and yielding: Effects on cognition and performance in functionally diverse innovation teams. *Negotiation and Conflict Management Research, 3*(4), 312–337. https://doi.org/10.1111/j.1750-4716.2010.00063.x

Weinhardt, J. M., & Vancouver, J. B. (2012). Computational models and organizational psychology: Opportunities abound. *Organizational Psychology Review, 2*(4), 267–292. https://doi.org/10.1177/2041386612450455

Wilensky, U., & Rand, W. (2015). *An introduction to agent-based modeling: Modeling natural, social, and engineered complex systems with NetLogo.* MIT Press. https://doi.org/10.1063/PT.3.2884

CHAPTER 3

MACHINE LEARNING AND THE SCIENCE OF TEAMS

Patrick J. Rosopa
Clemson University

ABSTRACT

Teams permeate every aspect of life including business, sports, military, healthcare, and music. Over the past few decades, much has been learned about how individual team characteristics (e.g., knowledge, skills) can affect team processes (e.g., coordination, shared situational awareness) and outcomes (e.g., team performance, innovation). However, researchers have highlighted the need for advances and innovations in methods and analytic tools to help better understand team-level constructs and the dynamic nature of teams. The field of data science is described, in general, and how inductive research and machine learning algorithms, in particular, can contribute to theory and practice in teams. In this chapter, supervised learning, unsupervised learning, and semi-supervised learning are described. Then, a specific algorithm in supervised learning and unsupervised learning is described along with applied examples related to research on teams. Limitations and recommendations are discussed.

Managing Team Centricity in Modern Organizations, pages 53–76
Copyright © 2022 by Information Age Publishing
www.infoagepub.com

Teams permeate every aspect of life including business, sports, military, healthcare, and music. Teams are two or more people that are interdependent, sharing responsibility to accomplish a common goal (Kozlowski, 2018; Salas & Cannon-Bowers, 2001). In organizations, effective teams can leverage the diverse abilities and characteristics of its team members, outperforming the simple aggregate of employees working individually. Although there are many theoretical models of teams and teamwork, most models are guided by McGrath's (1964) input-process-output (IPO) framework (Kozlowski, 2018). In general, inputs are characteristics of the individual members, the team, and the organization. Processes generally refer to how inputs are transformed through transition processes (e.g., goal specification), action processes (e.g., coordination), and interpersonal processes (e.g., conflict management) to produce valued outcomes (Marks et al., 2001).

Over the past few decades, much has been learned about how individual team characteristics (e.g., knowledge, skills) can affect team processes (e.g., coordination, shared situational awareness) and outcomes (e.g., team performance, innovation). However, researchers have highlighted the need for advances and innovations in methods, measures, designs, and analytic tools to help better understand team-level constructs (see e.g., Chan, 2019; Tannenbaum et al., 2012) and the dynamic nature of teams (Kozlowski, 2018). A cross-sectional study, for example, lacks the ability to capture the rich and complex interactions associated with team formation and team cognition, and how these contribute to team outcomes (e.g., team effectiveness in a dynamic decision-making environment). On the other hand, longitudinal designs with data collected from individual team members (e.g., unobtrusively with wearable sensors) over time, with measures and manipulations of an environment as teams perform in real-time, "in the wild," provide high fidelity data. However, longitudinal designs and studies that involve multiple events/scenarios/episodes and data from different sources (e.g., video, audio, navigation systems) in simulated or real-world settings leads to other challenges. Not only are there large volumes of data, but also diverse types of data (e.g., images, text, coordinates) and such data, whether from experiments, quasi-experiments, or archival data, must be accurately merged/joined, cleaned, processed (e.g., converting images to numbers) before being analyzed. In addition, the statistical methods commonly used in teams research may not be robust in capturing the nesting, dynamic, and sequential aspects of the data. Thus, statistical methods in teams research must evolve and adapt by exploring advanced algorithms. Notably, methods and algorithms commonly used in data science and machine learning have the potential to advance the science of teams. After discussing data science and machine learning, specific statistical algorithms are described along with applied examples related to research on teams.

DATA SCIENCE AND MACHINE LEARNING

Globalization and rapid advances in technology (e.g., software, telecommunications, cloud computing) has led to an unprecedented amount of data (volume) in a wide array of structured and unstructured data types (variety) compiled and updated in milliseconds (velocity; Tonidandel et al., 2018). Given the volume, variety, and velocity of data available in organizations, it is not surprising that the field of data science is playing an important role across a wide range of sectors including aerospace, education, healthcare, engineering, manufacturing, and retail. We first define data science and how it can contribute to theory and practice in teams research. Then, we provide a broad overview of machine learning and highlight some algorithms that can potentially advance the science of teams.

Data Science

Grus (2019) stated half-jokingly "a data scientist is someone who knows more statistics than a computer scientist and more computer science than a statistician" (p. 1). "Data science combines multiple fields, including statistics, scientific methods, artificial intelligence (AI), and data analysis, to extract value from data... [and] ... derive actionable insights" (Oracle, n.d.). Stated differently, data science uses systematic methods, statistics, computer programming, and subject matter knowledge to glean information from data. Data science is applied across a wide range of areas including bioinformatics, market research, medical diagnosis, and robotics. It is not uncommon to see other terms such as AI, machine learning, and deep learning used synonymously. Although they are related, Figure 3.1 provides a conceptual representation of how these areas overlap. AI involves having computers/technology mimic human decision-making, behavior, and emotions. AI is a large and diverse field (see e.g., Amabile, 2020; Raisch & Krakowski, 2021; Simon, 1995; Stranders et al., 2013) and is beyond the scope of this current chapter. Machine learning refers to the set of algorithms and methods that are applied to data to understand patterns, classify, and make predictions. Deep learning refers to a large class of algorithms that uses neural networks, in particular, to understand patterns, classify, and make predictions. Although there are a number of other tools and algorithms, deep learning can be thought of as a subset of machine learning.

Data science plays a role in all areas shown in Figure 3.1. Importantly, although data science is frequently used for business analytics (e.g., maximizing profit, minimizing cost, increasing the number of clicks on a website), data science can also contribute to research and theory-building (Lee et al., 2020; Shrestha et al., 2020; von Krogh, 2020).

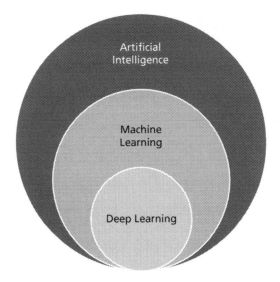

Figure 3.1 Conceptual relationships between artificial intelligence, machine learning, and deep learning.

Deductive and Inductive Research

Research in human resource management and organizational science disciplines use the hypothetico-deductive method to develop theories and improve our understanding of behavior in organizations (Locke, 2007). The hypothetico-deductive method connects theories derived through deductive reasoning to empirical data. According to Platt (1964), the hypothetico-deductive method begins with the relevant extant theory, which is used to deduce "intellectual inventions," or hypotheses that extend the theory logically. Then, the researcher collects data from a research study to determine whether the hypotheses are supported. If so, the results are interpreted and considered in relation to the underlying theory and expanded upon by future research.

Francis Bacon introduced induction, shifting the focus of research from theory extension to knowledge discovery (Mahootian & Eastman, 2009). In contrast to deduction, which begins with theory, induction begins with empirical observations. With induction, a pattern is extracted from observations/data and a theory is generated. The theory does not have to be directly based on previous supported theories or imply proof of a theory. Inductive methods can allow researchers to expose deductively generated hypotheses to greater falsifiability by allowing inductive methods to identify alternative explanations. Although research in academia follows deductive reasoning, researchers have argued for a more balanced approach, encouraging more inductive research (Locke, 2007; McAbee et al., 2017; Shrestha et al., 2020; Spector & Pindek, 2016; Spector et al., 2014).

As noted previously, data science employs scientific methods. Based on substantive knowledge, careful probability sampling of research units, and controlled experimental designs, in many ways, data science mirrors the deductive approach that serves as the foundation of academic research. However, data science also relies heavily on large quantities of existing and often unstructured data from multiple sources (e.g., wearable sensors, customer database, social media, employee records, navigation systems). Moreover, such data typically needs to be joined and preprocessed which constitutes *the* area where data scientists spend much of their time (Wickham & Grolemund, 2016). Although there is a lack of control with such data, by exploring, investigating patterns, and developing competing models to gain insight, data science also takes an inductive approach to understand phenomena because of its emphasis on prediction (Yarkoni & Westfall, 2017).

The deductive approach to research is well-established in academia as evidenced by the majority of articles published in journals (Spector et al., 2014). However, researchers have noted some concerns (Hambrick, 2007; Spector & Pindek, 2016; Yarkoni & Westfall, 2017).

> Unfortunately, in these days of over-reliance on theory generation, many if not most of our theories have been under-tested and receive few if any empirical tests beyond the original paper in which they appeared (Kacmar & Whitfield, 2000) ... theories can focus our approaches in certain directions to the exclusion of others, and discourage us from exploring new ways of thinking. If all of our studies must be based on a priori theory, there is no room in the literature for reports of new phenomena for which there are no theories, or for new ways of viewing phenomena that fail to fit any preconceived theoretical frameworks. (Spector et al., 2014, p. 499)

As a complement to deductive research, the inductive nature of data science and machine learning algorithms have the potential to contribute to theory and practice (Yarkoni & Westfall, 2017). Exploratory studies and novel findings from inductive research can serve as the "raw material for future theories" (Spector et al., 2014, p. 500). Having provided the motivation for inductive research, we next review machine learning.

Overview of Machine Learning

This section provides a brief introduction to machine learning and describes some basic algorithms with which human resource management and organizational scholars will be familiar. Machine learning algorithms can be broadly categorized into supervised learning, unsupervised learning, and semi-supervised learning.

Supervised Learning

With supervised learning, a researcher has a set of inputs and an output (James et al., 2013). In machine learning, these inputs are often referred to as features. In applied psychology and management, depending on the context, the inputs may be referred to as predictors, independent variables, factors, regressors, explanatory variables, mediators, moderators, confounders, covariates, or exogenous variables. An output is synonymous with criterion, dependent variable, response, outcome, end point, or endogenous variable. For example, the term independent variable is frequently used in the context of randomized experiments. As another example, depending on the context, a factor can refer to a categorical independent variable (e.g., in analysis of variance) or a factor might refer to a latent variable/construct (e.g., in structural equation modeling). Because inputs and features are somewhat generic terms, we will use them interchangeably. Conveniently, the IPO heuristic (McGrath, 1964) is a commonly used framework in research on teams (Kozlowski, 2018).

With supervised learning, the idea is to find a function that relates the inputs to the output based on some criterion (or loss function). If the output is continuous (e.g., team performance), the criterion might be to minimize the sum-of-squared errors in prediction. If the output is categorical (e.g., target detected vs. target not detected), the criterion might be to maximize classification accuracy. Thus, with supervised learning, the researcher must choose a function that appropriately combines the inputs and results in an output. This is a nontrivial issue given that many functions are available. As an additional challenge, inputs can be transformed in a variety of ways (e.g., natural logarithm, squared) prior to being used in a function.

With supervised learning, the researcher must also decide on the criterion used to make a decision about the quality of a model. For example, for a continuous output, which model results in the smallest mean square prediction error? Is the model overly complex and difficult to interpret? Is there another model with a similar mean square prediction error that is more interpretable?

The provided description of supervised learning may sound familiar. In fact, the most basic of supervised learning algorithms is multiple linear regression. Multiple linear regression is commonly used in human resource management, industrial-organizational psychology, and related fields (Rosopa et al., 2013). In multiple linear regression, the function takes a set of inputs to maximize the prediction of a continuous output. In other words, the set of inputs (e.g., conscientiousness, cognitive ability, cohesion, experience) are aggregated, using a weighted linear combination where the weights are estimated regression coefficients. The aggregate is a set of predicted scores on the output (e.g., predicted performance). In this regression context, we estimate a set of coefficients such that the maximum possible correlation between the predicted output and the observed output is obtained (Fox, 2016). This maximum possible correlation is known as the multiple correlation (R). When squared, this is known as the squared multiple correlation (R^2) or coefficient of determination (King et al., 2018). Researchers and practitioners must decide on what inputs to use in the function. Should some inputs be excluded? Should some inputs be transformed (e.g., squared term, or cross products for interaction effects)? Decisions such as these are typically based on a priori theory. If relevant inputs are not included (or measured), then R^2 and adjusted R^2 will be underestimated. Although R^2 and adjusted R^2 are commonly used indices to evaluate the performance of a model in the behavioral and social sciences, in the data science literature, cross-validated mean square prediction error is the typical metric for evaluating model performance (James et al., 2013).

Although multiple linear regression is commonly used in management and related fields (Scandura & Williams, 2000), many other supervised learning algorithms are available. Some are extensions of ordinary least squares multiple linear regression that attempt to address the tradeoff between having a small amount of bias in the estimated coefficients in exchange for more precision in the estimates (i.e., smaller standard errors; James et al., 2013). Hastie et al. (2009) and James and colleagues (2013) provide comprehensive coverage of various supervised learning algorithms (e.g., ridge regression, regression trees and random forests). Putka et al. (2018) provide a concise review of many supervised learning algorithms and compared their performance using data from 83 inputs (biodata items) and one continuous output collected from 9,257 individuals who entered the U.S. Army's Reserve Officer Training Corps Leadership Development and Assessment Course. Although many modern methods outperformed multiple linear regression, Putka and colleagues (2018) noted that some modern methods may be especially preferred for instances where there is multicollinearity and/or nonlinearity.

Supervised learning algorithms apply to labeled data. Labeled data simply means that the inputs are paired with an output. Thus, when exploring different supervised learning algorithms, there is some output that the algorithm is attempting to predict (for continuous output) or classify (for categorical output). When data are unlabeled, this indicates that there is no output (or outcome). Machine learning algorithms appropriate for unlabeled data is the realm of unsupervised learning.

Unsupervised Learning

With unsupervised learning, there exists a set of features and there is no output. Because the researcher simply has a collection of features, there is no output to predict or classify. Unsupervised learning can be conceptualized in two different ways.

With unsupervised learning, the researcher might group observations/rows (e.g., employees) based on their scores on the features. The researcher attempts to find homogeneous groups of observations. In other words, observations (e.g., employees) in the same group are very similar to one another while observations in different groups tend to be different from one another. This is known generally as clustering. Although there are a variety of approaches for clustering including hierarchical clustering, k-means clustering, and mixture models, each method attempts to find homogeneous groups of observations using the features. Note that because the data is unlabeled, we have no group to compare against to assess whether the clusters are "real" or "valid" in any sense, and we have no output to evaluate whether the clusters are able to optimally predict an outcome. As a concrete example, Gerlach et al. (2018) used unsupervised learning, specifically, clustering of personality data. Based on 1.5 million observations, they suggested the presence of four personality types.

Alternatively, with unsupervised learning, researchers may need to reduce many features (i.e., high-dimensional data) to a smaller set of new variables (i.e., two or three dimensions), where the new variables might be used in a subsequent analysis (e.g., supervised learning). As opposed to discovering groups of similar observations/rows, dimensionality reduction focuses on reducing the number of features. A popular method for dimension reduction is principal components analysis. Principal components analysis takes a set of p features and computes a new set of p variables called components that partitions the total variability in the data into p orthogonal chunks (Rencher & Christensen, 2012). Typically, in principal components analysis, the goal is to choose a smaller number of components (k) that explains as much variability in the original data as possible. Although principal components analysis has been used for dimension reduction (Jolliffe & Cadima, 2016), image compression (Ranade et al., 2007), and climate research (Hannachi et al., 2007), in management research, principal components analysis does not seem to be as commonly used as another closely related dimension reduction technique—factor analysis.

With factor analysis, a set of observed variables are believed to be caused by an underlying latent variable (Rencher & Christensen, 2012). Thus, the p observed variables might be reduced to two latent variables. It is important to note, however, that these latent variables are not the same as principal components. With principal components analysis, the p observed features are used to compute a linear combination on each of the principal components, where the number of principal components k is small and explains a large proportion of variance in the p features. If understanding and interpreting underlying latent factors is a major goal of an analysis, then factor analysis is more appropriate. If the goal is to reduce a large number of variables to a smaller set of more manageable variables, then principal components analysis may be more appropriate. Conway and Huffcutt (2003) provide a general review of these procedures and provide practical recommendations depending on whether interest lies in interpreting latent variables vs. dimension reduction.

Semi-Supervised Learning

Semi-supervised learning algorithms are targeted towards problems where there exist labeled and unlabeled data (van Engelen & Hoos, 2020). Although there are inputs, not all inputs have an associated output. In particular, the amount of unlabeled data is much larger than the amount of labeled data. Typically, labeled data has a higher cost or is difficult to obtain (James et al., 2013; van Engelen & Hoos, 2020). Although we are not aware of any applications of semi-supervised learning algorithms in human resource management in general, we suspect that semi-supervised learning algorithms could be applied to aerospace and healthcare.

Various inputs are available for aerospace teams (e.g., physical fitness assessments, stress, cognitive ability). However, important outputs may be primarily available only for teams in space. For teams still going through training, outputs "in the wild" are not available. Thus, this would be a situation where semi-supervised learning may be useful because the labeled data for teams could be used for learning what the output might be for the teams with unlabeled data.

Reinforcement learning can be thought of as a variation of semi-supervised learning. With reinforcement learning, an agent (or system) uses thousands of samples of data while interacting in its environment (e.g., an agent in a virtual game or a robot in the real world) and, depending on behavior, the agent is rewarded or punished as it pursues a goal. Although behavior initially may be guided by labeled data, when interacting in an environment, data (inputs) are received by the agent and the agent's behavior/action may be rewarded or penalized and, over time, the agent learns. Thus, an agent's behavior/action is paired with a reward or penalty, which does not necessarily occur immediately. Reinforcement learning has been used to teach a machine to walk (Garcia & Shafie, 2020) and teach an agent how to cooperate in a game (Tampuu et al., 2017). Reinforcement learning has also been applied in healthcare for optimal scheduling and resource allocation (Coronato et al., 2020). Although reinforcement learning appears to have many applications especially in AI, often there is one task or goal being learned as the agent interacts in an environment. Because teams typically have multiple goals and tasks, further advances in reinforcement learning may be needed (e.g., multi-objective optimization) for applications in teams research.

Summary

Although there are a host of ways that lessons learned from machine learning can contribute to the behavioral and social sciences (e.g., cross-validation to address the replication crisis, robust models with increased predictive power; Yarkoni & Westfall, 2017), the goal of this section was to provide a general introduction to data science and machine learning. In the next sections, specific algorithms are described that have the potential to make incremental contributions to the science of teams.

SUPERVISED LEARNING WITH NEURAL NETWORKS

Having provided an overview of three general areas of machine learning, I next focus on a specific class of algorithms widely used in industry. However, these algorithms are not commonly used in human resource management and organizational science. Specifically, neural networks and their basic architecture are described. Then, I discuss three reasons why neural networks may be useful in the study of teams.

Perceptron

To understand neural networks, I first discuss a foundational concept upon which all neural networks are based—the perceptron. Based on work by McCulloch and Pitts (1943), the perceptron was formalized by Rosenblatt (1958), a professor of neurobiology at Cornell University. A perceptron functions like a single neuron in the brain. Neurons receive signals (i.e., inputs) through dendrites. The signals are processed in the cell body, and electrochemical signals are then transmitted to other neurons via synapses (output). Although work on the perceptron was developed in the mid-1900s and was limited to binary outputs, advances in technology that could perform computer-intensive calculations helped fuel the growth and development of neural networks with numerous applications today including voice translation, computer vision, and self-driving cars (Aggarwal, 2018).

Figure 3.2 depicts a perceptron with three inputs. It deserves noting that the three inputs are weighted (using w_1, w_2, and w_3) and summed, and a bias term is added. The weights can be thought of as being similar to regression

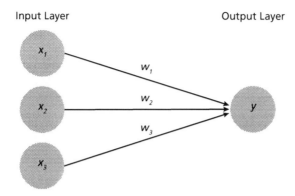

Figure 3.2 Single layer perceptron with three inputs and one output. *Note:* w_1, w_2, and w_3 are weights associated with each input node. The bias term was omitted.

coefficients and the bias term is analogous to an intercept. However, the resulting value is then transformed using an activation function. There are many activation functions (Hastie et al., 2009) and they are not reviewed here. However, it deserves noting that the activation function transforms what is simply a weighted linear combination of the inputs to a nonlinear "signal." This nonlinearity is a major reason that neural networks work well in prediction and classification (Aggarwal, 2018; Hastie et al., 2009) relative to conventional methods (e.g., multiple linear regression), particularly with high dimensional data and complex relationships. Overall, the single perceptron takes a set of inputs, processes the data, and makes a prediction (for continuous output) or classification (for categorical output). The circles depicted in Figure 3.2 are often referred to as nodes. The set of processes that occur between the input nodes and the output node can be expanded to allow for even more complex calculations.

Multilayer Perceptron

Figure 3.3 depicts a multilayer perceptron. The input layer, on the left, has three input nodes. There is one hidden layer that consists of four hidden nodes. Thus, the inputs are processed (weighted and summed) and an activation function applied at each of the four hidden nodes. Then, the results from the four hidden nodes serve as new inputs. These are processed (weighted and summed) and an activation function applied, and the final output is produced. Notice that there are two output nodes. Figure 3.4 depicts another multilayer perceptron but with two hidden layers. The input layer, on the left, has four input nodes. Note that the first hidden layer has

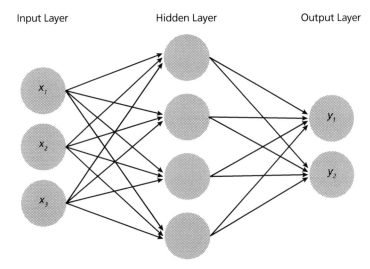

Figure 3.3 Multilayer perceptron with three inputs, one hidden layer, and two outputs. *Note:* The hidden layer consists of four hidden nodes. Weights and bias terms were omitted.

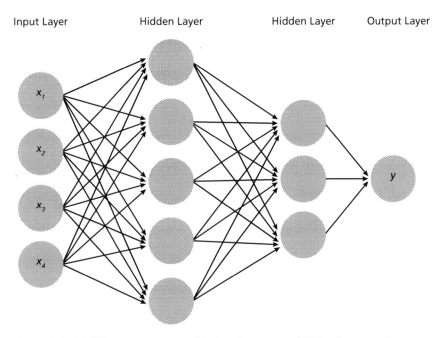

Figure 3.4 Multilayer perceptron with four inputs, two hidden layers, and one output. *Note:* The first hidden layer consists of five hidden nodes. The second hidden layer consists of three hidden nodes. Weights and bias terms were omitted.

five hidden nodes, and the second hidden layer has three hidden nodes. There is one output node.

Hidden layers extract characteristics from the inputs and, as noted by Hastie and colleagues (2009), substantive knowledge and experimentation can be used to decide on the number of hidden layers to build into the neural network architecture. As suggested by Hastie and colleagues (2009), it is generally better to have many hidden nodes than too few, because as part of testing and training the neural network some of the weights can be shrunken towards zero. Besides the computational time, there are no constraints on the number of input nodes in the input layer and output nodes in the output layer when building a neural network. However, with an arbitrarily large number of nodes, there may be convergence problems.

As an example, a neural network can be trained to recognize numbers from images. The neural network may have close to 1,000 inputs, depending on the number of pixels for each image in a sample. There may be two or more hidden layers with each hidden layer containing dozens of nodes. Because there are 10 digits (0, 1, 2, ... 9), there would be 10 outputs for such a problem. Depending on other decisions (e.g., type of activation function), this neural network is relatively easy to train and can classify new images with high accuracy (Aggarwal, 2018). In organizational research, Somers and Casal (2009) used a neural network with five inputs (e.g., job satisfaction, job search) and one continuous output (i.e., job performance) and found that one hidden layer was adequate to model nonlinearities, and the neural network outperformed multiple linear regression.

Reasons for Using Neural Networks

There are a number of characteristics that make neural networks a useful tool for conducting research on teams. I discuss improved prediction, nonlinearity, and dynamic theories.

Improved Prediction
Given the many benefits of effective teams, effect sizes in teams research are not large. In a meta-analysis on the effectiveness of team training in improving team performance, using 93 effect sizes across 2,650 teams, Salas and colleagues (2008) found the average meta-analytic correlation across various outcomes was .34, suggesting that team training explains on average approximately 11.6% of variance in outcomes. In a meta-analytic correlation matrix by Courtright et al. (2015), task interdependence and outcome interdependence correlated .13 and .27, respectively, with overall team performance. Thus, task interdependence explained approximately 1.7%

of variance in overall team performance while outcome interdependence explained approximately 7.3% of variance in overall team performance.

Given that neural networks have been found to explain more variability in an output compared to traditional multiple linear regression, it seems that neural networks could serve as a useful tool in teams research. As an example application, with training data predicting job performance using five inputs, Somers and Casal (2009) found that the optimal multilayer perceptron had an $R^2 = .396$ while multiple linear regression had an $R^2 = .038$. When applied to test data (i.e., new data), the optimal multilayer perceptron had an $R^2 = .150$ while multiple linear regression had an $R^2 = .005$. In a study predicting work stress using seven inputs, Somers, Birnbaum, and Casal (2001) found that a neural network using a radial basis activation function had an $R^2 = .41$ while multiple linear regression had an $R^2 = .27$ with training data. When applied to test data, the neural network had an $R^2 = .24$ while multiple linear regression had an $R^2 = .08$. Thus, in terms of predictive power, machine learning algorithms like neural networks could potentially improve the prediction of future behavior/outcomes (Yarkoni & Westfall, 2017) and this would be an especially important contribution in teams operating in high stress, high stakes situations like surgical teams and urban search and rescue teams.

Nonlinearity

Researchers theorize about the complex pattern of relationships between and among variables that result in effective team performance. Sui et al., (2016) investigated an inverted U-shaped relationship between leader-member exchange differentiation and team coordination. Among research and development teams, organizational tenure diversity had a curvilinear relationship with team innovation, particularly when team-oriented human resource practices were low, with $R^2 = .07$ and overall $R^2 = .52$ (Chi et al., 2009). Rapp and colleagues (2014) found that team self-efficacy and team performance followed an inverted U-shape pattern among sales teams, especially under high team goal monitoring, with $R^2 = .03$ and overall $R^2 = .29$. Although theories may suggest nonlinearities when modeling relationships among variables in teams research, many models are typically tested using multiple linear regression or structural equation modeling which lack the capability to model complex nonlinearities. This may partly explain the small effect sizes typically found in teams research.

Although polynomial terms can be added to linear regression and structural equation models, it is possible that the complexities of human interactions in teams may result in underlying functions far more complex than adding a squared term and/or a product term to a model. Current statistical models may not have the capability to capture the depth and complexity of the nonlinearities in teams research.

Neural networks are very flexible and can account for nonlinearities. The nonlinearity need not be restricted to U-shaped patterns or an interaction among inputs. The ability to account for nonlinearity is determined by the choice of activation function (Hastie et al., 2009). Recall that inputs are each multiplied by weights and a bias term added. The activation function is applied to the weighted sum. A popular activation function is the rectified linear activation function (ReLU), which would account for nonlinearity compared to linear activation functions like an identity function. As an example, Palocsay and White (2004) used a sigmoid activation function with seven input nodes predicting distributed justice. Somers (2001) found that a Bayesian neural network outperformed least square multiple linear regression when modeling nonlinearities in job performance using role conflict, role clarity, job involvement, and job satisfaction. Somers and colleagues (2021) modeled nonlinearities in a neural network also using a sigmoid activation function. They detected multiple complex nonlinearities between job search behavior, job satisfaction, and affective commitment with job performance. Some patterns were U-shaped and others were S-shaped. Note that their neural network accounted for 39.6% of variance compared to 3.8% when using multiple linear regression.

Dynamic Theories

Theory and research on teams highlight the "dynamic, emergent, and adaptive aspects of team member interactions with the environment, their task, and each other over time" (Kozlowski, 2018, p. 206). As dynamic systems, consistent with the IPO framework (McGrath, 1964), inputs combine in complex patterns that impact team processes, unfolding over time to impact team effectiveness (Kozlowski & Chao, 2018). Team processes and team performance can lead to important feedback loops (e.g., via guided team self-correction) that serve to further impact team processes and team performance (Smith-Jentsch et al., 2008).

Although the neural networks depicted in Figure 3.3 and Figure 3.4 can be used with static systems, another strength of neural networks beyond their flexibility to handle very complex nonlinearities is that they can also incorporate sequential data. With sequential data (inputs and outputs collected over time), imagine a neural network like that depicted in Figure 3.3, but layered over time. This is a recurrent neural network. Although the basic neural network architecture is similar to the multilayer perceptron in Figure 3.3, there are other aspects of the network that are added. Feedback loops in a recurrent neural network allow for outputs from an earlier state to influence inputs at a later state. Thus, an output at a later state is influenced not only by the inputs at the current state, but also the inputs at a previous state. In a way, the neural network has "memory" of the past. This may have various applications in teams research, for example, transactive memory systems (Lewis

& Herndon, 2011). Because data on teams is collected over time, a recurrent neural network may allow for more accurate modeling of the temporal dynamics and feedback loops described in theoretical models.

Neural Networks: An Applied Example

Because of the mixed findings on the role of personality in teams, researchers have theorized about different pathways through which personality affects team effectiveness (LePine et al., 2011). Neural networks may provide a robust method to model the relations between personality and team effectiveness. At the team level, for example, team personality composition would serve as inputs and team effectiveness would serve as the output. Note that neural networks allow for multiple outputs (see e.g., Figure 3.3). Although the researcher would need to explore the optimal number of hidden nodes, number of hidden layers, and choice of activation function (e.g., ReLU), in the end, this would serve to increase the predictive power of the neural network. For example, two hidden layers may be needed with multiple nodes to distill useful information about personality composition to predict team effectiveness. The choice of activation function would allow for complex nonlinearities (e.g., ReLU), beyond the conventional linear interactions tested in the behavioral sciences.

UNSUPERVISED LEARNING WITH PRINCIPAL COMPONENTS ANALYSIS

In the area of unsupervised learning, I suggest principal components analysis could be applied in research on teams. Although principal components analysis is well-established in engineering, physics, and climate research, its application in human resource management and teams research, in particular, seems limited. I first briefly discuss principal components analysis.

Principal Components Analysis

Given a set of p inputs or features, where p is large, the inputs may be used in an analysis. However, there are too many variables; that is, it is high-dimensional. Using an eigen decomposition (Jolliffe & Cadima, 2016), p new variables (components) can be computed that partition the total variability of the p inputs into p orthogonal components. Although the p inputs are correlated with one another (e.g., backup behavior, coordination, shared situational awareness), the p components will be uncorrelated with one another. Typically, instead of retaining all p components, a smaller number of k components are retained. For example, instead of needing $p = 15$ inputs to represent team processes, perhaps only $k = 3$ components would be used and would account for most of the variability in the 15×15 correlation matrix. It is important not to confuse principal components analysis with factor analysis. The example provided does not deal with latent factors. The total variability of the 15-dimensional data is now mostly contained in a lower dimensional subspace of three dimensions.

Reasons for Using Principal Components Analysis

There are at least two reasons for using principal components analysis in teams research. One is to reduce the dimensionality of the data so that it can be used in other analyses. The second relates to discovering patterns in the data.

Dimensionality Reduction

As noted, principal components analysis is typically used for dimension reduction. Unfortunately, a review of the literature has not revealed many applications of principal components analysis for dimension reduction in teams research. One reason for this is that data is clustered within teams. Thus, the measures on individual team members (i.e., composition) are nested within teams.

In most applications of principal components analysis, it is assumed that the observations/rows are independent. When multiple observations/rows are from the same team (e.g., platoon), then those observations will likely be dependent. Although this could cause problems with respect to dimension reduction, a multilevel principal components analysis could be conducted. Multilevel principal components analysis can separate variability between groups versus within groups. The lower dimensional component space could still be used as variables in other analyses. For example, these components could serve as inputs in a neural network.

Discovering Patterns

By using a few principal components, a large amount of the total variability in the data can be accounted for, but with fewer variables. Scores on the principal components can be used for visualization. For example, a scatterplot of the scores on the first two principal components could be used to check for outliers or irregular patterns in the data (Rencher & Christensen, 2012). Another application borrows from bioinformatics and analyzing gene expression data. With very high dimensional data, it is difficult if not impossible to detect clusters. After reducing data via principal components analysis and performing a clustering method like k-means clustering can aid in detecting genes that co-occur. The same approach can be taken in teams research. First, reduce noisy data using principal components analysis. Then, two or three components could be used as part of a clustering method (e.g., k-means clustering) to discover underlying groups. Overall, by combining two unsupervised learning algorithms, this may facilitate the discovery of unique patterns in the data.

Principal Components Analysis: An Applied Example

In teams research, all team members may be measured at the individual level on various characteristics. Because there are many characteristics and clustered by team, multilevel principal components analysis would be useful for reducing the dimensionality of the data at the team level and the individual level. Then, depending on whether a researcher is focusing on the individual level vs. the team level, principal components can be computed for the individual level and the team level. Such components scores could then be used as input for other analyses, for example, neural networks.

LIMITATIONS AND RECOMMENDATIONS

In the previous sections, I described how neural networks (supervised learning) and principal components (unsupervised learning) could be used in teams research to advance theory and practice. Here, some limitations are described and I offer recommendations for researchers and practitioners.

Neural Networks

Neural networks are simple to understand conceptually. However, the mathematics and computations involved in training and testing a neural network far exceed that of any multiple linear regression model. Because neural networks are not part of typical graduate training in human resource management and other organizational science disciplines, additional training will be needed to be able to develop and train such models. For example, when developing a neural network, there are various decisions to make. It is recommended that all inputs be treated equally (Hastie et al., 2009) by standardizing (i.e., transformed to z scores) or using a minimum-maximum normalization so that all inputs range between 0 and 1. Other approaches are available. Of the various activation functions (i.e., nonlinearity), which should a researcher use? In addition, the researcher must decide on the number of hidden layers and how many nodes in each hidden layer. A researcher must also decide on a parameter known as the learning rate. If the learning rate is too small, convergence may be slow; if the learning rate is too large, a solution may not be obtained as the algorithm oscillates in the solution space (Hastie et al., 2009). Thus, additional training in statistics, calculus, and computer programming may be useful. As suggested by Chan (2019), multidisciplinary collaborations with colleagues in statistics, engineering, and computer science will serve to strengthen the methods and theory in teams research.

Although neural networks may explain more variability in one or more outputs, interpreting the results can be challenging. In neural networks, interpreting the relative importance of the inputs is not the same as a least squares regression coefficient. Researchers in management and organizational behavior are familiar with the linear interpretation of coefficients associated with an input. In path analysis, if the estimated slope is positive, then this suggests that more of the input is associated with more of the output. However, as researchers in teams have noted, the complex and dynamic processes occurring within teams may not follow straightforward linear patterns (pun intended). Although there is no analog to the "beta weight" from multiple linear regression in neural networks, sensitivities can be calculated providing a relative rank among the inputs in terms of "importance." I also recommend an approach analogous to a squared semi-partial correlation (R^2). Specifically, after training a neural network and deciding on the final model, the overall R^2 can be calculated. Then, the researcher can refit the model but exclude one of the inputs. The R^2 from this model can be subtracted from the overall R^2, resulting in a pseudo-squared semi-partial correlation (R^2). This could be computed for each input, thus providing a sense of which inputs contribute most to the prediction of the output in the neural network. In addition, when interpreting the results of a neural network, I recommend that a conventional ordinary least squares regression model also be estimated. In this way, researchers and practitioners can compare the predictive power of the basic regression model with that of the final neural network.

Researchers should examine the number of hidden layers and the number of nodes in each hidden layer because this could provide insight into potential mediators or moderators. Specifically, in a neural network, if an input appears to have a large influence in predicting the output, but has a small bivariate correlation with the output, this could suggest that there may be a mediator operating between the input and output or that there is a moderator of the input and output relation. It is worth noting, however, that if the interaction is a standard linear interaction, then multiple linear regression should be able to detect this effect. On the other hand, if the interaction is of a complex nonlinear form, it is unlikely that multiple linear regression will be able to detect the nature of the interaction effect.

Principal Components Analysis

Principal components analysis can be performed on commonly available statistical software. However, a limitation may be that multilevel principal components analysis is not available in *SPSS*. Multilevel principal components analysis is available in *R* (R Core Team, 2021) and can be conducted using the *lavaan* package.

When using principal components analysis, it is recommended that scatterplots of the first few principal components be examined. As noted, the scatterplot of the first two principal components may suggest patterns in the data. If a grouping variable exists, using color or symbols to represent group membership would be useful. After deciding on the number of principal components to retain (k), the principal component scores can be stored and used for subsequent analyses (e.g., neural network).

CONCLUSION

There is a need for more robust data analytic tools in teams research. This chapter described the field of data science, in general, and how inductive research and machine learning algorithms, in particular, can contribute to theory and practice in teams. I discussed how a supervised learning (neural networks) and an unsupervised learning (principal components analysis) algorithm can be used. Consistent with Chan (2019), more multidisciplinary collaborations with engineering, computer science, and statistics is needed so that human resource management and organizational scholars can better model the complex nonlinear dynamic patterns in teams research.

AUTHOR NOTE

Correspondence concerning this chapter should be addressed to Patrick J. Rosopa, PhD, Department of Psychology, 418 Brackett Hall, Clemson University, Clemson, SC 29634. Email: prosopa@clemson.edu

REFERENCES

Aggarwal, C. C. (2018). *Neural networks and deep learning.* Springer.

Amabile, T. M. (2020). Creativity, artificial intelligence, and a world of surprises. *Academy of Management Discoveries, 6*(3), 351–354. https://doi.org/10.5465/amd.2019.0075

Chan, D. (2019). Team-level constructs. *Annual Review of Organizational Psychology and Organizational Behavior, 6*, 325–348. https://doi.org/10.1146/annurev-orgpsych-012218-015117

Chi, N. W., Huang, Y. M., & Lin, S. C. (2009). A double-edged sword? Exploring the curvilinear relationship between organizational tenure diversity and team innovation: The moderating role of team-oriented HR practices. *Group and Organization Management, 34*(6), 698–726. https://doi.org/10.1177/1059601109350985

Conway, J. M., & Huffcutt, A. I. (2003). A review and evaluation of exploratory factor analysis practices in organizational research. *Organizational Research Methods, 6*(2), 147–168. https://doi.org/10.1177/1094428103251541

Coronato, A., Naeem, M., De Pietro, G., & Paragliola, G. (2020). Reinforcement learning for intelligent healthcare applications: A survey. *Artificial Intelligence in Medicine, 109*, 101964. https://doi.org/10.1016/j.artmed.2020.101964

Courtright, S. H., Thurgood, G. R., Stewart, G. L., & Pierotti, A. J. (2015). Structural interdependence in teams: An integrative framework and meta-analysis. *Journal of Applied Psychology, 100*(6), 1825–1846. https://doi.org/10.1037/apl0000027

Fox, J. (2016). *Applied regression analysis and generalized linear models* (3rd ed.). SAGE Publications.

Garcia, J., & Shafie, D. (2020). Teaching a humanoid robot to walk faster through Safe Reinforcement Learning. *Engineering Applications of Artificial Intelligence, 88*, 103360. https://doi.org/10.1016/j.engappai.2019.103360

Gerlach, M., Farb, B., Revelle, W., & Amaral, L. A. N. (2018). A robust data-driven approach identifies four personality types across four large data sets. *Nature Human Behaviour, 2*(10), 735–742. https://doi.org/10.1038/s41562-018-0419-z

Grus, J. (2019). *Data science from scratch: First principles with python.* O'Reilly Media.

Hambrick, D. C. (2007). The field of management's devotion to theory: Too much of a good thing? *Academy of Management Journal, 50*(6), 1346–1352. https://doi.org/10.5465/AMJ.2007.28166119

Hannachi, A., Jolliffe, I. T., & Stephenson, D. B. (2007). Empirical orthogonal functions and related techniques in atmospheric science: A review. *International Journal of Climatology: A Journal of the Royal Meteorological Society, 27*(9), 1119–1152. https://doi.org/10.1002/joc.1499

Hastie, T., Tibshirani, R., & Friedman, J. (2009). *The elements of statistical learning: Data mining, inference, and prediction* (2nd ed.). Springer Science & Business Media.

James, G., Witten, D., Hastie, T., & Tibshirani, R. (2013). *An introduction to statistical learning with applications in R.* Springer.

Jolliffe, I. T., & Cadima, J. (2016). Principal component analysis: A review and recent developments. *Philosophical Transactions of the Royal Society A: Mathematical, Physical and Engineering Sciences, 374*(2065), 20150202.

Kacmar, K. M., & Whitfield, J. M. (2000). An additional rating method for journal articles in the field of management. *Organizational Research Methods, 3*(4), 392–406. https://doi.org/10.1177/109442810034005.

King, B. M., Rosopa, P. J., & Minium, E. W. (2018). *Statistical reasoning in the behavioral sciences* (7th ed.). Wiley.

Kozlowski, S. W. J. (2018). Enhancing the effectiveness of work groups and teams: A reflection. *Perspectives on Psychological Science, 13*(2), 205–212. https://doi.org/10.1177/1745691617697078

Kozlowski, S. W. J., & Chao, G. T. (2018). Unpacking team process dynamics and emergent phenomena: Challenges, conceptual advances, and innovative methods. *American Psychologist, 73*(4), 576–592. https://doi.org/10.1037/amp0000245

Lee, A., Inceoglu, I., Hauser, O., & Greene, M. (2020). Determining causal relationships in leadership research using Machine Learning: The powerful synergy of experiments and data science. *The Leadership Quarterly*, 101426. https://doi.org/10.1016/j.leaqua.2020.101426

LePine, J. A., Buckman, B. R., Crawford, E. R., & Methot, J. R. (2011). A review of research on personality in teams: Accounting for pathways spanning levels of theory and analysis. *Human Resource Management Review, 21*(4), 311–330.

Lewis, K., & Herndon, B. (2011). Transactive memory systems: Current issues and future research directions. *Organization Science, 22*(5), 1254–1265. https://doi.org/10.1287/orsc.1110.0647

Locke, E. A. (2007). The case for inductive theory building. *Journal of Management, 33*(6), 867–890. https://doi.org/10.1177/0149206307307636

Mahootian, F., & Eastman, T. E. (2009). Complementary frameworks of scientific inquiry: Hypothetico-deductive, hypothetico-inductive, and observational-inductive. *World Futures, 65*(1), 61–75.

Marks, M. A., Mathieu, J. E., & Zaccaro, S. J. (2001). A temporally based framework and taxonomy of team processes. *Academy of Management Review, 26*(3), 356–376. https://doi.org/10.5465/amr.2001.4845785

McAbee, S. T., Landis, R. S., & Burke, M. I. (2017). Inductive reasoning: The promise of big data. *Human Resource Management Review, 27*(2), 277–290. https://doi.org/10.1016/j.hrmr.2016.08.005

McCulloch, W. S., & Pitts, W. (1943). A logical calculus of the ideas immanent in nervous activity. *The Bulletin of Mathematical Biophysics, 5*(4), 115–133.

McGrath, J. E. (1964). *Social psychology: A brief introduction.* Holt, Rinehart, & Winston.

Oracle (n.d.). *What is data science?* Retrieved from https://www.oracle.com/data-science/what-is-data-science/

Palocsay, S. W., & White, M. M. (2004). Neural network modeling in cross-cultural research: A comparison with multiple regression. *Organizational Research Methods, 7*(4), 389–399. https://doi.org/10.1177/1094428104268030

Platt, J. R. (1964). Strong inference. *Science, 146*(3642), 347–353.

Putka, D. J., Beatty, A. S., & Reeder, M. C. (2018). Modern prediction methods: New perspectives on a common problem. *Organizational Research Methods, 21*(3), 689–732. https://doi.org/10.1177/1094428117697041

R Core Team. (2021). *R: A language and environment for statistical computing.* R Foundation for Statistical Computing. https://www.R-project.org/

Raisch, S., & Krakowski, S. (2021). Artificial intelligence and management: The automation–augmentation paradox. *Academy of Management Review, 46*(1), 192–210. https://doi.org/10.5465/amr.2018.0072

Ranade, A., Mahabalarao, S. S., & Kale, S. (2007). A variation on SVD based image compression. *Image and Vision Computing, 25*(6), 771–777. https://doi.org/10.1016/j.imavis.2006.07.004

Rapp, T. L., Bachrach, D. G., Rapp, A. A., & Mullins, R. (2014). The role of team goal monitoring in the curvilinear relationship between team efficacy and team performance. *Journal of Applied Psychology, 99*(5), 976–987. https://doi.org/10.1037/a0036978

Rencher, A. C., & Christensen, W. F. (2012). *Methods of multivariate analysis* (3rd ed.). Wiley.

Rosenblatt, F. (1958). The perceptron: A probabilistic model for information storage and organization in the brain. *Psychological Review, 65*(6), 386–408. https://doi.org/10.1037/h0042519

Rosopa, P. J., Schaffer, M. M., & Schroeder, A. N. (2013). Managing heteroscedasticity in general linear models. *Psychological Methods, 18*, 335–351.

Salas, E., & Cannon-Bowers, J. A. (2001). The science of training: A decade of progress. *Annual Review of Psychology, 52*, 471–499. https://doi.org/10.1146/annurev.psych.52.1.471

Salas, E., DiazGranados, D., Klein, C., Burke, C. S., Stagl, K. C., Goodwin, G. F., & Halpin, S. M. (2008). Does team training improve team performance? A meta-analysis. *Human factors, 50*(6), 903–933. https://doi.org/10.1518/001872008X375009

Scandura, T. A., & Williams, E. A. (2000). Research methodology in management: Current practices, trends, and implications for future research. *Academy of Management Journal, 43*(6), 1248–1264.

Shrestha, Y. R., He, V. F., Puranam, P., & von Krogh, G. (2020). Algorithm supported induction for building theory: How can we use prediction models to theorize? *Organization Science, 32*(3), 656–880.

Simon, H. A. (1995). Artificial intelligence: An empirical science. *Artificial Intelligence, 77*(1), 95–127. https://doi.org/10.1016/0004-3702(95)00039-H

Smith-Jentsch, K. A., Cannon-Bowers, J. A., Tannenbaum, S. I., & Salas, E. (2008). Guided team self-correction: Impacts on team mental models, processes, and effectiveness. *Small Group Research, 39*(3), 303–327. https://doi.org/10.1177/1046496408317794

Somers, M. J. (2001). Thinking differently: Assessing nonlinearities in the relationship between work attitudes and job performance using a Bayesian neural network. *Journal of Occupational and Organizational Psychology, 74*(1), 47–61. https://doi.org/10.1348/096317901167226

Somers, M. J., Birnbaum, D., & Casal, J. (2021). Supervisor support, control over work methods and employee well-being: New insights into nonlinearity from artificial neural networks. *The International Journal of Human Resource Management, 32*(7), 1620–1642. https://doi.org/10.1080/09585192.2018.1540442

Somers, M. J., & Casal, J. C. (2009). Using artificial neural networks to model nonlinearity: The case of the job satisfaction—Job performance relationship. *Organizational Research Methods, 12*(3), 403–417. https://doi.org/10.1177/1094428107309326

Spector, P. E., & Pindek, S. (2016). The future of research methods in work and occupational health psychology. *Applied Psychology: An International Review, 65*(2), 412–431. https://doi.org/10.1111/apps.12056

Spector, P. E., Rogelberg, S. G., Ryan, A. M., Schmitt, N., & Zedeck, S. (2014). Moving the pendulum back to the middle: Reflections on and introduction to the inductive research special issue of Journal of Business and Psychology. *Journal of Business and Psychology, 29*(4), 499–502. https://doi.org/10.1007/s10869-014-9372-7

Stranders, R., De Cote, E. M., Rogers, A., & Jennings, N. R. (2013). Near-optimal continuous patrolling with teams of mobile information gathering agents. *Artificial Intelligence, 195*, 63–105.

Sui, Y., Wang, H., Kirkman, B. L., & Li, N. (2016). Understanding the curvilinear relationships between LMX differentiation and team coordination and performance. *Personnel Psychology, 69*(3), 559–597. https://doi.org/10.1111/peps.12115

Tampuu, A., Matiisen, T., Kodelja, D., Kuzovkin, I., Korjus, K., Aru, J., Aru, J., & Vicente, R. (2017). Multiagent cooperation and competition with deep reinforcement learning. *PloS One, 12*(4), e0172395. https://doi.org/10.1371/journal.pone.0172395

Tannenbaum, S. I., Mathieu, J. E., Salas, E., & Cohen, D. (2012). Teams are changing: Are research and practice evolving fast enough? *Industrial and Organizational Psychology: Perspectives on Science and Practice, 5*(1), 2–24. http://doi.org/10.1111/j.1754-9434.2011.01396.x

Tonidandel, S., King, E. B., & Cortina, J. M. (2018). Big data methods: Leveraging modern data analytic techniques to build organizational science. *Organizational Research Methods, 21*(3), 525–547. https://doi.org/10.1177/1094428116677299

van Engelen, J. E., & Hoos, H. H. (2020). A survey on semi-supervised learning. *Machine Learning, 109*(2), 373–440. https://doi.org/10.1007/s10994-019-05855-6

von Krogh, G. (2020). Building capacity for empirical discovering in management and organization studies. *Academy of Management Discoveries, 6*(2), 159–164. https://doi.org/10.5465/amd.2020.0053

Wickham, H., & Grolemund, G. (2016). *R for data science: Import, tidy, transform, visualize, and model data.* O'Reilly Media, Inc.

Yarkoni, T., & Westfall, J. (2017). Choosing prediction over explanation in psychology: Lessons from machine learning. *Perspectives on Psychological Science, 12*(6), 1100–1122. https://doi.org/10.1177/1745691617693393

PART II

ENHANCING TEAM PERFORMANCE

CHAPTER 4

ENHANCING TEAM ENGAGEMENT IN TEAM-CENTRIC ORGANIZATIONS

An Integrative Model and Application

Gabriel Dickey
University of Northern Iowa

J. Lee Whittington
University of Dallas

Enoch Asare
University of Dallas

ABSTRACT

Many organizations are shifting towards a more team-centric approach as a response to an increasingly complex and dynamic business environment. This move toward a team-based structure requires consideration of team-oriented behaviors and processes. In this paper we develop a model that features team engagement as the central construct and a primary driver of

Managing Team Centricity in Modern Organizations, pages 79–114
Copyright © 2022 by Information Age Publishing
www.infoagepub.com

team performance in team-centric organizations. We emphasize the use of team performance management as a direct antecedent of team engagement. However, effective team performance management requires an integration of supportive leadership behaviors; therefore, we integrate the most salient full range leadership behaviors of the team leader across the specific phases of team performance management. The result is a conceptual model that can be utilized by both practitioners and researchers to evaluate how team engagement emerges in team-centric organizations. We illustrate the application of this model by discussing an integrative approach in the context of public accounting audit teams.

Drastic changes in the operating environment are forcing organizations to make crucial decisions about organizational design. This need is emphasized in the 2017 Deloitte Global Human Capital Trends survey of over 10,000 companies in 140 countries that identified organizational design as the most important issue facing the companies surveyed (Walsch & Volini, 2017). The dynamic complexity of the current environment has created a need for more organic organizational structures that provide greater agility to respond to the emerging market conditions and disruptions. Thus, organizational design has become a strategic imperative.

One response to these demands is a shift toward a more team-centric organization (Dulebohn & Murray, 2019; McDowell et al., 2016). The move towards team-centric organizations is also characterized by a higher representation of knowledge workers (Dulebohn & Hoch, 2017). As the level of knowledge related work increases, it is nearly impossible for one person to become an expert on every aspect of work that needs to be performed. Further, as repetitive task-based work becomes increasingly commoditized and replaceable by a variety of technologies, the sustainable competitive advantage of organizations has gravitated to a focus on knowledge creation that is efficiently accumulated and easily accessible. This shift augments the traditional task-based dimension of work with knowledge-based processes, and this new way of working must be accounted for by developing appropriate performance management processes. These distinct team-based performance management processes must be supplemented with leadership behaviors that focus on enhancing team-level attitudes and behaviors (Dulebohn & Murray, 2019).

The movement of knowledge-based organizations from an individual to a team-centric mode of operation also creates the need for special consideration of previously considered behavioral processes. For example, employee engagement has long been a concern for many organizations because the physical, cognitive, and emotional energies that characterize engaged employees are associated with high levels of individual task performance (Rich et al., 2010). As organizations become more team-centric, the persistent concerns about the engagement levels of individual employees must shift to the team level as well. Team engagement is a collective rather than individual construct that is distinguishable from employee engagement (Costa et al., 2014a). Although team members still perform their individual responsibilities, the accumulation of the sum of team members' individual engagement does not capture the shared perceptions of the whole team and "these shared perceptions are reflective of a shared organizational property" (Barrick et al., 2015, p. 113). Team engagement is also representative of the shared psychological connection that groups of individuals have towards each other and the results of their team (Sharma & Bhatnagar, 2017). We view team engagement as a primary driver of performance in team-centric organizations.

In this paper we develop a conceptual model of team performance with team engagement as our central construct. The conceptual model developed identifies team performance management and the behaviors of the team leader as crucial and interdependent factors that facilitate the emergence of team engagement. We present team performance management as a set of activities that encompass the entire cycle of a team's performance. The team performance management phases parallel the well-established individual performance management process (Aguinis, 2019; Asare, 2018; Asare et al., 2020; Locke & Latham, 1990). However, effective team performance management relies on the active involvement of the team leader (Dulebohn & Murray, 2019; Whittington & Galpin, 2010; Whittington et al., 2017). In team-centric organizations, the team leader's behaviors must have a team-oriented focus that goes beyond the individual level.

Our focus on team leader behavior is based on the full range leadership perspective because it uniquely reflects the fact that different mixtures of transactional and transformational leadership behaviors can be utilized during any stage of team development (Bell & Whittington, 2018). We integrate these transactional and transformational leadership behaviors across the phases of the team performance management process. We view the development of engaged teams as the result of an integrated set of team performance management processes and leadership behaviors.

By extending the individual performance management phases to the team level, this research makes four distinct contributions to the literature on team performance: First, we integrate the team leader's leadership behaviors into the specific phases of team performance management. Second, we emphasize the salience of the contingent reward (transactional) leadership behaviors of the team leader through each phase of team performance management. Third, we use the integrated team performance management process to develop a set of proposals into a conceptual model of team engagement that can be evaluated by researchers in a variety of different organizational domains. Fourth, we provide an application of the conceptual model by using audit teams as an exemplar knowledge-based team-centric organization. These practices can be generalized to other team-centric organizations.

TEAM ENGAGEMENT: THE CENTRAL CONSTRUCT

Engagement theory has been used to help researchers and practitioners better understand and evaluate performance. Kahn (1990) first defined employee engagement as "the degree to which individuals invest their physical, cognitive, and emotional energies into their role performance" (p. 694). Schaufeli et al. (2002) expanded upon Kahn's definition of employee engagement as "a positive work-related state comprised of vigor, dedication, and absorption" (p. 74). They clarify *vigor* as the high levels of energy with which one pursues his or her work-related tasks, *dedication* as the feelings of involvement in one's work, and *absorption* as the full concentration that one has when performing work-related tasks. Engaged employees have a psychological connection to their work and can invest themselves more fully in their job-related roles (Bakker et al., 2008). By fully investing and absorbing themselves into their work, highly engaged employees are energetically connected to their work (Gruman & Saks, 2011; Schaufeli & Salanova, 2007). Research has shown that higher levels of engagement are significantly related to enhanced individual job performance, higher organizational citizenship behavior, and lower turnover intention (Jha & Kumar, 2016; Rich et al., 2010; Shuck et al., 2011).

Although the engagement level of individuals remains an important issue, as organizations shift to team-based structures, the emphasis on engagement must also shift to the team level. Team engagement entails a referent shift from the "I" to the "we" and results in a shared state that cannot be found in individuals (Costa et al., 2014b). The shift to a team-based structure reflects a pattern of interdependencies as individual team members are required to coordinate and synchronize their roles and actions with other members of the team (Costa et al., 2014a). The success of teams is dependent upon the way team members interact because the team dynamic creates complex patterns of interactions among team members that go beyond individual contributions (Katz & Kahn, 1978; McGrath et al., 2000).

Team engagement is defined as a "shared, positive, fulfilling, motivational state of work-related well-being" (Costa et al., 2012, p. 35). Engaged teams create "a positive and activated climate that is characterized by feelings of pleasure" and thus can keep their motivational levels higher, which results in greater mutual commitment towards collective goals and outcomes (Costa et al., 2017, p. 207). An engaged team has members that are not only invested in their work but are also emotionally attached to each other (Sharma & Bhatnagar, 2017). This emotional attachment creates trust that facilitates a team climate of knowledge sharing where information flows more freely, and job-related issues and conflicts create energy rather than suppress it (Sharma & Bhatnagar, 2017). Team engagement considers these patterns of interactions and differs from individual employee engagement because the interactions of team members and team processes form a "whole" that has properties the individual parts do not (Costa et al., 2014a). Costa et al. (2014b) note that team engagement functions as a different construct because teams have different and more complex shared processes than individuals do in developing their own individual attitudes and behaviors.

The Impact of Team Engagement on Team Performance

Although individual employee engagement has been associated with a wide variety of individual level performance measures, research examining the effect that collective engagement has on group performance is limited. In an examination of 83 banks, Barrick et al. (2015) discovered that collective organizational engagement was positively associated with increased organizational profitability (as measured by return on assets). Costa et al. (2015) find that the availability of team resources influences team engagement, which in turn improves team performance. Torrente et al. (2012) found that team engagement mediates the relationship between team social resources and team performance.

The relationship between team engagement and team level outcomes is supported by Makikangas et al. (2016) and Tims (2013) who both report that shared job crafting among team members increases team engagement, which promotes team performance. Rahmadani et al. (2020) empirically demonstrate that engaging leadership (inspiring, strengthening, empowering, and connecting) and team engagement promote learning, innovation, and performance among team members.

Thus, we propose that team engagement is a central construct in team-centric organizations and will positively impact team performance.

Proposition 1: *Team engagement will be positively associated with team performance.*

ANTECEDENTS TO TEAM ENGAGEMENT

Team engagement is an emergent phenomenon that is a result of the interaction of several dynamic inputs and processes. Capra and Luisi (2014) define emergent properties as "the novel properties that arise when a higher level of complexity is reached by putting together components of lower complexity" (p. 154). They note that these properties emerge from the specific relationships and interactions among the parts in the organized ensemble (Capra & Luisi, 2014). These inputs and processes can vary, but team engagement does not just haphazardly emerge. A foundation must be set by having a team whose members know what is expected of them both individually and collectively and the environment must be conducive to allow the dynamic interactions to exist in a positive and productive manner. There are at least two crucial elements that help set a foundation for engaged teams to emerge: team performance management and the behaviors of the team's immediate leader. Each of these factors impacts the level of team engagement throughout the team's performance cycle.

Performance Management

Performance management is a process consisting of four interdependent phases: performance planning, implementation, evaluation, and consequences (Asare, 2018). The elements of individual employee performance management can be extended to teams (Aguinis, 2019). These phases extend across the performance cycle of the team, beginning with initial project scope assessment (including goal setting), implementation, concurrent process enhancement, and project completion. In this section we discuss a team performance management process that integrates the elements of team management developed by Hackman (1987) with the stages of the performance management process (Aguinis, 2019; Asare, 2018; Asare et al., 2020).

Performance planning entails setting clear, specific, and challenging goals that are attainable for employees. Performance implementation is concerned with employees executing the performance plan. Performance evaluation encompasses rating employees' performance by the employee and the manager. The evaluative criteria used in this phase are tied directly to the performance expectations and goals established in the performance planning phase. The final phase of this integrated performance management process allocates the consequences of meeting, or failing to meet, performance expectations. The consequence phase primarily involves the formal distribution of tangible rewards (or sanctions) and can also include less-tangible rewards such as affirmation and appreciation. Ideally, there are no surprises in the evaluation and consequences phases of the process because any deviations from expectations should have been addressed through the regular, concrete expectations-based feedback that the manager provided throughout the performance cycle.

Performance Management at the Team Level

Extending performance management to the team level introduces four complexities to the process that need to be managed (Aguinis, 2019). The first challenge is to identify an effective means of assessing an individual's contributions as compared to those of the team and its members. The second challenge is to identify team performance measures. The third challenge is to effectively motivate team members to achieve both their personal and team goals. Finally, employee rewards must be based on both individual and team performance (Aguinis, 2019).

Effectively addressing the challenges identified by Aguinis (2019) requires an intentional effort to structure the team task and allocate the necessary resources to support the team. Effective work teams have structured processes that make the roles and responsibilities of team members clear (Hackman, 1987). These processes ensure that appropriate resources are identified and utilized. These structure-creating processes set boundaries for behavioral norms and provide the basis for ongoing assistance and expectation-based feedback throughout the performance cycle. Hackman (1987) identified four stages of managerial work that are necessary for creating an effective team. Stage 1 is the pre-work stage where time is spent identifying tasks and critical task demands. Stage 2 is the creating performance conditions stage where resources and the necessary supports are identified as well as the make-up of the team. Stage 3 is the forming and building team stage where boundaries are set, and appropriate norms are developed. Stage 4 is providing ongoing assistance where mechanisms and behaviors for promoting synergy are established. Hackman's guidelines provide an actionable framework for addressing the challenges identified by Aguinis (2019).

Phase 1: Performance Planning

The team performance management process extends across a team's project life cycle and parallels individual performance management. Performance planning begins with pre-work planning, where the organization's strategic goals are cascaded down to individual employee and team level goals. In a team context, the pre-work includes considering the team's tasks and the demands of these tasks. This stage involves determining the structure of the tasks and identifying the resources that are necessary to support the team. In team-centric organizations, the staffing and team leader decisions flow from the identification of task requirements, including an assessment of task complexity and the risks associated with the project. The time and attention given to these preparatory activities create the boundary conditions for team performance (Hackman, 1987).

The pre-work sets the stage for determining specific performance goals for the team. This pre-work includes setting boundaries for team performance by clarifying task expectations and developing appropriate norms for interaction of the team members (Hackman, 1987). This should be a participatory process that includes identifying individual roles and expectations in the context of the team performance expectations in the form of specific goals (Aguinis, 2019; Asare et al., 2020; Kinicki et al., 2013). Effective goal setting also provides the role and task identification that are crucial to team performance (Cameran et al., 2018). The individual goals that reflect the individual roles and responsibilities should be aligned with the team's goals.

The goal setting aspects of the performance planning phase is foundational for the entire team performance management process. The goal setting process should result in a clear set of expectations that are used as the basis for concurrent feedback throughout the performance cycle. These goals should also function as the evaluative criteria in the formal team performance evaluation phase. The goal setting process should also encourage communication and coordination among team members. The importance of team goal setting is emphasized by Kramer et al. (2013) who identify eight factors that are critical to team goal setting. These factors are task interdependence, goal type, organizational culture, team identity, team size, individual differences, reward systems, and leadership.

Task interdependence represents the extent to which team members must interact with each other to complete their tasks and positively influences team collective efficacy and goal commitment, which in turn influences team performance (Aube & Rousseau, 2005; Gully et al., 2002). The team-based goals can be based on a variety of team-oriented objectives including quality, profitability, timing (e.g., deadlines and milestones), and client satisfaction.

Teams are embedded in the larger context of the organizations and the organization's culture plays a significant role in team development as it impacts the attitudes and behaviors of all members in the organization. Although the organizational culture has a strong influence on the team culture, each team can have its own unique identity. Team identity is important for team goal setting because the more team members identify with team goals, the harder they work to attain those goals (Kramer et al., 2013). Team size can also influence team performance because smaller team size discourages social loafing and promotes team goal commitment (Harkins & Petty, 1982; Karau & Williams, 1993; Latane et al., 1979).

Teams are comprised of individuals and recognizing individual differences in terms of goal orientation is essential in team goal setting. Individuals who primarily seek learning-oriented goals are more cooperative. Other team members may have a performance-oriented approach to goals. These individuals view goal achievement as outcomes that demonstrate personal competency. These individuals tend to be more competitive (Kramer et al.,

2013). The reward systems should be based on both individual and team-related factors and be designed in a way that promotes individual differences without sacrificing a team culture of cooperation.

Team goal setting should encourage members to participate in the goal setting. Allowing team members to participate in setting the team's goals provides them with voice in the form of opinions, means, timeframe, and resource requirements for goal attainment (Ashford & De Stobbeleir, 2013; Borgogni & Russo, 2013; Travers, 2013). Participative team goal setting promotes member self-efficacy and goal commitment (Cascio, 2006; Latham & Wexley, 1994; Shilts et al., 2013). Senecal et al. (2008) concluded that team goal setting promotes team cohesion. Aguinis (2019) notes that it is critical for leaders to encourage team members to try new behaviors and provide them information on team best practices. Additionally, it is important to give team members enough time to practice new skills and encourage them to try new ways of working together (Aguinis, 2019).

Phase 2: Performance Implementation

The planning stage sets the foundation for the implementation stage of team performance. The performance implementation phase is composed of performance execution of the roles and tasks identified in Phase 1, ongoing expectations-based performance feedback, and facilitation. Each team member's responsibility is to execute the performance plan by putting into action the agreed-upon performance requirements as they were defined at the performance planning stage (Latham & Wexley, 1994).

The implementation phase requires specific actions from the team leader. The team leader's role and responsibilities are to guide the employee through the performance execution process by using expectations-based feedback (Latham & Wexley, 1994; Whittington et al., 2017). This feedback should include not only corrective and constructional feedback (Avolio, 2011), but affirmational feedback for meeting project milestones (Whittington et al., 2017). The regular use of constructive and corrective feedback, along with affirmational recognition, keeps team members focused, and promotes ongoing goal commitment and attainment (Briscoe & Claus, 2008; Gruman & Saks, 2011; Kramer et al., 2013). This feedback is often informal yet must be timely (Galpin & Whittington, 2009, 2012).

The team leader is also responsible for facilitating the performance execution process by removing situational constraints that are preventing the team and its members from attaining their performance goals (Borgogni & Russo, 2013; Cascio, 2006). The team leader addresses situational constraints by providing the employee with resources such as requisite task information, materials, tools, and supplies that are necessary for goal attainment (Cascio, 2006; Latham & Arshoff, 2013). These responsibilities may also involve providing team-based resources such as additional team members and protecting the team from distractions due to changes in project scope or obligations to other organizational demands.

Phase 3: Performance Evaluation

Performance evaluation is the formal assessment of the employee's behavior and results during the performance cycle (Latham & Wexley, 1994). The team performance evaluation process can occur at a project milestone, end of team project, and/or end of the organizational performance cycle and the evaluation process should be formalized by the organization. Effective team performance management must include these formal performance assessments to evaluate and rate the team and individual team members' performance for the performance cycle. By using the goals established in the performance planning phase as the evaluative criteria for formal team performance evaluation reduces the contamination and deficiency problems often associated with performance appraisals (Whittington et al., 2017).

For fairness, trust, and ownership purposes, it is common to have ratings from both the team leader and the individual team members (Aguinis, 2019; Cascio, 2006; Pulakos, 2009). These comprehensive evaluations provide voice in the appraisal process and enhance the perceptions of the fairness of the performance appraisal process. These perceptions lead to higher levels of trust in both the performance management process and the leader of the team (Bol et al., 2010; Bol & Lill, 2015; Bol & Smith, 2011; Latham & Locke, 1990). For team-centric organizations, the use of peer evaluations also promotes workload sharing, cooperation, and high performance among team members (Aguinis, 2019).

The evaluation phase of the team performance management process concludes with feedback in the form of performance ratings to the team members and the team. This feedback "closes the loop" for the current performance cycle by evaluating the actual performance of the team against the performance expectations that were developed in the planning phase of the performance management process. Explicitly linking these assessments to the performance goals reinforces commitment to the performance management process. These formal assessments also provide the basis for individual and team goal setting for the next performance cycle (Aguinis, 2019; Asare et al., 2020).

Phase 4: Performance Consequences

The consequences phase of team performance management is concerned with linking tangible rewards with both individual and team performance. During the performance consequences phase, the organization applies rewards and sanctions as consequences for both team and individual performance. Research shows that rewards and sanctions should be applied right at the end of the current organizational performance cycle to promote high performance, engagement, job satisfaction, and affective commitment (Aguinis, 2009; Latham & Locke, 1990; Podsakoff et al., 1982). The primary rewards offered in the consequences phase are extrinsic rewards. Extrinsic rewards are defined as rewards given to an individual by another person or entity (Latham & Locke, 1990). Extrinsic rewards include financial incentives such as pay increases or bonuses and promotions.

The Impact of Team Performance Management on Team Engagement

Organizations seeking to cultivate an environment from which engaged teams can emerge need effective team performance management. The connection between individual performance management and employee engagement is supported in a recent series of field studies conducted by Whittington et al. (2017). In four separate studies, Whittington et al. (2017) report significant positive relationships between performance management and employee engagement (Asare et al., 2020; Whittington et al., 2017). Path analyses conducted by Mone and London (2009) and Mone et al. (2011) also confirm the positive association between performance management and employee engagement.

The connection between individual performance management and employee engagements has been extended to the team level. Researchers have found that the team goal setting aspect of team performance management impacts team performance. For example, Hoegl and Parboteeah (2003) found team goal setting to be directly related to team effectiveness. Aube et al. (2014) empirically demonstrate that team goal commitment mediates the relationship between team flow and team performance. Research by Van der Hoek et al. (2018) discovers that goal setting promotes team performance.

To foster and cultivate an organizational environment of highly engaged teams, team-centric organizations need to extend their performance management processes to the team level. By extending the performance management processes to teams, we expect that team performance management provides the necessary structure from which engaged teams can emerge.

Proposition 2: *Team performance management will be positively related to team engagement.*

Beyond Team Performance Management

Team performance management is crucial to the development of team engagement. However, the mere presence of team performance management is not sufficient for developing a high-performance team. The effectiveness of the performance management system is determined by the active involvement of the team leader. The importance of the leadership behaviors of the team's leader have recently been emphasized by the Gallup organization. Gallup suggests that the behaviors of an employee's immediate manager are key to the level of employee engagement (Clifton & Harter, 2019). In fact, Gallup states that "70% of the variance in employee engagement is determined solely by the manager" (Clifton & Harter, 2019, p. 12).

In team-centric environments, one-way dyad-based relationships that foster individual outcomes must be supplemented with team-oriented behaviors by the team leader. Kozlowski et al. (2016) note that team management requires a team-centric leadership approach such as transformational leadership. Transformational leadership is built on a foundation of transactional leadership and these two behaviors combine to form the full range leadership behaviors.

Given the importance of team leader behavior, we argue that the leader's behavior will moderate (enhance) the relationship between performance management and team engagement. In the next section, we discuss the elements of the full range of leadership behaviors (Avolio, 2011). Following this discussion, we integrate the various transformational and transactional facets of full range leadership with the phases of team performance management and then build this integration into the conceptual model of team engagement.

Full Range Leadership

The leadership behaviors of the team leader play a key role in the creation of an environment that fosters team engagement (Barrick et al., 2015; Costa et al., 2014a; Sharma & Bhatnagar, 2017). The leader must be versatile and have an acute understanding of the environment and context to appropriately exhibit the appropriate behaviors that can lead to an engaged team (Morgeson et al., 2010). The full range leadership model developed by Avolio and Bass (1991) effectively captures the essence of contextual leadership (Antonakis et al., 2003). Full range leadership suggests that the interaction between a leader and his or her followers could take two complementary and interdependent forms: transactional and transformational leadership.

Transactional leadership occurs when a leader exchanges something of economic, political, or psychological value with a follower (Goodwin et al., 2001). The exchanges are based on the leader identifying performance requirements and clarifying the conditions under which rewards are available for meeting these requirements. These exchanges create a psychological contract between the leader and followers. Contingent reward behaviors represent the active and constructive exchange part of the relationship between leaders and followers (Robinson & Boies, 2016). By clarifying expectations and keeping promises through rewards, contingent reward behaviors can help set an important foundation of trustworthiness for followers (Wofford et al., 1998).

The contingent reward behaviors exhibited by the team leader parallel several aspects of the performance management process. Clarifying performance expectations and setting clear goals occurs in the performance planning phase of team performance management. Contingent reward behaviors also include providing regular and concrete expectation-based feedback across the performance cycle. These behaviors are crucial during the implementation and execution phases of the performance management process.

The trust that arises from transactional leadership provides a necessary foundation for transformational leadership. Transformational leadership moves beyond the exchange-based nature of transactional leadership to build a relationship with subordinates and motivate them to attain their goals through specific leadership behaviors. Transformational leadership encourages the interaction of followers to engage in a way that achieves higher levels of motivation and morality beyond self-interest (Kozlowski et al., 2016). Transformational leadership behaviors "inspire followers to raise their performance beyond expectations" by encouraging followers to transcend their own self-interests, raising their level of consciousness concerning outcomes, and by raising or expanding follower needs levels" (Goodwin et al., 2011, p. 411).

A transformational leader exhibits at least one of the following characteristics but oftentimes a combination: idealized influence, inspirational motivation, intellectual stimulation, and individualized consideration (Bass & Avolio, 1993). Podsakoff et al. (1990) expanded the four "I's" framework by identifying six behaviors that make up the set of transformational leadership behaviors:

- *Identifying and articulating a vision (TFLV):* The transformational leader can effectively inspire team members with their plans for the future and get others committed to these plans.
- *Fostering the acceptance of group goals (TFLG):* The transformational leader can get the team members to work towards the same goals and develop a team attitude and spirit amongst the team.
- *Setting high performance expectations (TFLE):* The transformational leader sets high performance expectations for the team members by insisting on their best performance throughout the production cycle.
- *Providing an appropriate model (TFLM):* The transformational leader leads by example and demonstrates the appropriate behaviors by "doing" rather than simply "telling."
- *Providing individualized support (TFLS):* The transformational leader makes connections with individual team members and provides sup-

port to the members by showing respect for their personal feelings and behaving in a manner that is thoughtful of their personal needs.

- *Providing intellectual stimulation (TFLI):* The transformational leader is able to foster an intellectually stimulating environment by forcing members to rethink some of their own ideas and viewing old problems in new ways.

The Impact of Full Range Leadership on Team Engagement and Performance

Transformational leadership has a well-established connection with performance-level outcomes such as task performance, innovative behavior, creativity, organizational citizenship behaviors, and team learning (Aryee et al., 2012; Gong et al., 2009; Koeslag-Kreunen et al., 2018; Purvanova et al., 2006; Qu et al., 2015). Keller (2006) found transformation leadership characteristics to positively impact team cost performance and technical quality. Transformational leadership behaviors promote team potency, which in turn promotes team performance (Schaubroeck et al., 2007). Braun et al. (2013) find that transformational leadership characteristics build team trust, which results in higher team performance. Transformational leaders have been associated with higher levels of overall organizational performance as well (Colbert et al., 2008; Judge & Piccolo, 2004; Wang et al., 2011). Barrick et al. (2015) found that transformational leadership was positively associated with collective organizational engagement.

In a recent field study, Dickey (2019) found that team leader behavior was positively associated with team engagement. Specifically, Dickey reported that the full range of transformational and contingent reward behaviors were significantly related to team engagement. Furthermore, his results indicated that the impact of these leader behaviors on team performance was fully mediated by team engagement. The combination of transactional and transformational leadership behaviors by the team's immediate leader is an integral element in the development of highly engaged teams. By consistently exhibiting these behaviors throughout the phases of team performance management, the team leader fosters the trust, psychological connection, and team-oriented culture that is found in highly engaged teams.

ENHANCING TEAM PERFORMANCE MANAGEMENT

The team leader must exhibit the full range leadership behaviors throughout the phases of team performance management, however there are certain subdimensions of full range leadership that are more salient during the specific phases of team performance management. The following section integrates these subdimensions into the phases of team performance management.

Integrating the Full Range Leadership Behaviors

Phase 1: Performance Planning

The planning phase is incredibly important for any type of project. During the planning stage, leadership is critical in setting team goals and driving goal commitment. Effective leaders clearly define team goals, motivate, and develop members for goal attainment (Kramer et al., 2013; Zaccaro et al., 2001). The most salient leadership behaviors in the performance planning stage are articulating a vision, fostering the development of group (team) goals, and setting high performance expectations. The transformational setting of high-performance expectations complements the contingent reward behaviors that should be executed in the planning phase. These aspects of full range leadership should be embedded in every aspect of the goal setting process.

Effective team leaders have a thorough understanding of the organization's culture and how it aligns with the team's identity. The team leader uses his or her understanding of the organizational culture and team identity to articulate a compelling vision of what collective success means for each team member. Therefore, the leader's vision is a critical component to team engagement. In instances where the team's identity does not align with the organizational culture, the leader must guide the team to make necessary changes.

Fostering the acceptance of team goals adds formality to the vision articulation behaviors in the performance planning stage. After understanding, influencing, and articulating the vision for the team, the leader must ensure that the team goals are accepted by all team members. The primary goal is to have a successful completion of the team's overall objective(s); however, there are several other team and individual goals that should be established during the performance planning stage. The team leader must ensure that any individual and team goals are managed in such a way that they do not detract from the team's cohesiveness, engagement, and performance (Birnberg, 2011).

Crafting and articulating a compelling vision fosters acceptance of the team's goals. Together with contingent reward behaviors, these behaviors cascade into setting high performance expectations and behavioral norms that are crucial for team engagement. These expectations occur at both the individual and team levels. A team leader should recognize that individual team members may pursue a variety of goals (Griffith et al., 2016). The team leader's awareness of these individual goals should be used to work with the team members to ensure that their individual goals are difficult yet achievable. Similarly, team goals should be stretched to push the team and its members to high levels of performance, however the team goals must be attainable lest they lose their potency.

During the performance planning phase, contingent reward behaviors are the most crucial dimension of the full range of leadership behaviors. The effective use of contingent reward behaviors ensures that performance expectations in the form of specific and challenging goals are communicated and committed to. These expectations provide a clear target that focuses team performance and enhances goal commitment by specifying the extrinsic rewards associated with goal achievement. The performance criteria also set the stage for feedback that can be used throughout the audit process as teams and their members meet and exceed the established performance expectations.

Phase 2: Performance Implementation

The most salient full range leadership behaviors shift in Phase 2 as the performance plan is implemented and executed. In the second phase, the modeling behaviors of the team leader are important. The team leader sets the "tone at the top" of the team by being a positive example for team members to follow. The modeling behaviors may include applying professional judgment for dealing with adaptive challenges (Heifetz, 1994; Heifetz & Linskey, 2002) that emerge as the project evolves. The modeling behaviors may also include demonstrating high emotional intelligence in handling conflicts, and consistently exhibiting ethical conduct and moral reasoning. In this phase the leader should lead by "doing" rather than simply "telling," to facilitate the team's performance by removing potential bottlenecks and impediments that could hinder the team's performance.

Team leaders also facilitate team performance by equipping team members with the tools necessary for goal attainment (Pulakos, 2009; Zaccaro et al., 2001). During the performance implementation and execution phase, the leader should provide individualized support to the team members by behaving in a manner that is respectful and thoughtful to the needs of the individuals on the team. This support may involve helping team members develop their technical skills or guiding them to the appropriate resources. In addition, individualized support involves being cognizant of each team member's mood and emotional state as these can impact the judgment calls that are required in intensively interactive team-based tasks (Cianci & Bierstaker, 2009; Gaudine & Thorne, 2001).

Team leaders also provide intellectual stimulation for the team by challenging the way team members think about issues, problems, and ideas. If executed properly, this stimulation helps create a level of dynamic energy amongst the team members that is a necessary part of highly engaged teams. By engaging in these intellectually stimulating behaviors, leaders can also help the team members avoid the complacency that can lead to dysfunctional behaviors.

During Phase 2, the contingent reward behaviors are centered on providing ongoing feedback to the team members, both individually and collectively. A fully invested team leader is actively involved in soliciting feedback from the team members and using social cues to provide "in the moment" praise or constructive critique designed to improve both individual and team performance. This active feedback allows team members to understand how they are progressing, which creates trust by reinforcing the explicit performance expectations and the psychological contract established in Phase 1.

Phase 3: Performance Evaluation

Performance evaluation is an ongoing process of concurrent feedback throughout the team performance cycle. This feedback may include formal milestone reviews and should also include feedback sessions such as the personal management interviews suggested by Cameron (2012). These concurrent feedback sessions are important for providing affirmation, as well as constructive and corrective feedback (Avolio, 2011). However, the performance evaluation phase of the performance management process involves a formal appraisal of the team's performance. In this phase, the most salient leadership behaviors are primarily contingent rewards based on the performance goals set in the performance planning phase.

The second and third phases of team performance management may be continuous or discrete. Knowledge-based professions typically have project milestones that are evaluated throughout a project. Pre-established milestones create opportunities for more formalized contingent reward behaviors to be exhibited. The contingent rewards offered should be based on the expectations established in the first phase, however, go-forward expectations for subsequent milestones may be adjusted accordingly.

Phase 4: Performance Consequences

The final phase of team performance management is the consequences phase. During this phase, the use of extrinsic contingent reward behaviors by the team leader are most salient. These extrinsic rewards include compensation and promotions. Team-centric firms need to avoid relying solely on individual performances, however. Given team engagement is a shared motivational construct that is crucial to high team performance outcomes, extrinsic rewards that recognize only individual performance can create disincentives and distrust in team-oriented ideals that inhibit team engagement. Thus, the extrinsic contingent reward behaviors should include team-based performance criteria.

TABLE 4.1 Integrated Phases of Team Performance Management			
Phase 1: Performance Planning	**Phase 2: Performance Implementation**	**Phase 3: Performance Evaluation**	**Phase 4: Performance Consequences**
Full Range Leadership Behaviors:	Full Range Leadership Behaviors:	Full Range Leadership Behaviors:	Full Range Leadership Behaviors:
• Vision (TFLV) • Group Goals (TFLG) • High Performance Expectations (TFLE) • Contingent Reward (clarifying expectations)	• Individualized Support (TFLS) • Intellectual Stimulation (TFLI) • Modeling (TFLM) • Contingent Reward (providing on-going feedback)	• Contingent Reward (expectation-based evaluation)	• Contingent Reward (based on actual vs. expectation performance)

The integration of the full range leadership behaviors creates the integrated phases of team performance management depicted in Table 4.1.

Evaluating the Interaction of Team Performance Management and Leadership

Although the full range leadership behaviors of the team leader are integrated into the phases of team performance management, full range leadership represents a distinct set of behaviors whose specific impact on team engagement and team performance can be evaluated by both practitioners and researchers. The interaction of the full range leadership behaviors with team performance management is a key consideration in the emergence of engaged teams. While team performance management sets a foundation for highly engaged teams, the full range leadership behaviors of the team leader enhance the team performance management processes to ensure that the phases are effectively executed. Thus, we propose that these behaviors have a moderating (enhancing) effect on the relationship between team performance management and team engagement:

Proposition 3: *The use of full range leadership behaviors by the team leader will enhance the relationship between the team performance management and team engagement.*

Figure 4.1 illustrates the relationships among the three propositions.

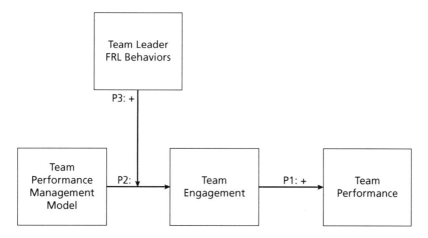

Figure 4.1 Proposed model.

APPLICATION OF THE INTEGRATED TEAM PERFORMANCE MANAGEMENT PHASES

In this section we provide an application of our conceptual model in the specific setting of public accounting audit teams. We demonstrate that the elements of the team performance management process can be mapped across the audit performance cycle. Additionally, we will discuss the importance of the full range of leadership behaviors of the audit team leader (the lead audit partner) throughout the audit cycle. Although we provide an application of our conceptual model in a specific context, we are confident that the model can be generalized to other team-centric organizations.

Knowledge-intensive project-based organizations that are organized around project teams provide opportunities to study the antecedents and consequences of team engagement. A good example of this type of organization is the certified public accounting firm. Financial statement auditing ("auditing" or "audit") is a profession that relies almost exclusively on knowledge workers, who must deal with an environment that is constantly in flux due to changes in regulations, technology, client-related factors, and economic conditions (Newmark et al., 2018).

Audit teams provide a particularly appropriate context for this research because auditing is an inherently team-based profession and the importance of the audit team is essential as the audit process is dependent on it (Dobre et al., 2012). Audit teams provide a potentially rich field for examination of team behaviors because individuals are typically on multiple audits and part of several teams under many different partners who have distinct managerial directives and leadership styles (Cameran et al., 2017). As a result, individual auditors are exposed to a wide variety of team cultures that form a solid basis for comparison in evaluating team dynamics. Therefore, we use the audit teams of certified public accounting firms as an exemplar knowledge-intensive, project-based, team-centric organization and embed our proposed team performance in an audit team related context.

Financial Statement Audit Overview

A financial statement audit is a project that consists of tasks, procedures, and responsibilities. The collection of tasks, procedures, and responsibilities performed throughout the audit form the audit process. An audit involves a set of highly interconnected processes where the results of procedures performed in one financial statement cycle and/or account can impact several different cycles and/or accounts (Arens et al., 2020).

These audits are typically conducted by teams. An audit team is a hierarchical assembly of individuals brought together for the purpose of performing a financial statement audit of the organizations being audited (Solomon, 1987). Audit teams are a part of certified public accounting firms that are members of a professional organization where the collective level of expertise provides the necessary legitimacy for the services they provide (Von Nordenflycht, 2010). The auditing standards require the members of the team to possess a level of expertise that allows them to properly perform their responsibilities (PCAOB, 2015).

Audit firms that have a significant number of teams failing to maintain minimum audit quality standards risk losing their legitimacy, therefore audit quality is the principal performance-related outcome for audit teams (Holm & Zaman, 2012; Persico, 2019). Developing a high-quality audit team goes beyond identifying and assembling qualified and competent individuals to execute the audit process. Individuals do not work in isolation and the interaction of team members plays an important role in how the audit teams operate (Cameran et al., 2018). The interactions among team members create dynamic patterns of collective behavior than can significantly impact the quality of an audit team's performance.

The Impact of Team Engagement on Audit Performance

The audit environment can be one of immense pressure as deadlines, process disruptions, and labor resource deficiencies can lead to dysfunctional auditor behaviors (Svanström, 2016). Research has demonstrated that engaged teams exhibit more resilience when encountering difficulties and drawbacks (Costa et al., 2017). Teams with higher levels of team engagement have more collective vitality, commitment, and focus with which to proactively investigate potential audit-related issues. This proactivity allows teams to identify and resolve issues earlier in the audit process, which gives adequate time for adjusting the audit approach if the results of the audit procedures do not go according to plan. The ability to identify and resolve issues earlier in the audit process creates an environment of greater quality, profitability, and client satisfaction.

Identifying and resolving issues can be complicated given the subjectivity of many audit and accounting related issues (Dickey, 2019). A high-quality audit team requires that the audit team members exercise their roles and responsibilities effectively. In addition, high-quality audit teams have members who trust each other with sensitive client related concerns and issues. Highly engaged teams operate in an environment where team members share more information (Sharma & Bhatnagar, 2017). An audit is highly integrated, which means that the issues found in one financial statement area can impact other areas (Arens et al., 2020). Sharing more information ultimately leads to better issue identification and resolution and therefore plays a significant role in high quality audits.

The team-centric, integrated, knowledge-based nature of financial statement auditing emphasizes the importance of the dynamic interactions that occur during an audit. A stagnated audit team is at greater risk of failing to comply with and adjust to the ever-changing regulatory, economic, and client environments. An audit team can also leverage the psychological connection that its team members have with their work and each other to design better audit processes and procedures that improve team performance. Thus, team engagement is a strategic imperative for team-centric organizations such as certified public accounting firms that operate in dynamic and complex business environments. In a recent field study, Dickey (2019) examined 82 audit teams and found that team engagement was positively associated with audit quality. These results indicate that team engagement is a crucial antecedent to team performance for knowledge-intensive team-centric organizations such as financial statement auditing.

Aligning the Audit Cycle With the Team Performance Management Phases

The phases of the team performance management cycle closely parallel those of the integrated financial statement audit cycle (Arens et al., 2020). The planning phase of the audit cycle involves the pre-work of assessing the size, complexity, and the risks associated with a particular audit. These assessments are then utilized to make decisions concerning the staffing of the audit team as well as setting both individual and team performance expectations.

The planning phase of the audit cycle corresponds with the performance planning phase (Phase 1) of team performance management.

The implementation phase (Phase 2) of team performance management corresponds with the execution phase of the audit cycle. For an audit, this phase includes performing a variety of tests related to internal controls, transactions, and account balances. The execution of audit testing can be an iterative process as the preliminary results oftentimes indicate the need for additional procedures. The evaluation phase (Phase 3) of team performance management can occur at various points during the execution phase of the audit (e.g., milestone dates) as well as during the completion phase of the audit. The audit cycle concludes with documenting the results of the audit procedures performed and communicating the results of the audit via the issuance of a formalized audit report. The consequences phase (Phase 4) of team performance management is based on the results of the audit in relation to previously established individual and team-based expectations.

Integrated Team Performance Management in Auditing

High performing certified public accounting firms have highly engaged audit teams. The foundation for team engagement must be established with sound structural team management processes and strong leadership behaviors from team leaders that facilitate the execution of these processes. Our conceptual model in Figure 4.1 leverages previous accounting context field studies conducted by Dickey (2019) and Asare (2018). Asare (2018) evaluated the behaviors of 105 individual accountants and discovered that performance management was positively related to engagement. In the field study of audit teams, Dickey (2019) found that the full range leadership behaviors of the lead audit partner were positively related to team engagement.

Phase One: Performance Planning

The audit planning phase begins by developing an understanding of the client and scope of the audit work. This step is usually performed by a more senior member of the audit team who has a solid understanding of the audit approach and how it applies to a given client. The scope of an audit is used to prepare a project budget, which documents the estimated number of hours for each team member and the expected areas where the team members are expected to incur their time. This scope assessment determines the resource needs of the audit team and plays a significant role in determining the staffing composition of the audit team. Failure to properly staff an audit team can inhibit team performance throughout the entirety of the audit process. Although experience is the primary determinant of team composition, the interests and motivations of potential team members should be a consideration as well. Team members with the necessary level of experience who also have a strong desire to be involved in a particular industry or on a specific audit client are more likely to be engaged (Wollard & Shuck, 2011).

Once the team composition has been determined, the goal setting process for the team should take place. Team goal setting processes that encourage participation from all team members will result in a mutual acceptance of team goals between the lead audit partner and the members of the audit team. There are a variety of team-related performance metrics that can be used to evaluate audit team performance such as quality, profitability, timing, and client-service. Although these results are not mutually exclusive, quality must always be a primary concern for audit teams because without a reputation of quality, the firm loses its regulatory legitimacy.

In the planning phase of any audit cycle, there is a great deal of emphasis on role and task identification. However, role and task ambiguity remain potential threats to audit performance (Cameran et al., 2018). Vera-Muñoz et al. (2006) note that the conflict related to ambiguity causes team members to spend more time coping with the resultant stress and less time performing their job-related responsibilities productively. The roles and responsibilities must be aligned with the overall team goals and objectives and should consider the individual goals and motivations of team members. A detailed task listing should be developed and aligned with the overall project budget to minimize the risk of role and task ambiguity.

The contingent reward behaviors of the lead audit partner are crucial in the planning phase of the audit cycle. The lead audit partner should clarify the roles and expectations of team members and reward those individuals who meet and exceed performance expectations. Clarification of expectations is especially important in an audit team setting because of the variety of different team members and experience levels. The rewards for meeting and exceeding these expectations must be explicitly stated and clearly articulated during the planning phase of the audit cycle. The rewards for performance should be related to both the individual and team levels. For instance, team members who underperform individually but are part of a well-performing team may be able to simultaneously share in team successes (e.g., a celebratory outing and/or team-related bonus) while also lacking in certain contingent rewards that accompany individual performance such as promotion or higher levels of merit-based pay.

In addition to the foundation that is set through effective contingent reward behaviors, there are certain transformational behaviors that are salient in the performance planning stage. The lead audit partner must ensure that there is commitment to the team goals from all team members. The primary goal is to finish the audit by the filing or issuance deadline, however there are several other team specific goals that can be established during the performance planning stage. For instance, teams may commit to tangible team goals such as meeting different performance-related milestones throughout the audit process.

Effective lead audit partners have a thorough understanding of the team's culture and how it aligns with an individual's identity. By articulating a compelling vision for the audit team, the lead audit partner not only understands this alignment but can also articulate the collective vision to the team's members. Research demonstrates that auditors pursue a variety of different individual goals (Griffith et al., 2016). In instances where an individual's identity or motivations do not align with the team culture, the lead audit partner must provide guidance for the individual to make necessary changes. For example, the team culture may be one of greater empowerment or flexibility which may be at odds with a team member who is uncomfortable delegating responsibility.

Finally, the lead audit partner should work with the team members to ensure that they are setting high performance expectations both individually and collectively during the planning phase. These goals should be difficult yet achievable and allow members to aspire to higher levels of performance. The setting of high expectations complements the contingent reward behaviors. The team-based quality, profitability, timing, and client-service metrics are used as motivational team performance-related factors.

Phase 2: Performance Implementation

The execution of the audit plan is commonly referred to as "fieldwork." Once the audit team's fieldwork begins, the team leader provides ongoing expectations-based feedback to team members through frequent updated meetings or "check-ins." These check-ins ensure that the roles and tasks being performed by team members are contributing to the goals and objectives that were set at the performance planning stage. The dynamic nature of an audit means that task requirements can change throughout the audit. Therefore, effective team performance management on an audit team requires that team members regularly update the detailed task listing that was developed in the first phase of team performance management. Throughout the audit process, the team leader should have a sound understanding of how the team is progressing and whether there are any impediments to performance. This understanding allows the lead audit partner to effectively use the contingent reward behaviors in an appropriate and timely manner.

The team leader's use of contingent reward behaviors is also crucial during the audit execution stage. Having set clear performance expectations in the audit planning phase, the lead audit partner must also provide the team with frequent expectations-based feedback as the team members perform their tasks. The feedback process allows the partner to motivate and coach team members to focus on the performance plan for goal attainment at the individual and team levels (Aguinis, 2019; Whittington et al., 2017).

If team members are meeting or exceeding their personal and team goals, the partner should affirm the progress in his or her feedback to the team. The purpose of the feedback is to keep team members focused to promote goal commitment and attainment (Briscoe & Claus, 2008; Gruman & Saks, 2011; Kramer et al., 2013).

The contingent reward leadership behaviors provide an opportunity for the lead audit partner to elevate team performance beyond expectations. For example, a team and its members may have developed an exceptional risk identification analysis or incorporated the use of a new technology that simultaneously improved quality and created efficiencies in scope. By taking advantage of opportunities to exhibit implicit rewards, the lead audit partner can specifically identify the best practices that go beyond what has previously been established as an agreed upon performance expectation. These behaviors also strengthen the psychological contract and increase the levels of trust and emotional connection that are found in highly engaged audit teams.

Another crucial aspect of team leadership involves equipping team members with the tools and providing the support that is necessary for goal attainment (Pulakos, 2009; Zaccaro et al., 2001). This equipping and support function begins during the planning phase and extends through the implementation phase of the audit cycle. During the execution phase, the lead audit partner should provide individualized support to the team members by behaving in a manner that is respectful and thoughtful to the needs of the individuals on the team. The lead audit partner may need to help team members develop their technical skills or guide them to the appropriate resources. The lead audit partner also needs to be cognizant of each team member's mood and emotional state as these can impact judgments made during an audit (Cianci & Bierstaker, 2009; Gaudine & Thorne, 2001). The support provided by the lead audit partner may also include resolving certain client-imposed constraints or approving the use of additional team members should the scope of the audit significantly change. The individual support reduces stress and affords team members the necessary confidence to focus on their audit-related responsibilities. With all team members focused, the levels of mutual commitment increase.

Performing high quality audits involves making judgment calls and requires the application of professional skepticism (Nelson, 2009). Despite this generally acknowledged auditing principle, Pierce and Sweeney (2004) found that 43% of auditors reported acceptance of limited client explanations and superficial analysis of client documents. Thus, it is incumbent on the lead audit partner to engage in the intellectually stimulating behaviors with team members. In the context of an audit, intellectual stimulation involves challenging the way auditors think about issues, problems, and ideas. These behaviors help the team members avoid complacency. Auditing is an inherently knowledge-based profession with ever-changing technologies, business environments, and accounting and auditing standards, therefore, the lead audit partner needs to ensure that the team members are making the necessary adaptations.

Finally, the audit team leader is ultimately responsible for setting the "tone at the top" of the audit team and the transformational modeling behaviors should consistently be exhibited throughout the execution phase of the audit. The lead audit partner must present a model of the appropriate team level mindset. In addition, sound ethical decision-making is a significant element of high audit quality and the lead audit partner must also present a model of the appropriate ethical mindset. Simply speaking to a team-oriented and ethical mindset is not enough, however; the lead audit partner must also provide a visible demonstration of how the execution of this mindset manifests. When reviewing the audit team's work and interacting with the team members and client, the lead audit partner provides direct evidence of the acceptable and appropriate behaviors for team members to follow. Alignment of the lead audit partner's "saying" with "doing" promotes the higher levels of trust that are found in highly engaged audit teams.

Phase 3: Performance Evaluation

Depending on the length of the audit, the third phase of team performance management may take place after milestones determined during the planning phase or at the end of the audit. The criteria for measuring profitability, timing, client service, and quality should be measured and evaluated. These measurements can come from profitability reports, time reports, client satisfaction reports, internal and external inspections, and independent reviewer evaluations.

The performance evaluation process adds a level of formality to the more "in the moment" contingent reward behaviors exhibited by the lead audit partner in the second phase of team performance management. By using formal metrics and multiple data points, the lead audit reinforces the performance goals and promotes the credibility of the performance management process. A milestone approach can be highly effective and if the evaluation is performed at a milestone date, the go-forward expectations can be revised to improve subsequent performance.

The completion phase of the audit provides an opportunity for the lead audit partner to perform a formal final evaluation. Both team and individual goals should be considered in evaluating performance. The goals and objectives established in the planning phase and revised (if applicable) during the implementation phase are used as the basis for evaluation and there should be no uncertainty about the terms of performance. Additionally, the lead audit partner should obtain as many perspectives of individual performance as possible, including gathering feedback from each team member and employees of the audit client who played a critical role in the audit process. Communication of the performance evaluation needs to be transparent and clearly articulated by the lead audit partner.

Phase 4: Performance Consequences

During the consequences phase of team performance management, the rewards are mostly extrinsic in the form of raises and promotions that are based on the evaluation process performed in the evaluation phase of team performance management. Celebratory team outings create opportunities to strengthen relationships and build the cohesiveness that will be beneficial for subsequent audit projects. Team bragging rights and "feel-good" attitudes are forms of intrinsic rewards that are experienced in audit teams. Finally, it should be stressed that team performance management is a cycle-based approach whereby the results of one cycle are used in the planning phase of the next cycle. Therefore, the audit team results directly impact the goal setting process for the following audit. The consequences should be structured in a manner that promotes either improvement or continued high-performance in subsequent performance cycles.

CONCLUSION

Our research has positioned team engagement as a primary driver of high performing teams in team-centric organizations. Team engagement is a construct that goes beyond the simple "sum of the parts" approach that has previously been the primary focus of engagement related research. Teams consist of a collection of individuals who have dynamic interactions and share emotions with each other. Team engagement is an emergent phenomenon that effectively captures the characteristics of shared motivational capabilities and strong psychological connections found in high performing teams. Given the theoretical and empirical findings to date, we propose that team-centric organizations should place a primary emphasis on team engagement in the development and evaluation of their teams.

The importance of team engagement in team-centric organizations creates the need to further the understanding of the factors that create a necessary foundation for team engagement to emerge. We have developed a conceptual team-based model with team engagement as the central construct. This conceptual model utilizes previous literature on individual performance management that includes the planning, implementation, evaluation, and consequences phases. We have extended these phases to the team level using a set of team management principles to create the phases of team performance management. We expect team performance management to have a direct and significant positive impact on the level of team engagement.

Further, we propose that team performance management is enhanced by team leaders who consistently exhibit the full range of transformational and transactional behaviors throughout the phases of team performance management. These full range leadership behaviors are not mutually exclusive, nor are they limited to a specific phase of team performance management. Effective leaders will use a combination of these behaviors across the lifecycle of the team; however, certain aspects of full range leadership are more salient at specific phases of team performance management. We identify the most salient dimensions of full range leadership in each of the phases of team performance management. This integration includes a strong emphasis on contingent reward leadership behaviors that are salient throughout the integrated phases of team performance management.

Team performance management and the full range leadership behaviors of the team leader represent two distinct constructs whose interaction is considered in our conceptual model. We propose that the leadership behaviors of the team leader moderate (enhance) the phases of team performance management. As depicted in Figure 4.1, this interaction sets a foundation for team engagement, which in turn leads to high team performance-related outcomes. Finally, empirical evidence on engagement at a team level unit of analysis has been extremely scarce. We leverage the limited prior research found in an audit team setting to develop a potential application of the complete model.

REFERENCES

Aguinis, H. (2009). An expanded view of performance management. In J. W. Smither & M. London (Eds.), *Performance management: Putting research in action* (pp. 1–43). Jossey-Bass.

Aguinis, H. (2019). *Performance management* (4th ed). Chicago Business Press.

Antonakis, J., Avolio, B. J., & Sivasubramaniam, N. (2003). Context and leadership: An examination of the nine-factor full-range leadership theory using the Multifactor Leadership Questionnaire. *The Leadership Quarterly, 14*(3), 261–295. https://doi.org/10.1016/S1048-9843(03)00030-4

Arens, A. A., Elder, R. J., Beasley, M. S., & Hogan, C. E. (2020). *Auditing and assurance services: An integrated approach* (17th ed.). Pearson Education.

Aryee, S., Walumbwa, F. O., Zhou, Q., & Hartnell, C. A. (2012). Transformational leadership, innovative behavior, and task performance: Test of mediation and moderation processes. *Human Performance, 25*(1), 1–25. https://doi.org/10.10 80/08959285.2011.631648

Asare, E. (2018). *Promoting employee engagement through performance management: A field study of accountants* [Doctoral dissertation, University of Dallas]. https:// digitalcommons.udallas.edu/edt/7

Asare, E. K., Whittington, J. L., & Walsh, R. (2020). Promoting desirable work attitudes and behaviors among accountants: A field study. *Journal of Business*

and Industrial Marketing, 35(10), 1591–1604. https://doi.org/10.1108/JBIM
-01-2019-0020

Ashford, S. J., & De Stobbeleir, K. M. (2013). Feedback, goal setting, and task performance revisited. In E. Locke & G. P. Latham (Eds.), *New developments in goal setting and task performance* (pp. 51–64). Routledge.

Aubé, C., Brunelle, E., & Rousseau, V. (2014). Flow experience and team performance: The role of team goal commitment and information exchange. *Motivation and Emotion, 38*(1), 120–130. https://doi.org/10.1007/s11031-013-9365-2

Aubé, C., & Rousseau, V. (2005). Team goal commitment and team effectiveness: The role of task interdependence and supportive behaviors. *Group Dynamics, 9*(3), 189–204. https://doi.org/10.1037/1089-2699.9.3.189

Avolio, B. (2011). *Full range leadership development.* (2nd ed.). SAGE Publishing.

Avolio, B. J., & Bass, B. M. (1991). *The full range leadership development programs: Basic and advanced manuals.* (2nd ed.). Bass, Avolio, & Associates.

Bakker, A. B., Schaufeli, W. B., Leiter, M. P., & Taris, T. W. (2008). Work engagement: An emerging concept in occupational health psychology. *Work & Stress. 22*(3), 187–200. https://doi.org/10.1080/02678370802393649

Barrick, M. R., Thurgood, G. R., Smith, T. A., & Courtright, S. H. (2015). Collective organizational engagement: Linking motivational antecedents, strategic implementation, and firm performance. *Academy of Management Journal, 58*(1), 111–135. https://doi.org/10.5465/amj.2013.0227

Bass, B. M., & Avolio, B. J. (1993). Transformational leadership and organizational culture. *Public Administration Quarterly, 17*(1), 112–121.

Bell, R. G., & Whittington, J. L. (2018). Exploring the full range of leadership across the organizational life cycle and growth states of entrepreneurial firms. In *Research handbook on entrepreneurship and leadership* (pp. 173–194). Edward Elgar.

Birnberg, J. G. (2011). A proposed framework for behavioral accounting research. *Behavioral Research in Accounting, 23*(1), 1–43. https://search.proquest.com/scholarly-journals/proposed-framework-behavioral-accounting-research/docview/849618964/se-2?accountid=7106.

Bol, J., Keune, T., Matsumura, E., & Shin, J. (2010). Supervisor discretion in target setting: An empirical investigation. *Accounting Review, 85*(6), 1861–1886. https://doi.org/10.2308/accr.2010.85.6.1861

Bol, J., & Lill, B. (2015). Performance target revisions in incentive contracts: Do information and trust reduce ratcheting and the ratchet effect? *Accounting Review, 90*(5), 1755–1778. https://doi.org/10.2308/accr-51050

Bol, J. C., & Smith, S. D. (2011). Spillover effects in subjective performance evaluation: Bias and the asymmetric influence of controllability. *The Accounting Review, 86*(4), 1213–1230. https://search.proquest.com/scholarly-journals/spillover-effects-subjective-performance/docview/880048074/se-2?accountid=7106

Borgogni, L., & Russo, Dello, S. (2013). A quantitative analysis of the high performance cycle in Italy. In E. A. Locke & G. P. Latham (Eds.), *New developments in goal setting and task performance* (pp. 270–283). Routledge.

Braun, S., Peus, C., Weisweiler, S., & Frey, D. (2013). Transformational leadership, job satisfaction, and team performance: A multilevel mediation model of trust. *Leadership Quarterly, 24*(1), 270–283. https://doi.org/10.1016/j.leaqua.2012.11.006

Briscoe, D. R., & Claus, L. M. (2008). Employee performance management: Policies and practices in multinational enterprises. In A. Varma, P. S. Budhwar, & A. DeNisi (Eds.), *Performance management: A global perspective* (pp. 15–39). Routledge.

Cameran, M., Ditillo, A., & Pettinicchio, A. (2017). *Auditing teams: Dynamics and efficiency.* Taylor & Francis.

Cameran, M., Ditillo, A., & Pettinicchio, A. (2018). Audit team attributes matter: How diversity affects audit quality. *European Accounting Review, 27*(4), 595–621. https://doi.org/10.1080/09638180.2017.1307131

Cameron, K. (2012). *Positive leadership: Strategies for extraordinary performance.* Berrett-Koehler Publishers.

Capra, F., & Luisi, P. L. (2014). *The systems view of life: A unifying vision.* Cambridge University Press.

Cascio, W. F. (2006). Global performance management systems. In G. K. Stahl & I. Bjorkman (Eds.), *Handbook of research in international human resource management* (pp. 176–196). Edward Elgar.

Cianci, A. M., & Bierstaker, J. L. (2009). The impact of positive and negative mood on the hypothesis generation and ethical judgments of auditors. *Auditing, 28*(2), 119–144. https://doi.org/10.2308/aud.2009.28.2.119

Clifton, J., & Harter, J. (2019). *It's the manager: Gallup finds the quality of managers and team leaders is the single biggest factor in your organization's long-term success.* Simon & Schuster Digital Sales.

Colbert, A. E., Kristof-Brown, A., Bradley, B. H., & Barrick, M. R. (2008). CEO transformational leadership. The role of goal importance congruence in top management teams. *Academy of Management Journal, 51*(1), 81–96. https://doi.org/10.5465/AMJ.2008.30717744

Costa, P. L., Passos, A. M., & Bakker, A. B. (2012). *Teamwork engagement: Considering team dynamics for engagement* (Working Papers Series 2 12-06, ISCTE-IUL). Business Research Unit (BRU-IUL).

Costa, P. L., Passos, A. M., & Bakker, A. B. (2014a). Teamwork engagement: A model of emergence. *Journal of Occupational & Organizational Psychology, 87*(2), 414–436. https://doi.org/10.1111/joop.12057

Costa, P. L., Passos, A. M., & Bakker, A. B. (2014b). Empirical validation of the teamwork engagement construct. *Journal of Personnel Psychology, 13*(1), 34–45. https://doi.org/10.1027/1866-5888/a000102

Costa, P. L., Passos, A. M., & Bakker, A. B. (2015). Direct and contextual influence of team conflict on team resources, team work engagement, and team performance. *Negotiation & Conflict Management Research, 8*(4), 211–227. https://doi.org/10.1111/ncmr.12061

Costa, P. L., Passos, A. M., Bakker, A. B., Romana, R., & Ferrão, C. (2017). Interactions in engaged work teams: A qualitative study. *Team Performance Management: An International Journal, 23*(5/6), 206–226. https://doi.org/10.1108/TPM-12-2016-0054

Dickey, G. (2019). *Exploring the human side of audit quality: Team engagement and partner leadership behaviors* [Doctoral dissertation, University of Dallas]. https://digitalcommons.udallas.edu

Dobre, F., Vilsanoiu, D., & Turlea, E. (2012). A multiple regression model for selecting audit team members. *Procedia Economics and Finance, 3*, 204–210. https://doi.org/10.1016/S2212-5671(12)00141-4

Dulebohn, J. H., & Hoch, J. E. (2017). Virtual teams in organizations. *Human Resource Management Review, 27*(4), 569–574. https://doi.org/10.1016/j.hrmr.2016.12.004

Dulebohn, J. H., & Murray, B. (2019). Leadership, performance management and team-centric organizations. In D. L. Stone & J. H. Dulebohn (Eds.), *The only constant in HRM today is change* (pp. 199–229). Information Age Publishing.

Galpin, T., & Whittington, J. L. (2009). Creating a culture of candor in the leadership classroom. *Journal of Leadership Education, 8*(2), 10–19. https://doi.org/10.12806/V8/I2/AB2

Galpin, T. J., & Whittington, J. L. (2012). Creating a culture of sustainability in entrepreneurial enterprises. In M. Wagner (Ed.), *Entrepreneurship, innovation and sustainability* (pp. 68–87). Taylor and Francis.

Gaudine, A., & Thorne, L. (2001). Emotion and ethical decision-making in organizations. *Journal of Business Ethics, 31*(2), 175–187. https://doi.org/10.1023/A:1010711413444

Gong, Y., Huang, J. C., & Farh, J. L. (2009). Employee learning orientation, transformational leadership, and employee creativity: The mediating role of employee creative self-efficacy. *Academy of Management Journal, 52*(4), 765–778. https://doi.org/10.5465/amj.2009.43670890

Goodwin, V. L., Whittington, J. L., Murray, B., & Nichols, T. (2011). Moderator or mediator? Examining the role of trust in the transformational leadership paradigm. *Journal of Managerial Issues, 23*(4), 409–425. https://www.jstor.org/stable/23209107

Goodwin, V. L., Wofford, J. C., & Whittington, J. L. (2001). A theoretical and empirical extension to the transformational leadership construct. *Journal of Organizational Behavior, 22*(7), 759–774. https://doi.org/10.1002/job.111

Griffith, E. E., Kadous, K., & Young, D. (2016). How insights from the "new" JDM research can improve auditor judgment: Fundamental research questions and methodological advice. *Auditing: A Journal of Practice & Theory, 35*(2), 1–22. https://doi.org/10.2308/ajpt-51347

Gruman, J. A., & Saks, A. M. (2011). Performance management and employee engagement. *Human Resource Management Review, 21*(2), 123–136. https://doi.org/10.1016/j.hrmr.2010.09.004

Gully, S. M., Incalcaterra, K. A., Joshi, A., & Beaubien, J. M. (2002). A meta-analysis of team-efficacy, potency, and performance: Interdependence and level of analysis as moderators of observed relationships. *Journal of Applied Psychology, 87*(5), 819–832. https://doi.org/10.1037/0021-9010.87.5.819

Hackman, J. (1987). The design of work teams. In J. Lorsch (Ed.), *Handbook of organizational behavior* (pp. 315–342). Prentice Hall.

Harkins, S. G., & Petty, R. E. (1982). Effects of task difficulty and task uniqueness on social loafing. *Journal of Personality and Social Psychology, 43*(6), 1214–1229. https://doi.org/10.1037/0022-3514.43.6.1214

Heifetz, R. (1994). *Leadership without easy answers.* Belknap Press.

Heifetz, R., & Linsky, M. (2002). *Leadership on the line: Staying alive through the dangers of leading.* Harvard Business School.

Hoegl, M., & Parboteeah, P. K. (2003). Goal setting and team performance in innovative projects: On the moderating role of teamwork quality. *Small Group Research, 34*(1), 3–19. https://doi.org/10.1177/1046496402239575

Holm, C., & Zaman, M. (2012). Regulating audit quality: Restoring trust and legitimacy. *Accounting Forum 36*(1), 51–61. https://doi.org/10.1016/j.accfor.2011.11.004

Jha, B., & Kumar, A. (2016). Employee engagement: A strategic tool to enhance performance. *DAWN: Journal for Contemporary Research in Management, 3*(2), 21–29.

Judge, T. A., & Piccolo, R. F. (2004). Transformational and transactional leadership: A meta-analytic test of their relative validity. *Journal of Applied Psychology, 89*(5), 755–768. https://doi.org/10.1037/0021-9010.89.5.755

Kahn, W. A. (1990). Psychological conditions of personal engagement and disengagement at work. *Academy of Management Journal, 33*(4), 692–724. https://doi.org/10.5465/256287

Karau, S. J., & Williams, K. D. (1993). Social loafing: A meta-analytic review and theoretical integration. *Journal of Personality and Social Psychology, 65*(4), 681–706. https://doi.org/10.1037/0022-3514.65.4.681

Katz, D., & Kahn, R. L. (1978). *The social psychology of organizations* (2nd ed.). John Wiley & Sons.

Keller, R. T. (2006). Transformational leadership, initiating structure, and substitutes for leadership: A longitudinal study of research and development project team performance. *Journal of Applied Psychology, 91*(1), 202–210. https://doi.org/10.1037/0021-9010.91.1.202

Kinicki, A. J., Jacobson, K. J. L., Peterson, S. J., & Prussia, G. E. (2013). Development and validation of the performance management behavior questionnaire. *Personnel Psychology, 66*(1), 1–45. https://doi.org/10.1111/peps.12013

Koeslag-Kreunen, M., Van den Bossche, P., Hoven, M., Van der Klink, M., & Gijselaers, W. (2018). When leadership powers team learning: A meta-analysis. *Small Group Research, 49*(4), 475–513. https://doi.org/10.1177/1046496418764824

Kozlowski, S. W., Mak, S., & Chao, G. T. (2016). Team-centric leadership: An integrative review. *Annual Review of Organizational Psychology and Organizational Behavior, 3*, 21–54. https://doi.org/10.1146/annurev-orgpsych-041015-062429

Kramer, W. S., Thayer, A. L., & Salas, E. (2013). Goal setting in teams. In E. Locke & G. P. Latham (Eds.), *New developments in goal setting and task performance* (pp. 287–310). Routledge.

Latane, B., Williams, K., & Harkins, S. (1979). Many hands make light the work: The causes and consequences of social loafing. *Journal of Personality and Social Psychology, 37*(6), 822–832. https://doi.org/10.1037/0022-3514.37.6.822

Latham, G. P., & Arshoff, A. S. (2013). The relevance of goal setting theory for human resource management. In E. Locke & G. P. Latham (Eds.), *New developments in goal setting and task performance* (pp. 331–342). Routledge.

Latham, G. P., & Locke, E. (1990). Work motivation and satisfaction: Light at the end of the tunnel. *Psychological Science, 1*(4), 240–246. https://doi.org/10.1111/j.1467-9280.1990.tb00207.x

Latham, G. P., & Wexley, K. N. (1994). *Increasing productivity through performance appraisal.* Addison-Wesley.

Locke, E. A., & Latham, G. P. (1990). *A theory of goal setting & task performance.* Prentice-Hall.

Makikangas, A., Aunola, K., Seppala, P., & Hakanen, J. (2016). Work engagement–team performance relationship: Shared job crafting as a moderator. *Journal of Occupational and Organizational Psychology, 89*(4), 772–790. https://doi.org/10.1111/joop.12154

McDowell, T., Agarwal, D., Miller, D., Okamoto, T., & Page, T. (2016). Organizational design: The rise of teams. *Deloitte Insights.* https://www2.deloitte.com/insights/us/en/focus/human-capital-trends/2016/organizational-models-network-of-teams.html

McGrath, J. E., Arrow, H., & Berdahl, J. L. (2000). The study of groups: Past, present, and future. *Personality and Social Psychology Review, 4*(1), 95–105. https://doi.org/10.1207/S15327957PSPR0401_8

Mone, E., Eisinger, C., Guggenheim, K., Price, B., & Stine, C. (2011). Performance management at the wheel: Driving employee engagement in organizations. *Journal of Business & Psychology, 26*(2), 205–212. https://doi.org/10.1007/s10869-011-9222-9

Mone, E., & London, M. (2009). *Employee engagement through effective performance management: A practical guide for managers.* Routledge.

Morgeson, F. P., DeRue, D. S., & Karam, E. P. (2010). Leadership in teams: A functional approach to understanding leadership structures and processes. *Journal of Management, 36*(1), 5–39. https://doi.org/10.1177/0149206309347376

Nelson, M. W. (2009). A model and literature review of professional skepticism in auditing. *Auditing: A Journal of Practice & Theory, 28*(2), 1–34. https://doi.org/10.2308/aud.2009.28.2.1

Newmark, R. I., Dickey, G., & Wilcox, W. E. (2018). Agility in audit: Could scrum improve the audit process? *Current Issues in Auditing, 12*(1), A18–A28. https://doi.org/10.2308/ciia-52148

Persico, F. (2019, October 10). *How a Quality Audit Enhances Trust.* EY.com. https://www.ey.com/en_us/assurance/how-a-quality-audit-enhances-trust

Pierce, B., & Sweeney, B. (2004). Cost–quality conflict in audit firms: An empirical investigation. *European Accounting Review, 13*(3), 415–441. https://doi.org/10.1080/0963818042000216794

Podsakoff, P. M., MacKenzie, S. B., Moorman, R. H., & Fetter, R. (1990). Transformational leader behaviors and their effects on followers' trust in leader, satisfaction, and organizational citizenship behaviors. *The Leadership Quarterly, 1*(2), 107–142. https://doi.org/10.1016/1048-9843(90)90009-7

Podsakoff, P. M., Todor, W. D., & Skov, R. (1982). Effects of leader contingent and noncontingent reward and punishment behaviors on subordinate performance and satisfaction. *Academy of Management Proceedings*, *25*(4), 810–821. https://doi.org/10.5465/256100

Public Company Accounting Oversight Board. (2015). Concept release on audit quality indicators (Release No. 2015-005). PCAOB. https://pcaob-assets .azureedge.net/pcaob-dev/docs/default-source/rulemaking/docket_041/ release_2015_005.pdf?sfvrsn=de838d9f_0

Pulakos, E. D. (2009). *Performance management: A new approach for driving business results*. Wiley-Blackwell.

Purvanova, R. K., Bono, J. E., & Dzieweczynski, J. (2006). Transformational leadership, job characteristics, and organizational citizenship performance. *Human Performance*, *19*(1), 1–22. https://doi.org/10.1207/s15327043hup1901_1

Qu, R., Janssen, O., & Shi, K. (2015). Transformational leadership and follower creativity: The mediating role of follower relational identification and the moderating role of leader creativity expectations. *The Leadership Quarterly*, *26*(2), 286–299. https://doi.org/10.1016/j.leaqua.2014.12.004

Rahmadani, V. G., Schaufeli, W. B., Stouten, J., Zhang, Z., & Zulkarain, Z. (2020). Engaging leadership and its implication for work engagement and job outcomes at the individual and team level: A multi-level longitudinal study. *International Journal of Environmental Research and Public Health*, *17*(3), 776. https://doi.org/10.3390/ijerph17030776

Rich, B. L., Lepine, J. A., & Crawford, E. R. (2010). Job engagement: Antecedents and effects on job performance. *Academy of Management Journal*. *53*(3), 617–635. https://doi.org/10.5465/AMJ.2010.51468988

Robinson, M. A., & Boies, K. (2016). Different ways to get the job done: Comparing the effects of intellectual stimulation and contingent reward leadership on task-related outcomes. *Journal of Applied Social Psychology*, *46*(6), 336–353. https://doi.org/10.1111/jasp.12367

Schaubroeck, J., Lam, S. S., & Cha, S. E. (2007). Embracing transformational leadership: team values and the impact of leader behavior on team performance. *Journal of Applied Psychology*, *92*(4), 1020–1030. https://doi.org/ 10.1037/0021-9010.92.4.1020

Schaufeli, W. B., & Salanova, M. (2007). Efficacy or inefficacy, that's the question: Burnout and work engagement and their relationships with efficacy beliefs. *Anxiety, Stress, and Coping*, *20(2)*, 177–196. https://doi.org/ 10.1080/10615800701217878

Schaufeli, W. B., Salanova, M., González-Romá, V., & Bakker, A. B. (2002). The measurement of engagement and burnout: A two sample confirmatory factor analytic approach. *Journal of Happiness Studies*, *3*(1), 71–92. https://doi.org/ 10.1023/A:1015630930326

Senecal, J., Loughead, T. M., & Bloom, G. A. (2008). A season-long team-building intervention: Examining the effect of team goal setting on cohesion. *Journal of Sports & Exercise Psychology*, *30*(2), 186–199. https://doi.org/10.1123/ jsep.30.2.186

Sharma, A., & Bhatnagar, J. (2017). Emergence of team engagement under time pressure: role of team leader and team climate. *Team Performance Management*, *23*(3), 171–185. https://doi.org/10.1108/TPM-06-2016-0031

Shilts, M. K., Townsend, M. S., & Dishman, R. K. (2013). Using goal setting to promote health behavior change: Diet and physical activity. In E. Locke & G. P. Latham (Eds.), *New developments in goal setting and task performance* (pp. 415–489). Routledge.

Shuck, B., Reio, T. G., & Rocco, T. S. (2011). Employee engagement: An examination of antecedent and outcome variables. *Human Resource Development International, 14*(4), 427–445. https://doi.org/10.1080/13678868.2011.601587

Solomon, I. (1987). Multi-auditor judgment/decision making research. *Journal of Accounting Literature, 6,* 1–25. https://search.proquest.com/scholarly-journals/multi-auditor-judgment-decision-making-research/docview/216313875/se-2?accountid=7106

Svanström, T. (2016). Time pressure, training activities, and dysfunctional auditor behavior: Evidence from small firms. *International Journal of Auditing, 20*(1), 42–51. https://doi.org/10.1111/ijau.12054

Tims, M., Bakker, A. B., & Rhenen, W. V. (2013). Job crafting at the team and individual level: Implications for work engagement and performance. *Group & Organization Management, 38*(4), 427–454. https://doi.org/10.1177/1059601113492421

Torrente, P., Salanova, M., Llorens, S., & Schaufeli, W. B. (2012). Teams make it work: How team work engagement mediates between social resources and performance in teams. *Psichothema, 24*(1), 106–112. ISSN: 0214-9915.

Travers, C. J. (2013). Using goal setting to promote personal development. In E. Locke & G. P. Latham (Eds.), *New developments in goal setting and task performance*. Routledge.

Walsch, B., & Volini, E. (2017). *Rewriting the rules for the digital age: 2017 Deloitte Global Human Capital Trends.* Deloitte University Press. https://www2.deloitte.com/content/dam/Deloitte/us/Documents/humancapital/hc-2017-global-human-capital-trends-gx.pdf

Van der Hoek, M., Groeneveld, S., & Kuipers, B. (2018). Goal setting in teams: Goal clarity and team performance in the public sector. *Review of Public Personnel Administration, 38*(4), 472–493. https://doi.org/10.1177/0734371X16682815

Vera-Muñoz, S. C., Ho, J. L., & Chow, C. W. (2006). Enhancing knowledge sharing in public accounting firms. *Accounting Horizons, 20*(2), 133–155. https://doi.org/10.2308/acch.2006.20.2.133

Von Nordenflycht, A. (2010). What is a professional service firm? Toward a theory and taxonomy of knowledge-intensive firms. *Academy of management Review, 35*(1), 155–174. https://doi.org/10.5465/amr.35.1.zok155

Wang, G., Oh, I. S., Courtright, S. H., & Colbert, A. E. (2011). Transformational leadership and performance across criteria and levels: A meta-analytic review of 25 years of research. *Group & Organization Management, 36*(2), 223–270. https://doi.org/10.1177/1059601111401017

Whittington, J. L., & Galpin, T. J. (2010). The engagement factor: Building a high-commitment organization in a low-commitment world. *Journal of Business Strategy, 31*(5), 14–24. https://doi.org/10.1108/02756661011076282

Whittington, J. L., Meskelis, S., Asare, E., & Beldona, S. (2017). *Enhancing employee engagement: An evidence-based approach.* Springer.

Wofford, J. C., Goodwin, V. L., & Whittington, J. L. (1998). A field study of a cognitive approach to understanding transformational and transactional leadership. *The Leadership Quarterly, 9*(1), 55–84. https://doi.org/10.1016/S10 48-9843(98)90042-X

Wollard, K. K., & Shuck, B. (2011). Antecedents to employee engagement: A structured review of the literature. *Advances in Developing Human Resources, 13*(4), 429–446. https://doi.org/10.1177%2F1523422311431220

Zaccaro, S. J., Rittman, A. L., & Marks, M. A. (2001). Team leadership. *Leadership Quarterly, 12*(4), 451–483. https://doi.org/10.1016/S1048-9843(01)00093-5

CHAPTER 5

WHEN DOES FEEDBACK ENHANCE PERFORMANCE IN TEAMS?

A Systematic Literature Review and Future Research Agenda

Akvilė Mockevičiūtė
Vrije Universiteit Amsterdam

Sabrine El Baroudi
Vrije Universiteit Amsterdam

Sergey Gorbatov
Vrije Universiteit Amsterdam

Svetlana N. Khapova
Vrije Universiteit Amsterdam

Managing Team Centricity in Modern Organizations, pages 115–164
Copyright © 2022 by Information Age Publishing
www.infoagepub.com

ABSTRACT

With the rising interest in the effect of feedback on performance in teams, theoretical models have been developed to explain when and how different factors influence the relationship between feedback and performance in teams. However, most of the extant conceptual models tend to neglect that in the context of the contemporary work environment, team processes are influenced by contextual factors that originate outside such teams and more generally outside organizations. The research has also acknowledged that such contextual factors influence the relationship between feedback and performance in teams, but there is currently no review paper that integrates these extant research findings to show how this process is likely to occur. To address this limitation, we systematically review the research on the relationship between feedback and performance in teams published up to 2021, integrate our findings into a multilevel model, and identify the research gaps. We provide a rationale for our multilevel analysis based on the multiple team membership perspective and spillover theory, which we also use to suggest avenues for future research to further advance the literature on feedback and performance in teams.

The past years have witnessed a rise in research on the relationship between feedback and performance in teams (e.g., Aakvik et al., 2017; Glikson et al., 2019; Hoever et al., 2018) as feedback is a critical enabler of performance management in team-centric organizations (Geister et al., 2006; Glikson et al., 2019; Kozlowski & Ilgen, 2006). Defined as a subset of information denoting how well individuals are meeting various goals at work (Herold & Greller, 1977), feedback is found to elevate performance (Heslin & Latham, 2004; Song et al., 2018), which can also be referred to as the job responsibilities that are formally required to be fulfilled (i.e., in-role performance; Katz & Khan, 1978) as well as voluntary extra work activities (i.e., extra-role performance; MacKenzie et al., 1998). However, the feedback–performance relationship in teams is rather a complex phenomenon that is heavily influenced by contextual factors (Aakvik et al., 2017; Peterson & Behfar, 2003; Van Thielen et al., 2018).

Several theoretical models have been developed to propose which contextual factors could potentially influence the feedback-performance relationship in teams (e.g., Gabelica & Popov, 2020; Gabelica et al., 2012; London & Sessa, 2006). While such models have been helpful in providing a comprehensive overview, emerging empirical evidence has signaled that they have at least two significant limitations. First, these models address the relationship between feedback and performance in teams from only individual and within-team levels of analysis. Therefore, the contextual factors that originate from outside of teams are not accounted for while the research does show that they influence the relationship between feedback and performance in teams (Ashford et al., 2018; Glikson et al., 2019;

Sánchez-Expósito & Naranjo-Gil, 2020). Thus, the extant models generally fail to take into consideration that in the contemporary work environment, team members tend to be part of more than one team at a time, referred to in the team literature as multiple team membership (O'Leary et al., 2011), and they increasingly work remotely (Kniffin et al., 2021). Therefore, contextual factors influencing team processes in the contemporary work environment operate not only at the intra-team level (i.e., within-team level) but also at the inter-team (i.e., between-team) and extra-team levels (i.e., contextual factors that originate beyond the team context; Sánchez-Expósito & Naranjo-Gil, 2020; Van Thielen et al., 2018; Wu et al., 2014). Second, these extant models were originally designed to propose a theory on the influences of contextual factors on feedback in teams without specifically identifying the contextual factors that have been found in the empirical research to influence the feedback–performance relationship in teams. Thus, to our knowledge, no systematic literature review yet exists that identifies multilevel contextual influences on the feedback-performance relationship in teams and integrates them in a model. This gap has led to misalignments of the empirical research on feedback in teams with contemporary modes of working and has caused fragmentation in this research field.

With this paper, we aim to address these limitations. We first synthesize the existing evidence on the contextual influences on the relationship between feedback and performance in teams incorporating a multilevel analysis. We do this by systematically reviewing 81 studies published up to 2021. In this way, we adjudicate and clarify the knowledge foundation of the field (Cronin & George, 2020). Next, we integrate our findings into a model and identify the research gaps in the literature. We advance the literature on feedback and performance in teams by proposing, based on spillover theory, a future research agenda for multilevel contextual influences that can be further empirically tested.

Rationale for a Multilevel Analysis

The theories that have been developed to explain the contextual influences on the relationship between feedback and performance in teams (Gabelica & Popov, 2020; Gabelica et al., 2012; London & Sessa, 2006) have focused only on addressing the contextual factors at the intra-team level, that is, the factors that are derived from within a team (Presbitero et al., 2017). For example, London and Sessa (2006) proposed a model on the relationship among feedback, learning, and performance in groups. The underlying idea of their model is that the way in which feedback is processed and used may be influenced by conditions that occur at both the individual and team levels such as demands and goals; accountability for performance; learning orientation;

and engagement in adaptive, generative, or transformative learning. London and Sessa's (2006) model was further extended by Gabelica et al. (2012) with influential feedback characteristics on teams such as level, type, and different combinations of feedback. More recently, Gabelica and Popov (2020) used the latter model to conceptualize how team members' cultural orientations influence the effect of feedback on performance in teams.

However, spillover theory (Edwards & Rothbard, 2000) illuminates the limitations of this approach as it is very narrow and does not fully represent how individuals work in contemporary teams. Spillover theory first originated in the work-life domain research to explain how the experiences of one person in one life domain, such as personal life, impact and transmit experiences into another life domain, such as work (Edwards & Rothbard, 2000). This spillover effect occurs through diverse mechanisms: (a) unintentionally due to cognitive and motivational processes such that positive moods derived from home enhance motivation and cognitive functioning at work, which in turn increase one's role performance (Staw et al., 1994) leading to more extrinsic rewards and positive moods at home; (b) due to scripts, that is, memorized knowledge structures of skills, behaviors, and values that spill over as they become ingrained and describe the correct sequence of events in familiar situations (Abelson, 1981), influencing one's behaviors across domains (Lord & Kernan, 1987).

More recently, spillover theory was also used to explain how team processes are influenced by the moods, experiences, skills, values, and behaviors that are transmitted from other teams and thereby influence how teams function. People are often part of multiple teams and gain unique experiences from working in different teams (Mathieu & Chen, 2011), which they bring together when transitioning from one team to another (Ashforth et al., 2000). This phenomenon is referred to as multiple team membership (O'Leary et al., 2011). Switching between teams initiates an inter-team spillover effect as experiences from the one team impact how the other team functions (Chen et al., 2019). Such contextual influences are identified in the literature as inter-team level contextual factors (Presbitero et al., 2017) and are thus also relevant for the feedback and performance relationship in teams.

In addition to inter-team level contextual factors, it is also reasonable to suggest that influences from outside of teams such as organizational human resource practices (Bednall et al., 2014) and influences from a broader environment are relevant for the feedback–performance relationship in teams. As individuals were forced to work from home during the Covid-19 pandemic, these experiences from the home sphere are now largely also influenced by the new work arrangements and could thus be brought into teams, thereby affecting how they function (Van der Lippe & Lippényi, 2020). In addition, other contextual factors that originate outside of teams, such as organizational characteristics, are worthwhile to consider in the feedback–performance relationship in teams. For instance, how organizational support is perceived by team members also influences inter-team dynamics and performance (Gelbard & Carmeli, 2009). Such contextual factors stem from outside teams, from either the organization or the broader environment outside of the organization, and they are referred to as extra-team level factors (Van Osch & Steinfield, 2016; Van Thielen et al., 2018).

METHOD

A systematic literature review is a literature review method that involves a systematic, replicable, and scientific search process with the purpose of identifying relevant articles in a fragmented area of research (Siddaway et al., 2019). By comparison, meta-analyses tend to focus more on assessing individual relationships between independent and dependent variables (e.g., Ritz et al., 2016; Rosenthal & DiMatteo, 2001). As our focus was on identifying contextual influences on the feedback-performance link in teams to explore gaps in the literature and to propose a model to be tested in future research, a systematic literature review was more appropriate (Cooper, 2010).

As recommended by Siddaway et al. (2019), we adhered to preferred reporting items for systematic reviews and meta-analyses (PRISMA) guidelines (Moher et al., 2009) in (a) planning the execution of this literature review and (b) summarizing the review method in a flow diagram (i.e., Figure 5.1), which is the best practice based on PRISMA (Daniels, 2019). We relied on these guidelines as they are the most applicable across various research areas (Siddaway et al., 2019). We then performed the literature review following Crossan and Apaydin (2010) in three steps: collecting the data, analyzing the data, and reporting the results.

Data Collection

To identify relevant studies for this systematic review, we performed an open search on all the empirical research on the relationship between feedback and performance in teams without specifying a time span to not limit its comprehensiveness. We then established the conceptual boundaries for the phenomena under investigation (Denyer & Tranfield, 2009). In particular, we set the boundary conditions for the concepts "feedback," "performance," and "team." We used Herold and Greller's (1977) definition of feedback because it captures the many definitions of feedback that are available in the literature (e.g., Kluger & DeNisi, 1996; Lam et al., 2011). Herold and Greller (1977) refer to feedback as

a subset of information available to individuals in their work environment. Feedback is the information that denotes how well individuals are meeting various goals. In the interpersonal realm, feedback involves information about how individual behaviors are perceived and evaluated by relevant others; (as cited in Ashford & Cummings, 1983, p. 3)

it can be both unsolicited and sought by individuals (Ashford & Cummings, 1983). "Feedback may pertain to both establishing the appropriate behaviors to achieve a goal and how well an individual is enacting those behaviors to achieve the goal" (as cited in Ashford & Cummings, 1983, p. 3). Such feedback can be formally and informally given by managers (e.g., Wang et al., 2009), informally given by peers (e.g., Druskat & Wolff, 1999), or proactively sought by individual team members (e.g., Ashford et al., 2018).

Next, we classified performance in teams in terms of in-role and extra-role performance. Team members' in-role performance concerns their job responsibilities that are formally required to be fulfilled (Katz & Khan, 1978), while extra-role performance concerns voluntary extra-work activities (MacKenzie et al., 1998). In teams, in-role and extra-role performance can take the form of individual or collective activities (e.g., DeShon et al., 2004) because team members may be assigned to work on individual tasks (e.g., Aakvik et al., 2017) and/or collaborative tasks (e.g., Geister et al., 2006).

Finally, we defined a team as "two or more individuals with specified roles interacting adaptively, interdependently, and dynamically toward a common and valued goal" (Salas et al., 1992, as cited in Salas et al., 2005, p. 559). Even though the concepts "team" and "group" are often used interchangeably in the literature (e.g., Keyton & Heylen, 2017), the most distinguishing difference between them is that compared to groups, teams consist of highly *interdependent* individuals who rely on each other to achieve performance (Ilgen et al., 2005; Kozlowski & Ilgen, 2006). Therefore, teams with high interdependence are "real teams" while those with low interdependence carry the label "working groups" (Katzenbach & Smith, 1993). In addition, this review focuses on teams in a work context only. Sports teams were excluded because the context of teams is very different in sports compared to the work context. For instance, in sports, performance measures are clearly defined while in a work environment, that is not the case (Harder, 1992). There are also clear practical distinctions between sports and work teams, for example, sports teams are structurally predetermined; therefore, individuals will always be part of a team, while employees in an organization can be assigned to perform both individual work and teamwork for different occasions (Barker et al., 2010). Third, self-managing teams are increasingly popular in business and medical contexts while a hierarchical structure is still prevalent in sports teams (Barker et al., 2010).

Once the boundary conditions were set, we performed a Boolean search using the terms "feedback AND performance AND team*." To ensure a rigorous search of peer-reviewed articles, we used the Institute for Scientific

Information (ISI) Web of Knowledge Social Sciences Citation Index (SSCI) database, which is the most comprehensive database for academic journals in multiple disciplines (Guz & Rushchitsky, 2009). We did not preselect based on disciplines as we aimed to gather relevant articles from various disciplines.

Data Analysis

The search process generated 1,761 articles. After eliminating duplicates, 1,756 articles remained. The abstracts of all these articles were manually screened. During this process, 1,573 abstracts were excluded for the following reasons: The articles focused on teams that were not studied in a work context (e.g., game players, sports), the articles were not empirical studies and feedback was not a clear independent variable (e.g., part of an intervention or an outcome variable/moderator), the articles did not focus on teams and feedback was not given among or to subjects (e.g., feedback on training), or performance was not a clear outcome variable. This manual screening procedure resulted in 183 suitable abstracts for full article review as the next step of the analysis. These 183 articles were also screened to explore other relevant references, which resulted in 15 articles that were added to the sample because they met our article inclusion criteria. After adding these 15 articles, 198 articles were subjected to full article review. These 198 articles were coded and analyzed based on the following criteria: (a) the definition of feedback, teams, and performance; (b) the type of feedback (e.g., formal versus informal, process versus performance-focused, individual versus team-oriented, positive versus negative); (c) the type of performance (i.e., in- versus extra-role); (d) team-level contextual factors (intra/inter/extra); (e) team characteristics (e.g., size, industry); (f) sample characteristics; (g) the methodology; (h) the main results; and (i) the discipline (e.g., psychology, management). Performance was categorized as in- or extra-role performance depending on whether it was expected (i.e., in-role performance) or unexpected (i.e., extra-role performance) from an employer's perspective (Balkin et al., 2015). We excluded 117 articles because their focus was out of the scope of our review, that is, they were not empirical studies, feedback was not an independent variable, performance was not a dependent variable, teams were not studied in a work context, the article was not written in English, or definitions of feedback and performance other than those employed in this study were used. In the latter case, an article was excluded, for example, because the independent variable was a team's failure to reach performance goals, which was not in line with Herold and Greller's (1977) definition. Similarly, articles that used other definitions of performance were excluded when the definition of their outcome variable was not in line with the definition of performance used in this review. Examples of such outcome variables were collective efficacy beliefs, the

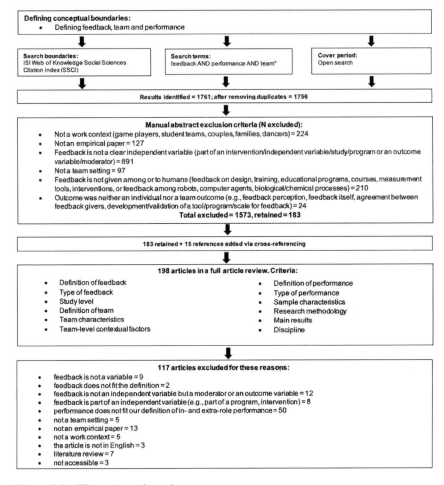

Figure 5.1   The systematic review process.

effectiveness of a feedback tool, team coordination, autonomy, communication skills, or knowledge sharing. Additionally, if feedback was a mediator, the article was included only if the direct relationship was also focused on feedback and performance. As a result, the final sample consisted of 81 empirical articles. Figure 5.1 displays the systematic review process.

Reporting the Results

Last, we present the results based on the categorization of contextual influences as first proposed by London and Sessa (2006); namely, feedback, individual, and team characteristics. Feedback characteristics include aspects such as feedback valence, source, purpose, and clarity; individual and team characteristics involve aspects such as demands, goals, perceptions, and the processing of feedback at both the individual and team levels; feedback orientation at the individual level and feedback culture at the team level. We identified and added more subcategories at the intra-, inter-, and extra-team levels that were not part of London and Sessa's (2006) model such as team processes, team emergent states, leader behavior, interaction among team members, the performance of other teams, organizational characteristics, and external organizational environment characteristics. We further distinguished between the categories based on conditions and mechanisms: Conditions are variables that specify when a particular effect between the predictor and the outcome variable holds while mechanisms explain why and how those effects occur (Baron & Kenny, 1986).

RESULTS

Feedback Influence on Performance in Teams Without Considering Contextual Factors

In our sample, the largest group of studies, that is, 63 empirical papers, found a positive direct relationship between feedback and performance in teams. Of these studies, 61 examined the relationship between feedback and in-role performance, while two examined extra-role performance, of which one study focused on overall employee creativity and one study focused on organizational citizenship behaviors (OCBs). Of the remaining 18 studies from our sample of 81 papers, only two found a negative relationship between feedback and in-role performance, seven found a nonsignificant relationship between feedback and performance in teams, and six did not investigate the direct relationship. Three studies of these remaining 18 papers in our sample employed qualitative methods, of which two argued for a positive relationship between feedback and performance and one did not find any influence of feedback on performance. Our analysis of these papers suggested that the effect of feedback on team performance also depends on a variety of contextual factors at the team level, upon which we elaborate in the following paragraphs.

Intra-Team Level Contextual Factors

We found that, in total, 26 articles investigated intra-team level contextual factors, that is, factors derived from within a team. Seventeen articles investigated contextual factors as conditions such as feedback, individual, and team characteristics, interaction among team members, team processes, and team emergent states. Twelve studies focused on examining the mechanisms to explain the ways through which feedback affects performance in teams such as team processes, team emergent states, and individual characteristics. Some intra-team level contextual factors were identified as both conditions and mechanisms (interpersonal trust and team reflexivity) in the feedback–performance relationship in teams.

Conditions

Feedback characteristics.   In two studies, timing, that is, *when* feedback is given, is an important condition influencing performance in teams. Druskat and Wolff (1999) showed that compared to the beginning or the end of a project, peer appraisal as a type of feedback is most effective when conducted midway through the project. Similarly, Kerr et al. (2005) showed that delaying or presenting feedback at the end attenuates *the Köhler effect* whereby a less capable individual works harder than another individual when working together, which suggests that to maximize performance gains in teams, feedback needs to be timely. In addition to timing, two studies show that the target, that is, the receiver(s) of feedback, is another important factor influencing the effect of feedback on performance in teams. For instance, Henning et al. (1997) found that providing feedback to two team members is better for performance than providing it to only one member. In a different study, Goomas et al. (2011) showed that providing aggregated group performance feedback in addition to individual feedback is beneficial to productivity. Finally, Lant and Hurley (1999) found that the valence of feedback, that is, positive or negative, influences the effect of performance feedback on the investment decision-making of top management teams such that the greater the extent to which performance exceeds aspiration (i.e., positive feedback), the greater the increase in investment in production as a result of performance feedback. Conversely, the greater the extent to which aspiration exceeds performance (i.e., negative feedback), the greater the decrease in investment as a result of performance feedback.

Individual characteristics.   One study found that individual characteristics, that is, team members' predispositions and abilities in a team, also influence the relationship between feedback and performance in teams. Wu et al. (2014) showed that feedback inquiry leads to higher performance in flexible work teams, particularly for team members high in attachment anxiety (i.e., members who perceive themselves as incapable and who therefore need approval), as opposed to attachment avoidance (i.e., members who do not trust others and who therefore avoid intimate relationships; Brennan & Bosson, 1998). Thus, attachment style influences the relationship between feedback inquiry and job performance in a team.

Team characteristics.

Team emergent states. Team emergent states, which are defined as "properties of the team that are typically dynamic in nature and vary as a function of team context, inputs, processes, and outcomes" (Marks et al., 2001, p. 357), were found to influence the feedback-performance relationship in one study. Specifically, Lampel and Jha (2017) found that nonperformance-based inertia, that is, team commitment, which is measured as the number of design competitions in which a team has participated, negatively moderates the relationship between performance feedback and design change as a performance criterion. Team commitment can be considered to be an emergent state because it can vary in terms of strength (i.e., strong versus weak).

Team processes. Team processes, which are defined as "members' interdependent acts that convert inputs to outcomes through cognitive, verbal, and behavioral activities directed toward organizing taskwork to achieve collective goals" (Marks et al., 2001, p. 357), affected the feedback-performance relationship in teams in two studies. Sakka et al. (2016) found that uncertainty and equivocality, that is, the lack of information and understanding about user requirements and technology in a team, respectively, influence the effect of feedback on project performance such that performance is enhanced when uncertainty and equivocality are high but deteriorates when they are low. In addition, Ertaç et al. (2019) showed that the relationship between private or public feedback and team performance is influenced by whether team performance is determined by the weakest or the strongest link in a team. If team performance is determined by the best performer, that is, team goals are achieved by high-ability members, then public and private feedback is better than no feedback. However, if team performance is determined by the weakest link in the team, then no feedback is better for team performance. This suggests that feedback has the greatest effect on performance only when teams have sufficient information, understanding, and high-ability members.

Team leader behavior. The results of five studies demonstrate the important role of the team leader on the effect of feedback on performance in teams. For instance, Gort et al. (2013) found that team leader behaviors, such as motivating team members and repeating project goals, contribute to the coordination of group activities, which positively influence performance in teams. Wang et al. (2009) showed that a team leader's feedback-giving approach influences the relationship between feedback and performance. The most effective approach in giving written feedback is a combination of empathetic and direction-giving approaches, that is, leaders simultaneously share emotion with team members to build interpersonal bonds, together with direction-giving language, that is, clarifying team members' goals and duties to minimize uncertainty in the team. Additionally, Fan et al. (2014) found that the effectiveness of a team leader feedback approach depends on how the team leader gives instructions to the team. A demanding feedback approach leads to more idea generation when teams receive direction-giving instructions, that is, instructions that clarify the task goals and requirements to diminish role and task ambiguity, while an encouraging feedback approach stimulates creativity when teams receive instructions written in more empathetic language, that is, by complimenting and inspiring team members' good work. Moreover, Iyengar and Schotter (2008) showed that subjects whose supervisors provided them with advice that was costly to ignore (i.e., the subjects were penalized for ignoring the supervisor's advice) learned better and were better at decision-making than those who could freely ignore their supervisor's advice. In addition, Hecht et al. (2019) examined team managers' discretion in providing relative performance feedback. They showed that team managers selectively use relative performance information, that is, they provide it to low-performing employees and withhold it from high-performing employees, which encourages low-performing employees to increase their effort and high-performing employees to sustain their effort, leading to greater collective effort in achieving team performance due to feedback.

Interaction among team members. Interaction among team members also has an influence on the feedback-performance link in teams as shown in three studies. Chang et al. (2008) found that instructor feedback on team performance is beneficial for improving task performance only when team cooperation and not individual effort is required. This suggests that interaction between team members is better for performance than no interaction (i.e., individual effort) and that feedback must be provided on those aspects of performance that are relevant for task completion (i.e., team cooperation instead of individual effort). In addition, Gabelica et al. (2014) found that team reflexivity, that is, team interactive discussion among team members immediately after receiving feedback on performance, increases the benefit of team performance feedback compared to teams that receive no feedback or only team feedback without such a team discussion. Similarly, Giesbers et al. (2016) found that nursing teams that use feedback to interact and reflect on performance are more effective in translating feedback into corrective behaviors than those that do not undertake such interaction and reflection. These studies show that feedback discussions among team members enhance the feedback effect on performance in teams.

In sum, at the intra-team level, various conditions were found to influence how feedback impacts performance in teams. Feedback characteristics, such as timing, target, and valence, influenced the feedback-performance link such that feedback was most effective in increasing performance when it was not delayed and was presented midway through a project. In addition, individual characteristics, such as attachment style, impacted the effect of feedback inquiry on performance such that feedback inquiry was most influential when individuals were high in attachment anxiety. Last, team emergent states (i.e., high team commitment), team processes (sufficient understanding and knowledge in a team), team leader behavior (i.e., leader's motivating, empathic and direction giving feedback approach and discretion in providing feedback), and the interaction among team members (i.e., discussion and reflection) all strengthened the feedback-performance relationship in teams.

Mechanisms

Our analysis revealed that several mechanisms were examined at the intra-team level. These mechanisms can be grouped according to their focus on team processes, team emergent states and individual characteristics.

Team processes. In six studies, we identified several team processes as mechanisms in the relationship between feedback and performance in teams. Eddy et al. (2013) related the use of an online guided team debriefing tool to improve performance through an indirect significant positive effect of team members' attention to teamwork and team self-correction. DeShon et al. (2004) found the relationship between feedback and team performance to be mediated by self-regulatory and team regulatory intentions and actions. Vashdi (2013) focused on guided team reflexivity, that is, a type of feedback in which team members identify and minimize the discrepancies between desired and actual performance, and found that the relationship between such feedback and performance occurred via a team's attention to detail. We also found several studies showing how team processes explain the feedback-performance link in teams but only under certain conditions. For instance, Hoever et al. (2018) found that informational diversity as a condition, that is, differences in team members' task-related knowledge, interacts with positive and negative feedback, which jointly affect team creativity via elaboration, that is, teams sharing and integrating their task-relevant information (Van Knippenberg et al., 2004), and generative information processing routes, that is, team members drawing on each other's input and sharing incomplete ideas (Dugosh et al., 2000). In particular, negative feedback increases team creativity via elaboration when team members are informationally diverse, while positive feedback enhances team creativity via generative processing when teams are not informationally diverse. In addition, Hollenbeck et al. (1998) showed that process feedback affects team decision-making accuracy via different mechanisms, specifically, hierarchical sensitivity, that is, the impression of how optimally the team leader uses their staff, and information distribution, that is, how well the team is informed about decisions. However, these mechanisms were stronger when teams had more experience working collaboratively. Last, in a study by Glikson et al. (2019), process feedback, which reflects how an individual performs a task in a team, positively affects team performance through the mediating effect of team effort only in virtual teams with a low proportion of highly conscientious team members, that is, those who are highly self-organized.

Team emergent states. We also identified emergent states as mechanisms in the relationship between feedback and performance in teams in five studies. For example, Mesch et al. (1994) found that collective goals mediate the positive relationship between negative feedback and team performance. Jung and Sosik (2003) showed that group potency and collective efficacy, which are dynamic collective perceptions about a group's capabilities (Marks et al., 2001), mediate the relationship between feedback and performance in teams. In a study by Geister et al. (2006), the relationship between team process feedback and team performance is mediated by interpersonal trust in virtual teams, which is a dynamic team state due to its unstable nature (i.e., more versus less trust). Tindale et al. (1991) found a positive mediating relationship between feedback, performance expectations, which are dynamic beliefs about future performance, and the performance of individuals in teams.

We also found one study showing how a team emergent state mediates the feedback-performance relationship in teams but only under a certain condition. Peterson and Behfar (2003) found that task and relationship conflict mediate the negative team performance feedback-performance link. However, if a team builds intra-group trust, such trust serves as a buffer to the negative effect of negative performance feedback on team performance.

Individual characteristics. Regarding individual characteristics, only one study, by Li et al. (2009), reported that team member satisfaction mediates the relationship between team performance feedback and team performance.

In sum, several mechanisms were found to explain the relationship between feedback and performance in teams, which are team processes (i.e., effort, information distribution, attention to teamwork and detail, and individual and team self-regulation), team emergent states (i.e., collective efficacy, inter-team trust, conflict, performance goals and expectations), and individual characteristics (i.e., team member satisfaction). Some of these mechanisms, such as team processes and emergent states, were effective only under certain conditions.

Inter-Team Level Contextual Factors

Conditions

Performance of other teams. Surprisingly, only two studies in our sample investigated inter-team level factors, that is, factors that present when different teams collaborate or communicate together (Presbitero et al., 2017), as conditions for the relationship between feedback and performance in teams. Sánchez-Expósito and Naranjo-Gil (2020) showed that relative performance feedback given to team members to compare their performance has a negative effect on the performance of individuals in teams but that this effect is mitigated by between-group relative performance feedback (i.e., comparing one's group performance to that of another group, thus creating social competition; Turner, 1975). This means that the performance of individuals in teams is lower only when within-group relative performance feedback is given compared to when both within- and between-group feedback are present. In addition, Lampel and Jha (2017) found that performance-based inertia, that is, reaching a performance level that marks an overall performance level of competing teams, negatively moderates the relationship between feedback and performance in a team.

In sum, the limited research on inter-team level contextual factors suggests that team members' awareness of how other teams perform can enhance the effect of feedback on performance. However, when team members aim to achieve the performance level of competing teams, this likely hinders the effect of feedback on performance in teams.

Extra-Team Level Contextual Factors

Our analysis revealed that research examining extra-team level factors as mechanisms or conditions is also scarce, identifying only five studies. These five studies can be grouped into organizational characteristics, that is, actions of the senior management, interdepartmental dynamics and organizational systems (Kirca & Hult, 2009) as well as external organizational environment characteristics (i.e., influences from outside the organization).

Conditions

Organizational characteristics.   Choi et al. (2019) found that board and management team outsiderness, that is, the proportion of nonemployee directors/executives tenured outside of the firm to the total directors/executives tenured in a year, moderates the relationship between feedback and performance such that higher outsiderness increases the responsiveness to performance feedback. Bednall et al. (2014) showed that the strength of organizational human resource management (HRM) practices improves the relationship between high-quality performance appraisal and employees' voluntary engagement in informal learning activities as a type of performance. Aakvik et al. (2017) found that incentives moderate the relationship between individual relative performance feedback and the productivity of individual employees in teams, such that the relationship is the strongest when bonuses depend on collective team performance and not on the performance of individuals in teams.

External organizational environment characteristics. Van Thielen et al. (2018) showed that environmental extremity, that is, the extent to which the external environment involves high risk, high environmental demands and consequences for low performance, influences the effect of constructive feedback on team effectiveness in police teams such that constructive feedback has a positive effect on team effectiveness and performance; however, this effect is constrained in teams working under high extremity.

Mechanisms

Organizational characteristics. Only one study investigated a mechanism operating only under certain conditions at the extra-team level. Ashford et al. (2018) found that CEO feedback-seeking leads to higher firm performance via top management team (TMT) potency, that is, beliefs about team capabilities (Gully et al., 2002) and that this relationship is moderated by the CEO's vision for the organization such that the mediating effect is the strongest when the CEO does not articulate a clear vision.

In sum, the research on extra-team level influential factors is also limited. Organizational characteristics are examined as conditions influencing the relationship between feedback and performance in teams such that the effect of feedback on performance was the greatest when the management team had members tenured outside of the organization, when the HRM practices were stronger, when bonuses depended on collective rather than individual performance, and when the CEO did not articulate a clear vision, feedback had its strongest effect via TMT potency. Only one external organizational environment characteristic (i.e., environmental extremity) is examined as a condition such that the feedback-performance link was the strongest when the team worked under low environmental extremity. Table 5.1 provides an overview of all the articles, definitions of feedback and performance, and contextual influences at the intra-, inter-, and extra-team levels identified in this review.

DISCUSSION

The purpose of this paper was (a) to provide a comprehensive review of intra-, inter-, and extra-team contextual influences for the feedback-performance relationship in teams; (b) to identify gaps; and (c) to propose future research directions to further enhance the literature on feedback and performance in teams. We accomplished these objectives by reviewing 81 articles on the relationship between feedback and performance in teams.

TABLE 5.1 Overview of All Studies Included

| Author(s) | Feedback Type | Influential Factor at the . . . | | | Performance Type |
		Intrateam Level	Interteam Level	Extrateam Level	
Aakvik et al. (2017)	Individual relative performance feedback "is feedback information about an individual team member's controllable contribution to the team, relative to other team members' contributions" (Hecht et al., 2019, p. 2).			Incentives based on individual or team performance	Individual productivity—"Productivity is a performance measure encompassing both efficiency and effectiveness" (Bhatti & Qureshi, 2007, p. 4).
Ashford et al. (2018)	Feedback seeking "is conscious devotion of effort toward determining the correctness and adequacy of behavior for attaining valued end states" (Ashford, 1986, p. 466).			CEO vision; Top management team potency	Firm performance
Ayieko et al. (2019)	Audit and feedback "in which professional performance is measured ("audit"), compared against targets or peers, and then fed back to the individual" (Patel et al., 2018, p. 1).				Adherence to treatment guidelines
Bachrach et al. (2001)	Relative performance feedback				Frequency of OCB—Three types of OCB were evaluated: "helping behavior is helping others with, or preventing the occurrence of, work-related problems; civic virtue indicates that the person responsibly participates in or is concerned about, the life of the organization;

(continued)

TABLE 5.1	Overview of All Studies Included (continued)				
		Influential Factor at the . . .			
Author(s)	Feedback Type	Intrateam Level	Interteam Level	Extrateam Level	Performance Type
					sportsmanship is willingness on the part of people to put up with minor inconveniences and tolerate less than ideal circumstances" (Bachrach et al., 2001, pp. 4–5)
Barton et al. (2020)	Individual performance feedback "is the provision of information about individual or group" (Salas et al., 2012, as cited in Glikson et al., 2019, p. 3) or institutional outcomes (Smeltzer et al., 2019).				Desired teaching behaviors
Bednall et al. (2014)	Performance appraisal "is a formal interview in which performance evaluations are communicated and future goals are agreed upon" (Pichler, 2012, as cited in Meinecke et al., 2017, p. 1).			Strength of HR practices	Engagement in informal learning activities—reflection on daily activities, knowledge sharing with colleagues, and innovative behavior. "Reflection includes activities such as assessing progress toward goals, identifying strengths and weaknesses, and devising approaches to overcome perceived obstacles. Knowledge sharing includes activities such as exchanging ideas with colleagues, discussing problems, and seeking advice. Innovative behavior includes generating (or adapting) novel solutions to problems, convincing colleagues to adopt new approaches, and ultimately implementing them within the organization" (Bednall et al., 2014, pp. 3–4).

(continued)

TABLE 5.1 Overview of All Studies Included (continued)

| Author(s) | Feedback Type | Influential Factor at the . . . | | | Performance Type |
		Intrateam Level	Interteam Level	Extrateam Level	
Boet et al. (2013)	Debriefing "is a reflective feedback process in which learners are encouraged to discuss the strengths and weaknesses of their performance" (Hattie & Timperley, 2007, as cited in Boet et al., 2013, p. 1); types of debriefing differ on whether it is guided by an instructor or a team and the extent of guidance on the content.				Team performance—"The extent to which a team accomplishes its goals or mission" (Devine & Philips, 2001, as cited in Bell, 2007, p. 1).
Bonner & Sillito (2011)	Individual performance feedback				Collective team estimation performance
Borgert et al. (2016)	Audit and feedback				Nurses' individual bundle compliance
Brindle et al. (2018)	Debriefing				Team and organizational outcomes
Brown et al. (2018)	Feedback via a CPR feedback device				CPR quality "is such metrics as compression rate, depth, and pauses" (Abella, 2016, p. 6).
Burns et al. (2008)	Team performance feedback				Implementation fidelity "is the degree to which...programs are implemented... as intended by the program developers" (Dusenbury et al., 2003, as cited in Carroll et al., 2007, p. 1).

(continued)

TABLE 5.1 Overview of All Studies Included (continued)

| Author(s) | Feedback Type | Influential Factor at the . . . | | | | Performance Type |
		Intrateam Level	Interteam Level	Extrateam Level		
Chang et al. (2008)	Performance feedback					Team performance
Chen et al. (2014)	Feedback about coworker's performance					Individual and team performance
Cheng et al. (2015)	Feedback via a CPR device					CPR quality
Cheng et al. (2018)	Feedback via a CPR device					CPR quality
Choi et al. (2019)	Performance feedback			Outsiderness of the board and the man-agement team		Search intensity by R&D
De Stobbeleir et al. (2020)	Feedback seeking					Team creativity "is the joint novelty and usefulness of a final product (Zhou & Shalley, 2011) developed by multiple interdependent actors" (as cited in Hoever et al., 2018, p. 8).
DeShon et al. (2004)	Individual and team performance feedback	Self and team regulatory intentions and actions				Individual and team performance
Druskat & Wolff (1999)	Peer appraisals "is a feedback method by which individuals review and evaluate potential or actual performance of their peers" (Fox et al., 1989, p. 1).	Appraisal tim-ing				Team members' perceptions of team communication, viability, social loafing

(continued)

TABLE 5.1 Overview of All Studies Included (continued)

Author(s)	Feedback Type	Influential Factor at the . . .			Performance Type
		Intrateam Level	Interteam Level	Extrateam Level	
Duncan et al. (2013)	Team feedback "is communication of information provided by (an) external agent(s) concerning actions, events, processes, or behaviors relative to task completion or teamwork" (Gabelica et al., 2012, p. 2); "Team feedback can be given at different levels: on an individual or on a team level (i.e., individual feedback aggregated on a team level and presented to the whole team)" (Geister et al., 2006, p. 4).				Radiation use
DuPont et al. (2011)	Audit and feedback				Severity of postpartum hemorrhages
Eddy et al., (2013)	Debriefing	Team processes			Team performance
Ertac et al. (2019)	Performance feedback	Performance is determined by the best or the worst performer			Team performance

(continued)

TABLE 5.1 Overview of All Studies Included (continued)

Author(s)	Feedback Type	Influential Factor at the . . .				Performance Type
		Intrateam Level	Interteam Level	Extrateam Level		
Fan et al. (2014)	Individual feedback	Leader's direction giving or empathetic approach in giving direction				Team members' creativity
Feller & Berendonk (2020)	Interprofessional feedback is feedback from other healthcare members (Feller & Berendonk, 2020).					Team collaboration is the willingness to learn together and share knowledge (Feller & Berendonk, 2020).
Gabelica et al. (2014)	Team feedback	Team reflexivity				Team performance
Gardner et al. (2017)	Debriefing	Individual or team goal setting				Team performance
Geister et al. (2006)	Team process feedback "is information regarding the way one is performing a task" (Salas et al., 2012, as cited in Glikson et al., 2019, p. 3).	Interpersonal trust				Team performance
Giesbers et al. (2016)	Feedback on quality measurements					Nurses' well-being and performance

(continued)

TABLE 5.1 Overview of All Studies Included (continued)

Author(s)	Feedback Type	Influential Factor at the . . .			Performance Type
		Intrateam Level	Interteam Level	Extrateam Level	
Glikson et al. (2019)	Process feedback	Team effort and team composition (i.e., conscientiousness)			Team performance
Goltz et al. (1990)	Individual and group feedback				Group handling performance
Goomas et al. (2011)	Team performance feedback				Team productivity "is the efficiency with which an organization or part of an organization uses its resources to meet its objectives" (Pritchard et al., 1988, p. 1)
Gort et al. (2013)	Use of performance indicators "is the design of the indicator system, data collection, data analysis and interpretation, discussion of insights, and developing suggestions for improvement" (Kleingeld et al., 2004, as cited in Gort et al., 2013, p. 2).				Team performance
Hecht et al. (2019)	Relative performance feedback	Team manager's discretion			Team members' effort

(continued)

TABLE 5.1 Overview of All Studies Included (continued)					
		Influential Factor at the . . .			
Author(s)	Feedback Type	Intrateam Level	Interteam Level	Extrateam Level	Performance Type
Henning et al. (1997)	Team feedback	Feedback delivered to one member or the whole team			Team productivity
Hoever et al. (2018)	Positive and negative feedback	Informational diversity and information processing route			Team creativity
Hollenbeck et al. (1998)	Process feedback	Team experience, hierarchical sensitivity and information distribution			Team decision-making accuracy "is the degree to which a leader's decision matched the correct decision, defined as the mean absolute error of the team's decision" (Hollenbeck et al., 1997, p. 8)
Hubner et al. (2017)	Standardized postresuscitation feedback				Quality of resuscitation
Hysong et al. (2017)	Audit and feedback				Adherence to treatment algorithm
Iyengar & Schotter (2008)	Supervisor's advice "is a type of persuasive address that focuses on proposals for action" (MacGeorge et al., 2004, as cited in Puutio et al., 2009, p. 6).	Cost of ignoring advice			Learning and decision-making

(continued)

TABLE 5.1 Overview of All Studies Included (continued)		Influential Factor at the …			
Author(s)	Feedback Type	Intrateam Level	Interteam Level	Extrateam Level	Performance Type
Johnston et al. (2011)	Performance feedback				Capacity for improvement
Jung & Sosik (2003)	Performance feedback	Collective efficacy and group potency			Group performance
Kerr et al. (2005)	Performance feedback	Feedback timing			Köhler effect "is a group motivation gain, wherein the less capable member of a dyad working conjunctively at a persistence task works harder than comparable individuals" (Kerr et al., 2005, p. 1)
Kim et al. (2017)	Debriefing				Team performance
Lampel & Jha (2017)	Performance feedback	Nonperformance-based inertia	Performance-based inertia		Magnitude of design change "is change in components and change in functional performance as a result of major subsystem or architectural change, and the interaction between the two levels over time" (Tidd, 1995, as cited in Lampel & Jha, 2017, p. 5)
Lant & Hurley (1999)	Performance feedback	Performance distance from aspiration			Investment decision-making

(continued)

TABLE 5.1 Overview of All Studies Included (continued)

Author(s)	Feedback Type	Influential Factor at the . . .				Performance Type
		Intrateam Level	Interteam Level	Extrateam Level		
Li et al. (2009)	Team task feedback "is the extent to which a team is given information on the quality of its work" (Strubler & York, 2007, as cited in Li et al., 2009, p. 4).	Team member satisfaction				Team performance
MacCormack & Verganti (2003)	Technical feedback "is how modules in the design interact"; market feedback "is information on the functioning of the product in the end-use context" (MacCormack & Verganti, 2003, p. 8).			Product or market uncertainty		Project performance "is the efficiency and effectiveness with which an ISD project is completed (Jun et al., 2011); efficiency refers to the level of success of the development process, i.e., the extent to which a project has been completed within budget and schedule; effectiveness can include various aspects of the delivered system, such as its reliability, ease of use, flexibility, and efficiency" (Na et al., 2004, as cited in Sakka et al., 2016, p. 3)
McLeod et al. (1992)	Process feedback					Team performance
Mesch et al. (1994)	Positive or negative feedback	Group goals				Task performance
Mellis et al. (2013)	Early performance feedback					Project performance
Mitrou et al. (2019)	Debriefing					Technical and nontechnical skills

(continued)

		Influential Factor at the...			
Author(s)	**Feedback Type**	**Intrateam Level**	**Interteam Level**	**Extrateam Level**	**Performance Type**
Nurudeen et al. (2015)	Multisource feedback "is gathering feedback from multiple people occupying varying roles in an individual's work environment and serves to generate a comprehensive perspective on performance" (Nurudeen et al., 2015, p. 2).				Behavioral change
Ostrander et al. (2020)	Individual and team feedback				Individual and team performance
Patel et al. (2018)	Audit and feedback				Patient quality care
Peterson & Behfar (2003)	Negative team performance feedback	Team conflict and team trust			Team performance
Pritchard et al. (1988)	Team performance feedback				Group productivity
Proude et al. (2008)	Individual or group feedback				Assessment and management of alcohol and tobacco use
Rasker et al. (2000)	Performance monitoring "is the ability of team members to give, seek, and receive task-clarifying feedback during a task execution				Team performance

(continued)

TABLE 5.1	Overview of All Studies Included (continued)				
		Influential Factor at the . . .			
Author(s)	Feedback Type	Intrateam Level	Interteam Level	Extrateam Level	Performance Type
	session" (Cannon-Bowers et al., 1995, as cited in Rasker et al., 2000); self-correction "is a process after a task execution session in which team members engage in reviewing events, correcting errors, discussing strategies, and planning for the next time" (Rasker et al., 2000).				
Sakka et al. (2016)	Feedback reports	A lack of information and a lack of understanding			Project performance
Sánchez-Expósito & Naranjo-Gil, (2020)	Relative performance feedback		Between-group relative performance feedback		Individual performance
Sametti et al. (2007)	Verbal and graphic feedback				Treatment integrity "is the degree to which an intervention is implemented as planned" (Hagermoser et al., 2007, p. 2)
Sawyer et al. (2012)	Debriefing				Resuscitation performance
Scherer et al. (2003)	Verbal or videotape review performance feedback				Individual performance

(continued)

TABLE 5.1 Overview of All Studies Included (continued)

| Author(s) | Feedback Type | Influential Factor at the . . . | | | Performance Type |
		Intrateam Level	Interteam Level	Extrateam Level	
Smeltzer et al. (2019)	Feedback on institutional performance				Patient survival rates
Smith-Jentsch et al. (2008)	Debriefing				Team performance
Sue-Chan & Latham (2004)	Coaching "is intervention to assess and improve individual and team performance" (Evered & Selman, 1989, p. 11).				Team performance
Tavoletti et al. (2019)	Peer evaluation				Team performance
Tindale et al. (1991)	Individual and group feedback	Performance expectations			Individual and group performance
Unger-Aviram et al. (2013)	Performance feedback				Project performance
Van Thielen et al. (2018)	Constructive feedback			Environmental extremity	Team effectiveness
Vashdi, (2013)	Guided team reflexivity "is encouraging members to systematically explore behavior-outcome linkages and member interactions in an open and safe context" (Gurtner et al., 2007, as cited in Vashdi, 2013, p. 8).	Team attention to detail			Team performance

(continued)

TABLE 5.1 Overview of All Studies Included (continued)

| Author(s) | Feedback Type | Influential Factor at the… | | | Performance Type |
		Intrateam Level	Interteam Level	Extrateam Level	
Villado & Arthur (2013)	After action review "is structured meeting that provides trainees with feedback, a chance to learn from past behavior, as well as to set goals and develop strategies for future performance" (Villado & Arthur, 2013, p. 2).				Team performance
Wang et al. (2009)	Feedback	Team leader's feedback-giving approach: empathetic or direction giving			Team creative performance
Wang et al. (2016)	Haptic and/or verbal feedback				Task completion
Wilkens & London (2006)	Feedback seeking				Creativity of outcomes
Wu et al. (2014)	Feedback seeking	attachment anxiety or attachment avoidance			Job performance

(continued)

TABLE 5.1 Overview of All Studies Included (continued)

Author(s)	Feedback Type	Influential Factor at the…			Performance Type
		Intrateam Level	Interteam Level	Extrateam Level	
Zajonc (1962)	Direct feedback "is knowledge of results regarding one's own individual performance in a group"; confounded feedback "is knowledge of the output of a group as a whole, where the group output is some combination of individual contributions" (Hall, 1957, as cited in Zajonc, 1962, p. 1).				Individual and group performance
Zohar & Polachek (2014)	Individual performance feedback				Safety behaviors

Based on our findings, we conclude that the research on intra-team influences is more advanced compared to the work that has been done at inter- and extra-team levels. With our comprehensive review, we contribute to the existing theoretical models on feedback and performance in teams in several ways. First, we extend the model of London and Sessa (2006) and Gabelica et al. (2012) by showing that diverse feedback characteristics are not only an independent variable but also a condition under which feedback has a stronger or weaker effect on performance in teams. Second, we demonstrate that contrary to the two existing models, the mechanisms through which feedback exerts its effect on performance in teams, are not only processing and perceptions of feedback but also various team processes, emergent states, and individual characteristics.

In addition, we extend the existing conceptual models (Gabelica et al., 2012; Gabelica & Popov, 2020; London & Sessa, 2006) by showing that inter-team contextual factors also influence the relationship between feedback and performance in teams. Although this stream of research is still at an early stage, our review demonstrates that other teams' performance influences the effect of feedback on performance within teams. This suggests that other teams and interactions with those teams alter within-team processes such as feedback. We also contribute to the existing conceptual models by adding relevant extra-team level contextual factors. Our review shows that factors at the organizational level, such as management team practices and characteristics, and factors from the external organizational environment also influence the effect of feedback on performance in teams. This means that influences outside of teams and organizations more broadly spill over to affect within-team processes.

However, we also identified that more research is needed to further unravel how the relationship between feedback and performance in teams is shaped by inter- and extra-team contextual factors. We contribute to the advancement of this stream of research by developing future research ideas based on the multiple team membership perspective and spillover theory.

Toward a Multilevel Model of Feedback and Performance in Teams: Future Research Suggestions

By drawing on spillover theory, the MTM perspective, and the findings of our literature review, we further discuss which other inter- and extra-team contextual factors can influence the feedback–performance relationship in teams. We suggest that some of the conditions and mechanisms that were found in our literature review at the intra-team level can be further examined at the inter-team level: specifically, inter-team processes, inter-team emergent states, and inter-team characteristics. We also identify factors at the extra-team level that can be further investigated in future research. Figure 5.2 displays

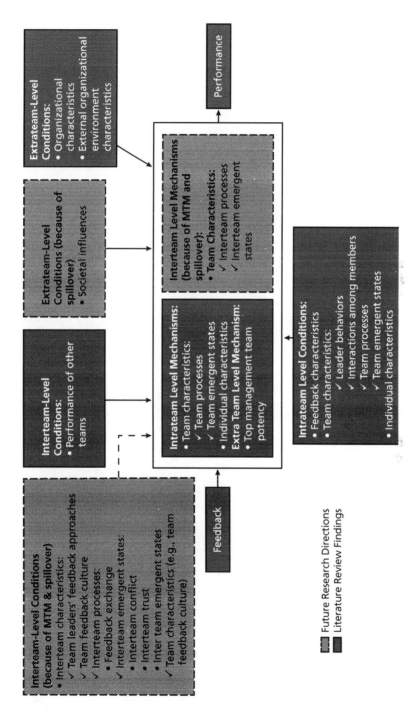

Figure 5.2 A multilevel model of feedback and performance in teams.

a multilevel model that integrates our literature review findings and suggestions for future research.

Inter-Team Level Contextual Factors

Inter-team characteristics.

Team leaders' feedback approaches. Team leaders provide feedback to their subordinates, which is important for effective performance in teams (e.g., Fan et al., 2014). As team leaders can lead multiple teams simultaneously (e.g., Luciano et al., 2014), they can apply the same effective leadership practices, such as providing feedback, across those teams (Morgeson et al., 2010). Indeed, as has been previously discussed, individuals encode certain behaviors and skills as scripts that are activated across similar situations, resulting in similar behaviors (Lord & Kernan, 1987). Thus, team leaders who lead multiple teams can transfer their experience with the provision of feedback from team to team, initiating an inter-team spillover effect that can consequentially affect how feedback influences performance in teams.

Team feedback culture. Teams have their own norms, processes, and characteristics, that is, team culture, which has a powerful influence on how team members complete their work (Hackman, 1992). Within an organization, various teams can have different team cultures (Cabana & Kaptein, 2019); thus, if an individual is a part of multiple teams simultaneously, they may be exposed to different team norms and expectations that they must manage (van de Brake et al., 2020). Team culture also has an effect on team members' performance and knowledge sharing (Shin et al., 2016), which indicates that it is possible to create a team feedback culture where feedback flows openly and is appreciated and sought out (London & Smither, 2002). Thus, the different extents to which team cultures promote feedback can be influential for the feedback-performance relationship in teams. Particularly because of the MTM and the spillover effect, team feedback cultures can spill over from one team to another, thereby influencing the feedback-performance process in teams.

Inter-team processes.

Frequency of feedback exchange between teams. In this review, we identified several studies on the effect of proactive feedback giving and seeking on performance in teams (e.g., De Stobbeleir et al., 2020). Proactive feedback seeking is a conscious effort to determine the adequacy of one's behaviors (Ashford, 1986) that increases team effectiveness (Bunderson & Boumgarden, 2010) and fosters creativity due to the diverse input obtained (De Stobbeleir et al., 2011). Following this reasoning, we argue that because of MTM, there are more opportunities to exchange valuable knowledge with team members who have collected diverse perspectives from other teams (Mortensen et al., 2007). Team members who are part of several teams may thus be more likely to engage in proactive feedback seeking and giving in teams, thereby creating more possibilities for improving performance in teams (Bunderson & Boumgarden, 2010). However, MTM can also hamper informal feedback giving and seeking in teams because team members who are part of multiple teams can perceive MTM as a job demand rather than a job resource due to their increased responsibilities (Pluut et al., 2014). Such team members may then be less willing to put forth extra effort to seek and give feedback as doing so would further increase their job demands, which could hamper performance in teams. Thus, future research can focus on the frequency of feedback exchange between different teams and examine how that affects the relationship between feedback and performance within teams when members are part of multiple teams.

Inter-team emergent states.

Inter-team conflict.   In our review, conflict in a team was identified as a mechanism between negative team performance feedback and performance (Peterson & Behfar, 2003). Such conflict not only occurs within a team (Jehn et al., 2013) but can also be transmitted from one team to another (Sassenberg et al., 2007). Van Bunderen et al. (2018) showed that due to conflicts between teams, a resource threat is transmitted to teams, that is, individuals' fear of personal resource deprivation. Therefore, a competitive mindset develops among team members, discouraging them from sharing resources with their teammates. One such beneficial resource that employees proactively seek and share is feedback (Ashford & Cummings, 1983). Thus, inter-team conflict could negatively influence the feedback–performance link as team members are less exposed to different perspectives that they can use to improve their performance (De Stobbeleir et al., 2011). However, conflicts between teams may also positively influence the feedback-performance link in teams. The research shows that under certain circumstances, low levels of task conflict can increase performance in teams (De Dreu & Weingart, 2003) as it encourages teams to explore different perspectives (Tjosvold, 1997), which can be gathered through proactive feedback giving and seeking in teams (De Stobbeleir et al., 2011). Thus, we suggest that future research incorporates inter-team conflict when studying the feedback-performance relationship in teams.

Inter-team trust.   Trust is defined as a positive expectation of another person's behavior (Palvia, 2009), and it is linked to positive team outcomes such as team performance (Dirks, 2000) and knowledge sharing (Lin & Huang, 2010). Trust in a team creates a safe climate for interpersonal risk-taking as it involves the perception of high team psychological safety (Bradley et al., 2012; Edmondson, 1999). The research further suggests that a safe environment facilitates open communication and interaction in a team (Baer & Frese, 2003) and encourages feedback-seeking behaviors (Ashford et al.,

2003), which in turn enhance team performance (De Stobbeleir et al., 2011). Spillover theory suggests that individuals perform habitual behaviors across similar contexts (Lord & Kernan, 1987; i.e., proactive feedback giving and seeking) and that positive feelings at one level of interaction spill over to other interactions (Staw et al., 1994; i.e., feelings of trust); thus, trust between teams can spill over to foster intra-team trust, thereby affecting the relationship between proactive feedback giving and seeking and performance. Therefore, future research can investigate the influence of inter-team trust on the relationship between feedback and performance in teams.

Extra-Team Level Contextual Factors

External organizational environment characteristics.

Societal influences. Due to the COVID-19 pandemic and the subsequent regulations issued by governments worldwide, many employees have turned to working remotely (Kniffin et al., 2021). The recent empirical work shows that remote work during the pandemic has caused distorted work–life balance (Hjálmsdóttir & Bjarnadóttir, 2020) and has led to more formal and less personal interaction with colleagues (Blanchard & McBride, 2019). Such work regulations issued from outside of teams, which cause work interactions to be more formal and less personal, can have profound implications on the feedback effect on performance in teams. Thus future research could investigate the impact that the COVID-19 and the associated restrictions have had on the feedback–performance link in teams. We hope that our work will inspire other researchers to further advance the research on feedback and performance in teams.

REFERENCES

Aakvik, A., Hansen, F., & Torsvik, G. (2017). Productivity dynamics, performance feedback and group incentives in a sales organization. *Labour Economics, 46,* 110–117. https://doi.org/10.1016/j.labeco.2016.12.003

Abella, B. S. (2016). High-quality cardiopulmonary resuscitation: Current and future directions. *Current Opinion in Critical Care, 22*(3), 218–224. https://doi.org/10.1097/MCC.0000000000000296

Abelson, R. P. (1981). Psychological status of the script concept. *American Psychologist, 36*(7), 715–729. https://doi.org/10.1037/0003-066X.36.7.715

Ashford, S. J. (1986). Feedback seeking in individual adaptation: A resource perspective. *Academy of Management Journal, 29*(3), 465–487. https://doi.org/10.5465/256219

Ashford, S. J., Blatt, R., & VandeWalle, D. (2003). Reflections on the looking glass: A review of research on feedback-seeking behavior in organizations. *Journal of Management, 29*(6), 773–799. https://doi.org/10.1016/S0149-2063(03)00079-5

Ashford, S. J., & Cummings, L. L. (1983). Feedback as an individual resource: Personal strategies of creating information. *Organizational Behavior and Human Performance, 32*(3), 370–398. https://doi.org/10.1016/0030-5073(83)90156-3

Ashford, S. J., Wellman, N., de Luque, M. S., De Stobbeleir, K. E. M., & Wollan, M. (2018). Two roads to effectiveness: CEO feedback seeking, vision articulation, and firm performance. *Journal of Organizational Behavior, 39*(1), 82–95. https://doi.org/10.1002/job.2211

Ashforth, B. E., Kreiner, G. E., & Fugate, M. (2000). All in a day's work: Boundaries and micro role transitions. *Academy of Management Review, 25*(3), 472–491. https://doi.org/10.5465/amr.2000.3363315

Ayieko, P., Irimu, G., Ogero, M., Mwaniki, P., Malla, L., Julius, T., Chepkirui, M., Mbevi, G., Oliwa, J., Agweyu, A., Akech, S., Were, F., English, M., & Clinical Information Network Authors. (2019). Effect of enhancing audit and feedback on uptake of childhood pneumonia treatment policy in hospitals that are part of a clinical network: A cluster randomized trial. *Implementation Science, 14,* 20–34. https://doi.org/10.1186/s13012-019-0868-4

Bachrach, D. G., Bendoly, E., & Podsakoff, P. M. (2001). Attributions of the "causes" of group performance as an alternative explanation of the relationship between organizational citizenship behavior and organizational performance. *Journal of Applied Psychology, 86*(6), 1285–1293. https://doi.org/10.1037//0021-9010.86.6.1285

Baer, M., & Frese, M. (2003). Innovation is not enough: Climates for initiative and psychological safety, process innovations, and firm performance. *Journal of Organizational Behavior: The International Journal of Industrial, Occupational and Organizational Psychology and Behavior, 24*(1), 45–68. https://doi.org:10.1002/job.179

Balkin, D. B., Roussel, P., & Werner, S. (2015). Performance contingent pay and autonomy: Implications for facilitating extra-role creativity. *Human Resource Management Review, 25*(4), 384–395. https://doi.org/10.1016/j.hrmr.2015.07.001

Barker, D., Rossi, A., & Pühse, U. (2010). Managing teams: Comparing organizational and sport psychological approaches to teamwork. In *Scandinavian Sport Studies Forum* (Vol. 1, pp. 115–132). Scandinavian Sport Studies Forum.

Baron, R. M., & Kenny, D. A. (1986). The moderator–mediator variable distinction in social psychological research: Conceptual, strategic, and statistical considerations. *Journal of Personality and Social Psychology, 51*(6), 1173–1182. https://doi.org/10.1037/0022-3514.51.6.1173

Barton, E. E., Velez, M., Pokorski, E. A., & Domingo, M. (2020). The effects of email performance-based feedback delivered to teaching teams: A systematic replication. *Journal of Early Intervention, (42)*2, 143–162. https://doi.org/10.1177/1053815119872451

Bednall, T. C., Sanders, K., & Runhaar, P. (2014). Stimulating informal learning activities through perceptions of performance appraisal quality and human resource management system strength: A two-wave study. *Academy of Management Learning & Education, 13*(1), 45–61. https://doi.org/10.5465/amle.2012.0162

Bell, S. T. (2007). Deep-level composition variables as predictors of team performance: A meta-analysis. *Journal of Applied Psychology, 92*(3), 595–615. https://doi.org/10.1037/0021-9010.92.3.595

Bhatti, K. K., & Qureshi, T. M. (2007). Impact of employee participation on job satisfaction, employee commitment and employee productivity. *International Review of Business Research Papers, 3*(2), 54–68.

Blanchard, A. L., & McBride, A. (2019). Putting the "group" in group meetings: Entitativity in face-to-face and online meetings. In A. L. Meinecke, J. A. Allen, & N. Lehmann-Willenbrock (Eds.), *Managing meetings in organizations* (pp. 71–92). Emerald Group. https://doi.org/10.1108/S1534-085620200000020004

Boet, S., Bould, M. D., Sharma, B., Revees, S., Naik, V. N., Triby, E., & Grantcharov, T. (2013). Within-team debriefing versus instructor-led debriefing for simulation-based education: A randomized controlled trial. *Annals of Surgery, 258*(1), 53–58. https://doi.org/10.1097/SLA.0b013e31829659e4

Bonner, B. L., & Sillito, S. D. (2011). Leveraging member knowledge in group decision-making: Expertise, extroversion, and feedback. *Group Dynamics-Theory Research and Practice, 15*(3), 233–245. https://doi.org/10.1037/a0022735

Borgert, M., Binnekade, J., Paulus, F., Goossens, A., Vroom, M., & Dongelmans, D. (2016). Timely individual audit and feedback significantly improves transfusion bundle compliance—A comparative study. *International Journal for Quality in Health Care, 28*(5), 601–607. https://doi.org/10.1093/intqhc/mzw071

Bradley, B. H., Postlethwaite, B. E., Klotz, A. C., Hamdani, M. R., & Brown, K. G. (2012). Reaping the benefits of task conflict in teams: The critical role of team psychological safety climate. *Journal of Applied Psychology, 97*(1), 151–158. https://doi.org:DOI:10.1037/a0024200

Brennan, K. A., & Bosson, J. K. (1998). Attachment-style differences in attitudes toward and reactions to feedback from romantic partners: An exploration of the relational bases of self-esteem. *Personality and Social Psychology Bulletin, 24*(7), 699–714. https://doi.org/10.1177/0146167298247003

Brindle, M. E., Henrich, N., Foster, A., Marks, S., Rose, M., Welsh, R., & Berry, W. (2018). Implementation of surgical debriefing programs in large health systems: An exploratory qualitative analysis. *BMC Health Services Research, 18*(1), 210–224. https://doi.org/10.1186/s12913-018-3003-3

Brown, L. L., Lin, Y. Q., Tofil, N. M., Overly, F., Duff, J. P., Bhanji, F., Nadkarni, V. M., Hunt, E. A., Bragg, A., Kessler, D., Bank, I., & Cheng, A. (2018). Impact of a CPR feedback device on healthcare provider workload during simulated cardiac arrest. *Resuscitation, 130*, 111–117. https://doi.org/10.1016/j.resuscitation.2018.06.035

Bunderson, J. S., & Boumgarden, P. (2010). Structure and learning in self-managed teams: Why "bureaucratic" teams can be better learners. *Organization Science, 21*(3), 593–801. https://doi.org/10.1287/orsc.1090.0483

Burns, M. K., Peters, R., & Noell, G. H. (2008). Using performance feedback to enhance implementation fidelity of the problem-solving team process. *Journal of School Psychology, 46*(5), 537–550. https://doi.org/10.1016/j.jsp.2008.04.001

Cabana, G. C., & Kaptein, M. (2019). Team ethical cultures within an organization: A differentiation perspective on their existence and relevance. *Journal of Business Ethics, 170*, 1–20. https://doi.org/10.1007/s10551-019-04376-5

Cannon-Bowers, J. A., Tannenbaum, E. S., Salas, E., & Volpe, C. E. (1995). Defining competencies and establishing team training requirements. In R. A. Guzzo & E. Salas (Eds.), *Team effectiveness and decision-making in organizations* (pp. 333–379). JosseyBass.

Carroll, C., Patterson, M., Wood, S., Booth, A., Rick, J., & Balain, S. (2007). A conceptual framework for implementation fidelity. *Implementation Science, 2*(1), 40–49. https://doi.org/10.1186/1748-5908-2-40

Chang, S. L., Erin, W., Martinec, D. V., Zheng, B., & Swanstrom, L. L. (2008). Verbal communication improves laparoscopic team performance. *Surgical Innovation, 15*(2), 143–147. https://doi.org/10.1177/1553350608318452

Chen, F., Zhang, L. M., & Latimer, J. (2014). How much has my co-worker contributed? The impact of anonymity and feedback on social loafing in asynchronous virtual collaboration. *International Journal of Information Management, 34*(5), 652–659. https://doi.org/10.1016/j.ijinfomgt.2014.05.001

Chen, G., Smith, T. A., Kirkman, B. L., Zhang, P., Lemoine, G. J., & Farh, J. L. (2019). Multiple team membership and empowerment spillover effects: Can empowerment processes cross team boundaries?. *Journal of Applied Psychology, 104*(3), 321–340. https://doi.org/10.1037/apl0000336

Cheng, A., Brown, L. L., Duff, J. P., Davidson, J., Overly, F., Tofil, N. M., Peterson, D. T., White, M. L., Bhanji, F., Bank, I., Gotesman, R., Adler, M., Zhong, J., Grant, V., Grant, D. J., Sudikoff, S. N., Marohn, K., Charnovich, A., Hunt, E. A., . . . Nadkarni, V. M. (2015). Improving cardiopulmonary resuscitation with a CPR feedback device and refresher simulations (CPR CARES Study): A randomized clinical trial. *Jama Pediatrics, 169*(2), 137–144. https://doi.org/10.1001/jamapediatrics.2014.2616

Cheng, A., Duff, J. P., Kessler, D., Tofil, N. M., Davidson, J., Lin, Y. Q., Chatfield, J., Brown, L. L., & Hunt, E. A. (2018). Optimizing CPR performance with CPR coaching for pediatric cardiac arrest: A randomized simulation-based clinical trial. *Resuscitation, 132*, 33–40. https://doi.org/10.1016/j.resuscitation.2018.08.021

Choi, J., Rhee, M., & Kim, Y. C. (2019). Performance feedback and problemistic search: The moderating effects of managerial and board outsiderness. *Journal of Business Research, 102*, 21–33. https://doi.org/10.1016/j.jbusres.2019.04.039

Cooper, H. (2010). Research synthesis and meta-analysis. *Applied social research methods series.* SAGE.

Cronin, M. A., & George, E. (2020). The why and how of the integrative review. *Organizational Research Methods*, 1–25. https://doi.org/10.1177/1094428120935507

Crossan, M. M., & Apaydin, M. (2010). A multi-dimensional framework of organizational innovation: A systematic review of the literature. *Journal of Management Studies, 47*(6), 1154–1191. https://doi.org/10.1111/j.1467-6486.2009.00880.x

Daniels, K. (2019). Guidance on conducting and reviewing systematic reviews (and meta-analyses) in work and organizational psychology. *European Journal of Work and Organizational Psychology, 28*(1), 1–10. https://doi.org/10.1080/1359432X.2018.1547708

De Dreu, C. K. W., & Weingart, L. R. (2003). Task versus relationship conflict, team member satisfaction, and team effectiveness: A meta-analysis. *Journal of Applied Psychology, 88*(4), 741–749. https://doi.org/10.1037/0021-9010.88.4.741

De Stobbeleir, K., Ashford, S., & Zhang, C. (2020). Shifting focus: Antecedents and outcomes of proactive feedback seeking from peers. *Human Relations, 73*(3), 303–325. https://doi.org/10.1177/0018726719828448

De Stobbeleir, K. E. M., Ashford, S. J., & Buyens, D. (2011). Self-regulation of creativity at work: The role of feedback-seeking behavior in creative performance. *Academy of Management Journal, 54*(4), 811–831. https://doi.org/10.5465/amj.2011.64870144

Denyer, D., & Tranfield, D. (2009). Producing a systematic review. In D. A. Buchanan & A. Bryman (Eds.), *The Sage handbook of organizational research methods* (pp. 671–689). SAGE Publications.

DeShon, R. P., Kozlowski, S. W. J., Schmidt, A. M., Milner, K. R., & Wiechmann, D. (2004). A multiple-goal, multilevel model of feedback effects on the regulation of individual and team performance. *Journal of Applied Psychology, 89*(6), 1035–1056. https://doi.org/10.1037/0021-9010.89.6.1035

Devine, D. J., & Philips, J. L. (2001). Do smarter teams do better: A meta-analysis of cognitive ability and team performance. *Small Group Research, 32*(5), 507–532. https://doi.org/10.1177/104649640103200501

Dirks, K. T. (2000). Trust in leadership and team performance: Evidence from NCAA basketball. *Journal of Applied Psychology, 85*(6), 1004–1012. https://doi.org/10.1037/0021-9010.85.6.1004

Druskat, V. U., & Wolff, S. B. (1999). Effects and timing of developmental peer appraisals in self-managing work groups. *Journal of Applied Psychology, 84*(1), 58–74. https://doi.org/10.1037/0021-9010.84.1.58

Dugosh, K. L., Paulus, P. B., Roland, E. J., & Yang, H. C. (2000). Cognitive stimulation in brainstorming. *Journal of Personality and Social Psychology, 79*(5), 722–735. https://doi.org/10.1037/0022-3514.79.5.722

Duncan, J. R., Street, M., Strother, M., & Picus, D. (2013). Optimizing radiation use during fluoroscopic procedures: A quality and safety improvement project. *Journal of the American College of Radiology, 10*(11), 847–853. https://doi.org/10.1016/j.jacr.2013.05.008

DuPont, C., Deneux-Tharaux, C., Touzet, S., Colin, C., Bouvier-Colle, M. H., Lansac, J., Thevenet, S., Boberie-Moyrand, C., Piccin, G., Fernandez, M., Rudigoz, R., For the Pithagore6 group, Bouvier-Colle, M., Chauleur, C., Colin, C., Deneux-Tharaux, C., Dupont, C., Harvey, T., Lansac, L., . . . Tessier, V. (2011). Clinical audit: A useful tool for reducing severe postpartum hemorrhages? *International Journal for Quality in Health Care, 23*(5), 583–589. https://doi.org/10.1093/intqhc/mzr042

Dusenbury, L., Brannigan, R., Falco, M., & Hansen, W. (2003). A review of research on fidelity of implementation: Implications for drug abuse prevention in school settings. *Health Education Research, 18*(2), 237–256. https://doi.org/10.1093/her/18.2.237

Eddy, E. R., Tannenbaum, S. I., & Mathieu, J. E. (2013). Helping teams to help themselves: Comparing two team-led debriefing methods. *Personnel Psychology, 66*(4), 975–1008. https://doi.org/10.1111/peps.12041

Edmondson, A. C. (1999). Psychological safety and learning behavior in work teams. *Administrative Science Quarterly, 44*(2), 350–383. https://doi.org/10 .2307/2666999

Edwards, J. R., & Rothbard, N. P. (2000). Mechanisms linking work and family: Clarifying the relationship between work and family constructs. *Academy of Management Review, 25*(1), 178–199. https://doi.org/10.5465/amr.2000.2791609

Ertaç, S., Gumren, M., & Kockesen, L. (2019). Strategic feedback in teams: Theory and experimental evidence. *Journal of Economic Behavior & Organization, 162,* 1–23. https://doi.org/10.1016/j.jebo.2019.04.005

Evered, R. D., & Selman, J. C. (1989). Coaching and the art of management. *Organizational Dynamics, 18*(2), 16–32. https://doi.org/10.1016/0090-2616(89)90040-5

Fan, K. T., Chen, Y. H., Wang, C. W., & Chen, M. D. (2014). E-leadership effectiveness in virtual teams: Motivating language perspective. *Industrial Management & Data Systems, 114*(3), 421–437. https://doi.org/10.1108/imds-07-2013-0294

Feller, K., & Berendonk, C. (2020). Identity matters–perceptions of inter-professional feedback in the context of workplace-based assessment in diabetology training: A qualitative study. *BMC Medical Education, 20*(1), 1–8. https://doi .org/10.1186/s12909-020-1932-0

Fox, S., Ben-Nahum, Z., & Yinon, Y. (1989). Perceived similarity and accuracy of peer ratings. *Journal of Applied Psychology, 74*(5), 781–786. https://doi.org/ 10.1037/0021-9010.74.5.781

Gabelica, C., & Popov, V. (2020). "One size does not fit all": Revisiting team feedback theories from a cultural dimensions perspective. *Group & Organization Management, 45*(2), 252–309. https://doi.org/10.1177/1059601120910859

Gabelica, C., Van den Bossche, P., De Maeyer, S., Segers, M., & Gijselaers, W. (2014). The effect of team feedback and guided reflexivity on team performance change. *Learning and Instruction, 34,* 86–96. https://doi.org/10.1016/j .learninstruc.2014.09.001

Gabelica, C., Van den Bossche, P., Segers, M., & Gijselaers, W. (2012). Feedback, a powerful lever in teams: A review. *Educational Research Review, 7*(2), 123–144. https://doi.org/10.1016/j.edurev.2011.11.003

Gardner, A. K., Kosemund, M., Hogg, D., Heymann, A., & Martinez, J. (2017). Setting goals, not just roles: Improving teamwork through goal-focused debriefing. *American Journal of Surgery, 213*(2), 249–252. https://doi.org/10.1016/j .amjsurg.2016.09.040

Geister, S., Konradt, U., & Hertel, G. (2006). Effects of process feedback on motivation, satisfaction, and performance in virtual teams. *Small Group Research, 37*(5), 459–489. https://doi.org/10.1177/1046496406292337

Gelbard, R., & Carmeli, A. (2009). The interactive effect of team dynamics and organizational support on ICT project success. *International Journal of Project Management, 27*(5), 464–470. https://doi.org/10.1016/j.ijproman.2008.07.005

Giesbers, A. P. M., Schouteten, R. L. J., Poutsma, E., van der Heijden, B., & van Achterberg, T. (2016). Nurses' perceptions of feedback to nursing teams on quality measurements: An embedded case study design. *International Journal of Nursing Studies, 64,* 120–129. https://doi.org/10.1016/j.ijnurstu.2016.10.003

Glikson, E., Woolley, A. W., Gupta, P., & Kim, Y. J. (2019). Visualized automatic feedback in virtual teams. *Frontiers in Psychology, 10,* 814–825. https://doi.org/10.3389/fpsyg.2019.00814

Goltz, S. M., Citera, M., Jensen, M., Favero, J., & Komaki, J. L. (1990). Individual feedback: Does it enhance effects of group feedback? *Journal of Organizational Behavior Management, 10*(2), 77–92. https://doi.org/10.1300/J075v10n02_06

Goomas, D. T., Smith, S. M., & Ludwig, T. D. (2011). Business activity monitoring: Real-time group goals and feedback using an overhead scoreboard in a distribution center. *Journal of Organizational Behavior Management, 31*(3), 196–209. https://doi.org/10.1080/01608061.2011.589715

Gort, M., Broekhuis, M., & Regts, G. (2013). How teams use indicators for quality improvement—A multiple-case study on the use of multiple indicators in multidisciplinary breast cancer teams. *Social Science & Medicine, 96,* 69–77. https://doi.org/10.1016/j.socscimed.2013.06.001

Gully, S. M., Incalcaterra, K. A., Joshi, A., & Beaubien, J. M. (2002). A meta-analysis of team-efficacy, potency, and performance: Interdependence and level of analysis as moderators of observed relationships. *Journal of Applied Psychology, 87*(5), 819–832. https://doi.org/10.1037/0021-9010.87.5.819

Gurtner, A., Tschan, F., Semmer, N. K., & Nägele, C. (2007). Getting groups to develop good strategies: Effects of reflexivity interventions on team process, team performance, and shared mental models. *Organizational Behavior and Human Decision Processes, 102*(2), 127–142. https://doi.org/10.1016/j.obhdp.2006.05.002

Guz, A. N., & Rushchitsky, J. J. (2009). Scopus: A system for the evaluation of scientific journals. *International Applied Mechanics, 45*(4), 351–362. http://doi.org/10.1007/s10778-009-0189-4

Hackman, J. R. (1992). *Group influences on individuals in organizations.* In M. D. Dunnette & L. M. Hough (Eds.), *Handbook of industrial and organizational psychology* (pp. 199–267). Consulting Psychologists Press.

Hagermoser Sanetti, L. M., Luiselli, J. K., & Handler, M. W. (2007). Effects of verbal and graphic performance feedback on behavior support plan implementation in a public elementary school. *Behavior Modification, 31*(4), 454–465. https://doi.org/10.1177/0145445506297583

Hall, R. L. (1957). Group performance under feedback that confounds responses of group members. *Sociometry, 20*(4), 297–305. https://doi.org/10.2307/2785982

Harder, J. W. (1992). Play for pay: Effects of inequity in a pay-for-performance context. *Administrative Science Quarterly, 37*(2), 321–335. https://doi.org/10.2307/2393227

Hattie, J., & Timperley, H. (2007). The power of feedback. *Review of Educational Research, 77*(1), 81–112. https://doi.org/10.3102/003465430298487

Hecht, G., Newman, A. H., & Tafkov, I. D. (2019). Managers' strategic use of discretion over relative performance information provision and implications for team-members' effort. *Management Accounting Research, 45,* 10638–10657. https://doi.org/10.1016/j.mar.2019.01.001

Henning, R. A., Bopp, M. I., Tucker, K. M., Knoph, R. D., & Ahlgren, J. (1997). Team-managed rest breaks during computer-supported cooperative work.

International Journal of Industrial Ergonomics, 20(1), 19–29. https://doi.org/10.1016/s0169-8141(96)00028-5

Herold, D. M., & Greller, M. M. (1977). Feedback the definition of a construct. *Academy of Management Journal,* 20(1), 142–147. https://doi.org/10.5465/255468

Heslin, P. A., & Latham, G. P. (2004). The effect of upward feedback on managerial behavior. *Applied Psychology,* 53(1), 23–37. https://doi.org/10.1111/j.1464-0597.2004.00159.x

Hjálmsdóttir, A., & Bjarnadóttir, V. S. (2020). "I have turned into a foreman here at home": Families and work–life balance in times of COVID-19 in a gender equality paradise. *Gender, Work & Organization,* 28(1), 68–83. https://doi.org/10.1111/gwao.12552

Hoever, I. J., Zhou, J., & van Knippenberg, D. (2018). Different strokes for different teams: The contingent effects of positive and negative feedback on the creativity of informationally homogeneous and diverse teams. *Academy of Management Journal,* 61(6), 2159–2181. https://doi.org/10.5465/amj.2016.0642

Hollenbeck, J. R., Ilgen, D. R., LePine, J. A., Colquitt, J. A., & Hedlund, J. (1998). Extending the multilevel theory of team decision making: Effects of feedback and experience in hierarchical teams. *Academy of Management Journal,* 41(3), 269–282. https://www.jstor.org/stable/256907

Hubner, P., Lobmeyr, E., Wallmuller, C., Poppe, M., Datler, P., Keferbock, M., Zeiner, S., Nürnberger, A., Zajicek, A., Laggner, A., Sterz, F., & Sulzgruber, P. (2017). Improvements in the quality of advanced life support and patient outcome after implementation of a standardized real-life post-resuscitation feedback system. *Resuscitation,* 120, 38–44. https://doi.org/10.1016/j.resuscitation.2017.08.235

Hysong, S. J., Kell, H. J., Petersen, L. A., Campbell, B. A., & Trautner, B. W. (2017). Theory-based and evidence-based design of audit and feedback programmes: Examples from two clinical intervention studies. *BMJ Quality & Safety,* 26(4), 323–334. https://doi.org/10.1136/bmjqs-2015-004796

Ilgen, D. R., Hollenbeck, J. R., Johnson, M., & Jundt, D. (2005). Teams in organizations: From input-process-output models to IMOI models. *Annual Review of Psychology,* 56, 517–543. https://doi.org/10.1146/annurev.psych.56.091103.070250

Iyengar, R., & Schotter, A. (2008). Learning under supervision: An experimental study. *Experimental Economics,* 11(2), 154–173. https://doi.org/10.1007/s10683-007-9164-2

Jehn, K., Rispens, S., Jonsen, K., & Greer, L. (2013). Conflict contagion: A temporal perspective on the development of conflict within teams. *International Journal of Conflict Management,* 24(4), 352–373. https://doi.org/10.1108/IJCMA-05-2011-0039

Johnston, S., Green, M., Thille, P., Savage, C., Roberts, L., Russell, G., & Hogg, W. (2011). Performance feedback: An exploratory study to examine the acceptability and impact for interdisciplinary primary care teams. *BMC Family Practice,* 12, 14–24. https://doi.org/10.1186/1471-2296-12-14

Jun, L., Qiuzhen, W., & Qingguo, M. (2011). The effects of project uncertainty and risk management on IS development project performance: A vendor perspective.

International Journal of Project Management, *29*(7), 923–933. https://doi
.org/10.1016/j.ijproman.2010.11.002

Jung, D. I., & Sosik, J. J. (2003). Group potency and collective efficacy: Examining
their predictive validity, level of analysis, and effects of performance feedback on future group performance. *Group & Organization Management*, *28*(3),
366–391. https://doi.org/10.1177/1059601102250821

Katz, D., & Kahn, R.L. (1978). *The social psychology of organizations*. Wiley.

Katzenbach, J. R., & Smith, D. K. (1993). The rules for managing cross-functional re-
engineering teams. *Planning Review*, *21*(2), 12–13. https://doi.org/10.1108/
eb054404

Kerr, N. L., Messé, L. A., Park, E. S., & Sambolec, E. J. (2005). Identifiability, performance feedback and the Köhler effect. *Group Processes & Intergroup Relations*,
8(4), 375–390. https://doi.org/10.1177/1368430205056466

Keyton, J., & Heylen, D. K. (2017). Pushing interdisciplinary in the study of
groups and teams. *Small Group Research*, *48*(5), 621–630. https://doi.org/
10.1177/1046496417732528

Kim, J. H., Kim, Y. M., Park, S. H., Ju, E. A., Choi, S. M., & Hong, T. Y. (2017).
Focused and corrective feedback versus structured and supported debriefing in a simulation-based cardiac arrest team training: A pilot randomized
controlled study. *Simulation in Healthcare-Journal of the Society for Simulation in
Healthcare*, *12*(3), 157–164. https://doi.org/10.1097/sih.0000000000000218

Kirca, A. H., & Hult, G. T. M. (2009). Intra-organizational factors and market orientation: Effects of national culture. *International Marketing Review*, *26*(6),
633–650. https://doi.org/10.1108/02651330911001323

Kleingeld, A. D., Van Tuijl, H., & Algera, J. A. (2004). Participation in the design of
performance management systems: A quasi-experimental field study. *Journal
of Organizational Behavior*, *25*(7), 831–851. https://doi.org/10.1002/job.266

Kluger, A. N., & DeNisi, A. (1996). The effects of feedback interventions on performance: A historical review, a meta-analysis, and a preliminary feedback
intervention theory. *Psychological Bulletin*, *119*(2), 254–284. https://doi.org/
10.1037/0033-2909.119.2.254

Kniffin, K. M., Narayanan, J., Anseel, F., Antonakis, J., Ashford, S. P., Bakker, A. B.,
Bamberger, P., Bapuji, H., Bhave, D. P., Choi, V. K., Creary, S. J., Demerouti,
E., Flynn, F. J., Gelfand, M. J., Greer, L. L., Johns, G., Kesebir, S., Klein, P.
J., Lee, S. Y.,...Vugt, M. v. (2021). COVID-19 and the workplace: Implica-
tions, issues, and insights for future research and action. *American Psychologist*,
76(1), 63–77. https://doi.org/10.1037/amp0000716

Kozlowski, S. W. J., & Ilgen, D. R. (2006). Enhancing the effectiveness of work groups
and teams. *Psychological Science in the Public Interest*, *7*(3), 77–124. https://doi
.org/10.1111/j.1529-1006.2006.00030.x

Lam, C. F., DeRue, D. S., Karam, E. P., & Hollenbeck, J. R. (2011). The impact
of feedback frequency on learning and task performance: Challenging the
"more is better" assumption. *Organizational Behavior and Human Decision Processes*, *116*(2), 217–228. https://doi.org/10.1016/j.obhdp.2011.05.002

Lampel, J., & Jha, P. P. (2017). Inertia, aspirations, and response to attainment discrepancy in design contests. *R&D Management*, *47*(4), 557–569. https://doi
.org/10.1111/radm.12240

Lant, T. K., & Hurley, A. E. (1999). A contingency model of response to performance feedback: Escalation of commitment and incremental adaptation in resource investment decisions. *Group & Organization Management, 24*(4), 421–437. https://doi.org/10.1177/1059601199244002

Li, F., Li, Y. J., & Wang, E. P. (2009). Task characteristics and team performance: The mediating effect of team member satisfaction. *Social Behavior and Personality, 37*(10), 1373–1382. https://doi.org/10.2224/sbp.2009.37.10.1373

Lin, T. C., & Huang, C. C. (2010). Withholding effort in knowledge contribution: The role of social exchange and social cognitive on project teams. *Information & Management, 47*(3), 188–196. https://doi.org/10.1016/j.im.2010.02.001

London, M., & Sessa, V. I. (2006). Group feedback for continuous learning. *Human Resource Development Review, 5*(3), 303–329. https://doi.org/10.1177/1534484306290226

London, M., & Smither, J. W. (2002). Feedback orientation, feedback culture, and the longitudinal performance management process. *Human Resource Management Review, 12*(1), 81–100. https://doi.org/10.1016/S1053-4822(01)00043-2

Lord, R. G., & Kernan, M. C. (1987). Scripts as determinants of purposeful behavior in organizations. *Academy of Management Review, 12*(2), 265–277. https://doi.org/10.5465/amr.1987.4307831

Luciano, M. M., Mathieu, J. E., & Ruddy, T. M. (2014). Leading multiple teams: Average and relative external leadership influences on team empowerment and effectiveness. *Journal of Applied Psychology, 99*(2), 322–331. https://doi.org/10.1037/a0035025

MacCormack, A., & Verganti, R. (2003). Managing the sources of uncertainty: Matching process and context in software development. *Journal of Product Innovation Management, 20*(3), 217–232. https://doi.org/10.1111/1540-5885.2003004

MacGeorge, E. L., Feng, B., Butler, G. L., & Budarz, S. K. (2004). Understanding advice in supportive interactions. Beyond the facework and message evaluation paradigm. *Human Communication Research, 30*(1), 42–70. https://doi.org/10.1111/j.1468-2958.2004.tb00724.x

MacKenzie, S. B., Podsakoff, P. M., & Ahearne, M. (1998). Some possible antecedents and consequences of in-role and extra-role salesperson performance. *Journal of Marketing, 62*(3), 87–98. https://doi.org/10.1177/002224299806200306

Marks, M. A., Mathieu, J. E., & Zaccaro, S. J. (2001). A temporally based framework and taxonomy of team processes. *Academy of Management Review, 26*(3), 356–376. https://doi.org/10.5465/amr.2001.4845785

Mathieu, J. E., & Chen, G. (2011). The etiology of the multilevel paradigm in management research. *Journal of Management, 37*(2), 610–641. https://doi.org/10.1177/0149206310364663

McLeod, P. L., Liker, J. K., & Lobel, S. A. (1992). Process feedback in task groups: An application of goal setting. *The Journal of Applied Behavioral Science, 28*(1), 15–41. https://doi.org/10.1177/0021886392281003

Meinecke, A. L., Lehmann-Willenbrock, N., & Kauffeld, S. (2017). What happens during annual appraisal interviews? How leader–follower interactions unfold and impact interview outcomes. *Journal of Applied Psychology, 102*(7), 1054–1074. http://doi.org/10.1037/apl0000219

Mellis, W., Loebbecke, C., & Baskerville, R. (2013). Requirements uncertainty in contract software development projects. *Journal of Computer Information Systems, 53*(3), 97–108. https://doi.org/10.1080/08874417.2013.11645636

Mesch, D. J., Farh, J. L., & Podsakoff, P. M. (1994). Effects of feedback sign on group goal setting, strategies, and performance. *Group & Organization Management, 19*(3), 309–333. https://doi.org/10.1177/1059601194193006

Mitrou, N., Elzinga, J., Cheng, J., Dobrin, A., Uppal, C. M., Leeper, T. J., Aguilar, A. B., & Leeper, W. R. (2019). Data driven competitive motivation strategies in a longitudinal simulation curriculum for trauma team training. *Journal of Surgical Education, 76*(4), 1122–1130. https://doi.org/10.1016/j.jsurg.2019.01.004

Moher, D., Liberati, A., Tetzlaff, J., Altman, D. G., & PRISMA Group. (2009). Preferred reporting items for systematic reviews and meta-analyses: The PRISMA statement. *BMJ, 339*, 332–336.

Morgeson, F. P., DeRue, D. S., & Karam, E. P. (2010). Leadership in teams: A functional approach to understanding leadership structures and processes. *Journal of Management, 36*(1), 5–39. https://doi.org/10.1177/0149206309347376

Mortensen, M., Woolley, A. W., & O'Leary, M. (2007). Conditions enabling effective multiple team membership. In *Virtuality and virtualization* (pp. 215–228). Springer. https://link.springer.com/content/pdf/10.1007%2F978-0-387-73025-7_16.pdf

Nurudeen, S. M., Kwakye, G., Berry, W. R., Chaikof, E. L., Lillemoe, K. D., Millham, F., Rubin, M., Schwaitzberg, S., Shamberger, R. C., Zinner, M. J., Sato, L., Lipsitz, S., Gawande, A. A., & Haynes, A. B. (2015). Can 360-degree reviews help surgeons? Evaluation of multisource feedback for surgeons in a multi-institutional quality improvement project. *Journal of the American College of Surgeons, 221*(4), 837–844. https://doi.org/10.1016/j.jamcollsurg.2015.06.017

O'Leary, M. B., Mortensen, M., & Woolley, A. W. (2011). Multiple team membership: A theoretical model of its effects on productivity and learning for individuals and teams. *Academy of Management Review, 36*(3), 461–478. https://doi.org/10.5465/amr.2009.0275

Ostrander, A., Bonner, D., Walton, J., Slavina, A., Ouverson, K., Kohl, A., Gilbert, S., Dorneich, M., Sinatra, A., & Winer, E. (2020). Evaluation of an intelligent team tutoring system for a collaborative two person problem: Surveillance. *Computers in Human Behavior, 104*, 1–11. https://doi.org/10.1016/j.chb.2019.01.006

Palvia, P. (2009). The role of trust in e-commerce relational exchange: A unified model. *Information & Management, 46*(4), 213–220. https://doi.org/10.1016/j.im.2009.02.003

Patel, S., Rajkomar, A., Harrison, J. D., Prasad, P. A., Valencia, V., Ranji, S. R., & Mourad, M. (2018). Next-generation audit and feedback for inpatient quality improvement using electronic health record data: A cluster randomized controlled trial. *Bmj Quality & Safety, 27*(9), 691–699. https://doi.org/10.1136/bmjqs-2017-007393

Peterson, R. S., & Behfar, K. J. (2003). The dynamic relationship between performance feedback, trust, and conflict in groups: A longitudinal study. *Organizational Behavior and Human Decision Processes, 92*(1/2), 102–112. https://doi.org/10.1016/s0749-5978(03)00090-6

Pichler, S. (2012). The social context of performance appraisal and appraisal reactions: A meta-analysis. *Human Resource Management, 51*(5), 709–732. http://doi.org/10.1002/hrm.21499

Pluut, H., Fleştea, A. M., & Curşeu, P. L. (2014). Multiple team membership: A demand or resource for employees? *Group Dynamics: Theory, Research, and Practice, 18*(4), 333–348. https://doi.org/10.1037/gdn0000016

Presbitero, A., Roxas, B., & Chadee, D. (2017). Effects of intra- and inter-team dynamics on organisational learning: Role of knowledge-sharing capability. *Knowledge Management Research & Practice, 15*(1), 146–154. https://doi.org/10.1057/kmrp.2015.15

Pritchard, R. D., Jones, S. D., Roth, P. L., Stuebing, K. K., & Ekeberg, S. E. (1988). Effects of group feedback, goal setting, and incentives on organizational productivity. *Journal of Applied Psychology, 73*(2), 337–358. https://doi.org/10.1037/0021-9010.73.2.337

Proude, E. M., Conigrave, K. M., Britton, A., & Haber, P. S. (2008). Improving alcohol and tobacco history taking by junior medical officers. *Alcohol and Alcoholism, 43*(3), 320–325. https://doi.org/10.1093/alcalc/agm182

Puutio, R., Kykyri, V. L., & Wahlström, J. (2009). The process and content of advice giving in support of reflective practice in management consulting. *Reflective Practice, 10*(4), 513–528. https://doi.org/10.1080/14623940903138381

Rasker, P. C., Post, W. M., & Schraagen, J. M. C. (2000). Effects of two types of intra-team feedback on developing a shared mental model in Command & Control teams. *Ergonomics, 43*(8), 1167–1189. https://doi.org/10.1080/00140130050084932

Ritz, A., Brewer, G. A., & Neumann, O. (2016). Public service motivation: A systematic literature review and outlook. *Public Administration Review, 76*(3), 414–426. https://doi.org/10.1111/puar.12505

Rosenthal, R., & DiMatteo, M. R. (2001). Meta-analysis: Recent developments in quantitative methods for literature reviews. *Annual Review of Psychology, 52,* 59–82. https://doi.org/10.1146/annurev.psych.52.1.59

Roberts, E., Dawoud, D. M., Hughes, D. A., & Cefai, C. (2015). Evaluation of a consultant audit and feedback programme to improve the quality of antimicrobial prescribing in acute medical admissions. *International Journal of Pharmacy Practice, 23*(5), 333–339. https://doi.org/10.1111/ijpp.12173

Sakka, O., Barki, H., & Cote, L. (2016). Relationship between the interactive use of control systems and the project performance: The moderating effect of uncertainty and equivocality. *International Journal of Project Management, 34*(3), 508–522. https://doi.org/10.1016/j.ijproman.2016.01.001

Salas, E., Dickenson, T. L., Converse, S. A., & Tannenbaum, S. I. (1992). Toward an understanding of team performance and training. In R. W. Swezey & E. Salas (Eds.), *Teams: Their training and performance* (pp. 3–29). Ablex.

Salas, E., Sims, D. E., & Burke, C. S. (2005). Is there a "big five" in teamwork? *Small Group Research, 36*(5), 555–599. https://doi.org/10.1177/1046496405277134

Salas, E., Tannenbaum, S. I., Kraiger, K., & Smith-Jentsch, K. A. (2012). The science of training and development in organizations: What matters in practice. *Psychological Science in the Public Interest, 13*(2), 74–101. https://doi.org/10.1177/1529100612436661

Sánchez-Expósito, M. J., & Naranjo-Gil, D. (2020). The effect of relative performance feedback on individual performance in team settings under group-based incentives. *Accounting and Business Research, (50)*4, 342–359. https://doi.org/10.1080/00014788.2020.1712548

Sanetti, L. M. H., Luiselli, J. K., & Handler, M. W. (2007). Effects of verbal and graphic performance feedback on behavior support plan implementation in a public elementary school. *Behavior Modification, 31*(4), 454–465. https://doi.org/10.1177/0145445506297583

Sassenberg, K., Moskowitz, G. B., Jacoby, J., & Hansen, N. (2007). The carry-over effect of competition: The impact of competition on prejudice towards uninvolved outgroups. *Journal of Experimental Social Psychology, 43*(4), 529–538. https://doi.org/10.1016/j.jesp.2006.05.009

Sawyer, T., Sierocka-Castaneda, A., Chan, D., Berg, B., Lustik, M., & Thompson, M. (2012). The effectiveness of video-assisted debriefing versus oral debriefing alone at improving neonatal resuscitation performance: A randomized trial. *Simulation in Healthcare: Journal of the Society for Simulation in Healthcare, 7*(4), 213–221. https://doi.org/10.1097/SIH.0b013e3182578eae

Scherer, L. A., Chang, M. C., Meredith, J. W., & Battistella, F. D. (2003). Videotape review leads to rapid and sustained learning. *American Journal of Surgery, 185*(6), 516–520. https://doi.org/10.1016/s0002-9610(03)00062-x

Shin, Y., Kim, M., Choi, J. N., & Lee, S. H. (2016). Does team culture matter? Roles of team culture and collective regulatory focus in team task and creative performance. *Group & Organization Management, 41*(2), 232–265. https://doi.org/10.1177/1059601115584998

Siddaway, A. P., Wood, A. M., & Hedges, L. V. (2019). How to do a systematic review: A best practice guide for conducting and reporting narrative reviews, meta-analyses, and meta-syntheses. *Annual Review of Psychology, 70*, 747–770. https://doi.org/10.1146/annurev-psych-010418-102803

Smeltzer, M. P., Faris, N. R., Ray, M. A., Fehnel, C., Houston-Harris, C., Ojeabulu, P., Akinbobola, O., Lee, Y., Meadows, M., Signore, R. S., Wiggins, L., Talton, D., Owen, E., Deese, L. E., Eubanks, R., Wolf, B. A., Levy, P., Robins, E. T., & Osarogiagbon, R. U. (2019). Survival before and after direct surgical quality feedback in a population-based lung cancer cohort. *Annals of Thoracic Surgery, 107*(5), 1487–1493. https://doi.org/10.1016/j.athoracsur.2018.11.058

Smith-Jentsch, K. A., Cannon-Bowers, J. A., Tannenbaum, S. I., & Salas, E. (2008). Guided team self-correction: Impacts on team mental models, processes, and effectiveness. *Small Group Research, 39*(3), 303–327. https://doi.org/10.1177/1046496408317794

Song, H., Tucker, A. L., Murrell, K. L., & Vinson, D. R. (2018). Closing the productivity gap: Improving worker productivity through public relative performance feedback and validation of best practices. *Management Science, 64*(6), 2628–2649. https://doi.org/10.1287/mnsc.2017.2745

Staw, B. M., Sutton, R. I., & Pelled, L. H. (1994). Employee positive emotion and favorable outcomes at the workplace. *Organization Science, 5*(1), 51–71. https://doi.org/10.1287/orsc.5.1.51

Strubler, D. C., & York, K. M. (2007). An exploratory study of the team characteristics model using organizational teams. *Small Group Research, 38*(6), 670–695. https://doi.org/10.1177/1046496407304338

Sue-Chan, C., & Latham, G. P. (2004). The relative effectiveness of external, peer, and self-coaches. *Applied Psychology-an International Review, 53*(2), 260–278. https://doi.org/10.1111/j.1464-0597.2004.00171.x

Tavoletti, E., Stephens, R. D., & Dong, L. (2019). The impact of peer evaluation on team effort, productivity, motivation and performance in global virtual teams. *Team Performance Management, 25*(5/6), 334–347. https://doi.org/10.1108/tpm-03-2019-0025

Tidd, J. (1995). Development of novel products through intraorganizational, and interorganizational networks: The case of home automation. *Journal of Product Innovation Management, 12*(4), 307–322. https://doi.org/10.1016/0737-6782(95)00026-P

Tindale, R. S., Kulik, C. T., & Scott, L. A. (1991). Individual and group feedback and performance: An attributional perspective. *Basic and Applied Social Psychology, 12*(1), 41–62. https://doi.org/10.1207/s15324834basp1201_4

Tjosvold, D. (1997). Conflict within interdependence: Its value for productivity and individuality. In C. K. W. De Dreu & E. Van de Vliert (Eds.), *Using conflict in organizations* (pp. 23–37). SAGE Publications.

Turner, J. C. (1975). Social comparison and social identity: Some prospects for intergroup behavior. *European Journal of Social Psychology, 5*(1), 5–34. https://doi.org/10.1002/ejsp.2420050102

Unger-Aviram, E., Zwikael, O., & Restubog, S. L. D. (2013). Revisiting goals, feedback, recognition, and performance success: The case of project teams. *Group & Organization Management, 38*(5), 570–600. https://doi.org/10.1177/1059601113500142

Van Bunderen, L., Greer, L. L., & Van Knippenberg, D. (2018). When interteam conflict spirals into intrateam power struggles: The pivotal role of team power structures. *Academy of Management Journal, 61*(3), 1100–1130. https://doi.org/10.5465/amj.2016.0182

Van de Brake, H. J., Walter, F., Rink, F. A., Essens, P. J., & van der Vegt, G. S. (2020). Benefits and disadvantages of individuals' multiple team membership: The moderating role of organizational tenure. *Journal of Management Studies, 57*(8), 1502–1530. https://doi.org/10.1111/joms.12539

Van der Lippe, T., & Lippényi, Z. (2020). Co-workers working from home and individual and team performance. *New Technology, Work and Employment, 35*(1), 60–79. https://doi.org/10.1111/ntwe.12153

Van Knippenberg, D., De Dreu, C. K. W., & Homan, A. C. (2004). Work group diversity and group performance: An integrative model and research agenda. *Journal of Applied Psychology, 89*(6), 1008–1022. https://doi.org/10.1037/0021-9010.89.6.1008

Van Osch, W., & Steinfield, C. W. (2016). Team boundary spanning: Strategic implications for the implementation and use of enterprise social media. *Journal of Information Technology, 31*(2), 207–225. https://doi.org/10.1057/jit.2016.12

Van Thielen, T., Decramer, A., Vanderstraeten, A., & Audenaert, M. (2018). When does performance management foster team effectiveness? A mixed-method field study on the influence of environmental extremity. *Journal of Organizational Behavior, 39*(6), 766–782. https://doi.org/10.1002/job.2297

Vashdi, D. R. (2013). Teams in public administration: A field study of team feedback and effectiveness in the Israeli public healthcare system. *International Public Management Journal, 16*(2), 275–306. https://doi.org/10.1080/10967494.2013.817255

Villado, A. J., & Arthur, W., Jr. (2013). The comparative effect of subjective and objective after-action reviews on team performance on a complex task. *Journal of Applied Psychology, 98*(3), 514–528. https://doi.org/10.1037/a0031510

Wang, C. W., Hsieh, C. T., Fan, K. T., & Menefee, M. L. (2009). Impact of motivating language on team creative performance. *Journal of Computer Information Systems, 50*(1), 133–140. https://www.tandfonline.com/doi/abs/10.1080/08874417.2009.11645370

Wang, J. L., Chellali, A., & Cao, C. G. L. (2016). Haptic communication in collaborative virtual environments. *Human Factors: The Journal of Human Factors and Ergonomics Society, 58*(3), 496–508. https://doi.org/10.1177/0018720815618808

Wilkens, R., & London, M. (2006). Relationships between climate, process, and performance in continuous quality improvement groups. *Journal of Vocational Behavior, 69*(3), 510–523. https://doi.org/10.1016/j.jvb.2006.05.005

Wu, C. H., Parker, S. K., & de Jong, J. P. J. (2014). Feedback seeking from peers: A positive strategy for insecurely attached team-workers. *Human Relations, 67*(4), 441–464. https://doi.org/10.1177/0018726713496124

Zajonc, R. B. (1962). The effects of feedback and probability of group success on individual and group performance. *Human Relations, 15*(2), 149–161. https://doi.org/10.1177/001872676201500204

Zhou, J., & Shalley, C. E. (2011). Deepening our understanding of creativity in the workplace: A review of different approaches to creativity research. In S. Zedeck (Ed.), *APA handbook of Industrial and organizational psychology* (pp. 275–302). APA. https://doi.org/10.1037/12169-009

Zohar, D., & Polachek, T. (2014). Discourse-based intervention for modifying supervisory communication as leverage for safety climate and performance improvement: A randomized field study. *Journal of Applied Psychology, 99*(1), 113–124. https://doi.org/10.1037/a0034096

CHAPTER 6

SITUATED EXPERTISE

The Extra-Team Outcomes of a Team Transactive Memory Intervention

John R. Austin
University of New England

ABSTRACT

Awareness of available expertise in a group directly influences the group's performance. Extensive empirical research on transactive memory systems has demonstrated this link. While there have been numerous research studies of this phenomenon, there is far less known about how interventions designed to increase transactive memory in natural continuing groups may have impacts beyond the groups. I provide an overview of transactive memory research and report on a team intervention designed around transactive memory systems theory. Post-intervention qualitative data was collected through group interviews with participants. The results of these interviews indicate that a significant impact of within-team transactive memory system awareness is in how team members change their interactions across the team. Situated expertise is introduced and defined as the combination of knowledge awareness, help-seeking actions, external benchmarking, and blurred boundaries needed to convert accurate team transactive memory systems into high quality extra-team expertise use.

Managing Team Centricity in Modern Organizations, pages 165–192
Copyright © 2022 by Information Age Publishing
www.infoagepub.com

165

How can members of groups within an organization system best use their available knowledge and track what new knowledge they need to be more effective? Researchers and practicing managers have worked to answer this question in many ways over the years. In this chapter, I examine the results of an intervention designed from research and applied in practice. The results of this intervention suggest researchers may need to look beyond the team level to fully understand how within-team transactive memory systems impact performance. Team centricity in organizations requires a mix of individual, team, and system level capabilities. I will provide an overview of transactive memory systems (TMS) research, describe the intervention designed with this research in mind, report on findings from some exploratory post-intervention interviews, and present a theoretical framework for future research. The proposed framework links individual and team-level expertise with proactive efforts to extend expertise networks beyond the team boundary.

This study is consistent with the call from Ployhart and Bartunek (2019) for theory tied to practice and represents the relational scholarship of integration advocated by Bartunek (2007). During the interventions described in this chapter, managers experimented with the data and created their own applications of the outputs. Their applications refine our understanding of how team TMS can have impacts at the extra-team level. While the focus of the initial intervention was to improve expertise use within the teams, subsequent qualitative interviews indicated behavioral changes well beyond the team boundaries. I introduce the concept of situated expertise to explain the extra-team impact of the team-level expertise intervention. Situated expertise is the extent to which individual or team-level knowledge is actively connected to the wider knowledge network through proactive efforts to locate, or situate, that knowledge within the organizational context and ensure it is available and current. Thus, situated expertise combines search and knowledge transfer processes. Search and knowledge transfer are two of four processes of organizational learning used by Argote et al. (2020) in a recent review of organizational learning research; knowledge creation and knowledge retention being the other two. I initially defined situated expertise in 2000 as a group's transactive memory system plus shared awareness of group member external ties (Austin, 2000). This earlier research highlighted that the advantage of knowing who knows what is limited if one does not know who to approach to tap into other social networks. By combining these two components, situated expertise provides a measure of how well group members can find existing knowledge in their situation as well as how well they can use social relationships to bring new information into the situation. However, this earlier work did not define the specific extra-team actions involved in bringing new information into the team.

TRANSACTIVE MEMORY SYSTEMS

The transactive memory concept emerged from research on how dyads manage knowledge between them. The laboratory studies sought to understand the blend of shared and individual knowledge within pairs of relative strangers and dating couples (Hollingshead, 1998, 2000). Members of these dyads developed systems for how they managed their own knowledge and drew from their knowledge of what the other member knew. The transactive memory of the individual dyad member included ways to encode, store, and retrieve information (Wegner, 1987). These early studies highlighted that it was not enough just to know who knows what. Individuals must also have ways to share relevant knowledge and access it when needed. This behavioral aspect of transactive memory distinguished it from other shared mental model research from the 1990s (Mohammed & Dumville, 2001) and offered a particularly valuable conceptual lens for team-level research. Individual and shared responsibility for maintaining knowledge is built into the transactive memory construct (Brandon & Hollingshead, 2004). While transactive memory can be viewed as a cognitive structure within an individual, a transactive memory system is a multi-person construct. It is a characteristic of a dyad or group (Wegner, 1987).

A transactive memory system is a measure of the extent to which group members are aware of the knowledge of other group members. Wegner (1987) defined a transactive memory system as a group information processing system consisting of group member knowledge combined with knowledge of other group members' knowledge. While Wegner initially envisioned transactive memory as an individual-level construct about a dyad, the notion of a group transactive memory system quickly took hold. Early research on TMS sought to define the construct (Hollingshead, 2000; Moreland et al., 1996; Wegner, 1987) and develop validated ways to measure it (Austin, 2003a; Lewis, 2003; Liang et al., 1995). Once these definitions and measures were established, transactive memory system research expanded to include a range of laboratory and field studies. These studies demonstrated a relationship between well-developed TMS and group coordination and performance (Austin, 2003a; Lewis, 2004; Liang et al., 1995; Moreland & Myaskovsky, 2000). Well-functioning TMS allow team members to specialize their personal knowledge while benefiting from efficient access to the specialized knowledge of other team members. This ability to combine specialization with efficient shared knowledge retrieval has been found to improve innovation (Peltokorpi & Hasu, 2016) and creativity (Gino et al., 2010).

Much TMS research focused on either the development of a TMS or the impact of TMS on performance outcomes. Because knowledge needs are always evolving, teams are faced with the need to constantly update their TMS. Outdated TMS can actually reduce performance of teams by leading to reliance on old TMS structures (Lewis et al., 2007). Maintaining TMS accuracy depends upon continued interactions (Brandon & Hollingshead, 2004), effective communication (Peltokorpi & Hood, 2019), and shared goals (Zhang et al., 2007). The multilevel interaction between interpersonal dynamics, individual knowledge stock, and shared knowledge distinguishes TMS from other approaches to shared knowledge (Lewis & Herndon, 2011).

There has been robust research on TMS over the past 20 years including several reviews of the field (Peltokorpi, 2012; Peltokorpi & Hood, 2019; Ren & Argote, 2011) and multiple meta-analytic studies (Bachrach et al., 2019; DeChurch & Mesmer-Magnus, 2010; Mesmer-Magnus et al., 2017; Turner et al., 2014). Bachrach et al.'s (2019) meta-analysis of 76 empirical studies linking TMS and team performance demonstrates the overwhelming evidence linking transactive memory with team performance. However, in doing so they also highlight how little we still know about this relationship. Specifically, the focus on the TMS-team outcome link in previous research has led to gaps in our understanding of how contextual factors contribute to transactive memory system development.

This study contributes to our understanding of how team TMS interacts with extra-team expertise networks. Teams that participated in a transactive memory development workshop were interviewed in order to learn how awareness of their team TMS influenced their actions. For many teams, the team workshop had the greatest impact on extra-team actions. By combining TMS awareness with help-seeking behaviors, external expertise benchmarking, and blurred team boundaries, teams were able to align team transactive memory with the broader expertise network. These actions form the basis of situated expertise.

PHASE 1: THE INTERVENTIONS

Two global companies contacted me requesting help to improve the effectiveness of work teams. In both cases, the aim was to help the teams better coordinate their actions within the team and make better use of the diverse knowledge of team members. Each team completed a transactive memory assessment and workshop. The interventions were designed as part of a consulting engagement and not as a research project. For this reason, the scoring of TMS cannot be used for research purposes. However, with support from the organizations, follow-up interviews with team members were conducted to learn from these interventions. These interviews revealed interesting patterns of action after the intervention and form the basis of this investigation. It is my hope this practice-based experience can inform the subsequent exploration of extra-team impacts of team expertise awareness. Figure 6.1 shows the timeline for this study. Follow-up interviews were

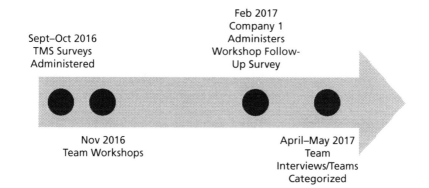

Figure 6.1 Intervention timeline.

conducted approximately 6 months after the workshop and 7 months after the initial surveys.

Designing an Intervention to Strengthen Group TMS

Three insights culled from research on expertise and group transactive memory informed the design of the study:

1. Structured conversations about team member expertise can increase expertise accuracy even in content areas not explicitly discussed (Littlepage et al., 1997).
2. Training team members together can increase accuracy of TMS and increase likelihood of its use (Rulke & Rau, 2000).
3. Focusing on context-specific transactive memory and linking it to social network knowledge can improve multiple measures of team performance (Austin, 2003a) while also developing a more generalized, abstract understanding of the knowledge domain (Lewis et al., 2005).

Identifying Group Experts

Research on how group members identify experts within the group suggests that in the absence of structured work to identify expertise, group members will identify experts based on characteristics not found to be correlated with actual expertise (Littlepage et al., 1995). Experts are identified based on how frequently they talk and use influence tactics, are acknowledged by other talkative group members, and use reason in their arguments (Littlepage & Mueller, 1997). Bunderson and Barton (2011) observed that expertise determination in groups is a status-organizing process in which greater competence (expertise) equates with greater status. Thus, status cues drive perceptions of expertise (Bunderson, 2003).

In order to break habits of selecting experts using inaccurate methods, group training ought to provide an alternate way to mindfully assess expertise of group members. Littlepage et al. (1997) found that group experience on a related task can facilitate recognition and utilization of expertise. Lewis et al. (2007) found that groups with membership changes sometimes relied on outdated TMS structures but when group "oldtimers" reflected on the collective knowledge in the group they were able to avoid the use of outdated shared knowledge structures. Therefore, engaging the team in expertise recognition tasks using context-relevant expertise could increase effectiveness of expertise use within a team. Austin's (2003a) process for measuring transactive memory is an example of a context-relevant expertise recognition task.

Training Teams Together to Build, Improve Expertise Use

Early TMS research found that training teams together improved team performance. TMS theory developed partially as a way to explain these findings. Liang et al.'s (1995) study of group transactive memory demonstrated that groups trained together outperformed groups in which the members trained separately. These groups worked on a task, assembling an AM radio, in which developing a group TMS could be expected to improve performance and in which a team would be unlikely to have a single member with dominant expertise. Other studies of groups during this time found similar results (Moreland et al., 1996; Moreland & Myaskovsky, 2000; Rulke & Rau, 2000). In essence, by experiencing the training together, group members can build trust in their knowledge of who knows what, seek out information from the right experts, and more effectively coordinate their actions. These studies found the mediating role of transactive memory system development could explain why teams trained together outperformed other teams. Rulke and Rau (2000) shed further light on the training process by coding group member communication patterns during the training phase of the project. They found that members developed their TMS by actively expressing their lack of knowledge and asking questions. Subsequently, individual members would claim expertise and others would evaluate those claims of expertise. Next, the groups would assign roles within the group. This study highlighted the importance of active communication and honest disclosure of expertise (or lack thereof) for the development of group TMS.

Prichard and Ashleigh (2007) further demonstrated that groups completing generic team-skills training on role allocation, goal setting, problem-solving, and interpersonal relationships demonstrated greater levels of team performance, transactive memory, and team skill. They noted it is not enough to know who knows what if the team does not have the skills needed to put that knowledge to use. In subsequent work, Ashleigh and Prichard (2012) propose trust as a key antecedent in the development of team TMS. Team training can provide a safe team space to build trust and enable team transactive memory development (Ashleigh & Prichard, 2011).

Context-Specific Transactive Memory

Researchers have operationalized transactive memory in multiple ways. Lewis (2003) categorized transactive memory assessments as recall, observation, and self-report measures. The early studies of dyads were primarily recall, and the radio assembly studies relied on a combination of observation and self-report. More recent meta-analysis studies show self-report measures to be the dominant measures for group TMS with Lewis' measure being the most widely used measure (Bachrach et al., 2019).

While self-report measures have become the standard for assessing TMS, there remains variance in what individuals are asked to report as part of the self-report. TMS has been roughly defined as knowledge of others' knowledge. Wegner's original definition of the TMS described it as group member knowledge combined with knowledge of other group members' knowledge. Self-report measures differ on the extent to which individual group member knowledge is included in the measure. The self-reporting of TMS could be an assessment of the group (Lewis, 2003) or an assessment of self, combined with knowledge of specific others (Austin, 2003a).

Another way TMS measures differ, is in their relative focus on general expertise or team-specific expertise. General TMS measures capture team member perceptions of knowledge sharing, accuracy, and application. These measures are not linked to specific expertise. The advantage of these measures is they enable comparison across studies and can be easily added into other research studies. Lewis' general TMS assessment in particular has enabled hundreds of researchers to add TMS measurement to studies of teams. Context-specific TMS measures link the measurement to specific expertise needed in a given team. The advantage of the context-specific measurement approach is it has a more immediate connection to the team's work. In theory, this connection should clarify the link between TMS and group performance as well as provide rich data about the network ties within the team. The disadvantage of this approach is context-specific measurement is labor and time intensive.

Because context-specific measures are labor and time intensive, this approach may be more suitable for studies in which TMS is the central construct being studied. However, the very reason dyadic, context-specific measurement is impractical for inclusion in large-scale survey research studies is what makes it potentially valuable as a TMS intervention in practice. It captures knowledge of knowledge down to the individual level and can be mapped at either the dyad or group level. It also focuses on knowledge areas identified as relevant to the specific group. This process offers a rich source of data to use for team member feedback and team development purposes.

Austin's study of cross-functional merchandising teams is an example of context-specific measurement (Austin, 2003a). The dyadic, context-specific measure in the 2003 study is a more direct measure of who knows what within a group than is a general TMS assessment. Austin's approach requires preliminary interviews to identify relevant expertise and a series of data transformations to calculate variable scores. Through preliminary semi-structured interviews with team stakeholders, 11 important knowledge areas/skills were identified. Group members were then asked to individually rate their expertise and each other team members' expertise in each of the 11 knowledge areas. This data was then used to calculate four transactive memory dimensions: group knowledge stock (sum of knowledge available within the group), knowledge specialization (degree to which different individuals are experts in different knowledge areas), transactive memory consensus (agreement on who the experts are within the group for each knowledge area), and transactive memory accuracy (degree to which other-ratings of expertise match self-ratings of expertise within the group). Depending on the goal of an intervention, each of these dimensions could provide useful feedback.

General and team-specific measures of TMS align with the distinction Geertz (1983) made between experience far and experience near knowledge. Experience far knowledge is knowledge that can be easily generalized across contexts. Experience near knowledge is knowledge tied to a specific context. Empirical research studies are often presented as experience far knowledge. Case studies and stories are often presented as experience near knowledge. For researchers, knowledge generalization is often the aim. For practicing managers, context application of knowledge is often the aim. Lewis' measure of TMS is a context-far type measure. Austin's measure of TMS is a context-near measure. Thus, the characteristic of Austin's design that makes it less useful for the researcher, makes it more useful for the practitioner. The intervention aim was to work with the team to improve its use of specific expertise within its work environment. The context-specific design best fits this project's aim.

The Organizations

Company 1 is a life sciences company based in the United States with additional locations in Europe and Asia. I was brought in by the director of learning to help develop critical thinking and team leadership capabilities. Thirteen teams participated in this project. The teams ranged in size from

8–14 members. Eight teams worked in the commercial side of the company and five worked in the research side.

Company 2 is a financial services company based in the United States with additional locations in Canada and the United Kingdom. I had worked with this organization for several years prior to this project as a facilitator and leadership development resource. Seven teams participated in this project. Teams ranged in size from 5–9 members. Four teams worked in IT and three teams provided internal financial analysis services.

Demographic variables were not collected during the survey process. One notable difference between the teams was the extent to which teams were global. Company 1 teams were global teams in which team coordination was managed through a combination of virtual and in-person meetings. Company 2 teams consisted of mostly co-located team members with a small number of team members located in other cities. All Company 2 employees in these teams were located in either the United States or Canada. All teams included in this study did include multiple in-person team meetings as part of their work processes.

The Team Development Intervention

The intervention involved stakeholder interviews, team member expertise surveys, and a team workshop. The design outlined in Austin (2003a) starts with interviews to identify the relevant expertise for the groups being studied and customized surveys built around the identified expertise and the specific people in the groups. The customized design allowed the consulting team to design feedback data for each team based on the specific expertise needs of the team. The consulting team followed instructions in the Appendix of Austin's 2003 article for the interview protocol and measurement of TMS.

Identifying Relevant Expertise
The consultants interviewed multiple stakeholders with knowledge of the teams' goals. Stakeholders included team leaders, team sponsors, internal coaches, external collaborators, and senior leaders. Through these interviews, the consultants identified 10–12 high priority expertise areas.

Collecting TMS Data
Each team member completed a TMS survey. For each of the high priority expertise areas, team members identified experts, rated the level of expertise available on the team, rated their own level of expertise, and rated their confidence that they would know how to find that expertise outside of the team.

Calculating TMS Measures

Team TMS scores were calculated following the procedures outlined in Austin's (2003a) Appendix.

Presenting Back to Teams

The results of the survey were presented to the teams during team development workshops. These workshops also covered other topics such as team decision-making, project management, and communication. The TMS survey formed the foundation of a session focused on team development and expertise use. To guide the discussion, each high priority expertise was charted on a 2x2 chart of accuracy vs. consensus for each team. Accuracy was defined as the extent to which expertise identified by group members aligned with self-reported assessment of expertise. Highly accurate expertise areas would be areas in which the group identified experts agree they are experts. Consensus was defined as agreement within the team about who the experts were. If there are many experts on the team in an area of expertise, consensus may be low if team members identified different people as top experts. Visualizing the results in this form allowed the teams to examine each expertise individually and focus on identifying strategies for improving team use of that expertise. In addition, the placement of all expertise data on a single chart enabled the team to consider more general strategies for improving transactive memory within the teams.

Figure 6.2 shows an example of an accuracy vs. consensus chart. Each of the quadrants prompted different types of discussions and actions. Facilitators guided the teams through a discussion of each quadrant. Team members discussed four questions for each quadrant: (a) "Do any of the results in this quadrant surprise you?"; (b) "What is an advantage of having these knowledge areas in this quadrant?"; (c) "What is an issue with having these knowledge areas in this quadrant?"; (d) "What actions can the team take to improve use of these knowledge areas?" Facilitators structured the discussion but did not give answers to any of these questions. The team members generated their own sensemaking and proposed actions from the data.

For high accuracy/high consensus expertise, the team would discuss the risk of having widely recognized experts on the team. Recognized experts on the team led to efficient use of expertise but also tended to put pressure on the experts to be accessible and could overwhelm the experts and put the team at risk if an expert were to leave. Teams would often propose mentoring and developing new experts as actions to improve team use of high accuracy/high consensus expertise.

For high accuracy/low consensus expertise, the team would consider why it was that there was disagreement about who was expert and yet for the most part team members were accurately identifying experts. Accurate but divergent expert identification often happened for expertise which was widely

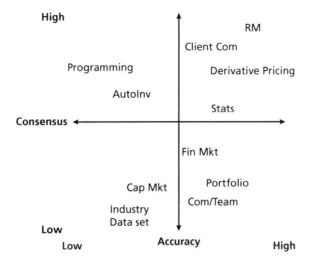

Key
AutoInv = Automated/computer driven investing
Cap Mkt = Capital markets
Client Com = Communicating with clients
Com/Team = Team process skills
Fin Mkt = Financial markets
Industry Data Set = Understanding and using industry databases
Portfolio = Portfolio management
Programming = Computer programming language
RM = Research methods
Stats = Statistical analysis

Figure 6.2 Accuracy vs. consensus chart.

held within the team. Such expertise may be required in order to be placed on the team in the first place. Conversations about these types of expertise would focus on how to ensure the team maintained its deep bench in these areas and how they would ensure the team knowledge remained up to date.

For low accuracy/low consensus expertise, the team would discuss why team members were essentially clueless about where the expertise was for these high priority expertise areas. Some reasons team members would give for the low level of shared understanding for these knowledge areas included lack of visibility for expertise use, awareness of external experts whom the team members would go to for help rather than reach out to a team member, or limited feedback about whether or not the identified expert was actually expert. Strategies for improving team awareness of expertise in these areas often involved public commitments by individual team members to develop expertise in these areas.

For low accuracy/high consensus expertise, the team would discuss why team members had a misperception that certain team members were experts when they were not. This dynamic would most often happen when there was one team member who knew "just a little more" than all the other team members. Newly emergent expertise areas (one example in several teams in the financial services company was artificial intelligence driven investing) or expertise areas in which low expertise would not immediately be evident in work quality would often end up in this quadrant. Team actions to improve use of these expertise areas included commitments to training and team member development and outreach to others within their organization to learn more about location of expertise within the organization.

The groups continued to revisit these expertise lists and team actions during their team meetings for several weeks after the workshop. Initial team assessments indicated all teams had begun to include discussions of expertise in their conversations about new projects in the weeks following this intervention.

PHASE 2: QUALITATIVE INTERVIEWS TO UNDERSTAND IMPACT

Over the next year, I continued to work with both organizations on different projects. Three months after the workshop, the director of learning for Company 1 sent a survey to the workshop participants. The results revealed a bifurcated impact. Some teams reported dramatic increases in perceived effectiveness attributed to the intervention. Other teams reported little to no perceived change. Even in the teams without perceived increases in effectiveness, team members reported an increase in awareness of their team's TMS. The director of learning contacted me and asked if I would be willing to explore these results and help her diagnose what led to the dramatic differences between teams. I agreed to conduct a series of semi-structured interviews and reached out to my contact at Company 2 and offered to conduct some similar interviews in their organization as well.

I conducted a series of group interviews with the teams. I arranged to join previously scheduled team meetings. These meetings were conducted via phone or video conference. I was able to participate in 16 team meetings. Four teams in Company 1 were unavailable. Two due to scheduling issues and two because the teams had been disbanded. The group interviews lasted between 20–30 minutes. Members of the teams who were not on the teams during the initial workshop were invited to sit in on the interviews but asked not to participate in the discussion.

The interviews were conducted using a write-speak protocol I developed as a consultant to conduct the team interviews. Write-speak is designed to maximize member participation and data content in time constrained group interviews. At the start, team members are told how many questions there will be and how long the interview will last. They are then given the following ground rules:

1. Individuals will have 1 minute to write their first response to the question.
2. For each question, once an individual speaks, they "move to the back of the line" and cannot speak again during that question until everyone else in the team has spoken or passed.
3. Each response is limited to 60 seconds and the interviewer enforces this rule.
4. Individuals are allowed and even encouraged to build on comments of a previous speaker.
5. The interviewer will determine when to move to the next question.

This process works well in continuing teams in which all team members already know each other. It generates responses to questions that are rich, nuanced, and include multiple answers. By limiting any individual speaker to 60 seconds, responses are often richer because other team members expand on the original response and individuals think before they speak so they can be concise.

In these interviews, I asked three questions using this protocol: (a) "What are your lasting impressions of the workshops?"; (b) "What actions (if any) have been taken to improve expertise use in the team since the workshops?"; and (c) "Reflect on why the team has or has not continued to focus on team expertise."

The group interviews were recorded and transcribed. The group interview transcripts were loaded into ATLAS.ti software to assist with the coding and identification of themes. I used an inductive approach to identify themes in the data (Braun & Clarke, 2006). Codes were assigned during a first data pass and then all interviews were reassessed against the full list of codes in a second data pass. Themes were identified related to within team and extra-team behaviors. Themes consist of an aggregation of codes into broad units of information representing shared ideas (Saldaña, 2016).

The internal learning professionals assigned each of the 16 teams as either a high impact or low impact team based on the post-workshop surveys of TMS impact on behavior. The director of learning at Company 1 agreed to share her survey with a learning manager in Company 2, who then administered the survey to the Company 2 teams. I was not aware of the team categorization as high or low impact until after I had completed the coding process. Ten teams were categorized as high impact and six teams were categorized as low impact. Of the four teams missing from the interview data, three would have been categorized as high impact and one as low impact. It is important to note that high/low impact does not indicate anything about team performance. It indicates the extent to which the team members self-reported team behavior changes due to the TMS assessment training. All 16 teams were meeting their performance goals. The performance variance between teams would not be large enough to justify using team performance as an outcome measure. In addition, the diversity of team goals would make performance comparisons difficult.

I then compared responses from teams reporting a high level of impact from the workshop to responses from teams reporting little impact from the workshop. Team behavior changes included team process actions as well as changed interactions with non-team members. Unexpectedly, the changes to interactions with non-team members were the most pervasive and were perceived to be the primary positive impact of the workshop. The changed interactions with non-team members were unexpected because our focus in the workshops was almost entirely on building expertise awareness within the teams. High impact teams and low impact teams both reported changes in internal team processes from the workshop. However, comments about changes to interactions with non-team members were pervasive within high impact teams and limited within low impact teams. I present a summary of the interview themes in Table 6.1.

Within Team Changes

Each of the 16 teams reported continued conversations about team member expertise after the workshops. Fourteen teams had built new routines into their team processes to keep their knowledge of team member expertise

TABLE 6.1 Team Interview Themes			
	High Impact Teams $N = 10$	Low Impact Teams $N = 6$	Total $N = 16$
Within Team Actions			
Expertise check-ins	9 (90%)	6 (100%)	15
Expertise-linked development goals	7 (70%)	3 (50%)	10
Using language of expertise	10 (100%)	6 (100%)	16
Use expertise process for hiring	3 (30%)	3 (50%)	6
External Actions			
Proactive help seeking	10 (100%)	2 (30%)	12
External expertise comparisons	9 (90%)	2 (30%)	11
Blurring team distinctions	6 (60%)	0 (0%)	6
Personal development without team coordination	2 (20%)	1 (10%)	3

current. This high number of teams reporting follow-up actions can be attributed to the active engagement after the workshops by the internal learning and development professionals. Actions teams reported included:

- Scheduling dedicated times in their team meetings to check in on expertise. Scheduled time was the most common reported action. In the training, teams talked about building expertise check-ins into team agendas. Teams reporting using this tactic to talk about how team members were assigned to tasks.
- Setting development goals linked with the expertise survey results. In several teams, the leaders required team members to refer to the team accuracy vs. consensus grid when developing their personal development goals for the year. In some teams, members established buddy systems to match experts with others who wanted to build their expertise as a form of expertise mentoring.
- Using the language of team expertise in subsequent trainings and retreats. All teams reported referring back to the workshop and using the expertise data in subsequent team training sessions and retreats. Referring back to the language of expertise had the effect of reinforcing the value of the expertise data and keeping it current.
- Use of expertise assessment in hiring. Six teams referred back to the results of the team expertise survey as part of their hiring processes during the year. Because not all teams hired and hiring was not specifically asked about in the interviews, we do not have data to indicate what percentage of hiring processes across teams made use of the expertise data.

External Interaction Changes

The high-impact teams changed their interactions with non-team members as well as with team members. Teams framed these new actions as ways to become more effective at connecting team member expertise with the available expertise in their environment. Three types of actions stood out as being implemented by the high-impact teams but not the low-impact teams: help-seeking behaviors, external benchmarking, and reducing distinctions between team and non-team members.

Dramatic Increases in Proactive Help-Seeking Behaviors
Awareness of team member knowledge is of limited use if team members do not actively use that knowledge. The single biggest difference between teams that reported positive impacts from the workshop and those teams that reported little impact was a reported increase in proactive help-seeking

behaviors. It should be noted that help-seeking was discussed as a strategy in the workshops. For this reason, it is not surprising that so many teams reported increased help-seeking activity after the workshop. The surprise was that proactive help-seeking appeared to drive the variance in workshop impact between teams and that this activity tended to involve team members seeking help from non-team members rather than from other team members. The frequency of external help seeking was unexpected because the help-seeking discussions in the workshops focused on seeking help within the team.

Benchmarking Within Team Expertise Against Available External Expertise

Limits of team expertise were discussed in the workshops. The high-impact teams reported actively comparing within team expertise with expertise available in other parts of the organization. External benchmarking occasionally informed new hire decisions and invitations to non-team members to join projects. These teams were using their focus on expertise as a way to continually assess the quality of the team stock of expertise and update it as needed.

Breaking Down Distinctions Between Team Member and Non-Team Member

Consistent with the increased external benchmarking, teams reported a blurring of team boundaries when confronting complex issues. Team members started to view the team as a subset of a larger expertise ecosystem. When confronted with new challenges, team members reported being more comfortable reaching out for help to experts outside the team. One member stated that the multiple discussions about team expertise made it easier to remember that every time a team member reached out to someone outside the team, they were actually increasing the stock of knowledge inside the team (through learning). External help seeking is thus reframed from being a failure of team expertise to being a process for growing team expertise.

SITUATED EXPERTISE: AN EXTRA-TEAM APPLICATION OF TEAM-LEVEL EXPERTISE

The interview findings that a within team expertise workshop triggered changes in boundary spanning activities suggests the need to consider extra-team explanations for how TMS impacts team performance. The team interviews indicate many positive outcomes of TMS will be missed if outcomes are only assessed at the team or individual level. All teams demonstrated increased awareness and use of within team expertise after the interventions. The teams that viewed the intervention as most influencing their team behavior reported additional changes to how they interreacted with their environment.

The team-level interventions reported here had the predicted team-level positive outcomes. It would be tempting to end the story there. In doing so, this application of TMS to practice becomes simply more evidence demonstrating that TMS is related to positive team outcomes. Previous TMS research would predict the increased awareness and use of team member expertise indicated in the interviews. The somewhat unexpected, and potentially more valuable, insights from these interventions were that the team-level TMS intervention had behavioral impacts beyond the team level. More significantly, these impacts beyond the team boundary appear to explain why some teams reported higher levels of impact from the intervention.

The combination of task-level organizing and individual help-seeking choices situates expertise within this extra-team system. This situated expertise is the extent to which individual or team-level knowledge is actively connected to the wider knowledge network through proactive efforts to locate, or situate, that knowledge within the organization and ensure it is available and current. Figure 6.3 illustrates the theoretical connections proposed in the situated expertise framework. Team transactive memory is just one element of a cognitive-behavioral process allowing expertise to remain current, actively used, and connected to the extra-team expertise network. The connections in Figure 6.3 lead to six propositions.

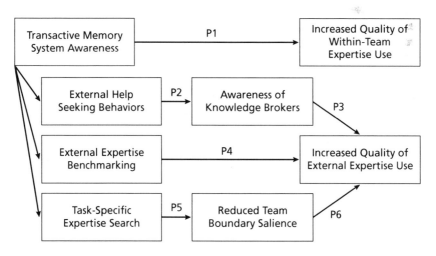

Figure 6.3 Situated expertise model of expertise use.

Awareness of Available Team Expertise

It is not a surprise that the intervention designed around transactive memory research would successfully increase team use of expertise in their work. The growing body of empirical evidence supports the value of TMS awareness. That all teams in this study reported increased use of team expertise in their work after the survey and workshop adds further evidence that knowing who knows what does lead to changes in team behavior. The focus on context specific TMS rather than general TMS in the initial survey may have increased the ability of team members to make connections with other expertise.

> **Proposition 1:** *Increasing team member awareness of the team transactive memory system will increase quality of within team expertise use.*

Individual Help-Seeking Actions

Lee (1997) identified three ways in which help seeking can be distinguished from other information search processes: (a) help seeking is associated with a specific problem, (b) help seeking is interpersonal, and (c) help seeking is proactive. Because help seeking is associated with a specific problem, it is commonly used to gather information in a unique or unanticipated situation. The proactive characteristic of help seeking indicates that the help seekers are in control of the behavior through their definition of the problem and selection of a helper (Austin, 2003b). Many organizational problems are ill-defined and not easily linked with written or digital sources of knowledge. These problems have conflicting interpretations and resolving them requires complex sensemaking and social interaction processes. Recent research suggests knowledge *seeking* may play a greater role in the diffusion of knowledge through social networks than has been acknowledged due to the more frequent research focus on knowledge *contributors* (Qiao et al., 2019).

The TMS intervention highlighted the connection between task and expertise. Help seeking in these situations is likely to be oriented around specific knowledge needs. Members of teams reporting high impacts from the intervention may have sought help more often because they had developed routines for looking for gaps in current knowledge. Knowledge brokers may play a particularly important role when help seeking goes beyond the team boundary. Brokers mediate between knowledge seekers and knowledge contributors (Lavis, 2006) and are important in a situation where new knowledge needs to be generated (Turnhout et al., 2013) or where new links need to be built. These individuals actively look for information gaps and find ways to bridge them (Bielak et al., 2008) suggests the important role brokers may play. As extra-team help-seeking activity increases, the value of knowledge brokers potentially increases as well. Lee et al. (2014) show the importance of transitive triads in explaining the relationship between TMS in teams and performance. A transitive triad is when information exchanges between two members of a network are facilitated by a third. Help-seeking activity can potentially address one of the tensions between effective internal team knowledge use and broader organizational knowledge use, namely that teams with deeper knowledge (multiple specialists) outperform teams of generalists (Lewis & Herndon, 2011). Norms of active help seeking can allow team members to continue to develop their specialized knowledge while more accurately tapping into the wider knowledge network.

Proposition 2: *Increased extra-team help-seeking activity will increase team awareness of knowledge brokers.*

Proposition 3: *Increased team awareness of knowledge brokers will increase the positive relationship between team transactive memory awareness and the quality of extra-team expertise use.*

Extra-Team Benchmarking

Teams in this study compared their team expertise to external expertise. It is possible that this benchmarking process enabled team members to continually refine their understanding of team expertise stock as well as their own awareness of where expertise resides in the network. Recent theorizing on the collective nature of individual knowledge offers an interesting lens for considering how individual expertise can link with collective knowledge within teams but also across teams. Rabb et al. (2019) make the distinction between individual in-depth knowledge (Type 1), superficial knowledge (Type II), and markers for the location of external knowledge (Type III). Well-developed TMS help build depth and accuracy of Type III knowledge. Unfortunately, the value of accurate Type III knowledge is limited by errors in individual ability to distinguish between Type I and Type II knowledge. If individuals think they know more than they really do on a topic, they will not seek out help. Type I/Type II error has been explored in studies of errors in explanatory depth (Rozenbilt & Keil, 2002). This error has been found to be more pronounced in areas where knowing something has perceived value (Gaviria et al., 2017) as would often be the case in work-related expertise. By introducing the idea of team shared knowledge, the intervention could prepare participants to reconsider their own depth of knowledge in relation to their team members.

The extra-team actions identified in the interviews could be understood as task-oriented behaviors designed to increase accuracy of Type III knowledge. The team TMS intervention combined with the increases in help-seeking behavior reduced Type I/Type II sensemaking errors while also improving accuracy of team member Type III knowledge. Active benchmarking of expertise further refines understanding of team and individual expertise.

Proposition 4: *External benchmarking of expertise will increase the positive relationship between team transactive memory awareness and quality of extra-team expertise use.*

Task-Based Expertise and Team Boundary Salience

Situated expertise is best understood by focusing at the task level rather than the team level. Researchers often use the team as their primary point of reference when examining team expertise. However, the task may be an appropriate point of reference in practice. Each individual team deals with multiple tasks that change over time. In order to apply an expertise-based framework for team process, team members must frequently reevaluate their process because, as tasks change, expertise demands change as well. Transactive memory plays a different role in different types of team tasks (Gupta & Hollingshead, 2010). External interactions by the teams were driven by specific task needs. More recent work has begun to explore the relationship between transactive memory and boundary spanning (Olabisi & Lewis, 2018). The very notion of a team boundary may be limiting when considering transactive memory as something that forms and reforms around tasks.

Team members in the intervention would initiate discussions of expertise within the context of specific new tasks. By linking the continued development of TMS with specific tasks, team members were able to focus on salient and relevant expertise. In addition, their orientation on the task meant they were not orienting on individuals. Such a task focus may have opened up the inquiry to include non-team members.

Brandon and Hollingshead offer a framework for linking this task-oriented framing with team member expertise (Brandon & Hollingshead, 2004). They proposed the task-expertise-person (TEP) unit as the basic construct for transactive memory. A full TEP unit would include knowledge about the task, expertise requirements for the task, and persons having expertise. Any missing information in a given TEP unit would need to be obtained in order for that unit to fully contribute to transactive memory in a group. Errors or missing information in any one of the three components can contribute to reduced efficacy in a group. They propose that transactive memory development involves the building of complete TEP units by group members. By shifting the unit of analysis away from the group or dyad, the TEP framing also opens up theorizing to consider a shifting location of TEP units. They can be within group or include a blend of group members and non-group members. The TEP unit shifts as the tasks shift.

> **Proposition 5:** *Team member focus on task-specific expertise will reduce the salience of team boundaries.*

> **Proposition 6:** *Reduced salience of team boundaries will increase the positive relationship between team transactive memory awareness and quality of extra-team expertise use.*

RELEVANCE OF SITUATED EXPERTISE FOR PRACTITIONERS

Because this study emerged from practitioner work, the relevance of situated expertise for practitioners is more direct than can often be the case in our research. Research emerging from practice offers this strength to our field. Each of the themes from the qualitative interviews can also be viewed as recommendations for practice. In addition to those themes, managers can explicitly connect extra-team implications to team-level development activities and establish expectations for help-seeking action.

Team-Level Development and Extra-Team Connections

Managers and team members seek to improve team performance in order to be more effective within a larger organizational system. The members of the high impact teams in this study recognized this aim. They translated the team-level workshops into actions that would make their team more effective at using the broader knowledge network. By doing so, these team members also could be thoughtful about how to develop their own expertise in areas needed within the knowledge network. Coaches and team leaders can encourage team members to routinely make connections between team development work and proactive efforts to move beyond the team boundary. In addition, teams can actively work to create knowledge brokers and use these brokers to expand team access to expertise.

Help Seeking Is Essential

Perhaps the most important implication of the situated expertise model for team members is acknowledging the central role of help seeking in developing and maintaining accurate and accessible expertise networks. Awareness of expertise is not enough. Expertise must be sought. Increasing help seeking may require shifts in team and organization culture and will not happen without sustained efforts by team and organization leaders. Help seeking beyond a team boundary does not just benefit the individual seeking help. It helps build the social knowledge of the team and extend the TMS. Austin's (2003a) initial studies of transactive memory included social expertise as well as task expertise. Social expertise had an impact on team performance. Help seeking builds social expertise by creating new brokerage connections.

RELEVANCE OF SITUATED EXPERTISE FOR RESEARCHERS

Measuring Extra-Team Outcomes in Team Research

The within-team impact of the intervention reported in this study was as would be predicted by previous TMS research. The unanticipated impact was at the extra-team level. Team-level research continues to assume team boundaries are clear and stable and therefore interpersonal dynamics end at that boundary. In practice, team boundaries are more fluid and becoming more so with shifting uses of collaboration technology. Team-level research would benefit from more focus on the shifting nature of team boundaries. TMS research has begun to make this shift with recent work exploring how TMS operates at different levels and across team boundaries (Olabisi & Lewis, 2018; Peltokorpi, 2014; Qiao et al., 2019). Knowledge integration crosses levels of analysis (Zahra et al., 2020) and rough categorizations of individual, team, organization may limit our ability to fully understand fluid knowledge networks. Recent research using the multi-teams system framework offers another useful framework for exploring situated expertise (Luciano et al., 2020). Extra-team expertise networks are not limited to multi-teams so future research could consider the different extra-team dynamics of multi-team systems, knowledge brokers, and individual help seekers. Intraorganizational learning (Argote & Ophir, 2017) offers a lens for understanding expertise networks that situates the team within the context rather than defining the edge of the context. If team boundaries are becoming less salient in expertise networks, new research can help us understand the implications.

Linking Help Seeking and Expertise

Help-seeking activities are key to organizational learning in a dynamic environment. Team members in this intervention used help seeking to bring new knowledge to the team as new tasks were encountered. However, current research on the link between organizational help seeking and knowledge flows is surprisingly scarce. As noted by Qiao et al. (2019), researchers have focused more on knowledge contributors than on knowledge seekers. Future research on help-seeking activities would benefit our understanding of expertise networks. TMS is accessed and refined when individuals seek help. Knowing what others know only matters if individuals proactively act on that knowledge.

Tracking Impact Over Time

This study was the result of a fortuitous invitation to revisit a previous intervention. The initial workshop and short-term assessment of impact did not reveal much variance between teams. The interesting pattern emerged over a longer period of time. Researchers may benefit from longer-term follow-up assessments at the completion of field studies. Our understanding of organizational dynamics could be richer with more explorations of how the impact of interventions evolve over time.

CONCLUSION

Situated expertise describes the extent to which individual or team-level knowledge is actively connected to the wider knowledge network through proactive efforts to locate, or situate, that knowledge within the organization and ensure it is available and current. The dynamic, changing nature of tasks within the system require shifting expertise needs. In order for local expertise systems to remain current, actors must continuously update not just their knowledge of who knows what (transactive memory) but also their knowledge of who knows who (social expertise). It is through proactive help-seeking activity that transactive memory and social expertise is situated within the extended knowledge network. The extended knowledge network cannot just become a larger single transactive memory system because doing so would require adding numerous person and knowledge nodes into the TMS. It would not take long for the accuracy of the TMS to degrade. Help seeking across boundaries creates a more fluid process for maintaining the relevancy of a given TMS and creating new knowledge brokers to link different TMSs.

A TMS is limited by our ability to know. Theoretically it is possible for TMS to extend beyond team boundaries. However, there is also a limit to how far such a system can extend and still maintain its connection to the initial definition of individual knowledge combined with shared knowledge.

As the number of potential connections grows, the potential for shared understanding drops. Organizations can overcome this limitation of TMS size by developing formal and informal coordinating mechanisms to link different TMS in an organization (Peltokorpi, 2014). Situated expertise can play a role as one of these coordinating mechanisms. Situated expertise is best understood by focusing at the task level rather than the team level, focusing on individual help-seeking actions rather than team actions, identifying the knowledge brokers, and understanding the process as anchored in individual sensemaking. Through the combination of knowledge awareness and help-seeking activity, expertise moves from one TMS to another, enabling new connections between knowledge networks. The process requires boundary spanning exploration, proactive help-seeking norms, and actions to update the shared knowledge directory in the original TMS. If any of these three behaviors is missing, the team systems will be less efficient. The results of this specific team intervention further suggest connecting team TMS with the wider knowledge network can reduce the extent to which TMS awareness fades over time.

REFERENCES

Argote, L., Lee, S., & Park, J. (2020). Organizational learning processes and outcomes: Major findings and future research directions. *Management Science, 67*(9), 5301–5967. https://doi.org/10.1287/mnsc.2020.3693

Argote, L., & Ophir, R. (2017). Intraorganizational learning. In J. A. C. Baum (Ed.), *The Blackwell companion to organizations* (pp. 181–207). Blackwell Publishers. https://doi.org/10.1002/9781405164061.ch8

Ashleigh, M., & Prichard, J. (2011). Enhancing trust through training. In R. H. Searle & D. Skinner (Eds.), *Trust and human resource management* (pp. 125–138). Edward Elgar Publishing. https://doi.org/10.4337/9780857932006.00015

Ashleigh, M., & Prichard, J. (2012). An integrative model of the role of trust in transactive memory development. *Group & Organization Management, 37*(1), 5–35. https://doi.org/10.1177/1059601111428449

Austin, J. R. (2000). Knowing what and whom other people know: Linking transactive memory with external connections in organizational groups. *Academy of Management Proceedings, 1*, F1–F6. https://doi.org/10.5465/apbpp.2000.5535165

Austin, J. R. (2003a). Transactive memory in organizational groups: The effects of content, consensus, specialization, and accuracy on group performance. *Journal of Applied Psychology, 88*(5), 866–878. https://doi.org/10.1037/0021-9010.88.5.866

Austin, J. R. (2003b). Expertise and friendship: Help seeking efficacy in groups. *Academy of Management Proceedings, 1*, H1–H6. https://doi.org/10.5465/ambpp.2003.13792500

Bachrach, D. G., Lewis, K., Kim, Y., Patel, P. C., Campion, M. C., & Thatcher, S. (2019). Transactive memory systems in context: A meta-analytic examination of contextual factors in transactive memory systems development and team performance. *Journal of Applied Psychology, 104*(3), 464–493. https://doi.org/10.1037/apl0000329

Bartunek, J. M. (2007). Academic-practitioner collaboration need not require joint or relevant research: Toward a relational scholarship of integration. *Academy of Management Journal, 50*(6), 1323–1333. https://doi.org/10.5465/amj.2007.28165912

Bielak, A. T., Campbell, A., Pope, S., Schaefer, K., & Shaxson, L. (2008). From science communication to knowledge brokering: The shift from 'science push' to 'policy pull.' In D. Cheng, M. Claessens, T. Gascoigne, J. Metcalfe, B. Schiele, & S. Shi (Eds.), *Communicating science in social contexts* (pp. 201–226). Springer Science + Business Media B. V. https://doi.org/10.1007/978-1-4020-8598-7_12

Brandon, D. P., & Hollingshead, A. B. (2004). Transactive memory systems in organizations: Matching tasks, expertise, and people. *Organization Science, 15*(6), 633–644. https://doi.org/10.1287/orsc.1040.0069

Braun, V., & Clarke, V. (2006). Using thematic analysis in psychology. *Qualitative Research in Psychology, 3*(2), 77–101. https://doi.org/10.1191/1478088706qp063oa

Bunderson, J. S. (2003). Recognizing and utilizing expertise in work groups: A status characteristics perspective. *Administrative Science Quarterly, 48*(4), 557–591. https://doi.org/10.2307/3556637

Bunderson, J. S., & Barton, M. A. (2011). Status cues and expertise assessment in groups: How group members size one another up…and why it matters. In J. Pearce (Ed.), *Status in management and organizations* (pp. 215–237). Cambridge. https://doi.org/10.1017/cbo9780511760525.014

DeChurch, L. A., & Mesmer-Magnus, J. R. (2010). Measuring shared team mental models: A meta-analysis. *Group Dynamics: Theory, Research, and Practice, 14*(1), 1–14. https://doi.org/10.1037/a0017455

Faraj, S., & Sproull, L. (2000). Coordinating expertise in software development teams. *Management Science, 46*(12), 1554–1568. https://doi.org/10.1287/mnsc.46.12.1554.12072

Gaviria, C., Corredor, J. A., & Zuluaga-Rendón, Z. (2017, July 16–29). "If it matters, I can explain it": Social desirability of knowledge increases the illusion of explanatory depth. In G. Gunzelmann, A. Howes, T. Tenbrink, & E. J. Davelaar, *Proceedings of the 39th Annual Conference of the Cognitive Science Society, CogSci 2017.* https://www.semanticscholar.org/paper/%22If-It-Matters%2C-I-Can-Explain-It%22%3A-Social-of-the-of-Gaviria-Corredor/26458da3a7afa04ed37f2b15edfa22c2f52b116d

Geertz, C. (1983). *Local knowledge: Further essays in interpretive anthropology.* Basic Books.

Gino, F., Argote, L., Miron-Spektor, E., & Todorova, G. (2010). First, get your feet wet: The effects of learning from direct and indirect experience on team creativity. *Organizational Behavior and Human Decision Processes, 111*(2), 102–115. https://doi.org/10.1016/j.obhdp.2009.11.002

Gupta, N., & Hollingshead, A. B. (2010). Differentiated versus integrated transactive memory effectiveness: It depends on the task. *Group Dynamics: Theory, Research, and Practice, 14*(4), 384–398. https://doi.org/10.1037/a0019992

Hollingshead, A. B. (1998). Retrieval processes in transactive memory systems. *Journal of Personality and Social Psychology, 74*(3), 659–671. https://doi.org/10.1037/0022-3514.74.3.659

Hollingshead, A. B. (2000). Perceptions of expertise and transactive memory in work relationships. *Group Processes and Intergroup Relations, 3*(3), 257–267. https://doi.org/10.1177/1368430200033002

Kozlowski, S. W. J., Chao, G. T., Grand, J. A., Braun, M. T., & Kuljanin, G. (2013). Advancing multilevel research design: Capturing the dynamics of emergence. *Organizational Research Methods, 16*(4), 581–615. https://doi.org/10.1177/1094428113493119

Lavis, J. N. (2006). Research, public policymaking, and knowledge-translation processes: Canadian efforts to build bridges. *Journal of Continuing Education in the Health Professions, 26*(1), 37–45. https://doi.org/10.1002/chp.49

Lee, F. (1997). When the going gets tough, do the tough ask for help? Help seeking and power motivation in organizations. *Organizational Behavior and Human Decision Processes, 72*(3), 336–363. https://doi.org/10.1006/obhd.1997.2746

Lee, J. Y., Bachrach, D. G., & Lewis, K. (2014). Social network ties, transactive memory, and performance in groups. *Organization Science, 25*(3), 951–967. https://doi.org/10.1287/orsc.2013.0884

Lewis, K. (2003). Measuring transactive memory systems in the field: Scale development and validation. *Journal of Applied Psychology, 88*(4), 587–604. https://doi.org/10.1037/0021-9010.88.4.587

Lewis, K. (2004). Knowledge and performance in knowledge-worker teams: A longitudinal study of transactive memory systems. *Management Science, 50*(11), 1519–1533. https://doi.org/10.1287/mnsc.1040.0257

Lewis, K., Belliveau, M., Herndon, B., & Keller, J. (2007). Group cognition, membership change, and performance: Investigating the benefits and detriments of collective knowledge. *Organizational Behavior and Human Decision Processes, 103*(2), 159–178. https://doi.org/10.1016/j.obhdp.2007.01.005

Lewis, K., & Herndon, B. (2011). Transactive memory systems: Current issues and future research directions. *Organization Science, 22*(5), 1254–1265. https://doi.org/10.1287/orsc.1110.0647

Lewis, K., Lange, D., & Gillis, L. (2005). Transactive memory systems, learning, and learning transfer. *Organization Science, 16*(6), 581–598. https://doi.org/10.1287/orsc.1050.0143

Liang, D. W., Moreland, R., & Argote, L. (1995). Group versus individual training and group performance: The mediating role of transactive memory. *Personality and Social Psychology Bulletin, 21*(4), 384–393. https://doi.org/10.1177/0146167295214009

Littlepage, G., Robison, W., & Reddington, K. (1997). Effects of task experience and group experience on group performance, member ability, and recognition of expertise. *Organizational Behavior and Human Decision Processes, 69*(2), 133–147. https://doi.org/10.1006/obhd.1997.2677

Littlepage, G. E., & Mueller, A. L. (1997). Recognition and utilization of expertise in problem-solving groups: Expert characteristics and behavior. *Group Dynamics: Theory, Research, and Practice, 1*(4), 324–328. https://doi.org/10.1037/1089-2699.1.4.324

Littlepage, G. E., Schmidt, G. W., Whisler, E. W., & Frost, A. G. (1995). An input-process-output analysis of influence and performance in problem-solving groups. *Journal of Personality and Social Psychology, 69*(5), 877–899. https://doi.org/10.1037/0022-3514.69.5.877

Luciano, M. M., Nahrgang, J. D., & Shropshire, C. (2020). Strategic leadership systems: Viewing top management teams and boards of directors from a multiteam systems perspective. *Academy of Management Review, 45*(3), 675–701. https://doi.org/10.5465/amr.2017.0485

Mesmer-Magnus, J., Niler, A. A., Plummer, G., Larson, L. E., & DeChurch, L. A. (2017). The cognitive underpinnings of effective teamwork: A continuation. *Career Development International, 22*(5), 507–519. https://doi.org/10.1108/cdi-08-2017-0140

Mohammed, S., & Dumville, B. C. (2001). Team mental models in a team knowledge framework: Expanding theory and measurement across disciplinary boundaries. *Journal of Organizational Behavior, 22*(2), 89–106. https://doi.org/10.1002/job.86

Moreland, R. L., Argote, L., & Krishnan, R. (1996). Socially shared cognition at work: Transactive memory and group performance. In J. L. Nye & A. M. Brower (Eds.), *What's social about social cognition? Research on socially shared cognition in small groups* (pp. 57–84). SAGE Publications. https://doi.org/10.4135/9781483327648.n3

Moreland, R. L., & Myaskovsky, L. (2000). Exploring the performance benefits of group training: Transactive memory or improved communication? *Organizational Behavior and Human Decision Processes, 82*(1), 117–133. https://doi.org/10.1006/obhd.2000.2891

Olabisi, J., & Lewis, K. (2018). Within- and between-team coordination via transactive memory systems and boundary spanning. *Group & Organization Management, 43*(5), 691–717. https://doi.org/10.1177/1059601118793750

Peltokorpi, V. (2012). Organizational transactive memory systems. *European Psychologist, 17*(1), 11–20. https://doi.org/10.1027/1016-9040/a000044

Peltokorpi, V. (2014). Transactive memory system coordination mechanisms in organizations: An exploratory case study. *Group & Organization Management, 39*(4), 444–471. https://doi.org/10.1177/1059601114538813

Peltokorpi, V., & Hasu, M. (2016). Transactive memory systems in research team innovation: A moderated mediation analysis. *Journal of Engineering and Technology Management, 39*, 1–12. https://doi.org/10.1016/j.jengtecman.2015.11.001

Peltokorpi, V., & Hood, A. C. (2019). Communication in theory and research on transactive memory systems: A literature review. *Topics in Cognitive Science, 11*(4), 644–667. https://doi.org/10.1111/tops.12359

Ployhart, R. E., & Bartunek, J. M. (2019). Editors' comments: There is nothing so theoretical as good practice—A call for phenomenal theory. *Academy of Management Review, 44*(3), 493–497.

Prichard, J. S., & Ashleigh, M. J. (2007). The effects of team-skills training on transactive memory and performance. *Small Group Research, 38*(6), 696–726. https://doi.org/10.1177/1046496407304923

Qiao, T., Shan, W., Zhang, M., & Liu, C. (2019). How to facilitate knowledge diffusion in complex networks: The roles of network structure, knowledge role distribution and selection rule. *International Journal of Information Management, 47*, 152–167. https://doi.org/10.1016/j.ijinfomgt.2019.01.016

Rabb, N., Fernbach, P. M., & Sloman, S. A. (2019). Individual representation in a community of knowledge. *Trends in Cognitive Sciences, 23*(10), 891–902. https://doi.org/10.1016/j.tics.2019.07.011

Ren, Y., & Argote, L. (2011). Transactive memory systems 1985–2010: An integrative framework of key dimensions, antecedents, and consequences. *Academy of Management Annals, 5*(1), 189–229. https://doi.org/10.1080/19416520.2011.590300

Rozenblit, L., & Keil, F. (2002). The misunderstood limits of folk science: An illusion of explanatory depth. *Cognitive Science, 26*(5), 521–562. https://doi.org/10.1207/s15516709cog2605_1

Rulke, D. L., & Rau, D. (2000). Investigating the encoding process of transactive memory development in group training. *Group and Organization Management, 25*(4), 373–396. https://doi.org/10.1177/1059601100254004

Saldaña, J. (2016). *The coding manual for qualitative researchers* (3rd ed.). SAGE Publications.

Turner, J. R., Chen, Q., & Danks, S. (2014). Team shared cognitive constructs: A meta-analysis exploring the effects of shared cognitive constructs on team performance. *Performance Improvement Quarterly, 27*(1), 83–117. https://doi.org/10.1002/piq.21163

Turnhout, E., Stuiver, M., Klostermann, J., Harms, B., & Leeuwis, C. (2013). New roles of science in society: Different repertoires of knowledge brokering. *Science and Public Policy, 40*(3), 354–365. https://doi.org/10.1093/scipol/scs114

Wegner, D. M. (1987). Transactive memory: A contemporary analysis of the group mind. In B. Mullen & G. R. Goethals (Eds.), *Theories of group behavior* (pp. 185–208). Springer. https://doi.org/10.1007/978-1-4612-4634-3_9

Zahra, S. A., Neubaum, D. O., & Hayton, J. (2020). What do we know about knowledge integration: Fusing micro-and macro-organizational perspectives. *Academy of Management Annals, 14*(1), 160–194. https://doi.org/10.5465/annals.2017.0093

Zhang, Z. X., Hempel, P. S., Han, Y. L., & Tjosvold, D. (2007). Transactive memory system links work team characteristics and performance. *Journal of Applied Psychology, 92*(6), 1722–1730. https://doi.org/10.1037/0021-9010.92.6.1722

PART III

WORK FLEXIBILITY AND THE TEAM

CHAPTER 7

TACKLING THE AUTONOMY PARADOX

A Team Perspective on the Individual Use of Time-Spatial Flexibility

Miriam K. Baumgärtner
University of St. Gallen

Martina Hartner-Tiefenthaler
Vienna University of Technology

ABSTRACT

In many organizations, the question is no longer whether employees should have the opportunity for time-spatial flexibility, but rather how to successfully organize it. At the individual level, time-spatial flexibility has been appreciated as an autonomy-enhancing factor (Gajendran & Harrison, 2007; McNall et al., 2010). However, the "autonomy paradox" (Mazmanian et al., 2013) illustrates that constant availability concurrently reduces personal autonomy. Even though knowledge professionals have gained more autonomy to choose when and where to work, prevailing team norms may make them feel obligated to be available, thereby limiting their ability to disconnect from work, with

Managing Team Centricity in Modern Organizations, pages 195–224
Copyright © 2022 by Information Age Publishing
www.infoagepub.com
All rights of reproduction in any form reserved.

detrimental effects on their recovery (Schlachter et al., 2018). At the team level, however, the great variety of strategies for using time-spatial flexibility poses a challenge for team coordination and the predictability of availability. In addition, as team members compare themselves to one another, perceptions of justice regarding availability practices may differ. Therefore, we argue that flexible teams need to purposefully shape their availability norms and suggest a guided team reflexivity process. This approach enables team members to establish shared mental models of the use of time-spatial flexibility, which define the cornerstones of individual time-spatial flexibility strategies. At the core of the process is the joint development of team-based interaction scripts of availability uncovering expectations regarding the use of time-spatial flexibility, thus reducing the uncertainty of availability, and allowing for recovery outside of work.

All over the globe, the current COVID-19 pandemic has accelerated and extended flexible working. Office workers moved their work mainly or even entirely to their homes, which also resulted in more work outside standard office hours (International Labour Organization, 2020). Experts agree that the "new normal" after lockdowns and forced home offices will be characterized by flexible working, making this topic more relevant than ever. The literature shows that being able to choose where to work is very positive for employees as it increases autonomy (Gajendran & Harrison, 2007; McNall et al., 2010). Unequivocal empirical evidence demonstrates that flexible working with regard to time and place positively relates to job satisfaction (Gajendran & Harrison, 2007). When employees are provided with time-spatial flexibility, their work is divided between the office and other locations to varying degrees. They decide (to a certain extent) where and when to work based on professional and private demands. Wessels and colleagues (2019) refer to this form of self-regulatory behavior as "*time-spatial* job crafting" and consider it to be a "future work skill" of knowledge employees (p. 1). Time-spatial job crafting is a *context-specific* form of job crafting referring to the use of flexibility on a daily basis, whereas the original concept of job crafting focuses on changing cognitive, task, and/or relational boundaries to modify the job's design and social environment (Wrześniewski & Dutton, 2001). We define teams whose members enact time-spatial job crafting in a hybrid setting as *flexible teams*, integrating elements of co-located and virtual teams (Fiol & O'Connor, 2005). In flexible teams, individuals "make conscious decisions regarding the time and spatial dimensions of their work to optimize a time/spatial-demands fit (i.e., the best time and location/place to work on a given task and given personal demands)" (Wessels et al., 2019, p. 2). From a work-design perspective, this proactive individual approach is very important since employees take initiative to create changes in their working environment (Grant & Parker, 2009).

However, relational perspectives (Grant & Parker, 2009) should also be taken into account because the sum of these varying strategies within the team may not result in optimal productivity at the team level (Schelling, 1978). While standard operating procedures are little affected by time-spatial job crafting, team coordination, is more difficult because of reduced face-to-face time (Wittenbaum et al., 2002). Spontaneous interactions like communication in the hallway about ongoing issues are less likely (Waerzner et al., 2017). This is even more marked when team members use different time-spatial job crafting strategies, resulting in varying individual availability strategies. In many cases, team members do not know whether someone is actually available at the office, which also makes availability less certain in general (Fiol & O'Connor, 2005). With insufficient understanding of their colleagues' time-spatial job crafting rationales, such as psychological needs and private demands, team members and supervisors may make team-level decisions or establish certain demands that have adverse effects for individuals.

Balancing the individual and team levels in flexible working contexts hinges on the active shaping of availability norms, at the collective level, that emerge from time-spatial job crafting at the individual level. Etymologically, "availability" is defined as the "capability of advantageous use" originated in 1803 (Etymology Dictionary, n.d.). As such, the term encompasses decisions regarding whether, when, and where to respond to communications (Mazmanian et al., 2013). Extending its original meaning, we conceptualize availability as broadly encompassing all aspects of formal and informal communicative behaviors within a flexible team. Being available includes attending formal meetings online and in person, but also responding to messages sent via information and communication technology. The increased opportunities to contact colleagues at all times thanks to a diverse set of tools also reduce the predictability of job contacts for employees and might create a feeling of uncertainty concerning when and how to reach colleagues. As employees try to reduce uncertainty, they may mirror the availability behavior of their team members and adjust their actions accordingly. Over time, constant availability norms may evolve around the behavioral patterns of individual team members' time-spatial job crafting. Thus, the opportunity to autonomously decide when and where to work might not be a free choice after all since collective expectations develop within teams, and a collective norm of constant availability limiting employees' autonomy may emerge. Being available around the clock through a variety of channels contradicts the intention of flexible working to provide autonomy, which affects the recovery experiences of all team members (Sonnentag & Fritz, 2015).

We argue that aligning the time-spatial job crafting of individuals in the team is necessary because individualistic behaviors might act at the expense of team demands or fellow team members, as well as harm personal recovery when team members make themselves continuously available. Moreover, variation in time-spatial job crafting and, thus, availability, might lead to feelings of injustice. If some team members comply with the norm of constant availability and others do not, those who do may feel exploited and those who do not might feel stigmatized (albeit they behave within formal policies), which may lead to justice differentiation within a team.

With our paper, we extend the existing work that focuses on the individual perspective when investigating the effects of flexible work by moving the attention to the interplay between rationales at the individual and team levels. Our aim is twofold. First, drawing from different research streams, we theoretically investigate the phenomenon of this potential tension between individual rationales for time-spatial job crafting and team-level processes. In more detail, we apply a justice lens on the flexible team context and discuss how varying time-spatial job-crafting strategies in flexible teams might create uncertainty and injustice that impair recovery in the long run. Thus, we draw on the concept of team interaction scripts that aim to foster positive change, build shared mental models of availability in the team, and reduce uncertainty, as well as justice differentiation.

Second, based on the cognitive-behavioral model of reflexivity in teams (Konradt et al., 2016), we propose a hands-on approach to how flexible teams can optimally balance individual preferences and needs with team demands by actively shaping team availability norms. The aim is to maximize the benefits of flexible work for individuals but defining cornerstones at the collective level to ensure that team rationales establish justice and allow for recovery within teams. Reducing uncertainty about availability expectations will help employees to recover from work and foster mental health in flexible teams in the long run.

UNCERTAINTY OF AVAILABILITY EXPECTATIONS AS A RESULT FROM TIME-SPATIAL JOB CRAFTING

Due to the high prevalence of time-spatial flexibility, the question in many organizations is no longer whether employees should have the opportunity for time-spatial job crafting, but rather how it can be implemented successfully at a team level to support healthy team functioning (Dutton & Ragins, 2007, 2017). Members of flexible teams are present at a physical office and have access to the office infrastructure, but their time of presence varies because time-spatial flexibility allows them to craft their working time and space arrangements individually according to their needs and demands.

Wessels et al. (2019) define time-spatial job crafting as "the extent to which employees [...] actively select workplaces, work locations, and working hours, and then potentially adapt the place/location of work and working hours or tasks and private demands to ensure that these still fit [...] each other" (p. 2).

Time-spatial job crafting differs from the similar construct of individualized deals or "i-deals" (Rousseau, 2005). I-deals refer to "voluntary, personalized agreements of a nonstandard nature negotiated between individual employees and their employers regarding terms that benefit each party" (Rousseau et al., 2006, p. 978). Both constructs refer to a nonstandardized working environment and are assumed to harmonize an employee's work with his or her personal life (Hornung et al., 2010). In contrast to i-deals, time-spatial job crafting is practiced within the scope of the flexibility granted to all or a certain group of employees. Consequently, time-spatial flexibility enables knowledge professionals to craft working time and place arrangements on a day-to-day basis by continuously optimizing their time/spatial-demands fit (Wessels et al., 2019). In contrast, i-deals are negotiated on an individual basis with the supervisor and usually differ from those of an employee's co-workers (Bal & Dorenbosch, 2015; Kroon et al., 2016; Rousseau, 2005; Rousseau et al., 2006). Once negotiated and agreed upon, i-deals do not change daily; rather, they usually hold until the employee initiates further negotiations with the supervisor. For example, it is considered time-spatial job crafting when an employee starts to work at 10:00 a.m., 2 hours later than usual, on *a particular* Friday to attend a meeting at his child's school but comes to work at 8:00 a.m. the following week for an early meeting. Whereas time-spatial job crafting consists in optimizing time-spatial flexibility on a daily basis, i-deals concentrate on individual negotiations about how work is done, which differ from co-workers' negotiations but may not necessarily be adaptable on a daily basis. Thus, a time i-deal would be an arrangement whereby the employee starts work *every* Friday at 10:00 a.m. instead of 8:00 a.m. to bring their child to school. Finally, when each team member can craft working time and space arrangements on a daily basis, the team context is more ambiguous and less certain (Fiol & O'Connor, 2005).

Individual time-spatial job crafting (Wessels et al., 2019) aims to satisfy individuals' basic psychological needs, such as autonomy, relatedness, and competence as defined in self-determination theory (Deci & Ryan, 1985). Thus, employees aim to satisfy their three basic needs at work and choose their working time and place arrangements accordingly. Whereas one employee might satisfy their strong need for autonomy by working from home as much as possible, another may base their choice of time-spatial job crafting on others because they prefer to be at the office with them.

The three psychological needs are correlated: when employees experience support for autonomy, they typically feel more connected to the organization, fulfilling their need for relatedness, and also more effective, which satisfies their need for competence (Deci et al., 2017). However, despite the potential increase in autonomy, time-spatial flexibility may impair the satisfaction of the need for relatedness (Van Yperen et al., 2014) because of social isolation, either when working at home (Golden, 2012) or when others are constantly working at home, and to reduced spontaneous communication in the hallway (Waerzner et al., 2017)—the so-called "water-cooler conversations." Thus, although autonomy is inherent in time-spatial flexibility, we argue that the need for relatedness and competence must not be neglected when designing flexible work in teams.

When members' individual time-spatial job crafting varies considerably within the flexible team, the availability of team members might be challenged at certain times. For example, if a team member tries to discuss an issue with a colleague in person and fails to do so because the other employee works from home, they might have the feeling that the other person is hardly available. Conversely, when the majority of team members work mainly from the office, others might feel insecure if they are expected to do so as well to demonstrate physical availability. Thus, there is a tension between individual time-spatial job crafting and the uncertainty of expectations concerning availability, which needs to be resolved.

Proposition 1: *Time-spatial job crafting creates availability uncertainty.*

The Emergence of Collective Norms of (Constant) Availability

> An individual cannot simply turn off his or her mobile e-mail device and not respond to e-mails if he/she is committed to succeeding in a social environment that expects accessibility. (Mazmanian, 2013, p. 1247)

With individual time-spatial job crafting, some team members may choose to work (mainly) in the office while others opt to work remotely. Some may prefer to work very early in the day while others prefer to work late into the evening. Although this situation enables employees to autonomously craft their working time and place arrangements based on individual preferences, it may impair their autonomy in the long run. Because individuals are not independent from their social environment, they are influenced by their peers' flexible working. For instance, when the office is half-empty, the incentive to work onsite declines due to a contagion effect (Rockmann & Pratt, 2015). Time-spatial job crafting also affects the periods outside individual working hours because the variation in approaches results in professional messages from colleagues being received outside of working hours. As stated in our opening quote, employees may feel the urge to respond to incoming requests immediately. One way to ensure avail-ability is to make oneself accessible to peers around the clock. However, this may shape collective expectations of availability after working hours as well and creates a paradoxical situation (Mazmanian et al., 2013): The phenom-enon whereby the use of mobile e-mail devices both increases and reduces personal autonomy is called the "autonomy paradox" by Mazmanian and colleagues (2013). Their research shows that despite knowledge profession-als' autonomy to choose when and where to work, they end up using mo-bile communication devices all the time and everywhere, which ultimately restricts their actual autonomy. Even though autonomy in the workplace implies the authority to define the boundaries of work, employees fail to do so in practice because they act according to perceived expectations—that is, availability outside of standard working hours.

Over time, behavioral patterns resulting from individual time-spatial job crafting will lead to the development of collective availability norms that "orient behavior, punish deviants, and influence social control" (Mazma-nian, 2013, p. 1226). These evolving norms will set the cornerstones for future behavior: "A critical element in norm development is the emergence of a generally held, group-based understanding of expected and accepted behavior" (Bettenhausen & Murnighan, 1985, p. 354). As team members interact, they either align their time-spatial job crafting with the implied norm, adapt it, or attempt to pull the group toward their own understand-ing of availability (cf. Bettenhausen & Murnighan, 1985).

In sum, behaviors of unmanaged availability will bring about norms that have emerged over time rather than norms that have been developed de-liberately. Mostly, these norms are not explicated or verbalized. Thus, they may reflect perceived expectations of availability that are not in line with rational team availability demands nor with the real expectations of supervi-sors or/and other team members.

Proposition 2: *Time-spatial job crafting leads to the emergence of collective availability norms that may set high availability expectations.*

Implications of Constant Availability for Recovery From Work

When employees are constantly available for work issues, their temporal and spatial boundaries disappear, and their ability to disconnect from work is limited (Mazmanian et al., 2013). This perceived obligation also impairs their well-being due to a lack of sufficient recovery from work (Barley et al., 2011; Derks & Bakker, 2014; Dettmers et al., 2016; Thomas et al., 2006;

Schlachter et al., 2018). According to the effort-recovery model (Geurts & Sonnentag, 2006), the lack of recovery is associated with a harmful process in which normal work reactions to work demands develop into more chronic load reactions, resulting in a destabilized psychophysiological system. In particular, the two recovery experiences of psychological detachment and control (Sonnentag & Fritz, 2007, 2015) were shown to be impaired by availability outside work (Dettmers et al., 2016). Psychological detachment refers to refraining from job-related activities and thoughts during nonworking time. When work regularly interferes with private time, employees cannot detach from it, and their well-being is likely to be impaired (Schlachter et al., 2018). Even when there are no actual work behaviors but a potential availability for contacts by colleagues, we assume that detachment is likely to be hindered.

With regard to the second recovery experience, control, a recent study (Park et al., 2020) shows that perceived boundary control makes a considerable difference for experienced recovery from work: When employees feel that they have more control over the boundary between work and nonwork, their psychological detachment is less affected by availability expectations (Park et al., 2020). Thus, employees must retain their boundary control to support their own recovery.

Psychological detachment and boundary control are likely to be impaired by employees' uncertainty about availability, such as when they are unsure how to reach colleagues outside the office or whether it is appropriate to be unreachable during standard working hours (or nonworking hours). In line with this, Dettmers et al. (2016) show that when job contacts outside work hours are predictable (i.e., when employees know in advance whether they will be contacted outside work hours), emotional exhaustion is lower. When expectations are clarified and team members have control over their (un)availability outside work, it should be easier for them to detach from work outside working hours, which is crucial to their recovery from work (Sonnentag & Fritz, 2015).

Proposition 3: *Reducing the uncertainty of availability via clarifying expectations increases recovery from work.*

Shaping Norms: Balancing Individual Needs With Team Demands via Team Interaction Scripts

Availability norms emerge as a function of collective behavior and evolve around shared beliefs that are reflected in habitual behavioral and interactional patterns. They are prevalent in a social group until someone questions their appropriateness (Bettenhausen & Murnighan, 1985). Thus, once norms that might impair recovery emerge in flexible teams, they need to be actively tackled and purposefully changed via interaction scripts.

Interaction scripts (Lee et al., 2020) are used to affect positive change in the relational dynamics of interpersonal sharing. They are defined as "internalized cognitive schemas that direct individuals as to the appropriate behavior for specific organizational situations or contexts" (Lee et al., 2020, p. 99). In contrast to the traditional understanding of individualized scripts (Ashforth & Fried, 1988; Gioia & Poole, 1984; Lord & Kernan, 1987), interaction scripts are rather used in novel situations, shall be explicitly defined, and focus exclusively on guidelines for interaction (Lee et al., 2020). Lee et al. (2020) describe how the use of interaction scripts can legitimate new forms of interpersonal sharing by specifying content parameters and participation rules. Thus, we regard them as a means to initiate new forms of organizing availability in flexible teams and shape the evolution of less detrimental norms that support recovery.

When shaping prevailing norms of availability, it is essential to clarify expectations before creating shared beliefs around how time-spatial flexibility should be practiced within the team. Hereby, our focus is to disentangle two types of demands. On the one hand, business-related demands that refer to the necessities of the job must be followed, such as the need for one person to be present at the office to deal with requests from colleagues. The team needs clarity about how this availability is organized. On the other hand, there are perceived demands that lack any grounded need for availability but hinder individuals' ability to recover from work. These demands do not necessarily result in increased performance output and have not been requested by the supervisor, but they reflect social-normative contexts or personal characteristics (Schlachter et al., 2018) of replying quickly to requests. For instance, e-mails received on weekends are answered immediately despite personal obligations and the lack of a rational need to do so; however, since this has become a habit, shared expectations evolve around it and others might count on immediate responses.

Team members must be aware of which aspects of the prevailing norms of availability refer to required, non-changeable demands that should be prioritized and which of these perceived demands have evolved over time without a substantial underlying necessity and may be modified as a result of team reflection. That is why the team-level perspective must be taken into account to align varying individual-level strategies of time-spatial job crafting. Individual needs have to be organized within the boundaries of team demands. The goal is to develop a shared understanding of availability incorporating individual and team needs. As a result, autonomy should become less paradoxical because the uncertainty regarding availability should be reduced for the benefit of recovery (Derks et al., 2014; Dettmers, 2017). Since interaction scripts legitimize counter-normative interactions (Lee et al., 2020), they support flexible teams to deviate from the evolved norms of availability and shape a new course of action. When defining interaction scripts, it is crucial to aim for providing both enough flexibility for the individual and clarity about availability expectations and team demands.

Proposition 4: *Team interaction scripts must balance individual and team needs, allowing enough space for individual needs while fulfilling team demands.*

Heterogenous Availability Norms and Perceived Justice

Allowing shared expectations of difference through a great variety of time-spatial job crafting practices in a flexible team rather than centering on deviance from the norm may be viewed as a way to avoid the trap of constant availability (Mazmanian, 2012). Heterogeneous patterns of time-spatial job crafting allow team members to bring their individual (private) needs more to the fore and follow the underlying idea of time-spatial job crafting in using flexibility as a resource to fulfill individual needs.

Although a heterogeneous norm might be a preferred solution to overcome the threat of the norm of constant availability, a high variation of individual time-spatial job crafting among team members may also generate feelings of injustice in some members due to comparisons of availability for working tasks. Some team members might take advantage of the lack of clarification, whereas others might over-fulfill expectations; for example, by being constantly available for their co-workers.

The immanent role of justice in work teams and organizations has been extensively researched (Cohen-Charash & Spector, 2001; Colquitt, 2001; Cropanzano & Ambrose, 2001; Greenberg, 1987, 1993), but its role in time-spatial flexibility has received little attention (Hakonen & Lipponen, 2008; Thatcher & Bagger, 2011), even though unorganized practices of time-spatial flexibility may produce injustice among team members (Fogarty et al., 2011), which can generate anger or guilt (Hillebrandt & Barclay, 2017). We argue that justice may be even more relevant in the flexible team context as justice perceptions are particularly relevant in uncertain contexts (Lind & Van den Bos, 2002; Van den Bos & Lind, 2002). When team members have the opportunity to craft their working time and space arrangements individually, there is greater uncertainty than in co-located or completely virtual teams.

Since it is essential that heterogeneous strategies of time-spatial job crafting are viewed as fair by all team members, we argue that the level of justice is important but also the *differentiation* of justice within the team (compare leader-member exchange differentiation; Nishii & Meyer, 2009). Thus, when perceived justice varies strongly within teams and justice perception differentiation is high, we assume detrimental effects potentially impairing team members' recovery. Although justice is rarely addressed in studies about workplace flexibility, we argue that it is crucial when members of flexible teams have the autonomy to engage in time-spatial job crafting. Furthermore, the homogeneity or divergence of justice perceptions within the team must be taken into account. If there is high differentiation in justice perceptions among team members, defining team interaction scripts may be more difficult. However, when justice differentiation is high, gaining clarity about what is allowed and expected and reducing individual members' uncertainty is even more important. The goal is to harmonize overall justice perceptions and define cornerstones that allow high justice perceptions among all team members, with low differentiation.

To conclude, given that time-spatial job crafting inherently allows autonomy by providing a certain extent of individualization, we argue in favor of the variation of availability in flexible teams to support individual basic needs as well as private demands. However, if this variation becomes too great within a team and some team members are unavailable at the cost of others' availability, a sense of injustice may arise. That is why flexible teams face the challenge of balancing their individual needs with team demands.

Proposition 5: *Flexible teams with heterogeneous availability norms are more likely to have greater justice differentiation.*

How Interaction Scripts Help to Build Shared Mental Models of Availability in Flexible Teams

Flexible teams need to operate in a context of higher uncertainty because of the increased autonomy of employees, which raises questions of coordination, communication, and social connections (Bartel et al., 2012; Rockmann & Pratt, 2015). Defining team interaction scripts is viewed as more challenging in a more uncertain context (i.e., higher individual autonomy with regard to time-spatial job crafting) but also as more beneficial. It allows the teams to strategically balance individual time-spatial job crafting approaches with team needs by maximizing the beneficial effects of time-spatial flexibility and minimizing its negative effects.

When collectively defining team interaction scripts (e.g., via a team reflexivity process), it is essential that the team creates a mutual understanding of individual needs and develops shared mental models for working together flexibly (Konradt et al., 2015). Whereas team interaction scripts target concrete behaviors that drive change (Lee et al., 2020), shared mental models represent their underlying cognitive basis, "a collective and accurate understanding about [...] procedures, strategies and about one another" (Konradt et al., 2016, p. 166). Shared mental models "allow all team members to similarly interpret team-relevant information and share expectations regarding the team context" (Fisher et al., 2012, p. 830). Thus, they encourage everybody to be "on the same page" (Fisher et al., 2012, p. 825). As such, shared mental models are the mechanism connecting team reflection with adaptation (Konradt et al., 2015). Without the cognitive understanding of these scripts, the success of their implementation will be limited. For this reason, we consider it essential that the underlying shared mental models are in line with the team interaction scripts. Once team members understand the purpose and reasoning of the defined interaction scripts, it is possible to purposefully shape availability norms and reduce uncertainty.

Proposition 6: *Team interaction scripts of availability help to purposefully create shared mental models of availability and, thus, decrease availability uncertainty.*

A Practical Guide to Shaping Availability Norms

On a practical level, we propose the cognitive-behavioral model of reflexivity in teams (Konradt et al., 2016; Schippers et al., 2003, 2013) to orchestrate individual time-spatial job crafting at the team level and shape prevailing availability norms. Integrating regulatory theory (DeShon et al., 2004) and reflexivity theory (West, 1996), this model proposes a guided reflexivity process (see Figure 7.1) encompassing three phases—(a) making norms explicit by clarifying availability expectations, (b) jointly developing team interaction scripts, and (c) implementing team interaction scripts—that build on each other. It should be understood as a dynamic process that leads to a continuous improvement of work cooperation (Hinsz et al., 1997; Konradt et al., 2016) and refers to "the extent toward which teams think about their strategies and behaviors and adapt their functioning, in particular when confronted with complex and unpredictable environments" (Konradt et al., 2016, p. 153). Thus, time-spatial flexibility must be considered from a dynamic perspective given that individual needs, team contexts, and justice perceptions change over time (Jones & Skarlicki, 2013).

Making Norms Explicit: Clarifying Availability Expectations and Understanding Individual Time-Spatial Job-Crafting Strategies

To shape the availability norms and allow heterogeneity by considering justice issues, team members need to discuss the prevailing norms of availability first. Underlying expectations and preferences for individual time-spatial job crafting should be clarified, and team members should reveal

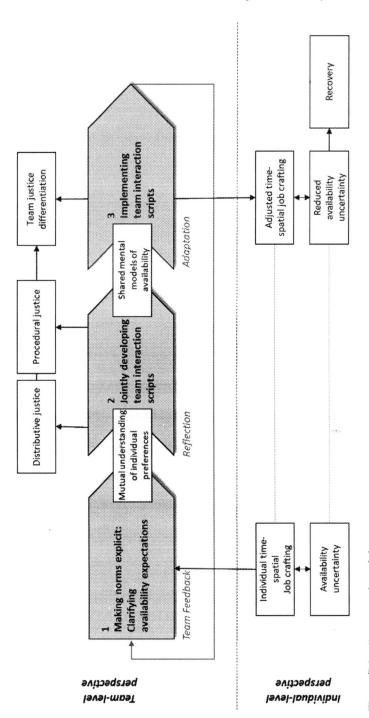

Figure 7.1 Conceptual model.

the reasoning behind their individual strategies (e.g., "I prefer to work early in the morning and do not like to be bothered with work after 7:00 p.m. because evening time is family time"). This informs other team members about personal needs and preferences regarding working times and locations and lays the groundwork for an honest and open exchange on the matter within the team.

The following issues are to be discussed: How many days of working outside the office are okay? Do team members have to announce them in advance and if yes, how many days in advance? Which time frame is expected/tolerated for responding to messages? How common is it to be contacted outside working hours? How to signal unavailability? Which (team) meetings require onsite presence? Which communication media are used for which purposes? How to contact fellow team members when outside the office?

In a second step, team members receive the opportunity to articulate and question their underlying expectations, which may contrast individual preferences with team demands. Individual preferences may be related to personal demands, such as picking up and looking after a child until the other parent can take over, but may also pertain to performance-related demands (e.g., working from home because one can better concentrate on a challenging task at home). Enabling individuals to take fellow team members' perspectives into account fosters understanding and helps them to make sense of their colleagues' time-spatial job crafting. It also creates mutual understanding, reduces uncertainty, and helps to build a better workplace (Parker et al., 2008) as predictability and transparency both play a crucial role in the process of coping with work demands (Dettmers et al., 2016; McGrath & Beehr, 1990; Sonnentag & Frese, 2003).

Reflection: Joint Development of Team Interaction Scripts

During the reflection phase, the focus moves from the individual to the team perspective and, thus, the team as a unit is the center of attention. Team members are instructed to reflect and plan strategy improvements (West, 2000). The goal is to achieve mutual agreement about the cornerstones of team demands to provide the boundaries that act as frameworks for employees' individual time-spatial job crafting and shape the prevailing norms of availability. Team members bring the experiences and knowledge they have exchanged, as well as different perspectives, into the team context (Konradt, et al., 2015, 2016) and discuss how they wish to work together. This involves establishing the scope of responsibilities—and the boundaries—that they give themselves as members of a flexible team, but also the boundaries imposed by the job or the organization.

Based on team members' expectations, teams jointly develop team interaction scripts (Lee et al., 2020) guiding their time-spatial job crafting behavior by considering team demands as well as the satisfaction of team members' needs. Although it is recommended to bring clarity to the team by documenting and writing down team interaction scripts, these scripts must leave enough room for individual time-spatial job crafting, as personal preferences, and contextual circumstances (including private life) vary.

The guiding idea is to define when team demands must be prioritized over personal needs (e.g., when scheduling meetings) to align individual goals with team goals through the development of team interaction scripts. This enables the team to go beyond individual adaptation strategies and take on the perspective of the whole team. Interaction scripts help to overcome uncertainty regarding supervisors' and co-workers' expectations of availability by creating shared mental models of availability (Konradt et al., 2016; Maynard & Gilson, 2014). Thanks to higher transparency and predictability of job contacts, they provide clarity on expectations (e.g., "My team members do not expect me to answer an e-mail at 11:00 p.m."), which can be used as a frame of reference for how to manage the blurred boundaries between work and the private sphere. Thus, behavioral change related to detachment from work is reinforced, providing room for recovery.

Adaptation: Implementing Team Interaction Scripts

Finally, in the third phase, team members implement the previously defined team interaction scripts and adapt their behavior accordingly. This transfers the content of the team interaction scripts into concrete behavioral actions, which are defined as "goal-oriented behaviors relevant to achieving the desired changes in team objectives, strategies, processes, organizations, or environments, identified during the stage of reflection" (West, 2000, p. 6). Depending on their initial time-spatial job-crafting strategies, team members may have to change their behaviors significantly to reduce the discrepancy with the written team interaction scripts that have been agreed upon by the team—that is, engage in interaction scripts-adjusted time-spatial job crafting (see Figure 7.1). This is the most critical determinant of success for the entire process (Konradt et al., 2015, 2016). The more team members' daily behaviors are aligned with the defined interaction scripts, the more stable and predictable the emerging behavioral patterns become over time (Bettenhausen & Murnighan, 1991).

Although the identification of the three phases may suggest that there are definitive starting and ending points to this process, we argue, in line with other scholars (e.g., Konradt et al., 2016), that this reflexivity process should be an iterative—or continuous—improvement process. As time passes following the adaptation phase, team members may acknowledge that their behaviors deviate from the interaction scripts defined initially as they come to recognize that certain guidelines, established to achieve certain target states, did not work as expected. For instance, the frustration of the need for relatedness may not become apparent until several weeks have passed, and as a consequence, isolation effects may emerge for some team members, which need to be dealt with. A new alignment process may then be initiated. Consequently, the interaction scripts will likely have to be reformulated after the adaptation/implementation phase.

The Role of Justice in the Reflexivity Process

One of the goals of the reflexivity process is to establish team interaction scripts that lead to lower justice differentiation with flexible teams. When team interaction scripts are perceived as fair, the likelihood of employees complying with them is higher. The perceived fairness of team interaction scripts is thus particularly relevant to the success of the reflexivity process. Since justice is so fundamental, we will put particular emphasis on this topic and discuss the role of different types of justice in defining team interaction scripts. The most researched type is *distributive justice*, which refers to "the perceived fairness of resources received" (Cropanzano & Ambrose, 2001, p. 121). For example, the resource of being able to independently craft working time and space arrangements must be negotiated within a flexible team. To do so, the underlying principles of distributive justice should be discussed. Three principles—equity, equality, and need—can justify the provision of time-spatial flexibility (Thatcher & Bagger, 2011) or, in other words, of the resource of autonomy. The *equity principle* is relevant when employees are allowed to work flexibly based on their prior performance. In their meta-analysis, Gajendran and Harrison (2007) have discussed that supervisors are more likely to grant flexibility to employees who are already performing well. Furthermore, one could also argue that all employees should be granted the same degree of flexibility following the *equality principle*, which applies when time-spatial flexibility is introduced on a large scale in the organization. Finally, the *need principle* could be used to argue that employees who spend more time commuting to the office should be given more opportunities to work flexibly. Although different arguments can be used, what is most important is that the underlying rationale for the decision is clear to team members. Indeed, research shows that the outcome of the reflexivity process is more favorable when employees perceive the procedures used as being fair (Lee & Sukoco, 2011). This perspective is defined as *procedural justice* and refers to the process of decision-making rather than the outcome of the decisions (Lerner et al., 1988). When the procedures regarding how resources are negotiated are perceived as fair, team collaboration is improved (Açikgöz, 2017). Thus, the process of negotiating team interaction scripts (i.e., procedural justice) is as important as the scripts themselves (i.e., distributive justice).

Boundary Conditions for the Reflexivity Process

To effectively define and implement team interaction scripts that will positively shape availability norms, several boundary conditions with the opportunity to foster or hamper the effectiveness of the intervention must be considered. In the following, we focus on the most important ones.

The Role of Leadership

Leaders play a central role in shaping the work environment of their followers as they also affect their team members' psychological well-being (Rousseau et al., 2008). Montano and colleagues (2017) conclude that leadership is "an important occupational health factor in its own right" (p. 344). Effective leadership should support autonomy by taking into account the basic psychological needs of employees (Hocine & Zhang, 2014). We assume that the success of the proposed team-based interaction script intervention is highly dependent on leadership style and leaders' attribution of usefulness to the intervention (Nielsen et al., 2017). Leaders act as role models of healthy work behavior (Kranabetter & Niessen, 2017) and shape team members' perceptions of how to deal with the autonomy paradox.

Leadership is relevant not only during the reflexivity process but also after as the leader has the power to sanction behavior that deviates from the interaction scripts negotiated. Scripts are considered strong when both behavioral expectations and the sequence of events are specified but regarded as weak when only expectations are specified (Gioia & Poole, 1984). Depending on how the leader enacts the implementation of the interaction scripts and complies with them, they can support the intervention with external legitimacy (Lee et al., 2020). At the initial stage of the process, particularly, the perceived legitimacy of the collectively defined interaction scripts affects how individual team members decide "how to enact the scripts and whether or not to engage in what they perceived to be socially risky behaviors" (Lee et al., 2020, p. 118). However, after some time, team members' behavior might increasingly deviate from the interaction scripts; thus, leaders should reclaim enactment or initiate a new reflexivity process. Consequently, the leader is an initiator providing the opportunity to iteratively and continuously reflect on the interaction scripts and address any discrepancies observed between the actual state and the defined target state.

The team reflexivity process is a continuous cycle enabling flexible teams to monitor and optimize their team coordination processes. Over time, the contextual situation of a flexible team may change (e.g., the intensity and prevalence of time-spatial job crafting, the intensity of digitalization, or habituation effects), and a reformulation of team interaction scripts may become necessary. We consider it the leader's responsibility to be aware of the need to reconsider the team interaction scripts and initiate a new reflexivity process. Finally, supporting employees' recovery and providing guidance about how to deal with the threat of the prevailing autonomy paradox can be regarded as a contemporary challenge for leaders.

The Role of an External Facilitator in the Reflexivity Process

Following Lee et al. (2020), we argue in favor of the inclusion of an external facilitator to support the development of interaction scripts, for three reasons. First, it enhances the separation of the intervention space from everyday work. Second, the facilitator's neutral status encourages unity and participation among all team members. Third, the facilitator provides immediate feedback and encouragement. We think that support from an external facilitator during the team reflexivity process is even more important when the leader is less participative or very authoritative because it enables team members to openly address underlying issues.

We also consider the role of an external facilitator particularly essential when there is a strong collective norm of constant availability. To question the prevailing norms, an outside perspective introducing insights about the practices of other organizations is particularly valuable and helps to derive team interaction scripts that enable more autonomous time-spatial job crafting.

Further, external facilitators are particularly valuable when it comes to justice issues since they bring in a neutral and more unbiased perspective without participating in workplace politics. When justice differentiation is high within the team, sharing different perspectives and creating mutual understanding might be challenging. Therefore, taking a neutral perspective is crucial for the success of this reflexivity process, which should not be carried out by any involved party.

The Role of Membership in Multiple Teams

Today, knowledge workers are frequently members of more than one team simultaneously. Estimations of the prevalence of this so-called "multi-team membership" among knowledge workers range between 65% and 95% (Margolis, 2019). When defining team interaction scripts, it is crucial to take into account employees' membership in other teams (and the relevant associated requirements regarding time-spatial job crafting) because multi-team environments pose several challenges at the individual and team levels (O'Leary et al., 2011). The underlying challenge for members with multi-team memberships is to allocate their attention, time, and information across several teams, which requires switching context and carries a risk of temporal misalignment. When managed poorly or differently, team demands conflict with one another, potentially leading to individual stress, impaired work-life balance, increased workload, and competing team identities (O'Leary et al., 2011). We assume that these challenges are even more pronounced in the flexible work context because direct, personal encounters between peers result less frequently. Furthermore, compared with the co-located work setting, leaders might be less aware of their team members' emotional exhaustion and need to reduce their constant connectivity.

The literature suggests that the number of team memberships matters and a moderate number of teams relates to higher productivity and learning at the individual and team levels, whereas the concurrent membership in either very few or very many project teams presents obstacles to both productivity and learning (O'Leary et al., 2011). A recent study (Berger et al., 2022) finds that only in organizations with higher multi-team membership does individual multi-team membership positively relate to emotional exhaustion. Thus, we conclude that demands from other teams need to be addressed openly, even more so in teams whose members have membership in many other teams. Generally, we suggest a separate team reflexivity process in each of these teams, requiring the participation of team members spanning multiple teams and bringing in other teams' demands during each process. Defining, for each team member, a focal team that receives priority over other teams might be useful when formalizing the interaction scripts. Finally, when implementing the scripts, each member should signal their availabilities and proactively communicate their needs across teams (e.g., stating their working times in e-mail signatures, indicating unavailability via out-of-office messages, etc.).

DISCUSSION

The COVID-19 pandemic has changed the design of work insofar as the focus is now on *how* time-spatial flexibility can be optimally implemented rather than whether it should be. Even before the COVID-19 crisis and the emergence of discussions about the role of face-to-face conversations at the watercooler and "Zoom fatigue" resulting from high volumes of digital communication, researchers have emphasized the social context of time-spatial flexibility, in which employees are embedded and which influences them (Grant & Parker, 2009). As flexible working is a key characteristic of the so-called "new normal" way of working, this conceptual paper targets the future working scenario for many organizations.

Existing research shows that time-spatial flexibility seems to be a double-edged sword, producing inconclusive findings. Research has uncovered positive effects, such as increased flexibility and autonomy (Kossek et al., 2006); as well as negative ones, such as stress or boundary blurring (Delanoeije et al., 2019), which impair recovery from work. However, traditional telework research has mainly examined the differences between users and non-users (Allen et al., 2015; Delanoeije & Verbruggen, 2020) and has rarely addressed contextual circumstances such as the team context.

Our theoretical paper extends the line of research focusing on time-spatial flexibility by providing insights on team processes taking place and interacting at the individual and team levels. It explains how certain outcomes of past flexibility studies—such as a lack of detachment from work outside working hours—emerge as a result of the interplay between time-spatial job crafting (Wessels et al., 2019) and the team context in which these proactive behaviors take place. Providing a holistic perspective on this interplay, we extend flexibility research by shedding light on team processes that lead to the development of certain availability norms, which are related to mutual expectations, justice perceptions, and opportunities for recovery. We view the reduction of availability uncertainty and the establishment of times of acceptable unavailability as one of the major challenges in fostering recovery and mental health in today's work environment.

Theoretical Implications

With this paper, we bring time-spatial job crafting to the team level by looking at the use of time-spatial job crafting more collectively and holistically. We conclude that individuals might gain autonomy through the opportunity to craft their working time and place arrangements, but these individual strategies pose challenges to team coordination, availability expectations, and the predictability of availability, which in turn affects individuals' recovery from work. Central to this potential tension between the individual and team levels are justice perceptions resulting from comparisons between team members. Shedding light on these team-level consequences of individual time-spatial job crafting, we also approach the implications on the team level as an issue of work design (Morgeson et al., 2013), which can be purposefully shaped via the definition of team interaction scripts and by changing the underlying shared mental models.

Theoretically, our two levels (i.e., individual and team) align with Grant and Parker's (2009) two central perspectives on work design (i.e., the relational and proactive perspectives), which both need to be taken into account. At the individual level, we assume a proactive perspective, which refers to employees taking initiative to shape their job design and work contexts (Grant & Parker, 2009), and we connect it to self-determination theory (Deci et al., 2017). With regard to flexibility, we focus on time-spatial job crafting (Wessels et al., 2019), that is, individuals optimizing their time and spatial needs by consciously deciding on their working time and place on a daily basis. To experience high levels of self-determination, the need for autonomy, competence, and relatedness should be satisfied. However, we argue that high time-spatial flexibility comes with challenges, for three reasons. First, need satisfaction is dependent on team members. Thus, employees in flexible teams may experience the frustration of the other two basic needs, competence and relatedness (Deci et al., 2017; Van Yperen et al., 2014), because the satisfaction of their individual needs depends on the behaviors of other team members. Second, according to the autonomy paradox, employees may feel pressured to be constantly available (Mazmanian et al., 2013), which may support the need for relatedness but also frustrates the need for autonomy. For instance, when a co-worker decides to write e-mails at 10:00 p.m., the recipients might feel that an immediate response is expected, and expectations of constant availability may thus be reinforced. Third (and relatedly), employees who have the option of time-spatial flexibility may be uncertain as to how intensively they should use it, which highlights the need to clarify what is expected from employees.

This struggle with uncertainties concerning others' expectations points to the social context of work and the "relational perspective" of work design (Grant & Parker, 2009) emphasizing the role of interpersonal relations and interdependencies at work. Hereby, we apply a justice lens (Colquitt & Zipay, 2015). When time-spatial job crafting within teams is unorganized, justice perceptions regarding the use of time-spatial flexibility may vary (Fogarty et al., 2011). Under high levels of uncertainty, justice issues become more salient to employees (Thau et al., 2009; Van den Bos & Lind, 2002) and potentially create tensions within teams. For example, some team members may take advantage of the lack of clarifications, whereas others might over-fulfill expectations by being constantly available. This phenomenon of varying perceptions of justice, which we call "justice differentiation," is a new perspective on the use of time-spatial flexibility in flexible teams.

We also advance team reflexivity research (Schippers et al., 2014; West, 1996). Previous research on the topic has mainly focused on the reflection phase while neglecting the need for adaptation (Konradt et al., 2016) for sustainable team functioning. Going beyond this, we shed light on adaptation strategies within the team process as they play a crucial role in behavioral change within teams (Konradt et al., 2016).

Practical Implications

With this paper, we address a real-world challenge that has a significant practical impact and has recently gained even greater relevance due to the increased prevalence of time-spatial job crafting possibilities brought about by COVID-19 restrictions and the related cultural change toward more flexible or hybrid working settings. By defining this guided team reflexivity process (Schippers et al., 2014; West, 1996) for flexible teams to dissolve the tension between individual rationales for applying time-spatial job crafting and collective consequences, we provide hands-on guidelines for organizations and leaders to design time-spatial flexibility at the team level that supports the alignment of team justice perceptions and fosters team members' recovery. Dealing with these issues is particularly important in current times as mental health problems are on the rise (Satici et al., 2020; Schmidt, et al., 2014; Schuller & Weiss, 2019).

The role of team leaders is central here. In making sure that coordination works smoothly in accordance with the individual use of time-spatial flexibility and related availabilities, a justice and health perspective is important to include. Although the goal is to keep the differentiation of justice perceptions low within the team, we particularly highlight the fact that this guided reflexivity process does not aim to restrict the autonomy provided by time-spatial flexibility but should rather enable flexible team members (and their leaders) to collectively define how they want to work together. It is not about defining strict behavioral rules that each team member must adhere to but rather creating an understanding of the rationales behind individual job-crafting strategies and setting the scope and boundaries of time-spatial flexibility in the team. This endeavor also shifts some of the responsibility for recovery from the individual to the leader as a designer of effective and healthy team structures and norms that allow for recovery periods. In this regard, leaders should openly address their teams' availability norms, make them explicit, reflect on them, and actively help to shape them (where appropriate) to foster clear expectations and reduce availability uncertainty.

CONCLUSION

Past work has shown that boundary blurring is a central mechanism through which time-spatial flexibility produces negative side effects (Cousins & Robey, 2015; Delanoeije et al., 2019), creating stress (Delanoeije & Verbruggen, 2020), and ultimately threatening employees' mental health (Golden, 2012). Therefore, time-spatial flexibility appears to be a double-edged sword yielding inconclusive findings and both positive and negative outcomes (Delanoeije & Verbruggen, 2020). Looking only at the individual perspective is insufficient; the team or relational perspective must also be taken into account (Grant & Parker, 2009). When team members' behavioral patterns of time-spatial flexibility lead to high availability norms, individual autonomy is threatened. Moreover, individual time-spatial job crafting challenges availability-related justice perceptions and team coordination. Offering an approach to dissolving the inherent tension between individuals' time-spatial job crafting and team coordination demands, we propose a guided reflexivity process consisting of three phases. The core objective is to develop shared mental models, which can be initiated via team-based interaction scripts of availability that define the scope and boundaries of individual time-spatial flexibility. Thus, this alignment process reduces the uncertainty of availability and justice differentiation within flexible teams and supports employees' recovery from work, ultimately managing the threat of the autonomy paradox and fostering better mental health.

AUTHOR NOTE

Both authors contributed equally to the writing of this chapter. The authors acknowledge the contribution of Stephan A. Boehm and Anneloes Raes for insightful discussions with regard to our topic.

REFERENCES

Açikgöz, A. (2017). The mediating role of team collaboration between procedural justice climate and new product development performance. *International Journal of Innovation Management, 21*(4), Article 1750039. https://doi .org/10.1142/S1363919617500396

Allen, T. D., Golden, T. D., & Shockley, K. M. (2015). How effective is telecommuting? Assessing the status of our scientific findings. *Psychological Science in the Public Interest, 16*(2), 40–68. https://doi.org/10.1177/1529100615593273

Ashforth, B. E., & Fried, Y. (1988). The mindlessness of organizational behaviors. *Human Relations, 41*(4), 305–329. https://doi.org/10.1177/001872678804100403

Bal, P. M., & Dorenbosch, L. (2015). Age-related differences in the relations between individualised HRM and organisational performance: A large-scale employer survey. *Human Resource Management, 25*(1), 41–61. https://doi.org/10.1111/1748-8583.12058

Barley, S. R., Meyerson, D. E., & Grodal, S. (2011). E-Mail as a source and symbol of stress. *Organization Science, 22*(4), 887–906. https://doi.org/10.1287/orsc.1100.0573

Bartel, C. A., Wrzesniewski, A., & Wiesenfeld, B. M. (2012). Knowing where you stand: Physical isolation, perceived respect, and organizational identification among virtual employees. *Organization Science, 23*(3), 743–757. https://doi .org/10.1287/orsc.1110.0661

Berger, S., Van de Brake, H. J., & Bruch, H. (2022). Resource leverage, resource depletion: A multilevel perspective on multiple team membership. *Journal of Applied Psychology, 107*(2), 298–309. https://doi.org/10.1037/apl0000889

Bettenhausen, K. L., & Murnighan, J. K. (1985). The emergence of norms in competitive decision-making groups. *Administrative Science Quarterly, 30*(3), 350–372. https://doi.org/10.2307/2392667

Bettenhausen, K. L., & Murnighan, J. K. (1991). The development of an intragroup norm and the effects of interpersonal and structural challenges. *Administrative Science Quarterly, 36*(1), 20–35. https://doi.org/10.2307/2393428

Cohen-Charash, Y., & Spector, P. E. (2001). The role of justice in organizations: A meta-analysis. *Organizational Behavior and Human Decision Processes, 86*(2), 278–321. https://doi.org/10.1006/obhd.2001.2958

Colquitt, J. A. (2001). On the dimensionality of organizational justice: A construct validation of a measure. *Journal of Applied Psychology, 86*(3), 386–400. https://doi.org/10.1037/0021-9010.86.3.386

Colquitt, J. A., & Zipay, K. P. (2015). Justice, fairness and employee reactions. *Annual Review of Organizational Psychology & Organizational Behavior, 2*, 75–99. https://doi.org/10.1146/annurev-orgpsych-032414-111457

Cousins, K., & Robey, D. (2015). Managing work-life boundaries with mobile technologies: An interpretive study of mobile work practices. *Information Technology & People, 28*(1), 34–71. https://doi.org/10.1108/ITP-08-2013-0155

Cropanzano, R., & Ambrose, M. L. (2001). Procedural and distributive justice are more similar than you think: A monistic perspective and a research agenda. In J. Greenberg, & R. Cropanzano (Eds.), *Advances in organizational justice* (pp. 119–151). Stanford University Press.

Deci, E. L., Olafsen, A. H., & Ryan, R. M. (2017). Self-determination theory in work organizations: The state of a science. *Annual Review of Organizational Psychology and Organizational Behavior, 4*, 19–43. https://doi.org/10.1146/annurev-orgpsych-032516-113108

Deci, E. L., & Ryan, R. M. (1985). The general causality orientations scale: Self-determination in personality. *Journal of Research in Personality, 19*(2), 109–134. https://doi.org/10.1016/0092-6566(85)90023-6

Delanoeije, J., & Verbruggen, M. (2020). Between-person and within-person effects of telework: A quasi-field experiment. *European Journal of Work and Organizational Psychology, 29*(6), 795–808. https://doi.org/10.1080/135943 2X.2020.1774557

Delanoeije, J., Verbruggen, M., & Germeys, L. (2019). Boundary role transitions: A day-to-day approach to explain the effects of home-based telework on work-to-home conflict and home-to-work conflict. *Human Relations, 72*(12), 1843–1868. https://doi.org/10.1177/0018726718823071

Derks, D., & Bakker, A. B. (2014). Smartphone use, work-home interference, and burnout: A diary study on the role of recovery. *Applied Psychology, 63*(3), 411–440. https://doi.org/10.1111/j.1464-0597.2012.00530.x

Derks, D., Van Mierlo, H., & Schmitz, E. B. (2014). A diary study on work-related smartphone use, psychological detachment and exhaustion: Examining the role of the perceived segmentation norm. *Journal of Occupational Health Psychology, 19*(1), 74–84. https://doi.org/10.1037/a0035076

DeShon, R. P., Kozlowski, S. W. J., Schmidt, A. M., Milner, K. R., & Wiechmann, D. (2004). A multiple-goal, multilevel model of feedback effects on the regulation of individual and team performance. *Journal of Applied Psychology, 89*(6), 1035–1056. https://doi.org/10.1037/0021-9010.89.6.1035

Dettmers, J. (2017). How extended work availability affects well-being: The mediating roles of psychological detachment and work-family-conflict. *Work & Stress, 31*(1), 24–41, https://doi.org/10.1080/02678373.2017.1298164

Dettmers, J., Bamberg, E., & Seffzek, K. (2016). Characteristics of extended availability for work: The role of demands and resources. *International Journal of Stress Management, 23*(3), 276–297. https://doi.org/10.1037/str0000014

Dutton, J. E., & Ragins, B. R. (2007). Moving forward: Positive relationships at work as a research frontier. In J. E. Dutton & B. R. Ragins (Eds.), *Exploring positive relationships at work: Building a theoretical and research foundation* (pp. 387–400). Lawrence Erlbaum Associates.

Dutton, J. E., & Ragins, B. R. (Eds.). (2017). *Exploring positive relationships at work: Building a theoretical and research foundation.* Psychology Press.

Fiol, C. M., & O'Connor, E. J. (2005). Identification in face-to-face, hybrid, and pure virtual teams: Untangling the contradictions. *Organization Science, 16*(1), 19–32. https://doi.org/10.1287/orsc.1040.0101

Fisher, D. M., Bell, S. T., Dierdorff, E. C., & Belohlav, J. A. (2012). Facet personality and surface-level diversity as team mental model antecedents: Implications for implicit coordination. *Journal of Applied Psychology, 97*(4), 825–841. https://doi.org/10.1037/a0027851

Fogarty, H., Scott, P., & Williams, S. (2011). The half-empty office: Dilemmas in managing locational flexibility. *New Technology, Work and Employment, 26*(3), 183–195. https://doi.org/10.1111/j.1468-005X.2011.00268.x

Gajendran, R. S., & Harrison, D. A. (2007). The good, the bad, and the unknown about telecommuting: Meta-analysis of psychological mediators and individual consequences. *Journal of Applied Psychology, 92*(6), 1524–1541. https://doi.org/10.1037/0021-9010.92.6.1524

Geurts, S. A. E., & Sonnentag, S. (2006). Recovery as an explanatory mechanism in the relation between acute stress reactions and chronic health impairment. *Scandinavian Journal of Work, Environment & Health, 32*(6), 482–492. https://doi.org/10.5271/sjweh.1053

Gioia, D. A., & Poole, P. P. (1984). Scripts in organizational behavior. *The Academy of Management Review, 9*(3), 449–459. https://doi.org/10.2307/258285

Golden, T. D. (2012). Altering the effects of work and family conflict on exhaustion: Telework during traditional and nontraditional work hours. *Journal of Business and Psychology, 27*(3), 255–269. https://doi.org/10.1007/s10869-011-9247-0

Grant, A. M., & Parker, S. K. (2009). Redesigning work design theories: The rise of relational and proactive perspectives. *The Academy of Management Annals, 3*(1), 317–375. https://doi.org/10.5465/19416520903047327

Greenberg, J. (1987). A taxonomy of organizational justice theories. *Academy of Management Review, 12*(1), 9–22. https://doi.org/10.5465/amr.1987.4306437

Greenberg, J. (1993). The social side of fairness: Interpersonal and informational classes of organizational justice. In R. Cropanzano (Ed.), *Justice in the workplace: Approaching fairness in human resources management* (pp. 79–103). Lawrence Erlbaum Associates.

Hakonen, M., & Lipponen, J. (2008). Procedural justice and identification with virtual teams: The moderating role of face-to-face meetings and geographical dispersion. *Social Justice Research*, 21, 164–178. https://doi.org/10.1007/s11211-008-0070-3

Hillebrandt, A., & Barclay, L. J. (2017). Observing others' anger and guilt can make you feel unfairly treated: The interpersonal effects of emotions on justice-related reactions. *Social Justice Research, 30*(3), 238–269. https://doi.org/10.1007/s11211-017-0290-5

Hinsz, V. B., Tindale, R. S., & Vollrath, D. A. (1997). The emerging conceptualization of groups as information processors. *Psychological Bulletin, 121*(1), 43–64. https://doi.org/10.1037/0033-2909.121.1.43

Hocine, Z., & Zhang, J. (2014). Autonomy supportive leadership: A new framework for understanding effective leadership through self-determination theory. *International Journal of Information Systems and Change Management, 7*(2), 135–149. https://doi.org/10.1504/IJISCM.2014.069397

Hornung, S., Rousseau, D. M., Glaser, J., Angerer, P., & Weigl, M. (2010). Beyond top-down and bottom-up work redesign: Customizing job content through idiosyncratic deals. *Journal of Organizational Behavior, 31*(2/3), 187–215. https://doi.org/10.1002/job.625

International Labour Organization. (2020, September 23). *ILO monitor: COVID-19 and the world of work.* https://www.ilo.org/wcmsp5/groups/public/@dgreports/@dcomm/documents/briefingnote/wcms_755910.pdf

Jones, D. A., & Skarlicki, D. P. (2013). How perceptions of fairness can change: A dynamic model of organizational justice. *Organizational Psychology Review, 3*(2) 138–160. https://doi.org/10.1177/2041386612461665

Konradt, U., Otte, K.-P., Schippers, M. C., & Steenfatt, C. (2016). Reflexivity in teams: A review and new perspectives. *The Journal of Psychology, 150*(2), 153–174. https://doi.org/10.1080/00223980.2015.1050977

Konradt, U., Schippers, M. C., Garbers, Y., & Steenfatt, C. (2015). Effects of guided reflexivity and team feedback on team performance improvement: The role of team regulatory processes and cognitive emergent states. *European Journal of Work and Organizational Psychology, 24*(5), 777–795. https://doi.org/10.1080/1359432X.2015.1005608

Kossek, E. E., Lautsch, B. A., & Eaton, S. (2006). Telecommuting, control, and boundary management: Correlates of policy use and practice, job control, and work–family effectiveness. *Journal of Vocational Behavior, 68*, 347–367. https://doi.org/10.1016/j.jvb.2005.07.002

Kranabetter, C., & Niessen, C. (2017). Managers as role models for health: Moderators of the relationship of transformational leadership with employee exhaustion and cynicism. *Journal of Occupational Health Psychology, 22*(4), 492–502. https://doi.org/10.1037/ocp0000044

Kroon, B., Freese, C., & Schalk, R. (2016). A strategic HRM perspective on i-deals. In M. Bal & D. M. Rousseau (Eds.), *Idiosyncratic deals between employees and organizations* (pp. 73–91). Routledge.

Lee, L. T.-S., & Sukoco, B. M. (2011). Reflexivity, stress, and unlearning in the new product development team: The moderating effect of procedural justice. *R&D Management, 41*(1), 410–423. https://doi.org/10.1111/j.1467-9310.2011.00645.x

Lee, M. Y., Mazmanian, M., & Perlow, L. (2020). Fostering positive relational dynamics: The power of spaces and interaction scripts. *Academy of Management Journal, 63*(1), 96–123. https://doi.org/10.5465/amj.2016.0685

Lind, E. A., & Tyler, T. R. (1988). *The social psychology of procedural justice.* Springer.

Lind, E. A., & Van den Bos, K. (2002). When fairness works: Toward a general theory of uncertainty management. *Research in Organizational Behavior, 24,* 181–223. https://doi.org/10.1016/S0191-3085(02)24006-X

Lord, R. G., & Kernan, M. C. (1987). Scripts as determinants of purposeful behavior in organizations. *The Academy of Management Review, 12*(2), 265–277. https://doi.org/10.2307/258534

Margolis, J. (2020). Multiple team membership: An integrative review. *Small Group Research, 51*(1), 48–86. https://doi.org/10.1177/1046496419883702

Maynard, M. T., & Gilson, L. L. (2014). The role of shared mental model development in understanding virtual team effectiveness. *Group & Organization Management, 39*(1), 3–32. https://doi.org/10.1177/1059601113475361

Mazmanian, M. (2012). Avoiding the trap of constant connectivity: When congruent frames allow for heterogeneous practices. *Academy of Management Journal, 56*(5), 1225–1250. https://doi.org/10.5465/amj.2010.0787

Mazmanian, M., Orlikowski, W. J., & Yates, J. (2013). The autonomy paradox: The implications of mobile email devices for knowledge professionals. *Organization Science, 24*(5), 1337–1357. https://doi.org/10.1287/orsc.1120.0806

McGrath, J. E., & Beehr, T. A. (1990). Time and the stress process: Some temporal issues in the conceptualization and measurement of stress. *Stress Medicine, 6*(2), 93–104. https://doi.org/10.1002/smi.2460060205

McNall, L. A., Nicklin, J. M., & Masuda, A. D. (2010). A meta-analytic review of the consequences associated with work–family enrichment. *Journal of Business and Psychology, 25,* 381–396. https://doi.org/10.1007/s10869-009-9141-1

Montano, D., Reeske, A., Franke, F., & Hüffmeier, J. (2016). Leadership, followers' mental health and job performance in organizations: A comprehensive meta-analysis from an occupational health perspective. *Journal of Organizational Behavior, 38,* 327–350.

Morgeson, F. P., Garza, A. S., & Campion, M. A. (2013). *Work design.* In N. W. Schmitt, S. Highhouse, & I. B. Weiner (Eds.), *Handbook of psychology: Industrial and organizational psychology* (2nd ed., Vol. 12, pp. 525–559). Wiley.

Nielsen, K., Randall, R., & Christensen, K. B. (2017). Do different training conditions facilitate team implementation? A quasi-experimental mixed methods study. *Journal of Mixed Methods Research, 11*(2), 223–247. https://doi.org/10.1177/1558689815589050

Nishii, L. W., & Mayer, D. M. (2009). Do inclusive leaders help to reduce turnover in diverse groups? The moderating role of leader–member exchange in the diversity to turnover relationship. *Journal of Applied Psychology, 94*(6), 1412–1426. https://doi.org/10.1037/a0017190

O'Leary, M. B., Mortensen, M., & Woolley, A. W. (2011). Multiple team membership: A theoretical model of its effects on productivity and learning for individuals and teams. *Academy of Management Review, 36*(3), 461–478. https://doi.org/10.5465/amr.2009.0275

Etymology Dictionary. (n.d.). Availability. In *Online Etymology Dictionary*. Retrieved May 5, 2021, from https://www.etymonline.com/word/availability?ref=etymonline_crossreference

Park, Y. A., Liu, Y., & Headrick, L. (2020). When work is wanted after hours: Testing weekly stress of information communication technology demands using boundary theory. *Journal of Organizational Behavior, 41*(6), 518–534. https://doi.org/https://doi.org/10.1002/job.2461

Parker, S. K., Atkins, P. W. B., & Axtell, C. M. (2008). Building better workplaces through individual perspective taking: A fresh look at a fundamental human process. In G. P. Hodgkinson, & J. K. Ford (Eds.), *International review of industrial and organizational psychology* (Vol. 23, pp. 149–196). Wiley.

Rockmann, K. W., & Pratt, M. G. (2015). Contagious offsite work and the lonely office: The unintended consequences of distributed work. *Academy of Management Discoveries, 1*(2), 150–164. https://doi.org/10.5465/amd.2014.0016

Rousseau, D. M. (2005). *I-deals: Idiosyncratic deals employees bargain for themselves*. M. E. Sharpe.

Rousseau, V., Aubé, C., Chiocchio, F., Boudrias, J.-S., & Morin, E. M. (2008). Social interactions at work and psychological health: The role of leader-member exchange and work group integration. *Journal of Applied Social Psychology, 38*(7), 1755–1777. https://doi.org/10.1111/j.1559-1816.2008.00368.x

Rousseau, D. M., Ho, V. T., & Greenberg, J. (2006). I-deals: Idiosyncratic terms in employment relationships. *Academy of Management Review, 31*(4), 977–994. https://doi.org/10.5465/amr.2006.22527470

Satici, B., Saricali, M., Satici, S. A., & Griffiths, M. D. (2020). Intolerance of uncertainty and mental wellbeing: Serial mediation by rumination and fear of COVID-19. *International Journal of Mental Health and Addiction,* 1–12. Advance online publication. https://doi.org/10.1007/s11469-020-00305-0

Schelling, T. C. (1978). *Micromotives and macrobehavior*. W. W. Norton.

Schippers, M. C., Den Hartog, D. N., Koopman, P. L., & Wienk, J. A. (2003). Diversity and team outcomes: The moderating effects of outcome interdependence and group longevity and the mediating effect of reflexivity. *Journal of Organizational Behavior, 24*(6), 779–802. https://doi.org/10.1002/job.220

Schippers, M. C., Edmondson, A. C., & West, M. A. (2014). Team reflexivity as an antidote to team information-processing failures. *Small Group Research, 45*(6), 731–769. https://doi.org/10.1177/1046496414553473

Schippers, M. C., Homan, A. C., & Van Knippenberg, D. (2013). To reflect or not to reflect: Prior team performance as a boundary condition of the effects of reflexivity on learning and final team performance. *Journal of Organizational Behavior, 34*(1), 6–23. https://doi.org/10.1002/job.1784

Schlachter, S., McDowall, A., Cropley, M., & Inceoglu, I. (2018). Voluntary work-related technology use during non-work time: A narrative synthesis of empirical research and research agenda. *International Journal of Management Reviews, 20*(4), 825–846. https://doi.org/10.1111/ijmr.12165

Schmidt, S., Roesler, U., Kusserow, T., & Rau, R. (2014). Uncertainty in the workplace: Examining role ambiguity and role conflict, and their link to depression—A meta-analysis. *European Journal of Work and Organizational Psychology, 23*(1), 91–106. https://doi.org/10.1080/1359432X.2012.711523

Schuller, K., & Weiss, F. (2019). The rise of mental health problems, inequality and the role of job strain in Germany. *Mental Health & Prevention*, 16, Article 200175. https://doi.org/10.1016/j.mhp.2019.200175

Sonnentag, S. (2003). Recovery, work engagement, and proactive behavior: A new look at the interface between nonwork and work. *Journal of Applied Psychology*, 88(3), 518–528. https://doi.org/10.1037/0021-9010.88.3.518

Sonnentag, S., & Frese, M. (2003). Stress in organizations. In I. B. Weiner (Ed.), *Handbook of psychology* (pp. 560–590). Wiley.

Sonnentag, S., & Fritz, C. (2007). The recovery experience questionnaire: Development and validation of a measure for assessing recuperation and unwinding from work. *Journal of Occupational Health Psychology*, 12(3), 204–221. https://doi.org/10.1037/1076-8998.12.3.204

Sonnentag, S., & Fritz, C. (2015). Recovery from job stress: The stressor-detachment model as an integrative framework. *Journal of Organizational Behavior*, 36(S1), S72–S103. https://doi.org/10.1002/job.1924

Thatcher, S. M. B., & Bagger, J. (2011). Working in pajamas: Telecommuting, unfairness sources, and unfairness perceptions. *Negotiation and Conflict Management Research*, 4(3), 248–276. https://doi.org/10.1111/j.1750-4716.2011.00082.x

Thau, S., Bennett, R. J., Mitchell, M. S., & Marrs, M. B. (2009). How management style moderates the relationship between abusive supervision and workplace deviance: An uncertainty management theory perspective. *Organizational Behavior and Human Decision Processes*, 108(1), 79–92. https://doi.org/10.1016/j.obhdp.2008.06.003

Thomas, G. F., King, C. L., Baroni, B., Cook, L., Keitelman, M., Miller, S., & Wardle, A. (2006). Reconceptualizing e-mail overload. *Journal of Business and Technical Communication*, 20(3), 252–287. https://doi.org/10.1177/1050651906287253

Van den Bos, K., & Lind, E. A. (2002). Uncertainty management by means of fairness judgments. In M. P. Zanna (Ed.), *Advances in experimental social psychology* (Vol. 34, pp. 1–60). Academic Press. https://doi.org/10.1016/S0065-2601(02)80003-X

Van Yperen, N. W., Rietzschel, E. F., & De Jonge, K. M. M. (2014). Blended working: For whom it may (not) work. *PLoS ONE* 9(7), Article e102921. https://doi.org/10.1371/journal.pone.0102921

Waerzner, A., Hartner-Tiefenthaler, M., & Koeszegi, S. T. (2017). Working anywhere and working anyhow? In Y. Blount & M. Gloet (Eds.), *Anywhere working and the new era of telecommuting* (pp. 90–112). IGI Global.

Wessels, C., Schippers, M. C., Stegmann, S., Bakker, A. B., Van Baalen, P. J., & Proper, K. I. (2019). Fostering flexibility in the new world of work: A model of time-spatial job crafting. *Frontiers in Psychology*, 10. https://doi.org/10.3389/fpsyg.2019.00505

West, M. A. (1996). Reflexivity and work group effectiveness: A conceptual integration. In M. A. West (Ed.), *The handbook of work group psychology* (pp. 555–579). Wiley.

West, M. A. (2000). Reflexivity, revolution and innovation in work teams. In M. Beyerlein, D. Johnson, & S. Beyerlein (Eds.), *Product development teams* (pp. 1–29). Emerald Group.

Wittenbaum, G. M., Vaughan, S. I., & Strasser, G. (2002). Coordination in task-performing groups. In R. S. Tindale, L. Heath, J. Edwards, E. J. Posavac, F. B. Bryant, Y. Suarez-Balcazar, E. Henderson-King, & J. Myers (Eds.), *Theory and research on small groups* (pp. 177–204). Springer. https://doi.org/10.1007/0-306-47144-2_9

Wrzesniewski, A., & Dutton, J. E. (2001). Crafting a job: Revisioning employees as active crafters of their work. *Academy of Management Review, 26,* 179–201. https://doi.org/10.2307/259118

CHAPTER 8

SERVANT LEADERSHIP AND IDIOSYNCRATIC DEALS

Influence on Individual and Team Performance

Chenwei Liao
Michigan State University

ABSTRACT

Idiosyncratic deals, or i-deals, are individualized work arrangements employees negotiate with their managers that are different from those of their coworkers. As a type of nonstandard human resource (HR) practice, i-deals represent a critical supplement to standardized HR practices in the workplace. In the current study, I simultaneously investigate antecedents and effects of i-deals at the individual and team levels. To this end, I draw on social cognitive theory (Bandura, 1986, 2001) to examine the relationship between servant leadership, i-deals, and subsequent individual and team efficacy and effectiveness. Two-wave, two-source, survey data collected from 189 employees and their managers working in 45 teams reveal multi-level motivation pathways for individuals and teams. Specifically, results show that servant leaders enhance employee self-efficacy and task performance by providing i-deals. At the team

Managing Team Centricity in Modern Organizations, pages 225–254

level, servant leaders promote team efficacy by allowing a high level of i-deals within teams, which in turn enhances team performance. This research enhances the theory building of servant leadership and i-deals, contributing to the broader integration of leadership and human resource management (HRM) in team research.

Idiosyncratic deals, or i-deals, represent a type of nonstandard human resource (HR) practice that facilitates the customization of work arrangements for employees (Liao et al., 2016; Rousseau, 2005). Specifically, i-deals are defined as personalized work arrangements (e.g., individualized work schedules, job tasks, and career development opportunities) negotiated between employees and managers that meet employees' personal needs while benefiting the employer (Liao et al., 2016; Rosen et al., 2013; Rousseau, 2005). Supplementing standardized HR policies, i-deals, as a nonstandard HR practice, allow employees to have work arrangements that are different from their coworkers (Liao et al., 2017). The emergence of i-deals in the contemporary workforce is not a coincidence. Rather, considering employees' needs in the current labor market has become increasingly pivotal because the increased competition for talents (Michaels et al., 2001), the reduction in collective bargaining (Farber & Western, 2000), and the greater initiative among employees to negotiate preferred work arrangements (Belkin, 2007; Freeman & Rogers, 1999) all call for managers' greater attention to employees' needs and uniqueness. Therefore, changes in the global work environment have made i-deals a useful and timely supplement to traditional standardized HR practices (Rousseau, 2005).

Despite the valuable insights on the nomological network of i-deals in the extant literature, there are two major limitations. First, while the critical role of managers in the i-deal negotiation process has been stressed in the definition, what is conspicuously lacking is research on how manager leadership style can influence the creation of i-deals (Liao et al., 2016). We are limited in our understanding of how leadership styles may promote or prohibit the use of i-deals in the workplace. Second, although it is explicitly defined that i-deals benefit both the recipients and the employer, existing research has predominantly focused on demonstrating the positive impact of i-deals on individual recipients, with no evidence supporting how individually negotiated deals may enhance unit effectiveness. To address these limitations, I simultaneously explore leader-related antecedents of i-deals and the effects of i-deals on individual and team performance.

First, I propose that servant leadership is uniquely related to the managers' enactment of i-deals. Servant leadership describes leaders who selflessly put others first, fulfill others' needs ahead of their own, and develop others to their fullest potential (Chiniara & Bentein, 2016; Eva et al., 2019; Greenleaf, 1970; Liden et al., 2008; Wu et al., 2021). The unique connection between servant leadership and i-deals lies in the alignment between the central tenet of servant leadership and the nature of i-deals. Specifically, the central tenet of servant leadership posits that servant leaders prioritize followers' needs and help them grow and succeed (Liden et al., 2015; Liden et al., 2008), while i-deals are individualized work arrangements created to meet the needs of employees (Liao et al., 2016). Therefore, it is reasonable to expect that servant leaders are willing to facilitate the creation of i-deals to fulfill employees' personal needs, develop their skills, and help them better perform their jobs. That is, there is a positive relationship between servant leadership and follower i-deals. Further, because of their high level of behavioral ethics, servant leaders do not just serve a select few; instead, servant leadership is targeted at every member of a team (Graham, 1991; Liden et al., 2008; Schaubroeck et al., 2011). Accordingly, servant leaders are likely to consider i-deals for all of the followers. Therefore, I expect that servant leadership is associated with a higher level of overall i-deals within the team.

Second, drawing on social cognitive theory (Bandura, 1986, 2001), I submit that both the experience of successfully negotiating i-deals with managers and the content of i-deals will give rise to followers' high self-efficacy and effectiveness at work. Social cognitive theory posits that people are agentic and engage in self-reflection and self-regulation processes. It is through these processes that individuals develop self-efficacy, which refers to individuals' cognitive beliefs of how capable they are in executing work-related activities (Bandura, 1997). Based on social cognitive theory, self-reflection of a successful i-deal negotiation process may lead to employees' perceptions of self-control at work, which enhances their self-efficacy. In addition, specific arrangements created by i-deals, or the content of i-deals, contribute to a better fit between the job and one's needs and interests, which also helps to enhance self-efficacy. At the team level, the prevalence of i-deals within a team emerges as a team-level phenomenon that contributes to team members' shared cognition about their control over work and the supervisor support they have as a team. A high level of overall i-deals within a team may therefore enhance team potency, which refers to team members' common belief about their capacities to be effective at executing work collectively. Hence, integrating servant leadership theory with social cognitive theory, I expect that servant leaders enhance individual and team efficacy and performance by granting i-deals to followers and allowing a high level of overall i-deals within a team. The hypothesized model is presented in Figure 8.1.

This study makes three contributions to the literature on i-deals and servant leadership. First, the present study offers an integrated perspective on how servant leaders enact HR practices to enhance individual and team efficacy and performance at work. Specifically, it shows that servant leaders are likely to work with all the followers in the creation of i-deals, a form of nonstandard HR practices that customize work arrangements for employees,

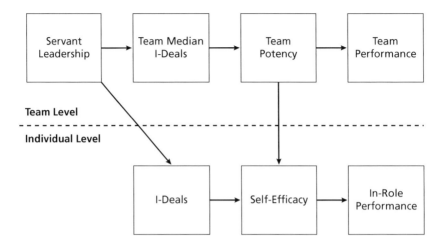

Figure 8.1 Theoretical model. *Note:* I-Deals = Idiosyncratic deals.

which result in the prevalence of i-deals within a team. As Liao and colleagues (2016) suggested, "As i-deal granters, leaders influence whether and the extent to which i-deals are permitted" (p. S16). Despite the important role of managers in the process of creating i-deals, little research has explored the effect of leadership styles. Thus, the current study advances our understanding of how leadership styles influence the creation of i-deals from a servant leadership perspective. Second, clearly stressed in the conceptualization of i-deals is a mutual benefit to both the i-deal recipients and the employer. However, empirical research has predominantly focused on demonstrating how i-deals benefit the recipients, with the impact of i-deals on the team and organization being largely unknown. Addressing this limitation, this study contributes to the i-deals literature by providing a direct test of the central tenet of i-deals that individually negotiated work arrangements can benefit a broader collective in the organization (Rousseau, 2005). Third, following Liden, Wayne, and colleagues' (2014) multi-level approach, the current research simultaneously investigates the influence of servant leadership and i-deals via social cognitive processes at the individual and team levels, adding to the multi-level theory building of servant leadership and i-deals.

THEORY AND HYPOTHESES

Servant Leadership and I-Deals

Distinct from traditional leadership theories that take a top-down approach, servant leadership puts a strong emphasis on setting aside leaders' self-interest for the betterment of all of their followers (Greenleaf, 1970). Such an unparalleled feature makes servant leadership theory well-suited for management in contemporary organizations (Liden, 2013). Indeed, extant research has consistently demonstrated a positive impact of servant leadership on individual and team effectiveness in the organization (Eva et al., 2019; Lee et al., 2020; Liden, Panaccio et al., 2014; van Dierendonck, 2011). Further, a recent meta-analysis supports the validity of servant leadership theory by showing that servant leadership can explain variations in important workplace outcomes above and beyond other leadership styles (e.g., transformational, ethical, and authentic leadership; Hoch et al., 2018).

There are seven dimensions of servant leadership (Liden et al., 2008). Not only do they possess *conceptual skills* to serve followers and teams, servant leaders also *provide followers with emotional support* and are *empowering*. They *put followers first* and *help them grow and succeed*. In addition, servant leaders maintain a high level of moral standards, *behave ethically*, and strive to *create value for the community* (Liden et al., 2008; Schaubroeck et al., 2011; Verdorfer et al., 2015). Leading by serving, servant leaders enhance performance for individuals and teams (e.g., Chen et al., 2015; Hu & Liden, 2011; Hunter et al., 2013; Liden, Wayne et al., 2014; Liden et al., 2015; Schaubroeck et al., 2011), by instilling in followers and teams a high level of confidence at work (Chen et al., 2015; Hu & Liden, 2011; Walumbwa et al., 2010). Despite these promising findings, we lack knowledge of the role servant leaders play in implementing human resource management (HRM) practices. Such an omission may limit our understanding of servant leadership functioning in the organization because managers' leadership styles are crucially associated with the way they enact HR practices (Kehoe & Han, 2020; Purcell & Hutchinson, 2007).

Specifically, while prior research has clearly shown promise of servant leadership's effectiveness, less is known regarding how servant leaders enact important HR practices to enhance individual and team performance. As agents of the HRM system, managers play an important role in carrying out HR duties that motivate employees (Kehoe & Han, 2020; Purcell & Hutchinson, 2007). The present study contends that servant leaders, because of their sensitivity to followers' needs and willingness to serve all the followers, actively implement HR practices to assist followers. Specifically, integrating servant leadership research with work on nonstandard HR practices, I submit that servant leaders work with followers to customize various aspects of employment arrangements and create i-deals for followers, enabling a better alignment between employees' work and their capabilities, interests, and needs.

I-deals are defined as personalized work agreements negotiated between employees and their managers regarding employment terms that benefit both employees and the employer (Rousseau et al., 2006). I-deals are considered as an effective nonstandard HR practice that enables employees to customize their employment arrangements (Liao et al., 2016). Distinct from dysfunctional person-specific employment practices (e.g., favoritism, unauthorized arrangements), i-deals represent a legitimate means for employees to meet their needs through personalizing their employment package (Rousseau, 2005; Rousseau et al., 2006). The content of i-deals may include flexible work schedules, customized task assignments, and special career development opportunities (Hornung et al., 2014; Rousseau, 2005; Rousseau et al., 2006). By enabling the customization of job elements for individual employees, i-deals lead to a better fit between job characteristics and employees' personal needs and strengths (Hornung, Rousseau et al., 2010; Hornung et al., 2014). Moreover, i-deals are also distinct from other individual-based employment practices (e.g., job crafting), due to the active role of managers in creating and maintaining the deals (Liao et al., 2016). For instance, job crafting describes the process by which employees make physical and cognitive changes to their jobs without obtaining the approval from their managers (Wrześniewski & Dutton, 2001). On the contrary, it is emphasized in the definition of i-deals that both managers and employees should be involved in the i-deal creation process to ensure mutual benefits for both employees and the employer (Rousseau, 2005; Rousseau et al., 2006). Because of the role of managers, a successful i-deal negotiation not only depends on managers' awareness of followers' needs and talents, but also revolves around managers' willingness to serve followers' needs and develop followers to their fullest potential. Therefore, managers' leadership styles are likely to influence i-deals (Liao et al., 2016). It is important to note that there is a clear conceptual distinction between servant leadership and i-deals. On the one hand, as a leadership style, servant leadership contains various behavioral dimensions that are characteristic to this unique pattern of leader behaviors, with a distinct feature to satisfy the needs of followers (Liden et al., 2008). On the other hand, i-deals are not behaviors per se; they are customized work arrangements that can be enacted to fulfill the needs of employees. Thus, i-deals are one of the means through which leaders serve their followers.

There are two reasons that servant leadership is positively associated with followers' i-deals. First, servant leaders are motivated and have the capacity to customize proper work arrangements for followers. Specifically, servant leaders are attentive to followers' needs, desires, goals, abilities, and potential, and assume the responsibility to bring out the best in their followers (Greenleaf, 1970; Liden et al., 2008). Thus, servant leaders' attention to followers allows them to better understand followers' perspectives in the process of i-deals negotiation. In addition, servant leaders possess task knowledge and problem-solving skills that help followers identify the best way to match job characteristics with their needs and interests (Liden et al., 2008;

van Dierendonck, 2011). Further, servant leaders put their followers first, help them grow and succeed, and are empowering (Liden, Wayne et al., 2014). Guided by such a serving mentality, servant leaders are likely to appreciate the initiative taken by followers in customizing their work arrangements. Therefore, servant leaders have a proclivity to attend to followers' requests for work schedules that meet their personal needs, work tasks that fit their interests and capabilities, and career development opportunities that help them grow professionally.

Second, servant leaders are determined to bring benefits to all stakeholders, including employees, the team, the organization, and the community (Liden et al., 2008). Thus, it is expected that servant leaders, while serving their followers, also consider the ramifications of any influence their behaviors have on other stakeholders. In the context of i-deals creation, when evaluating what flexible work schedules, special task assignments, or career development opportunities to offer, servant leaders take steps to prevent any customized arrangements from undermining the interests of the team and the organization. Such an emphasis on the welfare of all stakeholders in servant leadership helps to ensure that i-deals indeed bring mutual benefits to employees and the employer as articulated in the definition (Rousseau et al., 2006). In sum, servant leaders are willing to listen to employees' legitimate needs and help followers customize work arrangements (i.e., i-deals) that benefit both the organization and employees. Therefore, I expect servant leadership to be positively related to followers' successful negotiation of i-deals.

Hypothesis 1: *Servant leadership is positively related to employee i-deals.*

Not only do servant leaders care about the experience of individual members, they also ensure the effectiveness of overall team functioning (Hu & Liden, 2011). Empathetic and ethical (Liden et al., 2008), servant leaders strive to promote the welfare of others by supporting each of the individual members and minimizing potential relationship conflicts within a team (Chiniara & Bentein, 2018; Henderson et al., 2009; Schaubroeck et al., 2011). Research has shown that servant leaders create a servicing culture where helping others in the team is expected (Hunter et al., 2013; Liden, Wayne et al., 2014). In addition, servant leaders strive to develop high quality social exchange relationships with every team member (Chiniara & Bentein, 2018). Thus, it is unlikely that servant leaders, the role models to whom followers look up, would only serve some but not others, especially considering that it is the leaders who create the serving culture within teams.

The tendency of servant leaders to serve every team member has important implications on i-deals in teams. It is suggested that when i-deals are provided to only a few members, they will result in heterogeneity and may engender perceptions of favoritism and conflicts within teams (Rousseau et al., 2006). Therefore, servant leaders will strive to prohibit i-deals from being granted to only a few team members to protect the serving culture and team collaboration. Because servant leadership is focused on all followers, it is expected that servant leaders will not only recognize individual idiosyncrasy, but also maintain overall cohesiveness by assisting all followers when creating i-deals. Based on servant leaders' high proclivity to consider unique i-deals with each follower, it is argued that servant leadership is conducive to making i-deals prevalent in a team. Instead of serving a select few followers, servant leaders consider the needs of all, and bring out the potential in everyone in their team (Greenleaf, 1970). Leaders who are high on servant leadership tend to go the extra mile to create a flexible schedule for one follower, seek career development opportunity for another, and design customized tasks for a third follower. The result of such a practice is the prevalence of i-deals in the team. Therefore, in teams where leaders exhibit servant leadership, it is expected that there is a high level of overall i-deals.

Hypothesis 2: *Servant leadership is positively related to the overall level of i-deals within a team.*

I-Deals and Efficacy

Social cognitive theory (Bandura, 1986, 2001) posits that people are agentic, self-reflecting, and self-regulating organisms. In the process of interacting with the environment, individuals reflect upon their behaviors and form cognitions that guide their self-control processes (Bandura, 1997). The agency perspective of human beings explains why employees would initiate i-deal negotiation processes. Yet, depending on whether an i-deal negotiation is successful, employees' self-reflection upon their i-deal negotiation may lead to distinct cognitions. Central to social cognitive theory is the concept of self-efficacy. Specifically, self-efficacy refers to individuals' cognitive beliefs in their competence in executing work activities (Bandura, 1997). It is expected that successful negotiation of i-deals enhances one's self-efficacy, while failure in obtaining i-deals decreases self-efficacy.

There are three explanations for why i-deals are related to employee self-efficacy. First, the experience of successful initiation and negotiation of i-deals provides employees with a sense of control over their work. Having a sense of control at work enhances individuals' beliefs in their capabilities of completing tasks (Wood & Bandura, 1989). Second, granting i-deals to followers is a way to show leader support to followers. When employees feel they can negotiate with their managers and obtain their approval at work, they become more confident. Indeed, research has suggested that leader support facilitates the development of follower self-efficacy in the workplace (Wu & Parker, 2014). Third, specific content customized in i-deals is conducive to the enhancement of individual self-efficacy. For example, being able to work on personalized tasks that match individual abilities, skills, and interests raises one's confidence in accomplishing their work (Gist & Mitchell, 1992). Also, a flexible work schedule reduces tension and stress one might experience at work (Grzywacz et al., 2008), and thus should be positively related to self-efficacy. In addition, unique development opportunities designed to enhance employees' work skills directly contribute to their beliefs about their capacity to perform well. As illustrated in social cognitive theory, the acquirement of new skills and abilities contributes to one's self-efficacy (Bandura, 1986). Therefore, a positive relationship between i-deals and self-efficacy is expected.

Hypothesis 3: *I-deals are positively related to self-efficacy.*

Despite being negotiated between individual employees and their manager, the creation of i-deals takes place within a team context and may have implications on team functioning (Rousseau, 2005). Investigating multi-level implications of i-deals therefore becomes necessary for one to obtain a comprehensive understanding of how i-deals operate within an organization (Bal et al., 2012; Liao et al., 2017; Liao et al., 2016). Indeed, organizations are a multi-level system with employees nested within teams, which are nested within the organization (Rousseau, 1985). Scholars have called for multi-level consideration in organizational research to examine how phenomena occurring at the individual level may emerge and become meaningful team-level phenomena and how team-level characteristics may impact individual functioning within the organization (House et al., 1995; Klein et al., 1994; Rousseau, 1985). Specifically, employees working in the same team typically have task interdependence, interact socially within the team boundary, and share common goals (Kozlowski & Bell, 2003). Team boundaries, common goals, and interactions between members provide meanings for members such that team members see themselves and are seen by others outside the team as a social entity, forming the fundamentals for team-level phenomena to occur (Cohen & Bailey, 1997; Guzzo & Dickson, 1996; Sundstrom et al., 1990).

In a team where only one member can obtain i-deals, the overall level of i-deals within that team is low. In contrast, i-deals become prevalent when multiple team members are successful in creating customized work arrangements, resulting in a high overall level of i-deals. Taking from a multi-level perspective, the overall level of i-deals within a team emerges as a meaningful team-level phenomenon and serves as a basis upon which members develop shared perceptions about their teams. Specifically, the social interaction among employees working in the same team enables them to observe how other members are treated and allows them to share perceptions about the work environment (Klein et al., 2001). When viewed collectively at the team level, the overall level of i-deals within a team provides members with a sense of leader support and their overall level of control at work. In teams with a high level of overall i-deals, members observe that as a team they tend to have a high level of control. This information obtained through such vicarious experience (Bandura, 1986) is in turn positively factored in the members' shared cognitive process of forming their belief of how capable they are as a team. Indeed, according to social cognitive theory, when people work in teams and operate collectively, they tend to share beliefs about their capacities to be effective (Bandura, 1986), which refers to team potency (Gully et al., 2002). In addition, exchanging information regarding their experience of successfully obtaining i-deals may give rise to shared perceptions of leader support, which in turn enhance their team potency (Guzzo et al., 1993). On the contrary, a low level of overall i-deals within a team may result in perceptions that overall members have little voice in the work environment and that there is little leader support, which subsequently undermines their efficacy of how effective they can be collectively. In sum, I expect the overall level of i-deals in a team to shape members' shared belief of their collective capacity to exert efforts and to achieve desired team outcomes spanning tasks and situations.

Hypothesis 4: *The overall level of i-deals within a team is positively related to team potency.*

Team-shared confidence positively influences individual efficacy. Specifically, people in teams not only see themselves as individuals but also incorporate group membership to their definition of self (Tajfel & Turner, 1985). Social cognitive theory (Bandura, 1997) posits that motivation processes can be contagious. Members are more likely to believe that they are capable of performing their tasks when they belong to teams that are believed to be effective (Chen et al., 2007). Such a motivation contagion pathway enables the link between team potency and individual self-efficacy. Indeed, team potency shared by members may serve as an additional source of support that helps individuals become resilient and enhance individual confidence in challenging situations. Thus, team potency plays an important role in team members' individual competence beliefs, motivation, goals, and efforts (Lindsley et al., 1995). Therefore, it is expected that there is a cross-level direct relationship between team potency and self-efficacy.

Hypothesis 5: *Team potency is positively related to employee self-efficacy.*

Mediational Relationships Between Servant Leadership and Performance

The central role of self-efficacy to social cognitive theory (Bandura, 1986) is attributed to its positive influence on human functioning. "What people think, believe, and feel affects how they behave" (Bandura, 1986, p. 25). Compared with those who do not believe in their capabilities to complete the task, individuals with high self-efficacy tend to perform better. According to Bandura (1986), individuals are more comfortable to work on tasks where their efficacy is high, because people are more willing to put efforts toward tasks when they believe desired outcomes will be attained. Further, self-efficacy is closely related to effort expenditure and persistence such that individuals with a higher level of self-efficacy are more likely to exert their effort and be persistent. Empirical evidence has confirmed that self-efficacy can enhance employees' performance (Stajkovic & Luthans, 1998), even after controlling for their abilities and past performance (Bandura & Locke, 2003). Therefore, self-efficacy is positively related to individual performance.

Servant leadership has been found to be positively related to employee performance (Liden, Panaccio, et al., 2014; van Dierendonck, 2011). Walumbwa and colleagues (2010) showed that the positive effect of servant leadership on individual outcomes was mediated by self-efficacy. Similarly, Chiniara and Bentein (2016) demonstrated that servant leaders fulfill followers' needs for competence which in turn related positively to task performance. Considering such findings and Hypotheses 1 and 3 in the current article, servant leaders may enhance individual self-efficacy through a process of granting i-deals to followers, which in turn leads to high individual performance. Thus, i-deals and self-efficacy are expected to sequentially connect the linkage between servant leadership and individual performance.

Hypothesis 6: *I-deals and employee self-efficacy sequentially mediate the positive relationship between servant leadership and employee in-role performance.*

At the team level, when team potency is high, members share the belief that their team can be effective in achieving desired outcomes spanning tasks and situations. According to social cognitive theory (Bandura, 1986), a strong belief in collective capacity enhances team task performance. Indeed, this positive relationship between team potency and team performance was supported in empirical studies (Guzzo et al., 1993; Howell & Shea, 2006; Hu & Liden, 2011) and was confirmed in meta-analytic reviews (Gully et al., 2002; Stajkovic et al., 2009).

The effect of servant leadership on team-level outcomes is evident in past research (Ehrhart, 2004; Hu & Liden, 2011; Schaubroeck et al., 2011). In addition, team potency was found to mediate the relationship between servant leadership and team performance (Hu & Liden, 2011). Considering Hu and Liden's findings and Hypotheses 2 and 4 in the current study, servant leaders may promote team potency by being attentive to the needs of every follower and allowing a high level of i-deals within the team. Therefore, the relationship between servant leadership and team performance is expected to be sequentially mediated by the overall level of i-deals and team potency.

Hypothesis 7: *The overall level of i-deals within a team and team potency sequentially mediates the relationship between servant leadership and team performance.*

METHOD

Sample and Procedure

Data for the current investigation were obtained by surveying full-time employees and managers of a manufacturing company located in one of the four original special economic zones in the Southeast region of China. Based on the discussion with the director of HR, I extended invitations to participate in the research to employees and managers who worked in teams where managers had the authority to provide customized work arrangements (i.e., flexible work schedule, special task assignments, and career development opportunities). The survey process involved two waves. At Time 1, employees filled out a survey on-site during their paid working hours, providing responses to questions pertaining to servant leadership, i-deals, self-efficacy, team potency, and demographics. At Time 2, 3 weeks after employees completed their surveys, team managers evaluated employee in-role performance and team performance.

A total of 189 employees (response rate = 88%) and managers (response rate = 100%) from 45 teams completed the survey. Team sizes ranged from 3 to 10. All teams in the final sample met the minimum within-group response rate of 60% (Liden et al., 2006), with a range between 67% and 100%. With respect to gender, 30.2% of the employees were female, 65.6% were male, and 4.2% did not provide their answers. The average employee age, organizational tenure, job tenure, and tenure with the manager were 33.34 ($SD = 6.57$), 5.50 ($SD = 4.85$), 9.45 ($SD = 6.73$), and 3.20 ($SD = 3.01$) years, respectively. In terms of employee education, 15.9% had a degree of high school or below, 16.4% had an associate's degree, 59.8% had a bachelor's degree, 5.8% had a master's degree or above, and 3.2% did not respond.

Measures

All response scales were on a seven-point Likert scale ranging from 1 = *strongly disagree* to 7 = *strongly agree*. Higher scores indicate higher levels of that variable. Survey questions were first translated to Chinese and then back-translated to English using Brislin's (1980) recommended procedures.

Servant Leadership

Servant leadership was measured with the seven-item scale (SL-7) from Liden, Wayne et al. (2014; $\alpha = .92$). This measure captures all seven dimensions of servant leadership identified in Liden et al. (2008). The psychometric properties of the SL-7 scale are further demonstrated in Liden and colleagues (2015). A sample item is, "My manager gives me the freedom to handle difficult situations in the way that I feel is best."

I-Deals

I-deals were measured with the nine-item scale ($\alpha = .93$) from Hornung et al. (2014). It was made clear to the respondents that individuals can have employment arrangements that differ from their coworkers (e.g., different schedules, job duties, or development opportunities). The respondents were instructed to rate the extent to which they had successfully negotiated any of the listed personalized work arrangements with their manager by the time of the survey. The listed items include work arrangements regarding career, tasks, and flexibility. A sample item is, "job tasks that fit my personal interests."

Overall Level of I-Deals Within a Team

The overall level of i-deals within a team was obtained by taking the median of i-deals within each team. In the current study, median is selected to indicate the central tendency of i-deals in a team for two reasons.[1] First, i-deals at the team level have configural unit properties such that the operationalization at the team level does not require an agreement among individual i-deals (Kozlowski & Klein, 2000). That is, the overall tendency of i-deals at the team level can be directly aggregated based on measures at the individual level. Second, median is chosen over mean because mean is sensitive to outliers. Representing a team-level construct by taking its group mean can be problematic when agreement is not required (Liden et al., 2006). Kozlowski and Klein (2000) also recommended avoiding using group mean if agreement is not expected. Therefore, median is used to serve as a team-level indicator of the overall level of i-deals.

Self-Efficacy

Employees reported self-efficacy with the three-item measure ($\alpha = .82$) from Spreitzer (1995). The three items were originally from Jones (1986) and were adapted by Spreitzer (1995) to reflect one's current job rather than a new job. An example item is, "I am confident about my ability to do my job."

Team Potency

Team potency was reported by employees using the three-item scale ($\alpha = .88$) from Kirkman and colleagues (2004). A sample item is, "My team can get a lot done when it works hard."

In-Role Performance

Managers provided evaluations of their subordinates' in-role performance using five items ($\alpha = .92$) adapted from the scale in Tsui and colleagues (1997). A sample item is, "Compared with other employees, this employee's quality of work is much higher."

Team Performance

Team performance was evaluated by managers using the four-item measure ($\alpha = .81$) from Gibson and colleagues (2009). An example item is, "This team is consistently a high performing team."

Control Variables

Consistent with prior research examining leadership and employee performance (Hannah et al., 2016), the effect of employee dyad tenure with the manager (i.e., the amount of time employees had worked with their manager) on in-role performance was controlled for. Also, because variations in employees' exposure to the manager may affect their interaction and team performance (Cole et al., 2013; Keller, 2006), team members' average dyadic tenure was controlled for at the team level on team performance.

Data Aggregation and Level of Analysis

The measurement of servant leadership followed a direct consensus model (Chan, 1998), which requires the meaning of higher-level construct to be in the consensus among lower-level reports. Team potency was measured at the individual level using the referent-shift consensus model (Chan, 1998), which also requires one to show agreement among individual responses of a higher-level construct before aggregating the lower-level data to represent a higher level construct. To assess whether there was sufficient within-group agreement among employee responses regarding these two variables, three statistics were examined: One-way analysis of variance (ANOVA), intraclass correlations (ICCs), and within-group interrater reliability (r_{wg}; James et al., 1984). The ANVOA results provided initial support for aggregation, with $F(44, 144) = 1.93$, $p < .01$ and $F = (44, 143) = 1.94$, $p < .01$ for servant leadership and team efficacy, respectively. Such results indicate that there was significant between-team variance for these two variables, relative to the within-team variance. Additionally, ICC(1) (i.e., the relative amount of variance that resides between versus within teams) and ICC(2) (i.e., the reliability of between-team measures) were .18 and .48 for servant leadership and .18 and .48 for team efficacy, providing additional support for aggregation. Lastly, r_{wg}, the within-group interrater reliability, was calculated based on several theoretically possible distributions (i.e., uniform, small skew, and moderate skew; LeBreton & Senter, 2008), with an average r_{wg} of .96 for servant leadership and .97 for team potency. These values all exceed the conventional cutoff of .70 (James, 1988). In conjunction, these results indicated that it was appropriate to aggregate servant leadership and team potency to the team level.

Analytic Strategy

The proposed multi-level model was tested using Mplus 7 (Muthén & Muthén, 2012), which allowed a simultaneous estimation of the hypothesized multi-level relationships. Also, the use of the MLR estimator (Muthén & Muthén, 2012) provided robust standard errors for coefficient estimates. Indirect effects were evaluated using the Monte Carlo method recommended in MacKinnon et al. (2004). For each indirect effect, 20,000 Monte Carlo replications were generated to create its corresponding confidence interval. An interval excluding zero indicates a significant indirect relationship.

RESULTS

Confirmatory Factor Analysis

I ran several confirmatory factor analyses (CFAs) with Mplus 7 (Muthén & Muthén, 2012) to examine whether the measures included in the studies captured distinct constructs. Results of the CFAs are presented in Table 8.1. First, to test for the fit of the hypothesized 6-factor model, all of the observed items and dimensions were specified to load on their respective latent factors, with dimensional scores indicating the multidimensional construct (i.e., i-deals) and item scores indicating unidimensional constructs. The hypothesized model had a χ^2 (260, $N = 189$) = 503.79, CFI = .93, TLI = .92, RMSEA = .07, and SRMR = .06. The loadings ranged from .61 to .96 (mean = .82). Second, CFAs based on three alternative models of theoretical interest were compared to the original measurement model. Results in Table 8.1 show that the hypothesized model was superior,

TABLE 8.1   Confirmatory Factor Analysis Results

	χ^2	df	Δ_{χ^2}	$df_{\Delta(\chi2)}$	CFI	TLI	RMSEA	SRMR
Hypothesized Model	503.79	260	—	—	.93	.92	.07	.06
Alternative Model 1	813.81	263	310.02	3	.84	.82	.11	.22
Alternative Model 2	786.30	263	282.51	3	.85	.83	.10	.14
Alternative Model 3	613.51	263	109.72	3	.90	.88	.08	.07

Note: $N = 189$. *df* = Degrees of freedom. $\Delta_{\chi^2} = \chi^2$ differences between the hypothesized model and alternative models. CFI = Comparative fit index. TLI = Tucker-Lewis index. RMSEA = Root-mean-square error of approximation. SRMR = Standardized root-mean-square residual. For the multidimensional scale (i.e., i-deals), dimensional scores were used to indicate the construct, while other unidimensional scales were indicated by their items. The first alternative model was a 5-factor model with self-efficacy and team potency correlating at 1.0. The second alternative model was a 5-factor model with employee in-role performance and team performance correlating at 1.0. The third model was a 5-factor model with servant leadership and i-deals correlating at 1.0.

with $109.72 \leq \Delta_{\chi2(189, 3)} \leq 310.02$. These results in combination suggest that the measures included in the present study captured distinct constructs as anticipated.

Model Estimation

Table 8.2 lists the means, standard deviations, and bivariate correlations among the individual-level and team-level variables. In the model estimation, paths from i-deals to self-efficacy and from self-efficacy to in-role performance were specified to be random, while the control variable, dyad tenure, was specified to have a fixed effect on in-role performance. Because of the inclusion of random effects in the multi-level model, only unstandardized path coefficients were available. All the variables were group-mean centered, except for outcome variables (i.e., in-role performance and team performance). Pseudo R^2 ($\sim R^2$) was calculated using Snijders and Bosker's (1999) formulas to indicate the magnitude of variations in the individual- and team-level outcome variables that were accounted for by the hypothesized model. In total, the proportion of variance explained by the model was 21% for employee in-role performance and 20% for team performance.

Hypothesis Testing

Figure 8.2 presents the unstandardized estimated coefficients for the direct paths specified in the model. As shown in Figure 8.2, servant leadership was positively related to employee i-deals ($\beta = .89$, $p < .01$) and the overall

TABLE 8.2 Means, Standard Deviations, Bivariate Correlations, and Internal Consistency Coefficients

Variables	M	SD	1	2	3	4	5
Team Level							
1. Servant leadership	4.84	0.82	.81				
2. Overall i-deals (median)	4.31	0.91	.79**	—			
3. Team efficacy	5.53	0.61	.70**	.63**	.88		
4. Team performance	5.18	0.91	.01	.01	.24†	.89	
5. Average dyad tenure (years)	3.04	1.94	−.08	−.11	.15	.35*	—
Individual Level							
1. I-deals	4.31	1.31	.93				
2. Self-efficacy	5.85	0.75	.17*	.82			
3. In-role performance	5.53	1.02	.12	.13†	.92		
4. Dyad tenure (years)	3.20	3.01	−.01	.08	.09	—	

Note: N = 169–189 at the individual level. N = 45 at the team level. Internal consistency coefficients (Cronbach's alphas) are reported in bold on the diagonal. I-deals = Idiosyncratic deals. **$p < .01$; *$p < .05$. †$p < .10$.

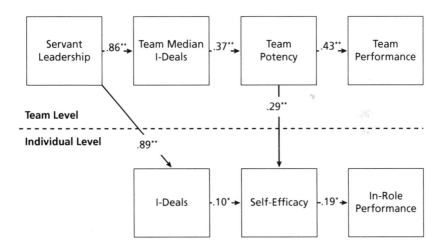

Figure 8.2 Multilevel path analysis results for the hypothesized model. *Note:* I-Deals = Idiosyncratic deals. Unstandardized path coefficients. **$p < .01$; *$p < .05$.

level of ideals within a team (i.e., team median i-deals, $\gamma = .86$, $p < .01$), providing support for Hypotheses 1 and 2. Further, supporting Hypothesis 3, i-deals related positively to employee self-efficacy ($\beta = .10$, $p < .05$). The significant positive relationship between team median i-deals and team potency ($\gamma = .37$, $p < .01$) provided evidence supporting Hypothesis 4. The cross-level direct path from team potency to self-efficacy was also significant ($\gamma = .29$, $p < .01$), providing support to Hypothesis 5.

To estimate the indirect relationships between servant leadership and individual and team performance proposed in Hypotheses 6 and 7, the Monte Carlo strategy recommended by MacKinnon et al. (2004) was used. Specifically, 20,000 Monte Carlo replications were generated for the hypothesized indirect effects to create corresponding confidence intervals. A confidence interval excluding zero indicates that the effect is significant. Supporting Hypothesis 6, results show a significant positive indirect effect from servant leadership to employee in-role performance via i-deals and self-efficacy sequentially, with the indirect effect = .02 (95% *CI*: .01, .03). At the team level, the indirect effect from servant leadership to team performance through team median i-deals and team potency was .14 (95% *CI*: .05, .23). Thus, Hypothesis 7 was supported.

GENERAL DISCUSSION

Drawing on servant leadership theory (Greenleaf, 1970; Liden et al., 2008) and social cognitive theory (Bandura, 1986, 2001), the current study investigated i-deals as a nonstandard HR practice through which servant leaders enhance individual and team efficacy and performance. Results based on multi-level analysis of data from 189 employees and managers in 45 teams demonstrated that servant leaders were more likely to provide followers with i-deals and allowed a high level of overall i-deals within the team, which enhanced the confidence and performance of individuals and teams. Such results have important theoretical and practical implications.

Theoretical Implications

This chapter makes several contributions to research on i-deals and servant leadership. First, by identifying servant leadership as an important factor that determines individual i-deals and the level of i-deals within teams, this study contributes to the research on antecedents of i-deals. Prior research has confirmed the important role of managers in making i-deals possible by showing that a good relationship between the manager and employee can facilitate the creation of i-deals (Rosen et al., 2013). Beyond a relational perspective, it is suggested that leadership styles can also be pivotal in influencing the creation of i-deals (e.g., Liao et al., 2016). Nevertheless, research has yet to accumulate empirical evidence that links any leadership style as an antecedent to i-deals. The current finding of the positive relationship between servant leadership and i-deals fills this gap. Therefore, adding to research that demonstrates the influence of managers on followers' i-deals, the current research reveals the crucial role of servant leadership in the creation of i-deals.

Further, the demonstration of servant leadership as a key antecedent to i-deals echoes the idea that servant leaders encourage follower voice (Liao et al., 2021). It also contributes to the broader literature integrating leadership and HR practices (Harris, 2001; Hutchinson & Wood, 1995; Kehoe & Han, 2020; Purcell & Hutchinson, 2007). Results from the current investigation show that servant leaders enhance employee and team competence through HR practices of customizing employee work arrangements. Consistent with social cognitive theory (Bandura, 1986, 2001), such results provide us with a closer examination of processes through which servant leadership influences individual and team performance. While the extant literature has recognized the critical role of managers with supervisory responsibilities in implementing HR practices, the current study represents the first effort to examine the role of servant leaders in enacting a nonstandard HR practice. In the current context, although i-deals represent a creative HR strategy that recognizes employees' proactivity and initiative, the role of managers is crucial because one of the major distinctions between i-deals and other employee job modification strategies (e.g., job crafting; Wrześniewski & Dutton, 2001) is that the creation of i-deals requires managers' approval. By allowing followers to participate in the process of changing their work arrangements, servant leaders share power with followers and advance their confidence and performance. Thus, managers' leadership styles are influential on whether they are willing to work with employees, grant i-deals to them, and allow for a high level of i-deals within teams.

Second, the results of the current study demonstrate that individually negotiated arrangements in an aggregated form may enhance the functioning of a team. Considering that i-deals are customizations of individual employees' work arrangements that help fulfill their needs and align job content with their strengths and interests (Rousseau, 2005), it is not surprising researchers have traditionally focused on understanding how i-deals influence the recipients at the individual level (Conway & Coyle-Shapiro, 2015; Liao et al., 2016). That said, there is a central tenet of i-deals that has yet to be tested: I-deals also benefit the employer, or the broader collective that i-deal recipients belong to (Rousseau, 2005; Rousseau et al., 2006). In the current investigation, I reveal that individually negotiated i-deals may have implications at the team level, such that members discern the frequency and prevalence of i-deals within a team. When there is a high level of i-deals, members witness frequent occurrences of i-deals in their team, which enhances their perceptions that the leader is supportive and their voice is heard. When viewed collectively at the team level, the extent to which i-deals are allowed within groups becomes a meaningful phenomenon and is powerful in shaping team processes. As confirmed in the present study, when more team members are allowed to modify work arrangements to fit their needs and strengths, they are more likely to share the cognition that their collective capacity is effective. Such enhanced team potency relates positively to team performance. Therefore, the current research supports that i-deals not only impact individual members of a team, but have implications on team processes and outcomes when viewed in combination, providing a direct test of the central tenet of i-deals regarding its mutual benefit to the recipients and the employer. Empirical support for this central tenet is of particular importance because i-deals are considered as differentiated HR practices that can potentially undermine team functioning (Kehoe & Han, 2020; Rousseau et al., 2006). The current study shows that when all team members can have certain forms of deals, teams are set to perform better.

Third, the current study contributes to the multi-level theory building of i-deals and servant leadership. Organizations are multi-level in nature and leadership operates within this multi-level context (Liao, 2017; Rousseau, 1985). That said, except for a few studies (e.g., Hunter et al., 2013; Liden, Wayne et al., 2014), research has mostly examined the influence of servant leadership on either team-level (e.g., Chiniara & Bentein, 2018; Ehrhart, 2004; Hu & Liden, 2011; Schaubroeck et al., 2011) or individual-level outcomes (e.g., Chen et al., 2015; Chiniara & Bentein, 2016; Neubert et al., 2016; Walumbwa et al., 2010) in isolation. While results from single-level investigations provide valuable insights on the effectiveness of servant leadership, it is necessary to study how servant leadership functions at multiple levels simultaneously within the organization to understand what to expect from this leadership style and how to apply it within the multi-level organizational context (Hunter et al., 2013). Contributing to multi-level theory of i-deals and servant leadership, the current research shows that servant leaders not only create customized work arrangements for followers and elevate the confidence level of those individuals but also enhance team potency by allowing a high level of i-deals within a team. In addition, the enhanced team potency also augments self-efficacy for individuals in the team. Integrating social cognitive theory with servant leadership theories from a multi-level perspective, this study indicates that servant leaders, because of their high concerns for follower development, utilize such specific HR practices to cultivate employee and team competence and help them become agentic, purposive, and proactive regulators of their actions. These results reveal multi-level pathways through which servant leadership and i-deals motivate individual followers and teams.

Practical Implications

Helping employees and teams succeed is central to managerial roles. In terms of practical implications, results of the current study confirm that managers who adopt a servant leadership style are best positioned to employ i-deals, a nonstandard HR practice, to enhance individual and team performance. Specifically, to enhance employee and team confidence in accomplishing tasks, managers are recommended to consider employees' legitimate needs and grant customized work arrangements to every employee in the team. Employees will gain a sense of confidence at work when they have a work schedule that avoids potential conflicts, work on tasks that match their strengths and interests, and acquire knowledge and skills that advance their capacities to perform their work.

It is also noteworthy that managers are recommended to consider such customized work arrangements for all followers in their teams rather than only a select few. It is expected that different members within the same team might have different needs regarding work schedules, task assignments, and opportunities for development. If everyone's needs are thoroughly discussed and considered, the entire team will perceive that they have the capacity to work effectively as a team, leading to a higher level of team performance. Thus, it is recommended that managers engage in servant leader behaviors when they enact nonstandard HR practices to enhance the overall positive effect within a team. Despite the positive impact of servant leadership on individual and team performance, precautions need to be taken when engaging in servant leader behaviors to prevent leaders from feeling depleted (Liao et al., 2020).

Strengths, Limitations, and Direction for Future Research

There are a few strengths of the study design that enhance the rigorousness of the current research. First, the multi-level design with two-wave data collected from two sources (i.e., employees and managers) helped to reduce common method bias. That said, employee reported variables were still subject to the same source influence, which threatened the validity of the mediational tests. Second, the data were collected on-site during paid working hours with a researcher present to answer questions during survey time. Such a data collection process not only increased response rates but also ensured response accuracy.

This study also has limitations. First, despite a multi-level time-lagged design, one needs to be cautious not to draw any causal inferences. Particularly regarding the mediational processes tested in the current research, it is likely that servant leaders may enhance the efficacy of individual followers, which in turn makes them more likely to negotiate customized work arrangements. Unfortunately, the reversed causality cannot be ruled out with the current cross-sectional design. In order to obtain causal conclusions with confidence, longitudinal studies with repeated measures collected on substantive variables are recommended.

Second, the current research focuses on servant leadership and shows that servant leaders utilize i-deals as an HR practice to enhance follower efficacy and team potency and effectiveness. It is recommended that future research examine multiple leadership styles simultaneously. For example, one of the four dimensions of transformational leadership is individualized consideration (Bass, 1985), which is relevant to the context of individualized work arrangements. It is probable that transformational leaders would also negotiate i-deals with followers in order to help followers transcend themselves. It will be worthwhile to model servant leadership and transformational leadership as antecedents of i-deals in the same model to understand how each may be uniquely associated with such an individualized HR practice. Based on the meta-analytic findings from Hoch et al. (2018), it is expected that servant leadership may have the most unique predictability regarding i-deals.

Third, while the current research has found significant effects of servant leadership and i-deals on individual and team efficacy and performance, I caution that such results be interpreted in the context of practical significance. Specifically, at the individual level, the indirect relationship between servant leadership and individual performance mediated by i-deals and self-efficacy was .02, raising a question of how much difference one would see in employee performance when i-deals are granted by servant leaders. The small value is likely due to the fact that only self-efficacy was examined as a mediation process. The total impact of servant leadership and i-deals on individual performance will be more substantial when other processes, such as social exchange, are jointly examined.

In terms of future research, one direction to extend the current study is to include outcomes at the organization level. As a leadership style adopted by top level executives, servant leadership has a direct positive relationship with firm performance (Peterson et al., 2012). Yet little is known regarding underlying mechanisms that relate servant leadership to firm level outcomes. In light of the findings from this study, i-deals may be an HR practice that eventually leads to the betterment of the entire organization. Rousseau (2005) suggests that i-deals overtime may receive institutional support and be integrated into organizational policies. Likewise, as Kroon and colleagues (2015) suggested, i-deals can be part and parcel of a firm's strategic HRM system. At the firm level, therefore, one can examine whether top management servant leadership is related to a higher level of i-deals within an organization. Further, more questions may be answered regarding the extent to which firm performance and the retention rate of talent is affected by the overall level of i-deals within a firm; and whether i-deals promote workforce employability, considering the direct and indirect costs of administering i-deals.

In addition, researchers may extend the current research by exploring the role of servant leaders in obtaining external support to serve their teams. Specifically, employees working in a team may share common needs based on their collective teamwork and are likely to desire customized work arrangements for their team. Such a phenomenon is called "we-deals," which refer to special work arrangements negotiated for an entire team (Hornung et al., 2009). It is expected that managers sometimes may not be able to directly make desired adjustments to team arrangements and instead need to act on behalf of the entire team to negotiate with higher management for possible resources and opportunities. Future research is encouraged to consider we-deals and investigate the relationship between servant leadership, we-deals, and outcomes at multiple levels within the organization.

Finally, another fruitful direction is to consider the role of i-deals differentiation in a team context (Saldivar & Liao, in press). Since the inception of i-deals,[2] fairness has been a concern (Greenberg et al., 2004; Rousseau et al., 2006). The justice issue related to i-deals is largely incurred by the nature of i-deals being nonstandardized and customized. When examined at the team level, i-deals can result in two types of differentiation that add to the differences among members. First, team members may have different numbers of deals. That is, some employees may have i-deals, while others do not; Or some employees have more i-deals than others. Second, i-deals negotiated by team members may differ in content. For example, one employee may have an i-deal that enables customized elements in tasks, another may have a flexible schedule i-deal, and the third may enjoy special career development opportunity as an i-deal. When administered with secrecy (Rousseau, 2005), this content difference in i-deals can also be interpreted by team members as signals of differential treatment that undermines overall fairness in a team. While there have been valuable attempts to address the fairness issue by examining how coworkers may react to the customized arrangements received by i-dealers (e.g., Lai et al., 2009), i-deals differentiation, referred to as the overall variability of i-deals within a team, may offer a unique lens to investigate its implications on teams.

CONCLUSION

I-deals are a form of important nonstandard HR practice that enables employees in the same team to have different work arrangements that satisfy their needs. Bridging servant leadership and i-deals research, the current study demonstrates that servant leaders enhance employee and team performance through i-deals. Such an integration reveals the role of servant leadership as an important antecedent of i-deals and contributes to the literature that examines managers' involvement in HRM. The results also provide empirical evidence confirming that individually negotiated i-deals can benefit a broader collective at the team level. I suggest that future research continue to enrich our understanding of how managers enact formal and informal HR practices to motivate individuals and teams.

NOTES

1. The model with team mean to indicate overall i-deals in a team produced comparable estimates.
2. Thanks to an anonymous reviewer for this idea.

REFERENCES

Bal, P. M., De Jong, S. B., Jansen, P. G. W., & Bakker, A. B. (2012). Motivating employees to work beyond retirement: A multi-level study of the role of I-deals and unit climate. *Journal of Management Studies, 49*(2), 306–331. https://doi.org/10.1111/j.1467-6486.2011.01026.x

Bandura, A. (1986). *Social foundations of thought and action: A social cognitive theory.* Prentice-Hall.

Bandura, A. (1997). *Self-efficacy: The exercise of control.* Worth.

Bandura, A. (2001). Social cognitive theory: An agentic perspective. *Annual Review of Psychology, 52*(1), 1–26. https://doi.org/10.1146/annurev.psych.52.1.1

Bandura, A., & Locke, E. A. (2003). Negative self-efficacy and goal effects revisited. *Journal of Applied Psychology, 88*(1), 87–99. https://doi.apa.org/doi/10.1037/0021-9010.88.1.87

Bass, B. M. (1985). *Leadership and performance beyond expectations.* Free Press.

Belkin, L. (2007, July 26). When whippersnappers and geezers collide. *The New York Times.* https://www.nytimes.com/2007/07/26/fashion/26work.html

Brislin, R. W. (1980). Translation and content analysis of oral and written material. In H. C. Triandis & J. W. Berry (Eds.), *Handbook of cross-cultural psychology: Methodology.* (Vol. 2, pp. 389–444). Allyn & Bacon.

Chan, D. (1998). Functional relations among constructs in the same content domain at different levels of analysis: A typology of composition models. *Journal of Applied Psychology, 83*(2), 234–246. https://doi.org/10.1037/0021-9010.83.2.234

Chen, G., Kirkman, B. L., Kanfer, R., Allen, D., & Rosen, B. (2007). A multilevel study of leadership, empowerment, and performance in teams. *Journal of Applied Psychology, 92*(2), 331–346. https://doi.apa.org/doi/10.1037/0021-9010.92.2.331

Chen, Z., Zhu, J., & Zhou, M. (2015). How does a servant leader fuel the service fire? A multilevel model of servant leadership, individual self identity, group competition climate, and customer service performance. *Journal of Applied Psychology, 100*(2), 511–521. https://doi.org/10.1037/a0038036

Chiniara, M., & Bentein, K. (2016). Linking servant leadership to individual performance: Differentiating the mediating role of autonomy, competence and relatedness need satisfaction. *The Leadership Quarterly, 27*(1), 124–141. https://doi.org/10.1016/j.leaqua.2015.08.004

Chiniara, M., & Bentein, K. (2018). The servant leadership advantage: When perceiving low differentiation in leader-member relationship quality influences team cohesion, team task performance and service OCB. *The Leadership Quarterly, 29*(2), 333–345. https://doi.org/10.1016/j.leaqua.2017.05.002

Cohen, S. G., & Bailey, D. E. (1997). What makes teams work: Group effectiveness research from the shop floor to the executive suite. *Journal of Management, 23*(3), 239–290. https://doi.org/10.1177%2F014920639702300303

Cole, M. S., Carter, M. Z., & Zhang, Z. (2013). Leader–team congruence in power distance values and team effectiveness: The mediating role of procedural justice climate. *Journal of Applied Psychology, 98*(6), 962–973. https://doi.apa.org/doi/10.1037/a0034269

Conway, N., & Coyle-Shapiro., J. (2015). Not so i-deal: A critical review of idiosyncratic deals theory and research. In P. M. Bal & D. M. Rousseau (Eds.), *Idiosyncratic deals between employees and organizations: Conceptual issues, applications, and the role of coworkers* (pp. 36–64). Routledge. http://dx.doi.org/10.4324/9781315771496-4

Ehrhart, M. G. (2004). Leadership and procedural justice climate as antecedents of unit-level organizational citizenship behavior. *Personnel Psychology, 57*(1), 61–94. https://doi.org/10.1111/j.1744-6570.2004.tb02484.x

Eva, N., Robin, M., Sendjaya, S., van Dierendonck, D., & Liden, R. C. (2019). Servant leadership: A systematic review and call for future research. *The Leadership Quarterly, 30*(1), 111–132. https://doi.org/10.1016/j.leaqua.2018.07.004

Farber, H. S., & Western, B. (2000). *Roundup the usual suspects: The decline of unions in the private sector, 1973–1998* [Working paper No. 437]. Princeton University. https://doi.org/10.2139/ssrn.229810

Freeman, R., & Rogers, J. (1999). *What workers want.* Russell Sage Foundation.

Gibson, C. B., Cooper, C. D., & Conger, J. A. (2009). Do you see what we see? The complex effects of perceptual distance between leaders and teams. *Journal of Applied Psychology, 94*(1), 62–76. https://doi.apa.org/doi/10.1037/a0013073

Gist, M. E., & Mitchell, T. R. (1992). Self-efficacy: A theoretical analysis of its determinants and malleability. *Academy of Management Review, 17*(2), 183–211. https://doi.org/10.5465/amr.1992.4279530

Graham, J. W. (1991). Servant-leadership in organizations: Inspirational and moral. *The Leadership Quarterly, 2*(2), 105–119. https://doi.org/10.1016/1048-9843(91)90025-W

Greenberg, J., Roberge, M. E., Ho, V. T., & Rousseau, D. M. (2004). Fairness as an "i-deal": Justice in under-the-table employment arrangements. *Research in Personnel and Human Resources Management, 22*, 1–34. https://doi.org/10.1016/S0742-7301(04)23001-8

Greenleaf, R. K. (1970). *The servant as leader.* The Robert K. Greenleaf Center.

Grzywacz, J. G., Carlson, D. S., & Shulkin, S. (2008). Schedule flexibility and stress: Linking formal flexible arrangements and perceived flexibility to employee health. *Community, Work and Family, 11*(2), 199–214. https://doi.org/10.1080/13668800802024652

Gully, S. M., Incalcaterra, K. A., Joshi, A., & Beaubien, J. M. (2002). A meta-analysis of team-efficacy, potency, and performance: Interdependence and level of analysis as moderators of observed relationships. *Journal of Applied Psychology, 87*(5), 819–832. https://doi.apa.org/doi/10.1037/0021-9010.87.5.819

Guzzo, R. A., & Dickson, M. W. (1996). Teams in organizations: Recent research on performance and effectiveness. *Annual Review of Psychology, 47*(1), 307–338. https://doi.org/10.1146/annurev.psych.47.1.307

Guzzo, R. A., Yost, P. R., Campbell, R. J., & Shea, G. P. (1993). Potency in groups: Articulating a construct. *British Journal of Social Psychology, 32*(1), 87–106. https://doi.org/10.1111/j.2044-8309.1993.tb00987.x

Hannah, S. T., Schaubroeck, J. M., & Peng, A. C. (2016). Transforming followers' value internalization and role self-efficacy: Dual processes promoting performance and peer norm-enforcement. *Journal of Applied Psychology, 101*(2), 252–266. https://doi.apa.org/doi/10.1037/apl0000038

Harris, L. (2001). Rewarding employee performance: Line managers' values, beliefs and perspectives. *International Journal of Human Resource Management, 12*(7), 1182–1192. https://doi.org/10.1080/09585190110068386

Henderson, D. J., Liden, R. C., Glibkowski, B. C., & Chaudhry, A. (2009). LMX differentiation: A multilevel review and examination of its antecedents and outcomes. *The Leadership Quarterly, 20*(4), 517–534. https://doi.org/10.1016/j.leaqua.2009.04.003

Hoch, J. E., Bommer, W. H., Dulebohn, J. H., & Wu, D. (2018). Do ethical, authentic, and servant leadership explain variance above and beyond transformational leadership? A meta-analysis. *Journal of Management, 44*(2), 501–529. https://doi.org/10.1177%2F0149206316665461

Hornung, S., Rousseau, D. M., & Glaser, J. (2009). Why supervisors make idiosyncratic deals: Antecedents and outcomes of i-deals from a managerial perspective. *Journal of Managerial Psychology, 24*, 738–764. https://doi.org/10.1108/02683940910996770

Hornung, S., Rousseau, D. M., Glaser, J., Angerer, P., & Weigl, M. (2010). Beyond top-down and bottom-up work redesign: Customizing job content through idiosyncratic deals. *Journal of Organizational Behavior, 31*(2–3), 187–215. https://doi.org/10.1002/job.625

Hornung, S., Rousseau, D. M., Weigl, M., Müller, A., & Glaser, J. (2014). Redesigning work through idiosyncratic deals. *European Journal of Work and Organizational Psychology, 23*(4), 608–626. https://doi.org/10.1080/1359432X.2012.740171

House, R. J., Rousseau, D. M., & Thomas-Hunt, M. (1995). The meso paradigm: A framework for the integration of micro and macro organizational behavior. In L. L. Cumings & B. M. Staw (Eds.), *Research in organizational behavior* (Vol. 17, pp. 71–114). JAI Press.

Howell, J. M., & Shea, C. M. (2006). Effects of champion behavior, team potency, and external communication activities on predicting team performance. *Group & Organization Management, 31*(2), 180–211. https://doi.org/10.1177%2F1059601104273067

Hu, J., & Liden, R. C. (2011). Antecedents of team potency and team effectiveness: An examination of goal and process clarity and servant leadership. *Journal of Applied Psychology*, *96*(4), 851–862. https://doi.apa.org/doi/10.1037/a0022465

Hunter, E. M., Neubert, M. J., Perry, S. J., Witt, L. A., Penney, L. M., & Weinberger, E. (2013). Servant leaders inspire servant followers: Antecedents and outcomes for employees and the organization. *The Leadership Quarterly*, *24*(2), 316–331. https://doi.org/10.1016/j.leaqua.2012.12.001

Hutchinson, S., & Wood, S. (1995). *Personnel and the line: Developing a new relationship.* Institute of Personnel and Development.

James, L. R. (1988). Organizational climate: Another look at a potentially important construct. In S. G. Cole & R. G. Demaree (Eds.), *Applications of interactionist psychology: Essays in honor of Saul B. Sells* (pp. 253–282). Lawrence Erlbaum.

James, L. R., Demaree, R. G., & Wolf, G. (1984). Estimating within-group interrater reliability with and without response bias. *Journal of Applied Psychology*, *69*(1), 85–98. https://doi.apa.org/doi/10.1037/0021-9010.69.1.85

Jones, G. R. (1986). Socialization tactics, self-efficacy, and newcomers' adjustments to organizations. *Academy of Management Journal*, *29*(2), 262–279. https://doi.org/10.5465/256188

Kehoe, R. R., & Han, J. H. (2020). An expanded conceptualization of line managers' involvement in human resource management. *Journal of Applied Psychology*, *105*(2), 111–129. https://doi.apa.org/doi/10.1037/apl0000426

Keller, R. T. (2006). Transformational leadership, initiating structure, and substitutes for leadership: A longitudinal study of research and development project team performance. *Journal of Applied Psychology*, *91*(1), 202–210. https://doi.apa.org/doi/10.1037/0021-9010.91.1.202

Kirkman, B. L., Rosen, B., Tesluk, P. E., & Gibson, C. B. (2004). The impact of team empowerment on virtual team performance: The moderating role of face-to-face interaction. *Academy of Management Journal*, *47*(2), 175–192. https://doi.org/10.5465/20159571

Klein, K. J., Conn, A. B., Smith, D. B., & Sorra, J. S. (2001). Is everyone in agreement? An exploration of within-group agreement in employee perceptions of the work environment. *Journal of Applied Psychology*, *86*(1), 3–16. https://doi.apa.org/doi/10.1037/0021-9010.86.1.3

Klein, K. J., Dansereau, F., & Hall, R. J. (1994). Levels issues in theory development, data collection, and analysis. *Academy of Management Review*, *19*(2), 195–229. https://doi.org/10.5465/amr.1994.9410210745

Kozlowski, S. W. J., & Bell, B. S. (2003). Work groups and teams in organizations. In I. B. Weiner, N. W. Schmitt, & S. Highhouse (Eds.), *Handbook of psychology* (2nd ed., pp. 333–375). Wiley. https://doi.org/10.1002/0471264385.wei1214

Kozlowski, S. W. J., & Klein, K. J. (2000). A multilevel approach to theory and research in organizations: Contextual, temporal, and emergent processes. In K. J. Klein & S. W. J. Kozlowski (Eds.), *Multilevel theory, research, and methods in organizations: Foundations, extensions, and new directions* (pp. 3–90). Jossey-Bass.

Kroon, B., Freese, C., & Schalk, R. (2015). A strategic HRM perspective on i-deals. In P. M. Bal & D. M. Rousseau (Eds.), *Idiosyncratic deals between employees and organizations: Conceptual issues, applications, and the role of coworkers* (pp. 73–91). Routledge. http://dx.doi.org/10.4324/9781315771496-6

Lai, L., Rousseau, D. M., & Chang, K. T. T. (2009). Idiosyncratic deals: Coworkers as interested third parties. *Journal of Applied Psychology, 94*(2), 547–556. https://doi.org/10.1037/a0013506

LeBreton, J. M., & Senter, J. L. (2008). Answers to 20 questions about interrater reliability and interrater agreement. *Organizational Research Methods, 11*(4), 815–852. https://doi.org/10.1177%2F1094428106296642

Lee, A., Lyubovnikova, J., Tian, A. W., & Knight, C. (2020). Servant leadership: A meta-analytic examination of incremental contribution, moderation, and mediation. *Journal of Occupational and Organizational Psychology, 93*(1), 1–44. https://doi.org/10.1111/joop.12265

Liao, C. (2017). Leadership in virtual teams: A multilevel perspective. *Human Resource Management Review, 27*(4), 648–659. https://doi.org/10.1016/j.hrmr.2016.12.010

Liao, C., Lee, H. W., Johnson, R. E., & Lin, S. H. (2020). Serving you depletes me? A leader-centric examination of servant leadership behaviors. *Journal of Management, 47*(5), 1185–1218. https://doi.org/10.1177%2F0149206320906883

Liao, C., Liden, R. C., Liu, Y., & Wu, J. (2021). Blessing or curse: The moderating role of political skill in the relationship between servant leadership, voice, and voice endorsement. *Journal of Organizational Behavior, 42*(8), 987–1004. https://doi.org/10.1002/job.2544

Liao, C., Wayne, S. J., Liden, R. C., & Meuser, J. D. (2017). Idiosyncratic deals and individual effectiveness: The moderating role of leader-member exchange differentiation. *Leadership Quarterly, 28*(3), 438–450. https://doi.org/10.1016/j.leaqua.2016.10.014

Liao, C., Wayne, S. J., & Rousseau, D. M. (2016). Idiosyncratic deals in contemporary organizations: A qualitative and meta-analytical review. *Journal of Organizational Behavior, 37*(S1), S9–S29. https://doi.org/10.1002/job.1959

Liden, R. C. (2013). Servant Leadership. In Kessler, E. H. (Ed.), *Encyclopedia of management theory* (pp. 698–702). SAGE.

Liden, R. C., Erdogan, B., Wayne, S. J., & Sparrowe, R. T. (2006). Leader-member exchange, differentiation, and task interdependence: Implications for individual and group performance. *Journal of Organizational Behavior, 27*(6), 723–746. https://doi.org/10.1002/job.409

Liden, R. C., Panaccio, A., Meuser, J. D., Hu, J., & Wayne, S. J. (2014). Servant leadership: Antecedents, processes, and outcomes. In D. V. Day (Ed.) *The Oxford handbook of leadership and organizations* (pp. 357–379). Oxford University Press. https://doi.org/10.1093/oxfordhb/9780199755615.013.018

Liden, R. C., Wayne, S. J., Liao, C., & Meuser, J. D. (2014). Servant leadership and serving culture: Influence on individual and unit performance. *Academy of Management Journal, 57*(5), 1434–1452. https://doi.org/10.5465/amj.2013.0034

Liden, R. C., Wayne, S. J., Meuser, J. D., Hu, J., Wu, J., & Liao, C. (2015). Servant leadership: Validation of a short form of the SL-28. *The Leadership Quarterly, 26*(2), 254–269. https://doi.org/10.1016/j.leaqua.2014.12.002

Liden, R. C., Wayne, S. J., Zhao, H., & Henderson, D. (2008). Servant leadership: Development of a multidimensional measure and multilevel assessment. *The Leadership Quarterly, 19*(2), 161–177. https://doi.org/10.1016/j .leaqua.2008.01.006

Lindsley, D. H., Brass, D. J., & Thomas, J. B. (1995). Efficacy-performance spirals: A multilevel perspective. *Academy of Management Review, 20*(3), 645–678. https://doi.org/10.2307/258790

MacKinnon, D. P., Lockwood, C. M., & Williams, J. (2004). Confidence limits for the indirect effect: Distribution of the product and resampling methods. *Multivariate Behavioral Research, 39*(1), 99–128. https://doi.org/10.1207/s1532 7906mbr3901_4

Michaels, E., Handfield-Jones, H., & Axelrod, B. (2001). *The war for talent.* Harvard Business School.

Muthén, L. K., & Muthén, B. O. (2012). *Mplus User's Guide* (version 7). Muthén & Muthén.

Neubert, M. J., Hunter, E. M., & Tolentino, R. C. (2016). A servant leader and their stakeholders: When does organizational structure enhance a leader's influence? *The Leadership Quarterly, 27*(6), 896–910. https://doi.org/10.1016/j .leaqua.2016.05.005

Peterson, S. J., Galvin, B. M., & Lange, D. (2012). CEO servant leadership: Exploring executive characteristics and firm performance. *Personnel Psychology, 65*(3), 565–596. https://doi.org/10.1111/j.1744-6570.2012.01253.x

Purcell, J., & Hutchinson, S. (2007). Front-line managers as agents in the HRM-performance causal chain: Theory, analysis and evidence. *Human Resource Management Journal, 17*(1), 3–20. https://doi.org/10.1111/j.1748-8583.2007.00022.x

Rosen, C. C., Slater, D. J., Chang, C. H., & Johnson, R. E. (2013). Let's make a deal: Development and validation of the ex post i-deals scale. *Journal of Management, 39*(3), 709–742. https://doi.org/10.1177%2F0149206310394865

Rousseau, D. M. (1985). Issues of level in organizational research: Multi-level and cross-level perspectives. *Research in Organizational Behavior, 7*(1), 1–37. https://psycnet.apa.org/record/1986-02679-001

Rousseau, D. M. (2005). *I-deals: Idiosyncratic deals employees bargain for themselves.* M. E. Sharpe.

Rousseau, D. M., & Ho, V. T., & Greenberg, J. (2006). I-deals: Idiosyncratic terms in employment relationships. *Academy of Management Review, 31*(4), 977–994. https://doi.org/10.5465/amr.2006.22527470

Saldivar, U., & Liao, C. (in press). Differentiation of idiosyncratic deals in teams: A multilevel perspective. *Group and Organization Management.* https://doi.org/10 .1177/10596011221108546

Schaubroeck, J., Lam, S. S. K., & Peng, A. C. (2011). Cognition-based and affect-based trust as mediators of leader behavior influences on team performance. *Journal of Applied Psychology, 96,* 863–871. https://doi.apa.org/doi/10.1037/ a0022625

Snijders, T. A. B., & Bosker, R. J. (1999). *Multilevel analysis: An introduction to basic and advanced multilevel modeling.* SAGE.

Spreitzer, G. M. (1995). Psychological empowerment in the workplace: Dimensions, measurement, and validation. *Academy of Management Journal, 38*(5), 1442–1465. https://doi.org/10.5465/256865

Stajkovic, A. D., Lee, D., & Nyberg, A. J. (2009). Collective efficacy, group potency, and group performance: Meta-analyses of their relationships, and test of a mediation model. *Journal of Applied Psychology, 94*(3), 814–828. https://doi .apa.org/doi/10.1037/a0015659

Stajkovic, A. D., & Luthans, F. (1998). Self-efficacy and work-related performance: A meta-analysis. *Psychological Bulletin, 124*(2), 240–261. https://doi.apa.org/ doi/10.1037/0033-2909.124.2.240

Sundstrom, E., De Meuse, K. P., & Futrell, D. (1990). Work teams: Applications and effectiveness. *American Psychologist, 45*(2), 120–133. https://doi.apa.org/ doi/10.1037/0003-066X.45.2.120

Tajfel, H., & Turner, J. C. (1985). The social identity theory of intergroup behavior. In S. Worchel & W. G. Austin (Eds.). *Psychology of intergroup relations* (2nd ed., pp. 7–24). Nelson Hall.

Tsui, A. S., Pearce, J. L., Porter, L. W., & Tripoli, A. M. (1997). Alternative approaches to the employee-organization relationship: Does investment in employees pay off? *Academy of Management Journal, 40*(5), 1089–1121. https://doi. org/10.5465/256928

van Dierendonck, D. (2011). Servant leadership: A review and synthesis. *Journal of Management, 37*(4), 1228–1261. https://doi.org/10.1177%2F0149206310380462

Verdorfer, A. P., Steinheider, B., & Burkus, D. (2015). Exploring the socio-moral climate in organizations: An empirical examination of determinants, consequences, and mediating mechanisms. *Journal of Business Ethics, 132*(1), 233–248. https://doi.org/10.1007/s10551-014-2319-0

Walumbwa, F. O., Hartnell, C. A., & Oke, A. (2010). Servant leadership, procedural justice climate, service climate, employee attitudes, and organizational citizenship behavior: A cross level investigation. *Journal of Applied Psychology, 95*(3), 517–529. https://doi.apa.org/doi/10.1037/a0018867

Wood, R., & Bandura, A. (1989). Impact of conceptions of ability on self-regulatory mechanisms and complex decision making. *Journal of Personality and Social Psychology, 56*(3), 407–415. https://doi.apa.org/doi/10.1037/0022-3514.56.3.407

Wrzesniewski, A., & Dutton, J. E. (2001). Crafting a job: Revisioning employees as active crafters of their work. *Academy of Management Review, 26*(2), 179–201. https://doi.org/10.2307/259118

Wu, C. H., & Parker, S. K. (2014). The role of leader support in facilitating proactive work behavior: A perspective from attachment theory. *Journal of Management, 43*(4), 1025–1049. https://doi.org/10.1177%2F0149206314544745

Wu, J., Liden, R. C., Liao, C., & Wayne, S. J. (2021). Does manager servant leadership lead to follower serving behaviors? It depends on follower self-interest. *Journal of Applied Psychology, 106*(1), 152–167. https://doi.apa.org/doi/10.1037/ apl0000500

PART IV

VIRTUAL TEAM ELECTRONIC COMMUNICATION AND DIVERSITY

CHAPTER 9

THE MODERATING EFFECT OF ELECTRONIC COMMUNICATION TECHNOLOGY ON THE RELATIONS BETWEEN DIVERSITY AND VIRTUAL TEAM PROCESSES

Julio C. Canedo
University of Houston–Downtown

Dianna L. Stone
Universities of New Mexico, Albany, and Virginia Tech

Kimberly M. Lukaszewski
Wright State University

Managing Team Centricity in Modern Organizations, pages 257–291
Copyright © 2022 by Information Age Publishing
www.infoagepub.com
All rights of reproduction in any form reserved.

ABSTRACT

There has been a dramatic rise in the use of virtual teams (VTs) in organizations (Driskell et al., 2003; Han & Beyerlein, 2016), and these teams are characterized by their geographic dispersion, use of electronic media to communicate, and diverse composition (Gibson et al., 2014). Research has shown that the use of electronic technology and diversity are two major factors that impact VT processes and outcomes (Han & Beyerlein, 2016). For instance, a review of the research revealed that diversity often has a negative impact on (a) communication in VTs, because diverse members have very different communication styles; (b) cooperation and cohesiveness, because the use of electronic communication lacks social cues and weakens affective bonds and interpersonal relations (Weisband & Atwater, 1999); and (c) conflict, because differences in language, cultural values, and use of electronic technology may frustrate team members and prevent them from completing tasks (Gibson et al., 2014). Similarly, research has shown that the use of electronic technology in VTs may create misunderstandings, reduce cooperation and cohesiveness, and increase conflict in these teams. However, some recent research has indicated that the use of electronic technology may alleviate some of the negative effects of diversity (Gibson et al., 2014) by reducing stereotypes, decreasing status differences, and increasing balanced participation in these teams. Thus, we present a model of the interaction of diversity and electronic communication technology on VT processes, and offer propositions to guide future research on these issues. In addition, we consider several practical implications for overcoming the problems associated with diversity and the use of electronic communication in VTs.

There has been a dramatic rise in the use of virtual teams in recent years (Driskell, et al., 2003; Dulebohn & Hoch, 2017; Gibson et al., 2014). Virtual teams (VTs) are typically defined as "groups of geographically and/or organizationally dispersed co-workers that are assembled using a combination of telecommunications and information technologies to accomplish an organizational task" (e.g., Townsend et al., 1998, p. 18). Research has shown that there are a number of advantages of VTs, including the fact that they can (a) share knowledge and communicate across geographic boundaries using electronic technology (Driskell et al., 2003), (b) reduce time in tedious face-to-face (FTF) meetings (Gibson et al., 2014), (c) work on projects around the clock (24/7; Han & Beyerlein, 2016), and (d) reduce travel time and costs (Gibson et al., 2014). Further, they allow individuals with specialized or unique knowledge, skills, and abilities to collaborate on projects even though they are not in the same location (Driskell et al., 2003; Gibson et al., 2014). As a result, VTs can include subject matter experts from around the world, which should greatly enhance their overall effectiveness (Han & Beyerlein, 2016).

Although there are many advantages of VTs, research has indicated that they may also pose a number of challenges (Gibson et al., 2014). For example, VTs often create difficulties with communication and coordination (Driskell et al., 2003), because electronic communication typically has low levels of media richness (e.g., fewer nonverbal cues), which can lead to miscommunication and misinterpretation of messages (Daft & Lengel, 1986). Studies have also shown that they may have lower levels of team engagement and socioemotional outcomes, including lower levels of trust, satisfaction, and shared responsibility (Gibson et al., 2014; Martins et al., 2004). In addition, they are often composed of culturally and nationally diverse team members and differences in members' backgrounds, abilities, culture, and language may create opportunities and challenges for communication and coordination (Gibson et al., 2014; Martins et al., 2004). Some research has indicated that differences in members' linguistic and cultural values can create misunderstandings in communication, and result in task or relationship conflict (Kankanhalli et al., 2006). In addition, studies have revealed that culturally diverse teams often lack shared beliefs and experiences, so they have problems agreeing on shared goals, roles, and norms (McDonough et al., 2003). Thus, researchers have argued that the effectiveness of diverse VTs may depend on other factors associated with these teams (e.g., type of technologies used) and the attributes of team members (e.g., differences in cultural values, language, proficiency in technology; Han & Beyerlein, 2016; Martins et al., 2004). For instance, when VTs are composed of members who use different languages, they may have more trouble communicating via electronic media (e.g., email or text) than those in traditional FTF teams (Han & Beyerlein, 2016; Martins et al., 2004).

Given that VTs are often composed of domestically diverse or globally diverse members, it is important to understand how diversity influences the effectiveness of VTs. Diversity deals with differences among individuals on any attribute that may lead to the perception that another person is different from the group (e.g., racial, cultural, gender, or age differences; e.g., Harrison & Klein, 2007; Triandis, 1994). To date, there has been considerable research in organizational behavior (OB) and human resource management (HRM) on diversity in traditional teams, and the results of that research have revealed that there are both positive and negative consequences associated with diversity in teams (Van Knippenberg et al., 2004). For example, diverse teams have a larger pool of task-relevant information and expertise than homogeneous teams, and differences in members' perspectives and abilities often enhance creativity and innovation in teams (Van Knippenberg et al., 2004). However, research has also shown that there are a number of disadvantages of diverse teams (Van Knippenberg et al., 2004). For instance, they typically have greater levels of initial conflict and misunderstandings, and lower levels of team cohesion than homogeneous teams (Roberge & van Dick, 2010). In addition, differences in cultural values, communication styles, and other factors may frustrate team members and prevent them from completing tasks (Gibson et al., 2014). As a result, some research showed that diversity had a negative effect on team development (Tyran & Gibson, 2008), and other studies revealed that diversity resulted in decreased performance and/or productivity in teams (e.g., Kirkman & Shapiro, 2001; Roberge & van Dick, 2010).

In view of the challenges often associated with diverse teams, we believe that diverse VTs may experience more difficulties in terms of VT processes like communication, cohesion, trust, and conflict than FTF teams. Despite these arguments, there has been relatively little empirical research on diversity in VTs (Gibson et al., 2014; Martins et al., 2004). Therefore, the primary purposes of this paper are to (a) review the existing research on diversity in VTs, (b) present a model of how diversity interacts with the use of electronic communication technology (hereinafter labeled electronic technology) to influence VT processes (e.g., communication, coordination/ cohesion, and conflict) and outcomes (e.g., performance, creativity), (c) identify needed research and offer propositions to guide future research, and (d) suggest several strategies to overcome diversity related challenges in VTs. We provide a brief review of the research on diversity in VTs in the section that follows (Gibson et al., 2014; Han & Beyerlein, 2016).

REVIEW OF THE RESEARCH ON DIVERSITY AND THE USE OF ELECTRONIC TECHNOLOGY IN VTS

Although there is widespread use of diverse VTs in organizations, relatively little theory and research has focused on the effects of these major factors on VT processes and outcomes (e.g., Gibson et al., 2014; Han & Beyerlein, 2016). For example, there are several models of VTs (Schiller & Mandviwalla, 2007) in the fields of management and management information systems (MIS; e.g., Driskell et al., 2003; Dulebohn & Hoch, 2017; Lin et al., 2008; Martins et al., 2004; Naik & Kim, 2010), but only two of these models consider the influence of diversity on VT outcomes (i.e., Dulebohn & Hoch, 2017; Martins et al., 2004). However, some research, albeit limited, has focused on the interactive effects of diversity and electronic technology on the effectiveness of VTs (Gibson et al., 2014; Martins et al., 2004). Thus, in the following sections we provide a brief review of the research on how diversity and the use of electronic technology influences the effectiveness of VTs. It merits emphasis that most of the articles included in our review come from the fields of management, OB, HRM, and psychology (e.g., Gibson et al., 2014; Martins & Shalley, 2011). We do not include all of the research in MIS because that research does not always focus on behavioral processes or outcomes.

The management-related models on VTs are based on the assumptions that input factors determine process factors, and, in turn, process factors affect VT outcomes. In this paper, we focus on two input categories (e.g., diversity and electronic communication technology), and consider how they affect three process factors (i.e.., communication, cooperation, cohesion, and conflict), and three outcome variables (i.e., performance, creativity, and member satisfaction).

Research on Influence of Diversity on VT Processes

Research has consistently shown that diversity has both positive and negative effects on VTs and FTF teams (Roberge & van Dick, 2010). For instance, results of research revealed that diversity in FTF teams has a negative impact on (a) communication, (b) collaboration, (c) cohesiveness, (d) social integration, and (e) member satisfaction (van Knippenberg & Schippers, 2007). Studies have also shown that these factors are important determinants of the success of diverse VTs (Gilson et al., 2015). For example, research has suggested that effective VTs have productive communication, balanced input among members, cohesiveness, shared knowledge, and the ability to manage conflict effectively (Gilson et al., 2015). Thus, the negative outcomes associated with diversity in VT composition are likely to lower the overall performance of diverse teams (Roberge & Van Dick, 2010). However, research has indicated that diversity in VTs also introduces differences in knowledge, ideas, and perspectives, and these factors lead to higher levels of creativity than in homogeneous VTs (Martins & Shalley, 2011).

It merits noting, however, that researchers have argued that diversity does not always lead to decreased effectiveness in communication in VTs (Gilson et al., 2015). Recent research has shown that the use of electronic communication methods may modify the degree to which diversity has a negative impact on communication (Gibson et al., 2014). For example, research has shown that the use of electronic technology may decrease prejudice against diverse team members because the physical characteristics and voice tones of these individuals are not seen or heard by others and will not evoke stereotypes (Walther, 2009; Zhou & Shi, 2011). Given that electronic technology may mitigate the problems often associated with diversity in teams, we review the research on the impact of diversity on four VT processes (i.e., communication, cooperation, cohesion, and conflict), and consider the degree to which electronic technology mitigates problems that may be brought about by diversity. Prior to discussing the impact of diversity on VT processes, it merits noting that we consider the following challenges posed by diversity in this paper: prejudice, stereotyping, status differences, biases based on lack of contact, miscommunication, and misunderstandings (Roberge & van Dick, 2010).

Communication

Effective communication among team members is critical for VT success because members are geographically dispersed, and the use of electronic communication technology may make it more difficult to share thoughts and ideas with others than FTF communication (Driskell et al., 2003). However, clear, open, and transparent communication is important so that team members can work together without misunderstandings. Several factors are thought to affect the clarity of VT communication, and one of the most significant factors is diversity in team composition. Diverse team members have differences in language, communication styles, and cultural values, and these factors often serve as barriers to effective communication in VTs (Driskell et al., 2003; Gibson et al., 2014).

Despite these arguments, results of research on the effects of diversity on communication in VTs have been mixed (Gibson et al., 2014). Some research has shown that culturally diverse VTs have more communication process challenges, which have a negative impact on members' ability to work together effectively (Au & Marks, 2012). One reason for this is that there are cross-cultural misinterpretations in VTs due to language, accents, and communication style differences (Han & Beyerlein, 2016). For example, research in anthropology has shown that European Americans and African Americans have direct communication styles whereas Asian Americans (hereinafter Asians), Hispanic Americans (hereinafter Hispanics), and Native Americans use very indirect communication styles (Hall & Hall, 1984; Kochman, 1981). These differences in the directness of communication are likely to create misunderstandings in teams because some members may not be able to understand the meaning of indirect messages, and others may view direct messages as coarse or rude.

Another reason that cultural differences in language or the absence of communication (i.e., silence) serve as barriers to communication is that team members decipher others' communication through their own cultural lens (Au & Marks, 2012). For instance, Asian and Native American cultures emphasize silence and stress that one should only speak in a meeting when the person has something significant to add to a discussion (Kochman, 1981). However, European American and African American cultures prescribe that one should be assertive and speak up in meetings (Kochman, 1981). As a result, European Americans and others may perceive that Asians and Native Americans are not involved in a project because they are not speaking during a meeting. However, in Asian and Native American cultures, silence does not mean a lack of involvement or engagement. Even though these team members may be silent, they may also be very passionate about an issue, and are just complying with their cultural norms that emphasize they should remain quiet (Kochman, 1981). Thus, team members may judge others' communication based on their own cultures, and make attribution errors about communication or silence in team conversations (Kochman, 1981).

Despite these findings, some recent research has found that the use of computer mediated communication (i.e., electronic technology) may actually moderate the relations between diversity and communication in VTs (Kiesler et al., 1984). For example, research has shown that electronic technology may enhance communication in diverse VTs because team members' physical characteristics and voice tones cannot be seen or heard when text messages are used and this reduces prejudice in teams (Kiesler et al., 1984). Similarly, research has revealed that when team members work together via electronic technology, they communicate more frequently than when they work FTF (Walther, 2009). Thus, they may actually get to know each other better in virtual than FTF teams (Walther, 2009). Even though there has been some research on the moderating effect of electronic technology on the relation between diversity and team communication, we believe, as do others (e.g., Gibson et al. 2014), that additional research is needed to examine these relations for different diversity groups and different types of technology.

Cooperation and Cohesion

Cooperation and cohesion can be considered two of the most important factors that affect VT performance. Cooperation is often defined as the act or willingness to work together, support, or help other team members achieve a common goal, and cohesion can be viewed as the total field of forces which act on members to remain in the group (Festinger et al., 1950, p. 164). Research has shown that cohesive teams have a number of benefits because they have greater levels of cooperation (Back, 1951), are more likely to agree on issues (Lott & Lott, 1961), and report greater satisfaction with the team than non-cohesive teams (Curtis & Miller, 1986). Researchers have also argued that VTs have greater difficulty developing cohesiveness and trust than FTF teams (Jarvenpaa & Leidner, 1999). The primary reason for this is that the use of electronic communication lacks social cues, weakens affective bonds, and reduces interpersonal relations among team members (Weisband & Atwater, 1999).

Consistent with the arguments just noted, research has shown that there are lower levels of constructive interaction and collaboration in diverse VTs than in heterogeneous FTF teams (Hambley et al., 2007). Further, research has indicated that the use of electronic rather than FTF communication in VTs has a negative impact on cohesion (Driskell et al., 2003). However, recent research has shown that some types of electronic technology (e.g., videoconferencing) may be more likely to foster cohesion in VTs than other types (e.g., email, instant messages; Ehsan et al., 2008). The reason for this is that videoconferencing technology is more likely to convey facial images, and social or personal cues than other forms of electronic communication technology (e.g., email). As a result, the use of videoconferencing is more likely than other forms of technology (e.g., email, text messages) to give team members access to facial expressions and nonverbal behaviors, which helps recipients understand messages and foster positive interpersonal interactions with others (Ehsan et al., 2008).

Another major factor thought to affect cooperation and cohesion is the diversity in team composition (Gera, 2013). There are a number of potential explanations for this. One reason is that diverse members in VTs may be less likely to have shared beliefs, experiences, norms, or similar mental models, and these differences often have a negative effect on team members' cooperation in teams (Gera, 2013). For example, research has shown that individuals with differences in cultural values often have dissimilar work scripts or role expectations, and these differences have a negative impact on cooperation and performance in VTs (Stone-Romero et al., 2003).

Apart from the factors just noted, another determinant of cooperation and cohesion in VTs is that ethnic and national differences often elicit negative stereotypes about team members, and this process reduces social integration and trust (Han & Beyerlein, 2016). Theory and research on social identity (Tajfel & Turner, 1985) has supported these arguments, and research on diverse VTs has found that ethnic and national differences often have a negative impact on cooperation and cohesion in these types of teams (Gibson et al., 2014). For instance, dominant team members may use negative stereotypes to assign diverse members to low status outgroups, and denigrate them in order to enhance the status of their own group (Tajfel & Turner, 1985). Further, they are likely to disparage outgroup members and ignore their contributions to the team (Tajfel & Turner, 1985). Considerable research on social identity theory has provided support for these effects (Tajfel & Turner, 1985).

Although most of the research has shown that diversity reduces cooperation and cohesion in VTs (Han & Beyerlein, 2016), some recent research has revealed that the use of electronic communication technology may alleviate some of the negative effects of diversity in these teams (Walther, 2009). For instance, research on computer mediated communication (CMC) has shown that the use of some types of electronic technology mitigates the lack of trust in diverse VTs (Krebs et al., 2006). Further, research has found that CMC facilitates relationships when there is within-group diversity (Walther, 2009). CMC typically refers to human communication that is networked through computers, but the term electronic technology is broader (Lee & Oh, 2017). In particular, the term electronic technology includes communication through use of computer hardware and software, operating systems, web-based applications, telephones and telecommunications, kiosks, and office products (e.g., fax machines; Washington University, n.d.). Even though there has been some research on the effects of CMC on trust and relationship formation in diverse VTs, we believe that additional research is needed to understand under what conditions electronic technology might enhance cooperation in diverse VTs.

Conflict

Diversity in team composition is also thought to increase conflict in VTs because the differences in language, cultural values, communication styles, and other factors may frustrate team members and prevent them from accomplishing their goals (Gibson et al., 2014). Further, increased conflict in VTs is thought to have a negative impact on overall VT performance and effectiveness (Gibson et al., 2014). In support of these arguments, results of research revealed that diversity increases process and interpersonal conflict in VTs, and other research found that diversity in VTs led to greater levels of conflict than in diverse FTF teams (Gera, 2013). Similarly, research by Staples and Zhao (2006) found that differences in language and cultural values increased conflict and decreased levels of satisfaction and cohesion in VTs. However, the same study found that the overall performance in heterogeneous VTs was greater than in heterogeneous FTF teams (Staples & Zhao, 2006).

In addition, conflict can arise in VTs because there are ethnic and cultural differences in how team members resolve conflict (Holt & DeVore, 2005; Montoya-Weiss et al., 2001). For instance, some individuals have cultural values that emphasize the avoidance of conflict, and view compromise as unacceptable (Montoya-Weiss et al., 2001). However, other cultural values stress that people should confront conflict or compete with other teams or their own team members (Montoya-Weiss et al., 2001). Research on these differences has shown that diverse VTs that use compromise to manage conflict have lower levels of team performance than those that use competition or confrontation to handle conflict (Montoya-Weiss et al., 2001).

Research has also revealed that communication delays, time zone differences, and lack of FTF contact hinders the development of understanding and interpersonal relationships, which increases conflict in diverse VTs (Kankanhalli et al., 2006). Likewise, cultural diversity in language and nationality creates weaknesses in interpersonal relations, which results in task and relationship conflict (Han & Beyerlein, 2016; Kankanhalli et al., 2006). In addition, research has indicated that geographic dispersion and the use of electronic media are important determinants of conflict in VTs (Hinds & Bailey, 2003; Hinds & Mortensen, 2005; Kankanhalli et al., 2006). For example, Kankanhalli and his colleagues (2006) found that asynchronous electronic communication resulted in conflict because there were delays in responses and feedback from others. Finally, research also revealed that process conflict had a negative impact on overall performance in diverse VTs (de Jong et al., 2008).

Even though most research has indicated that diversity in team composition increases conflict in VTs, research on CMCs has shown that the use of electronic technology may alleviate this problem (Kiesler et al., 1984). For instance, research has revealed that if electronic communication focuses on the task, then team members get to know each other personally through messages that are used to accomplish the task (Mortensen & Hinds, 2001). As a result, when team members get to know one another there will be lower levels of conflict in the diverse VTs than when they do not know each other (Mortensen & Hinds 2001). Thus, the interplay of diversity and the use of electronic technology may eliminate some of the sources of conflict in VTs. This interaction will be considered in more detail next.

Impact of Diversity on Overall VT Performance

As noted previously, models of VTs argue that if diversity decreases communication, cooperation, or cohesion, and increases conflict in VTs then it will also reduce the overall VT performance (Dulebohn & Hoch, 2017; Martins et al., 2004). Next, we review the research on the influence of diversity on overall VT performance.

Results of research on the impact of diversity on VT performance have revealed very inconsistent findings (Gibson et al., 2014; Staples & Zhao, 2006). Some studies found that diversity or differences in members' cultural values decreased the overall performance and effectiveness of VTs (Gibson et al., 2014). Other research indicated that there was no relation between diversity and VT performance (Edwards & Sridhar, 2005), and still other studies found that diversity was positively related to performance in VTs (Staples & Zhao, 2006). We consider each of these sets of findings in the sections that follow.

Studies Showing Diversity Decreases VT Performance

Several studies found that diversity in VT composition has a negative impact on overall team performance (Gibson et al., 2014). For example, a study of virtual dyads in the United States and Turkey by Swigger et al. (2004) found that these dyads were less effective when they were composed of individuals with different cultural values than when they were composed of members with homogeneous cultural values. This study also revealed that subtle differences in cultural values had a large impact on team performance. Results of another study found that differences in nationality were negatively related to VT performance (Martins et al., 2004). Further, research by Scott and Wildman (2015) revealed that differences in national culture, language, and regional culture were all negatively related to VT performance. However, the same study found that the negative effects of diversity on VT performance could be mitigated if team members understood and accepted cultural differences (Scott & Wildman, 2015).

Although most studies on the relation between diversity and VT performance have focused on overall team performance, a few studies have examined the impact of diversity in VTs on creativity (Martins & Shalley, 2011). These studies were based on two opposing viewpoints (Martins & Shalley, 2011). One framework was labeled the information decision making perspective, and argued that differences in perspectives should result in a greater range of ideas and approaches, enhancing creativity (Martins & Shalley, 2011). The other framework titled the social categorization—similarity-attraction perspective maintains that demographic differences lead to process losses and decreases in team performance or creativity (Martins & Shalley, 2011). Results of research on these two different frameworks found that diversity interacted with a number of VT-related factors to affect creativity (e.g., increased rapport, equal participation, process conflict, and members' technical expertise; Martins & Shalley, 2011). For instance, the relations between demographic differences and creativity were positive when there were high levels of rapport, equal participation, low levels of process conflict, and few differences in technical expertise between members (Martins & Shalley, 2011). However, the relations between demographic differences and creativity were negative when there were low levels of rapport or equal participation, and high levels of process conflict and large differences in technical expertise between members (Martins & Shalley, 2011). Results also indicated that differences in members' race or sex were not related to creativity. The overall findings of this research suggest that creativity in VTs may depend on the interaction of diversity in team membership and a number of team processes (e.g., high levels of rapport, equal participation, low levels of conflict, and members' technical expertise). As a result, much more research is needed to examine how diversity interacts with other team-related factors (e.g., good interpersonal relations, cooperation) to affect creativity and overall team performance.

Studies Showing Diversity Was Unrelated to VT Performance

A few studies have shown that diversity is unrelated to overall VT performance. For instance, research by Edwards and Sridhar (2005) found that VT members' diversity in cultural values had no relation to members' learning, satisfaction, or overall performance. Another study of 45 teams of graduate students in 10 countries found that national diversity was unrelated to team conflict or trust in diverse VTs (Polzer et al., 2006). However,

268 • J. C. CANEDO, D. L. STONE, & K. M. LUKASZEWSKI

the same study found that geographic differences heightened conflict and reduced trust in these types of teams.

Studies Showing Diversity Enhances VT Performance

Some studies have found that diversity is actually positively related to VT performance. For instance, a study by Kirkman et al. (2013) found that national diversity was curvilinearly related to overall VT performance, and the relation was moderated by psychological safety and the richness of the communication media used. Results of their study indicated that the relation between national diversity and performance became more positive when there were high levels of psychological safety and media richness, but the relation became more negative when there were low levels of the same variables (Kirkman et al., 2013). Consistent with studies already described, results of this study suggest that the relation between diversity and VT performance depends on other team-related factors (e.g., media richness). Similarly, a study by Staples and Zhao (2006) found that VTs that were heterogeneous performed at higher levels than FTF teams that were heterogeneous.

Even though the results of research on the relation between diversity and VT performance are mixed, we believe that several patterns emerged from our review of the literature. For example, one pattern that materialized was that diversity interacted with a number of team process variables (e.g., media richness, team rapport, levels of process conflict, and participation) to affect overall VT performance and creativity. Thus, we believe that additional research is needed to examine the degree to which diversity interacts with VT factors (e.g., media richness, team rapport, electronic technology) or team processes to affect overall performance.

Influence of Electronic Technology on VT Processes and Outcomes

Apart from diversity, another important factor that may affect the performance and effectiveness of VTs is the use of electronic communication technology (e.g., email, instant messages, electronic bulletin boards, videoconferencing). Although it is often thought that the use of electronic technology has a negative impact on VT processes (e.g., communication, cooperation, and cohesion; Gibson & Gibbs, 2006), results of research have found that the use of electronic technology may have both positive and negative effects on VT processes and outcomes (Walther, 2009). To date, there has been considerable research on the effects of CMC on team processes and outcomes (Kiesler et al., 1984; Walther, 2009). As a result, we incorporate the results of this research in our review of the effects of electronic technology on VT processes and outcomes.

Negative Effects of Electronic Technology on VT Outcomes

It has long been thought that the use of electronic technology has a negative impact on VT processes and outcomes because technology is impersonal and lacks social cues and media richness (Driskell et al., 2003). Research on the use of electronic media on diverse VTs has indicated that it can hamper information exchange (Powell et al., 2006), serve as a barrier to relationship building, and reduce overall team effectiveness (Kirkman et al., 2004). One reason for this is that the use of electronic technology or CMC does not include rich information about social contexts, social cues, or nuances, which results in misinterpretation of messages (Driskell et al., 2003; Han & Beyerlein, 2016). Further, studies have found that virtuality has negative effects on overall team processes (e.g., communication, cohesion; Gibson & Gibbs, 2006), and other research has shown that the lack of technical skills among members has a detrimental impact on VT effectiveness and can create conflict in these teams (Sarker & Sahay, 2003). As a result, researchers have argued that all VT members should receive technical training in order to facilitate communication, reduce conflict, and improve the overall VT effectiveness (Tan et al., 2000).

Positive Effects of Electronic Technology on VT Outcomes

Apart from the negative effects of electronic technology on VT outcomes, some researchers have argued that the use of electronic technology may also have positive effects on VT processes, and mitigate some of the negative outcomes associated with diversity in VTs (e.g., prejudice, miscommunication; Gibson et al., 2014). For example, research has shown that the use of electronic technology actually increases the frequency of communication in diverse VTs so team members get to know one another better through electronic messages than in FTF (Mortensen & Hinds, 2001). Similarly, the use of electronic technology gives team members the opportunity to communicate at any time of the day or night, which fosters interpersonal relations (Walther, 2009). Consistent with this argument, Mesmer-Magnus et al. (2011) found that virtuality increased the sharing of unique information among team members. Other studies found that sharing information in VTs led to higher levels of trust and interpersonal relations (Puiia, 2015).

Further, when text-based electronic technology is used, team members are more likely to be perceived as equals, and there are fewer status differences than in FTF teams (Walther, 2009). As a result, there should be more balanced participation in diverse VTs when text based electronic technology is used to communicate rather than other types of technologies. Research has also shown that the use of asynchronous (not occurring at the same time) or synchronous (occurring at the same time) communication affects VT processes (Morrison-Smith & Ruiz, 2020). However, the research on the use of asynchronous and synchronous communication has been mixed (Morrison-Smith & Ruiz, 2020). Some research found that asynchronous communication has a positive effect on communication, and reduces intercultural miscommunication because team members have more time to understand and process messages from other members (Han & Beyerlein, 2016). However, other research found that asynchronous communication is more likely to create misunderstandings because recipients cannot clarify the information when the message is sent (Morrison-Smith & Ruiz, 2020). Thus, synchronous communication may help team members clarify messages in a timely way, but it may not always be possible because of geographic differences, or time and scheduling differences (Morrison-Smith-Ruiz, 2020).

Taken together, the research just reviewed on the effects of electronic technology on VT processes and outcomes suggests that electronic technology may alleviate some of the problems associated with the effects of diversity in VTs (e.g., stereotyping, miscommunication, status differences). Thus, we believe, as do others, that the effects of diversity on VTs will depend on the use and type of electronic media employed in these teams (Gibson et al., 2014; Robert et al., 2018). Even though some researchers (e.g., Gibson et al., 2014) have argued that this interaction may be an important determinant of VT effectiveness, we know of only one empirical study that has examined this prediction (Robert et al., 2018). Thus, we present a model that can be used to enhance our understanding of how electronic technology might mitigate the challenges posed by diversity in VTs.

MODEL OF THE MODERATING EFFECTS OF ELECTRONIC TECHNOLOGY ON THE RELATIONS BETWEEN DIVERSITY AND VT PROCESSES AND OUTCOMES

Our model predicts that the interaction of diversity in VT composition and the use of electronic technology are key determinants of VT processes (e.g., communication, cohesion) and outcomes (e.g., performance, member satisfaction). It also suggests that diversity in VTs elicits a number of challenges (e.g., prejudice, stereotyping, miscommunication), and these challenges serve as intervening factors between diversity and VT processes. Our model also predicts that electronic technology moderates the relation between diversity and these intervening factors, so that the use of technology alleviates some of the difficulties caused by diversity in VTs. For example, research has shown that the use of text-based technology (e.g., email, text messages) reduces the challenges associated with prejudice and stereotyping (Walther, 2009). Further, our model predicts that the intervening factors have a major influence on VT communication, cohesion, and conflict. For instance, if prejudice against diverse members is decreased, then VT members are more likely to communicate and cooperate with one another

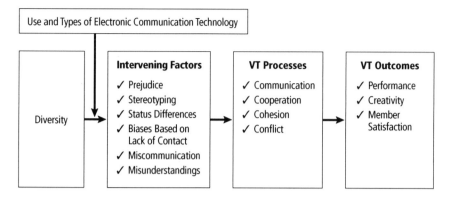

Figure 9.1 Model of the moderating effect of electronic communication technology on the relation between diversity and intervening factors in VTs.

and less likely to engage in conflict. A depiction of the model is presented in Figure 9.1.

We believe that our model makes a unique contribution to theory and research on diversity in VTs (e.g., Driskell et al., 2003; Dulebohn & Hoch, 2017; Martins et al., 2004), because it suggests that electronic technology ameliorates some of the challenges elicited by diversity in these teams. It also predicts that different types of electronic technology may be needed to address specific challenges. For instance, the use of text-based technology may decrease prejudice in diverse VTs more than videoconferencing, because text does not display physical characteristics like videoconferencing.

The Effects of Diversity on Challenges in VTs

In the following section, we provide a more detailed description of how diversity elicits challenges in VTs, and discuss how the use and types of electronic technology might mitigate these challenges. Our discussion considers how diversity produces challenges associated with prejudice, stereotyping, status differences, unequal participation, and cultural value differences.

One of the major challenges evoked by diversity in VTs is that diverse members are often stereotyped negatively, and viewed as less intelligent, less capable, and less motivated than others. Stereotypes can be considered largely false, overgeneralized beliefs about a member of a group that are not based on facts (Ashmore & Del Boca, 1981). One consequence of stereotyping is that diverse members are denigrated and excluded from team discussions or activities. Thus, even though diverse members have many talents and skills that they bring to VTs, stereotypes serve as a barrier to their participation, and their ideas are often discounted by other team members.

In order to address this challenge, our model predicts that electronic technology might be used to alleviate the stereotyping of diverse members in VTs. The primary reason for this is that some research on CMC has shown that the use of text-based technology reduces stereotyping because it does not convey members' physical characteristics or vocal tones which often evoke stereotypes (Walther, 2009).

Another challenge created by diversity in VTs is that diverse members may be assigned to low status outgroups which decreases their prestige, respect, worth, and esteem in the team. If diverse members are perceived as having low status, they will have less influence in the team, and may be given less credit or fewer rewards for their work than those who have high status. In addition, high status team members may disparage low status others in order to enhance their own self-esteem (Tajfel, 1982). In an effort to attend to this problem, our model predicts that the use of electronic technology may reduce status and power differences in teams, and decrease the extent to which diverse members are relegated to low status outgroups (Kiesler et al., 1984; Walther, 2009). The primary reason for this is that electronic technology creates visual anonymity, which diverts attention from diverse members' idiosyncratic characteristics and reduces status differences (Kiesler et al., 1984; Walther, 2009). In support of these arguments, research has shown that team members are more likely to view others as equals when text-based electronic technology is used rather than FTF communication (Kiesler et al., 1984). Stated differently, team members are less likely to pay attention to diverse members' personal characteristics when text-based technology is used compared to FTF communication, and this reduces the importance of status differences (Kiesler et al., 1984; Walther, 2009).

A third challenge created by diverse teams is that members may denigrate diverse members because they have had little previous contact with them, and view these members as part of a negatively stereotyped outgroup (Stone-Romero et al., 2003). Thus, if a team member is categorized as Hispanic American then they are assigned to a Hispanic category, and this categorization evokes stereotypes about the person (e.g., individual is lazy, unintelligent, and a dishonest criminal; Stone-Romero et al., 2003). However, theory and research has indicated that increased contact with diverse members can dispel these erroneous stereotypes, and ensure that diverse members are viewed as individuals, not members of a negatively categorized group (Allport, 1954). For example, increased contact with diverse members allows others to get to know them as individuals, not just as members of an undesirable group. If the contact is positive, others are more likely to view the diverse member favorably, and include them in the team. Our model indicates that the use of electronic technology may enhance positive contact and decrease biases associated with diverse team members. For example, research found that the use of electronic technology in VTs gave team members more frequent contact with diverse members, and they often got to know them better than in FTF teams (Mortensen & Hinds, 2001). This allows team members to get to know diverse members as individuals, which decreases prejudice and discrimination (Allport, 1954). Thus, text-based electronic technology may give team members greater opportunities to gather individuating information about diverse members, which enhances trust and close interpersonal relations (Walther, 2009).

Another major challenge created by diversity in VTs is that majority team members often dominate team discussions, which does not give diverse members an opportunity to share their ideas and suggestions (Kiesler et al., 1984; Walther, 2009). When discussions are dominated by a few majority members, then diverse VTs may not have balanced or equal participation, which decreases overall performance and creativity. Consistent with this argument, our model indicates that the use of text-based electronic technology may decrease the degree to which any one team member dominates discussions because others can enter or type their ideas and suggestions at any time (Mortensen & Hinds, 2001). As a result, electronic technology gives diverse members the opportunity to express their views even if majority members try to dominate the discussion, and this enhances the effectiveness of VTs.

A final challenge created by diversity in VTs is that team members often have very different cultural values (e.g., individualism/collectivism), which means that diverse members have unique communication styles and conflict resolution methods. For instance, research has shown that, on average, members of the various domestic diverse groups in the United States (e.g., Asians, Hispanics, Native Americans, African Americans) are more likely to value collectivism than members of the majority group in the United States (i.e., European Americans; Harrison & Stone, 2018). Team members who value collectivism typically prioritize the good of the group over the individual, and place emphasis on cooperation and consensus in teams (Triandis, 1994). They are also more likely to prefer group decision-making, conflict avoidance, low risk-taking, and collaboration than those who value individualism (Triandis, 1994). In contrast, team members who value individualism are likely to believe that the interests of individuals should take precedence over the group, and they emphasize independence, autonomy, rugged individualism, freedom, and stress confronting conflict.

As a result of these cultural value differences team members often have distinct communication styles (e.g., direct vs. indirect, emotional vs. unemotional), which are likely to create misunderstandings and miscommunication in VTs. For instance, team members who are individualistic typically prefer direct communication styles that emphasize rationality, emotional detachment, and focus on tasks rather than on relationships (Kochman, 1981). In contrast, team members who value collectivism prefer indirect communication styles that emphasize the use of metaphors, emotionality, and development of relationships (Smith, 2011). Even though we indicate that there are between-group differences in communication styles, it merits emphasis that there are also within-group differences in collectivistic or individualistic communication styles. Thus, all individuals in a group or subgroup do not use one same style (Betancourt & Lopez, 1993). As a result, inferences about communication styles apply, on average, not in absolute terms.

In order to address differences in communication or conflict resolution styles, our model suggests that the use of electronic technology may mitigate some of these problems in diverse VTs. For example, the use of videoconferencing may decrease misunderstandings in diverse VTs because it gives team members access to facial expressions, nonverbal behaviors, or tone of voice, which should increase their understanding of different types of messages. Similarly, the use of synchronous communication technology may help team members clarify messages or give them a chance to ask questions about messages in real time. Further, we believe that various types of collaboration technology (e.g., groupware, electronic team rooms) might be used to help team members work together and gain an understanding over time of different styles of communication.

Collaboration technology offers team members the chance to use multiple forms of technology to facilitate communication. Typically, this includes email, audio and video conferencing, chatrooms, electronic team rooms, chatbots, threaded discussions, and other types of technologies. Most of these technologies are well known, but we believe that a definition of team rooms may be needed. These types of electronic rooms are usually web-based virtual meeting rooms that allow team members to collaborate in real time, and they often include a variety of collaboration methods including audio- and videoconferencing, chat applications, instant messaging, document sharing, and so forth (Roseman & Greenberg, 1996).

Apart from the impact of cultural values on communication style, these values may also affect VT members' preference for conflict resolution methods (Triandis, 1994). For instance, team members with different cultural values often have dissimilar views about how to make decisions or resolve conflict. On average, individuals from collective cultures prefer compromising, avoiding, or collaborative (problem-solving) styles more than those from individualistic cultures (Triandis, 1994). However, those who value individualism are more likely to prefer confrontative, competitive, and dominating conflict styles that place emphasis on autonomy and give them control over the situation than collectivists (Triandis, 1994). These differences in conflict resolution styles are likely to serve as barriers to developing shared norms and guidelines in diverse VTs, and they may have a negative impact on interpersonal relations, communication, and overall VT performance (Kankanhalli et al., 2006). Thus, it is important to identify strategies to overcome these differences, and find ways of smoothing inter-personal relations in diverse VTs.

Our model suggests that different types of electronic technology may help diverse VTs alleviate conflict-related problems. For example, diverse VTs may use web-based team rooms to help members facilitate discussions and build rapport. Similarly, they might use collaborative technology and online team building games to build relationships and identify superordinate goals, which typically motivate teams to work together. Collaborative technologies may be useful for resolving conflict because they can help teams share concerns, de-velop strategies to overcome them, and vote on the preferred strategy to solve them (Kankanhalli et al., 2006). Although these arguments seem plausible, we know of no empirical research that has examined the effects of collabora-tive technologies on conflict resolution in diverse VTs.

In summary, our model predicts that electronic communication tech-nology will moderate the relations between diversity and intervening fac-tors (e.g., prejudice, stereotyping, miscommunication), and VT processes and outcomes. Stated differently, our model indicates that the use of dif-ferent types of electronic technology is likely to (a) reduce prejudice and stereotyping, (b) decrease status differences, (c) enhance contact between diverse and other team members, (d) augment diverse members' participa-tion in team discussions, and (e) alleviate miscommunication and conflict caused by cross-cultural differences in these teams. Given these arguments, we consider the extent to which research has supported the predicted rela-tions in our model, and offer propositions to guide future research in the next section. We also identify various types of electronic technology that may help decrease some of the diversity challenges faced in VTs.

The Moderating Effect of Electronic Technology on the Relation Between Diversity and Intervening Factors

As previously noted, our model predicts that the use of electronic tech-nology will moderate the relations between diversity and intervening fac-tors and VT processes. Given this argument, we will review the research on these predicted relations in our model.

Relation Between Diversity and Stereotyping

The model in Figure 9.1 indicates that diversity influences the degree to which team members negatively stereotype diverse team members. Not sur-prisingly, stereotyping of diverse members has detrimental effects on inter-personal relations, communication, and cohesion in diverse VTs. Further, if diverse members are stereotyped negatively, team members will discount their ideas, and this will have a negative impact on overall VT performance.

Our model predicts that the use of text-based electronic technology can be used to reduce stereotyping in diverse VTs because team members do not have access to the information (e.g., physical characteristics) that evokes stereotypes (Walther, 2009). Although some research has supported these arguments, the overall results on this relation have been mixed (Walther, 2009). For instance, some studies have found that the use of text-based technology in diverse VTs results in greater knowledge sharing (Robert et al., 2018) and less prejudice than FTF communication (Carte & Chidambaram, 2004; Giambatista & Bhappu, 2010). Research has also shown that decreases in stereotyping has a positive impact on communication and cohesiveness in these teams (Walther, 2009). However, other studies have indicated that the use of text-based communication had no effect on stereotyping in diverse teams (Staples & Zhao, 2006), and still other research indicated that it exacerbated prejudice and stereotyping in these types of teams (Adrianson, 2001).

Given the importance of reducing stereotyping in diverse VTs, and the inconsistent research findings on this issue, we believe that additional research is needed to examine the degree to which electronic technology ameliorates the problems associated with stereotyping in diverse VTs. Thus, we offer the following propositions to foster future research:

Proposition 1: *The use and type of electronic technology will moderate the relations between diversity and stereotyping in diverse VTs so that the use of text-based technology will decrease stereotyping in these teams.*

Proposition 2: *When stereotyping of diverse members is reduced in diverse VTs there will be (a) more effective communication, (b) greater cooperation and team cohesion, and (c) lower levels of conflict in these types of teams.*

Type of electronic technology needed. Our model also hypothesizes that some types of technology may be more likely to reduce stereotyping in VTs than others. For example, based on previous research, it can be argued that text-based technology (e.g., email, instant messages) may be more effective than visual or audio technology in reducing stereotypes because it does not reveal members' physical and vocal characteristics (Walther, 2009). However, it merits noting that we know of only one empirical study that has examined the extent to which the type of technology reduces stereotyping and enhances knowledge sharing in diverse VTs (Robert et al., 2018). Thus, we believe that additional research is needed to examine these moderating effects. As a result, we offer the following proposition to guide future research.

Proposition 3: *The use of text-based technology will be more likely to reduce stereotyping in diverse VTs than the use of visual or auditory technology.*

Relation Between Diversity and Status Differences

Studies have consistently shown that high status team members often denigrate or ignore the suggestions of low status members in diverse VTs (Driskell et al., 2003). As a result, members' status differences may serve as a barrier to diverse members' influence in VTs, and it may prevent teams from benefiting from the unique ideas and suggestions that these individuals bring to the team. Interestingly, some research has found that the use of CMCs may reduce the importance of status differences, decrease domination by a few high status members, and ensure that diverse members' views are considered in VTs (Kiesler et al., 1984). The primary reason for this is that the use of text-based CMC does not reveal members' status, prestige, or power, and leads all members to perceive others as having equal power in VTs (Kiesler et al., 1984). Similarly, research has shown that the use of CMC may decrease status differences because technology does not relay expressive communication, voice tone, or nonverbal behaviors (e.g., strong eye contact) that are indirect indices of status (Kiesler et al., 1984). Thus, there should be greater equalization of power in teams that use text-based electronic technology, and it should decrease the influence of charismatic and high status members, which should encourage all members to participate in discussions (Kiesler et al., 1984).

Although some studies have found that CMC reduces status differences in VTs, the results of research on this effect have been inconsistent. For instance, several studies revealed that social equalization was higher when CMC was used in VTs (Siegel et al., 1986). Results of other studies indicated CMC can reduce status effects during team discussions even between members from different cultures (e.g., Singapore vs. United States; Tan et al., 2015). Further, Sproull and Kiesler (1986) found that the use of email breaks down status differences in VTs, resulting in a greater equalization of participation in these teams. Despite these findings, other research has found that status differences were not lower in CMC than FTF teams, and status differences persisted in both CMC and FTF teams over time (Silver et al., 1994; Weisband et al., 2017).

Even though the research has been mixed on the degree to which the use of electronic technology can decrease status differences, most of the studies on this topic have been conducted in social, not organizational, settings (Kiesler et al., 1984). Thus, we believe that additional research is needed to assess these relations in organizational contexts. As a result, we offer the following propositions to guide future research on the topic.

Proposition 4: *The use of text-based electronic technology will moderate the relations between diversity and (a) the reduction of members' status differences and (b) the degree to which diverse members participate in VT discussions.*

Proposition 5: *When VT members' status differences are reduced, there will be (a) more effective communication, (b) greater cooperation and team cohesion, and (c) lower levels of conflict.*

Type of electronic technology needed. In the previous section we argued that the use of text-based technology (e.g., email, text messages) may be more likely to reduce status differences among diverse members than visual or auditory technology (e.g., videoconferencing, telephonic messages). To our knowledge, no empirical research has examined the degree to which text-based technology reduces status differences more than visual or auditory technologies in diverse VTs in organizations. Thus, we present the following proposition to guide research.

Proposition 6: *The use of text-based technology will be more likely to (a) reduce status differences and (b) enhance diverse members' participation in diverse VTs than the use of other forms of technology that display visual or auditory cues.*

Relation Between Diversity and Biases Based on Lack of Contact

Our model also suggests that diversity often results in biases because majority team members may not have had previous contact with diverse members, and they use unfounded stereotypes to form beliefs about them. For example, when team members have had little or no previous contact with someone who is Hispanic American, they are likely to base their views about the person on stereotypes associated with this group. This leads them to make biased inferences about the person (e.g., person is lazy, unintelligent, and criminal), which has a detrimental effect on communication and cohesion in VTs. However, our model predicts that increased positive contact with diverse members allows others to see them as individuals, which prevents them from using erroneous stereotypes to make inferences about their diverse teammates (Allport, 1954). For example, European Americans who have had little contact with Hispanic Americans may perceive that they are all lazy, unintelligent, and criminals. However, when they get to know a Hispanic teammate, they are likely to see the person as an individual who is intelligent, hardworking, and conscientious. Thus, positive contact with diverse VT members is thought to dispel unfounded stereotypes and enhance interpersonal relations between team members.

As noted previously, our model argues that electronic technology can be used to increase positive contact between diverse team members and others (Walther, 2009). However, the overall results of research on this issue have been mixed. Some research found that electronic technology can be used to increase positive contact and reduce interethnic conflict in VTs (Amichai-Hamburger & McKenna, 2006; Mortensen & Hinds, 2001). The primary reason for this is that electronic technology diverts attention from idiosyncratic characteristics which enhances trust and liking (Mortensen & Hinds, 2001). Further, research has indicated that the use of electronic technology facilitates positive contact because it (a) gives team members online anonymity which reduces feelings of vulnerability, (b) enhances trust of diverse members, and (c) makes it easier for team members to determine shared interests and values (Krebs et al., 2006; McKenna & Bargh, 2000; McKenna & Green 2002). However, other research found that the use of electronic technology actually exacerbated culturally based disagreements between Jews and Palestinians, which promoted higher levels of intergroup conflict (Ellis & Moaz, 2007).

Although the research on the effects of electronic technology on positive contact has been inconsistent, most of the studies on this effect have been conducted in social, not organizational, settings. Thus, we believe that research is needed to test these effects in organizational contexts. Therefore, we offer the following propositions to guide future research.

Proposition 7: *The use and type of electronic communication technology in VTs will moderate the relations between diversity and (a) positive contact with diverse members, (b) decrease stereotyping about them, and (c) enhance liking and positive interpersonal relations between VT members.*

Proposition 8: *When VT ingroup members have positive contact with diverse members there will be (a) more effective communication, (b) greater cooperation and team cohesion, and (c) lower levels of conflict.*

Type of electronic technology needed.   As noted previously, our model hypothesizes that the type of technology used will affect the degree to which team members will experience positive contact with diverse members. Further, we believe that the use of only text-based (e.g., email) technology may not give team members the chance to get to know diverse members well and may not overcome the preconceived stereotypes associated with these individuals. Thus, we predict that the use of a variety of technologies including visual, auditory, collaborative, and team-building technologies may be more likely to enhance positive contact and positive relations than the use of text-based technology alone. We know of no empirical research on this issue so we offer the following proposition to guide future research.

Proposition 9: *The use of a variety of visual, auditory, and collaborative technologies will be more likely to enhance (a) positive contact and (b) positive relations between VT members than the use of only text-based technologies.*

Relation Between Diversity and Culturally Based Miscommunication and Misunderstandings

A final set of challenges created by diversity in VTs is that team members often have very dissimilar cultural values (e.g., individualism or collectivism), which means that they have distinct communication and conflict resolution styles, and these differences are likely to result in miscommunication and misunderstandings in VTs (Kankanhalli et al., 2006). Our model suggests that the use of electronic technology may help alleviate some of these problems. For example, the use of synchronous communication technology may help team members clarify messages or give them a chance to ask questions in real time which could reduce miscommunication. Further, the use of various types of collaboration technology (e.g., discussion boards, electronic team rooms) might alleviate misunderstandings by giving members an opportunity to express their concerns or frustrations, and come to an agreement on methods that can be used to resolve problems. In addition, when VT members speak different languages, web-based translators may be used to translate messages, so everyone can participate in team discussions.

A recent review of the literature supports our contention that cross-cultural differences in VTs often result in greater levels of miscommunication and misunderstandings, and lower levels of satisfaction and cohesion than in homogeneous VTs (Morrison-Smith & Ruiz, 2020). For example, results of research indicated that sociocultural differences were positively related to conflict in VTs, and negatively related to communication, interactions, and team performance (Gibson et al., 2014). In addition, studies have shown that when VTs have high levels of sociocultural distance, they are more likely to have process challenges and lower team performance than when they have low levels of sociocultural distance (Gibson et al., 2014). Sociocultural distance is a measure of team members' perceptions about co-workers' values and norms (Morrison-Smith & Ruiz, 2020).

Research has also shown that perceived differences in race, education, or attitudes are negatively associated with cooperation and coordination in VTs (Eisenberg & Krishnan, 2018). Likewise, similarities in sociocultural beliefs were positively related to collaboration in VTs (Eisenberg & Krishnan, 2018). Studies also revealed that team members with collectivistic values were more likely to use collaboration in VTs than those who were individualistic (Paul, Samarah et al., 2004). A similar study found that when VTs were composed primarily of collectivistic members (e.g., Japan), they outperformed VTs composed of individualistic team members (e.g., United States; Mesquita & Popescu, 2014). Further, team members' individualism/collectivism was associated with greater sociocultural distance, higher levels of conflict and lower satisfaction, cohesion, and performance (Morrison-Smith & Ruiz, 2020).

Our model predicts that the use of electronic technologies is likely to mitigate some of the challenges posed by cross-cultural differences in VTs, and there has been some research on this issue. For instance, a study found that collectivistic team members were less likely to use electronic technology, and when they used technology they were more likely to choose synchronous technology than those who were individualistic (Kramer et al., 2017). The primary reason for this was that synchronous technology provides a higher level of relationship value because members can communicate in real time (Kramer et al., 2017). In contrast, those high in individualism were more likely to use electronic technology for their work and they preferred asynchronous technology so they could think about their answers before responding to others (Kramer et al., 2017).

Other research has examined how different technologies might decrease miscommunication and misunderstandings in diverse VTs. For instance, an interview study by Shachaf (2008) found that email helped team members overcome differences in verbal and nonverbal communication. The reason for this was that straightforward text did not include emotions or distractions, and was easier to understand than verbal messages alone (Shachaf, 2008). Similarly, Shachaf (2008) found that the use of web-based team rooms helped team members identify with the team and overcome the negative impact of communication style differences on understanding messages. She also found that chat rooms allowed team members to communicate spontaneously, and videoconferencing gave them the opportunity to observe others' facial expressions and nonverbal behaviors, which increased their understanding of others' messages (Shachaf, 2008). Research also found that videoconferencing with shared mental models was as effective as FTF communication (Guo et al., 2009). However, research by Hightower et al. (2007) revealed that the use of electronic technology does not always facilitate communication in VTs and is typically more formal, took longer to communicate, resulted in lower levels of member satisfaction, and did not enhance interpersonal relations in diverse VTs (Hightower et al., 2007).

Apart from the studies previously discussed, we know of only a few studies on the effects of electronic technology on culturally based conflict resolution. The results of one study found that group decision support systems were useful because they allowed team members to discuss options, voice their preferences, and vote on the final option (Paul, Seetharaman, et al., 2004). This study also revealed that group decision support systems had a positive impact on satisfaction with the decision-making process and the team. Another study by Denton (2006) found that the use of intranet groupware helped team members work together toward a common goal.

Although there has been some research on the effects of cross-cultural differences on miscommunication, misunderstandings, and VT processes, we believe that much more research is needed on these topics. Thus, we present the following propositions to guide research.

> **Proposition 10:** *Electronic technology will moderate the relation between diversity and cross-cultural communication so that technology will decrease the extent to which there is miscommunication between diverse VT members and others.*

> **Proposition 11:** *Electronic technology will moderate the relation between diversity and cross-cultural conflict resolution so that technology will increase the degree to which VT members voice concerns and resolve conflict.*

> **Proposition 12:** *When team members can understand cross-cultural communications there will be (a) greater cooperation and team cohesion and (b) lower levels of conflict in VTs than when they cannot understand cross-cultural communication.*

> **Proposition 13:** *When VT members have resolved cross-cultural conflict, there will be greater (a) communication, (b) levels of cooperation, and (c) team cohesion than when they have not resolved conflict.*

Type of electronic technology needed. We discussed the various types of technology that might be useful in cross-cultural teams in a previous section, so we will not repeat those issues here. In summary, there has been some research on the degree to which electronic technology moderates the relations between diversity and (a) stereotyping, (b) status differences, (c) participation in VTs, and (d) cross-cultural differences in communication and conflict. With a few exceptions, most of this research found that electronic technology can mitigate the diversity challenges associated with diverse VTs. We also found that specific types of technologies may be needed to meet different challenges. For example, text-based technology may alleviate stereotyping and status differences, but video, audio, or collaborative technologies may be needed to establish positive contact, or resolve miscommunication and misunderstandings in cross-cultural VTs.

STRATEGIES FOR OVERCOMING DIVERSITY CHALLENGES IN VTS

Although we have argued throughout this chapter that electronic technology is likely to ameliorate diversity problems in VTs, we want to emphasize that we do not believe that it is a panacea. Other types of strategies may also be useful to overcome diversity-related challenges in VTs. Next, we consider some strategies organizations might use to mitigate diversity problems in VTs.

Cross-Cultural and Diversity Training

Diversity is thought to have a negative impact on VT processes and outcomes. The primary reason for this is that diverse members have different cultural values, norms, role expectations, and communication styles. These factors increase miscommunication and conflict and decrease interpersonal relations and cohesion in these teams. For instance, members of different ethnic subgroups, women, and older workers have different communication styles than their counterparts, and these differences increase misunderstandings and misperceptions in VTs. We argued that electronic technology might be used to mitigate these problems, but we also believe that cross-cultural or diversity training may help VT members work together effectively. This type of training could help members understand differences in cultural values, norms, communication, and conflict resolution styles. It could also be used to change their expectations and provide them with new strategies for working in diverse VTs.

Technology Training

Another key challenge associated with diversity in VTs is that team members may have very different levels of skills and experience with technology, and VTs need members with high levels of expertise in technology to be successful. As a result, we contend that team members should be given the opportunity to complete training in different types of technology so that VTs can be more effective. For instance, older workers (e.g., baby boomers) may have lower levels of understanding of collaborative technologies (e.g., social media, virtual conferencing, team rooms, team games, decision support systems) than younger workers. In addition, they may not be familiar with emojis, acronyms, and images used by Millennials and members of Generation Z. Further, younger workers may have less experience with email than older workers because they are more likely to use text messages and social media to communicate than older workers. As a result, technology training may be needed to ensure that all members have the skills needed to use available technologies.

Use Team-Based Reward Systems

A common problem in organizations is that they use individual reward systems (e.g., individual pay for performance) but expect that these rewards will motivate people to work together in teams (Kerr, 1975). As a result, we believe that team-based rewards, rather than just individual rewards, are needed to motivate members to work collaboratively in diverse VTs. Thus, reward systems need to be aligned with the goals of VTs. For instance, organizations should reward team members who (a) facilitate cooperation with diverse team members, (b) share knowledge with other members, (c) encourage balanced participation in discussions so diverse members have a voice, and (d) foster the inclusion of all team members. Of course, organizations can use reward systems that motivate all types of behavior in diverse VTs, but we believe that enhancing cooperation and cohesion in these types of teams is essential.

Team Building

Given that many VTs involve diverse team members who have never worked together, we believe that team building might be used to enhance cooperation and cohesion in these teams. Team building typically asks members to participate in various collaborative activities that allow them to get to know one another, define roles, and improve interpersonal relations. Team building also emphasizes enhancing team processes and interpersonal relations, and is different from team training that stresses team efficiency and productivity (Cummings & Worley, 2014). Interestingly, team building can now be conducted online because there are numerous team games and activities that can be performed using electronic technology. Although team building seems to be a plausible way of improving VT performance, it merits noting that research has not shown that team building enhances team performance (Porras & Robertson, 1992). Thus, even though the strategies we proposed may increase the effectiveness of VTs, research needed to examine their success rates.

CONCLUSION

Given the rise in the use of diverse VTs, we presented a model that examines the extent to which electronic technology moderates the relations between diversity and VT processes and outcomes. Our model predicts that diversity poses a number of challenges in VTs (e.g., prejudice, stereotyping, status differences), and electronic technology can help alleviate some of these challenges and have a positive impact on VT processes (e.g., communication, cooperation, cohesion). Our model also suggests that specific types of electronic technology may be needed to address different challenges (e.g., text-based technology may be used to overcome prejudice more than visual technologies). We also reviewed the literature on the predicted relations in the model and offered propositions to guide future research on the issues. In addition, we considered several practical strategies that might be used to deal with diversity-related challenges in VTs.

We hope that our paper will increase our understanding of the challenges facing diverse VTs, and the degree to which electronic technology might be used to alleviate these challenges. We also hope that it will help organizations increase the inclusion of diverse members in VTs, and enable all team members to work together more effectively.

REFERENCES

Adrianson, L. (2001). Gender and computer-mediated communication: Group processes in problem solving. *Computers in Human Behavior, 17*(1), 71–94. https://doi.org/10.1016/S0747-5632(00)00033-9

Allport, G. W. (1954). *The nature of prejudice.* Addison-Wesley. https://psycnet.apa.org/record/1954-07324-000

Amichai-Hamburger, Y., & McKenna, K. Y. A. (2006). The contact hypothesis reconsidered: Interacting via the Internet. *Journal of Computer-Mediated Communication, 11*(3), 825–843. https://doi.org/10.1111/j.1083-6101.2006.00037.x

Ashmore, R., & Del Boca, F. K. (1981). Conceptual approaches to stereotypes and stereotyping. In D. L. Hamilton (Ed.), *Cognitive processes in stereotyping and intergroup behavior* (pp. 1–36). Psychology Press.

Au, Y., & Marks, A. (2012). "Virtual teams are literally and metaphorically invisible": Forging identity in culturally diverse virtual teams. *Employee Relations, 34(3),* 271–287. https://doi.org/10.1108/01425451211217707

Back, K. W. (1951). Influence through social communication. *The Journal of Abnormal and Social Psychology, 46*(1), 9–23. https://doi.org/10.1037/h0058629

Betancourt, H., & López, S. R. (1993). The study of culture, ethnicity, and race in American psychology. *American Psychologist, 48*(6), 629–637. https://doi.org/10.1037/0003-066X.48.6.629

Carte, T., & Chidambaram, L. (2004). A capabilities-based theory of technology deployment in diverse teams: Leapfrogging the pitfalls of diversity and leveraging its potential with collaborative technology. *Journal of the Association for Information Systems, 5*(11), 448–471. https://doi.org/10.17705/1jais.00060

Cummings, T. G., & Worley, C. G. (2014). *Organization development and change.* Cengage.

Curtis, R. C., & Miller, K. (1986). Believing another likes or dislikes you: Behaviors making the beliefs come true. *Journal of Personality and Social Psychology, 51*(2), 284–290. https://doi.org/10.1037/0022-3514.51.2.284

Daft, R. L., & Lengel, R. H. (1986). Organizational information requirements, media richness and structural design. *Management Science, 32*(5), 554–571. https://doi.org/10.1287/mnsc.32.5.554

de Jong, R., Schalk, R., & Curşeu, P. L. (2008). Virtual communicating, conflicts and performance in teams. *Team Performance Management, 14*(7/8), 364–380. https://doi.org/10.1108/13527590810912331

Denton, D. K. (2006). Using intranets to make virtual teams effective. *Team Performance Management, 12*(7/8), 253–257. https://doi.org/10.1108/1352759 0610711804

Driskell, J. E., Radtke, P. H., & Salas, E. (2003). Virtual teams: Effects of technological mediation on team performance. *Group Dynamics: Theory, Research, and Practice, 7*(4), 297–323. https://doi.org/10.1037/1089-2699.7.4.297

Dulebohn, J. H., & Hoch, J. E. (2017). Virtual teams in organizations. *Human Resource Management Review, 27*(4), 569–574. https://doi.org/10.1016/j .hrmr.2016.12.004

Edwards, H. K., & Sridhar, V. (2005). Analysis of software requirements engineering exercises in a global virtual team setup. *Journal of Global Information Management, 13*(2), 21–41. https://doi.org/10.4018/jgim.2005040102

Ehsan, N., Mirza, E., & Ahmad, M. (2008, August). Impact of computer-mediated communication on virtual teams' performance: An empirical study. *In Proceedings of the International Symposium on Information Technology,* Kuala Lumpur, Malaysia, 1–8. https://doi.org/10.1109/ITSIM.2008.4632068

Eisenberg, J., & Krishnan, A. (2018). Addressing virtual work challenges: Learning from the field. *Organization Management Journal, 15*(2), 78–94. https://doi .org/10.1080/15416518.2018.1471976

Ellis, D. G., & Moaz, I. (2007). Online argument between Israeli Jews and Palestinians. *Human Communication Research, 33*(3), 291–309. https://www.learntechlib .org/p/70199/

Festinger, L., Schachter, S., & Back, K. (1950). *Social pressures in informal groups: A study of human factors in housing.* Harper. https://psycnet.apa.org/record/1951 -02994-000

Gera, S. (2013). Virtual teams versus face to face teams: A review of literature. *Journal of Business and Management, 11(2),* 1–4. https://doi.org/10.9790/487X-1120104

Giambatista, R. C., & Bhappu, A. D. (2010). Diversity's harvest: Interactions of diversity sources and communication technology on creative group performance. *Organizational Behavior and Human Decision Processes, 111*(2), 116–126. https://doi.org/10.1016/j.obhdp.2009.11.003

Gibson, C. B., & Gibbs, J. L. (2006). Unpacking the concept of virtuality: The effects of geographic dispersion, electronic dependence, dynamic structure, and national diversity on team innovation. *Administrative Science Quarterly, 51*(3), 451–495. https://doi.org/10.2189/asqu.51.3.451

Gibson, C. B., Huang, L., Kirkman, B. L., & Shapiro, D. L. (2014). Where global and virtual meet: The value of examining the intersection of these elements in twenty-first-century teams. *Annual Review of Organizational Psychology and Organizational Behavior, 1(1),* 217–244. https://doi.org/10.1146/annurev -orgpsych-031413-091240

Gilson, L. L., Maynard, M. T., Jones Young, N. C., Vartiainen, M., & Hakonen, M. (2015). Virtual teams research: 10 years, 10 themes, and 10 opportunities. *Journal of Management, 41*(5), 1313–1337. https://doi.org/10.1177/ 0149206314559946

Guo, Z., D'ambra, J., Turner, T., & Zhang, H. (2009). Improving the effectiveness of virtual teams: A comparison of video-conferencing and face-to-face communication in China. *IEEE Transactions on Professional Communication, 52*(1), 1–16. https://doi.org/10.1109/TPC.2008.2012284

Hambley, L. A., O'Neill, T. A., & Kline, T. J. B. (2007). Virtual team leadership: The effects of leadership style and communication medium on team interaction styles and outcomes. *Organizational Behavior and Human Decision Processes, 103*(1), 1–20. https://doi.org/10.1016/j.obhdp.2006.09.004

Han, S. J., & Beyerlein, M. (2016). Framing the effects of multinational cultural diversity on virtual team processes. *Small Group Research, 47*(4), 351–383. https://doi.org/10.1177/1046496416653480

Harrison, D. A., & Klein, K. J. (2007). What's the difference? Diversity constructs as separation, variety, or disparity in organizations. *Academy of Management Review, 32*(4), 1199–1228. https://doi.org/10.5465/amr.2007.26586096

Harrison, T., & Stone, D. L. (2018). Effects of organizational values and employee contact on e-recruiting. *Journal of Managerial Psychology, 33*(3), 311–324. https://doi.org/10.1108/JMP-03-2017-0118

Hightower, R., Sayeed, L., & Warkentin, M. (2007). A longitudinal study of information exchange in computer-mediated and face-to-face groups. In U. Kulkarni, D. J. Power, & R. Sharda (Eds.), *Decision support for global enterprises* (pp. 93–112). Springer.

Hinds, P. J., & Bailey, D. E. (2003). Out of sight, out of sync: Understanding conflict in distributed teams. *Organization Science, 14*(6), 615–632. https://doi.org/10.1287/orsc.14.6.615.24872

Hinds, P. J., & Mortensen, M. (2005). Understanding conflict in geographically distributed teams: The moderating effects of shared identity, shared context, and spontaneous communication. *Organization Science, 16*(3), 290–307. https://doi.org/10.1287/orsc.1050.0122

Holt, J. L., & DeVore, C. J. (2005). Culture, gender, organizational role, and styles of conflict resolution: A meta-analysis. *International Journal of Intercultural Relations, 29*(2), 165–196. https://doi.org/10.1016/j.ijintrel.2005.06.002

Jarvenpaa, S. L., & Leidner, D. E. (1999). Communication and trust in global virtual teams. *Organization Science, 10*(6), 791–815. https://doi.org/10.1287/orsc.10.6.791

Kankanhalli, A., Tan, B. C. Y., & Wei, K. K. (2006). Conflict and performance in global virtual teams. *Journal of Management Information Systems, 23*(3), 237–274. https://doi.org/10.2753/MIS0742-1222230309

Kerr, S. (1975). On the folly of rewarding A, while hoping for B. *Academy of Management Journal, 18*(4), 769–783. https://doi.org/10.5465/255378

Kiesler, S., Siegel, J., & McGuire, T. W. (1984). Social psychological aspects of computer-mediated communication. *American Psychologist, 39*(10), 1123–1134. https://doi.org/10.1037/0003-066X.39.10.1123

Kirkman, B. L., Cordery, J. L., Mathieu, J., Rosen, B., & Kukenberger, M. (2013). Global organizational communities of practice: The effects of nationality diversity, psychological safety, and media richness on community performance. *Human Relations, 66*(3), 333–362. https://doi.org/10.1177/0018726712464076

Kirkman, B. L., Rosen, B., Tesluk, P. E., & Gibson, C. B. (2004). The impact of team empowerment on virtual team performance: The moderating role of face-to-face interaction. *Academy of Management Journal, 47*(2), 175–192. https://doi.org/10.5465/20159571

Kirkman, B. L., & Shapiro, D. L. (2001). The impact of cultural values on job satisfaction and organizational commitment in self-managing work teams: The mediating role of employee resistance. *Academy of Management Journal, 44(3),* 557–569. https://doi.org/10.5465/3069370

Kochman, T. (1981). *Black and White styles in conflict.* The University of Chicago Press.

Kramer, W. S., Shuffler, M. L., & Feitosa, J. (2017). The world is not flat: Examining the interactive multidimensionality of culture and virtuality in teams. *Human Resource Management Review, 27*(4), 604–620. https://doi.org/10.1016/j.hrmr.2016.12.007

Krebs, S. A., Hobman, E. V., & Bordia, P. (2006). Virtual teams and group member dissimilarity: Consequences for the development of trust. *Small Group Research, 37(6),* 721–741. https://doi.org/10.1177/1046496406294886

Lee, E-J, & Oh, S. Y. (2017). Computer-mediated communication. *Oxford Bibliographies.* https://doi.org/10.1093/OBO/9780199756841-0160

Lin, C., Standing, C., & Liu, Y. C. (2008). A model to develop effective virtual teams. *Decision Support Systems, 45*(4), 1031–1045. https://doi.org/10.1016/j.dss.2008.04.002

Lott, A. J., & Lott, B. E. (1961). Group cohesiveness, communication level, and conformity. *The Journal of Abnormal and Social Psychology, 62*(2), 408–412. https://doi.org/10.1037/h0041109

Martins, L. L., Gilson, L. L., & Maynard, M. T. (2004). Virtual teams: What do we know and where do we go from here? *Journal of Management, 30*(6), 805–835. https://doi.org/10.1016/j.jm.2004.05.002

Martins, L. L., & Shalley, C. E. (2011). Creativity in virtual work: Effects of demographic differences. *Small Group Research, 42*(5), 536–561. https://doi.org/10.1177/1046496410397382

McDonough, E. F., Kahnb, K. B., & Barczaka, G. (2003). An investigation of the use of global, virtual, and colocated new product development teams. *Journal of Product Innovation Management, 18*(2), 110–120. https://doi.org/10.1111/1540-5885.1820110

McKenna, K. Y. A., & Bargh, J. A. (2000). Plan 9 from cyberspace: The implications of the Internet for personality and social psychology. *Personality and Social Psychology Review, 4*(1), 57–75. https://doi.org/10.1207/S15327957PSPR0401_6

McKenna, K. Y. A., & Green, A. S. (2002). Virtual group dynamics. *Group Dynamics: Theory, Research, and Practice, 6(1),* 116–127. https://doi.org/10.1037/1089-2699.6.1.116

Mesmer-Magnus, J. R., DeChurch, L. A., Jimenez-Rodriguez, M., Wildman, J., & Shuffler, M. (2011). A meta-analytic investigation of virtuality and information sharing in teams. *Organizational Behavior and Human Decision Processes, 115*(2), 214–225. https://doi.org/10.1016/j.obhdp.2011.03.002

Mesquita, A., & Popescu, T. (2014). Universities in the business environment. *Faima Business & Management Journal, 2*(4), 5–13.

Montoya-Weiss, M. M., Massey, A. P., & Song, M. (2001). Getting it together: Temporal coordination and conflict management in global virtual teams. *Academy of Management Journal, 44*(6), 1251–1262. https://doi.org/10.5465/3069399

Morrison-Smith, S., & Ruiz, J. (2020). Challenges and barriers in virtual teams: A literature review. *SN Applied Sciences, 2*(6), 1–33. https://doi.org/10.1007/s42452 -020-2801-5

Mortensen, M., & Hinds, P. J. (2001). Conflict and shared identity in geographically distributed teams. *International Journal of Conflict Management, 12*(3), 212–238. https://doi.org/10.1108/eb022856

Naik, N., & Kim, D. J. (2010). Virtual team success: Towards a theory of performance in virtual teams. *AMCIS 2010 Proceedings 429.* https://aisel.aisnet.org/ amcis2010/429

Paul, S., Samarah, I. M., Seetharaman, P., & Mykytyn, P. P., Jr.. (2004). An empirical investigation of collaborative conflict management style in group support system-based global virtual teams. *Journal of Management Information Systems, 21*(3), 185–222. https://doi.org/10.1080/07421222.2004.11045809

Paul, S., Seetharaman, P., Samarah, I., & Mykytyn, P., Jr. (2004, December). Conflict in GSS-based Virtual Teams: Findings from an Experiment. *AMCIS 2004 Proceedings.* Retrieved from https://aisel.aisnet.org/amcis2004/249

Polzer, J. T., Crisp, C. B., Jarvenpaa, S. L., & Kim, J. W. (2006). Extending the faultline model to geographically dispersed teams: How colocated subgroups can impair group functioning. *Academy of Management Journal, 49*(4), 679–692. https://doi.org/10.5465/amj.2006.22083024

Porras, J. I., & Robertson, P. J. (1992). *Organizational development: Theory, practice, and research* (pp. 719–822). Consulting Psychologists Press.

Powell, A., Galvin, J., & Piccoli, G. (2006). Antecedents to team member commitment from near and far: A comparison between collocated and virtual teams. *Information Technology & People, 19*(4), 299–322. https://doi.org/10 .1108/09593840610718018

Puiia, L. (2015). Virtual team interactions: Do they help or hinder interpersonal communication? [Doctoral dissertation, University of Southern Maine]. https://digitalcommons.usm.maine.edu/etd/57

Roberge, M. E., & van Dick, R. (2010). Recognizing the benefits of diversity: When and how does diversity increase group performance? *Human Resource Management Review, 20*(4), 295–308. https://doi.org/10.1016/j.hrmr.2009.09.002

Robert, L. P., Jr., Dennis, A. R., & Ahuja, M. K. (2018). Differences are different: Examining the effects of communication media on the impacts of racial and gender diversity in decision-making teams. *Information Systems Research, 29*(3), 525–545. https://doi.org/10.1287/isre.2018.0773

Roseman, M., & Greenberg, S. (1996, November). TeamRooms: Network places for collaboration. *Proceedings of the ACM Conference on Computer Supported Cooperative Work* (pp. 325–333). ACM Press. https://doi.org/10.1145/240080.240319

Sarker, S., & Sahay, S. (2003). Understanding virtual team development: An interpretive study. *Journal of the Association for Information Systems, 4*(1), 247–285. https://doi.org/10.17705/1jais.00028

Schiller, S. Z., & Mandviwalla, M. (2007). Virtual team research: An analysis of theory use and a framework for theory appropriation. *Small Group Research, 38*(1), 12–59. https://doi.org/10.1177/1046496406297035

Scott, C. P. R., & Wildman, J. L. (2015). Culture, communication, and conflict: A review of the global virtual team literature. In J. L. Wildman & R. L. Griffith

(Eds.), *Leading global teams: Translating multidisciplinary science to practice* (pp. 13–32). Springer. https://doi.org/10.1007/978-1-4939-2050-1_2

Shachaf, P. (2008). Cultural diversity and information and communication technology impacts on global virtual teams: An exploratory study. *Information & Management, 45*(2), 131–142. https://doi.org/10.1016/j.im.2007.12.003

Siegel, J., Dubrovsky, V., Kiesler, S., & McGuire, T. W. (1986). Group processes in computer-mediated communication. *Organizational Behavior and Human Decision Processes, 37*(2), 157–187. https://doi.org/10.1016/0749-5978(86)90050-6

Silver, S. D., Cohen, B. P., & Crutchfield, J. H. (1994). Status differentiation and information exchange in face-to-face and computer-mediated idea generation. *Social Psychology Quarterly, 57*(2), 108–123. https://doi.org/10.2307/2786705

Smith, P. B. (2011). Communication styles as dimensions of national culture. *Journal of Cross-cultural Psychology, 42*(2), 216–233.

Sproull, L., & Kiesler, S. (1986). Reducing social context cues: Electronic mail in organizational communication. *Management Science, 32*(11), 1492–1512. https://doi.org/10.1287/mnsc.32.11.1492

Staples, D. S., & Zhao, L. (2006). The effects of cultural diversity in virtual teams versus face-to-face teams. *Group Decision and Negotiation, 15*(4), 389–406. https://doi.org/10.1007/s10726-006-9042-x

Stone-Romero, E. F., Stone, D. L., & Salas, E. (2003). The influence of culture on role conceptions and role behavior in organizations. *Applied Psychology, 52*(3), 328–362. https://doi.org/10.1111/1464-0597.00139

Swigger, K., Alpaslan, F., Brazile, R., & Monticino, M. (2004). Effects of culture on computer-supported international collaborations. *International Journal of Human-Computer Studies, 60*(3), 365–380. https://doi.org/10.1016/j.ijhcs.2003.10.006

Tajfel, H. (1982). Social psychology of intergroup relations. *Annual Review of Psychology, 33*(1), 1–39. https://doi.org/10.1146/annurev.ps.33.020182.000245

Tajfel, H., & Turner, J. C. (1985). The social identity theory of intergroup behavior. In S. Worchel & W. G. Austin (Eds.), *Psychology of Intergroup Relations* (2nd ed., pp. 7–24). Nelson Hall.

Tan, B. C. Y., Wei, K. K., Huang, W. W., & Ng, G. N. (2000). A dialogue technique to enhance electronic communication in virtual teams. *IEEE Transactions on Professional Communication, 43*(2), 153–165. https://doi.org/10.1109/47.843643

Tan, B. C. Y., Wei, K. K., Watson, R. T., & Walczuch, R. M. (2015). Reducing status effects with computer-mediated communication: Evidence from two distinct national cultures. *Journal of Management Information Systems, 15*(1), 119–141. https://doi.org/10.1080/07421222.1998.11518199

Townsend, A. M., DeMarie, S. M., & Hendrickson, A. R. (1998). Virtual teams: Technology and the workplace of the future. *Academy of Management Perspectives, 12*(3), 17–29. https://doi.org/10.5465/ame.1998.1109047

Triandis, H. C. (1994). *Culture and social behavior.* McGraw-Hill.

Tyran K. L., & Gibson C. B. (2008). Is what you see what you get? The relationship among surface- and deep-level heterogeneity characteristics, group efficacy, and team reputation. *Group & Organization Management, 33*(1), 46–76. https://doi.org/10.1177/1059601106287111

Washington University. (n.d.). What are examples of accessible electronic and information technology in education? Access Computing. https://www.washington.edu/accesscomputing/what-are-examples-accessible-electronic-and-information-technology-education

Van Knippenberg, D., De Dreu, C. K. W., & Homan, A. C. (2004). Work group diversity and group performance: An integrative model and research agenda. *Journal of Applied Psychology, 89*(6), 1008–1022. https://doi.org/10.1037/0021-9010.89.6.1008

Van Knippenberg, D., & Schippers, M. C. (2007). Work group diversity. *Annual Review of Psychology, 58*(1), 515–541. https://doi.org/10.1146/annurev.psych.58.110405.085546

Walther, J. B. (2009). Computer-mediated communication and virtual groups: Applications to interethnic conflict. *Journal of Applied Communication Research, 37*(3), 225–238. https://doi.org/10.1080/00909880903025937

Weisband, S., & Atwater, L. (1999). Evaluating self and others in electronic and face-to-face groups. *Journal of Applied Psychology, 84*(4), 632–639. https://doi.org/10.1037/0021-9010.84.4.632

Weisband, S. P., Schneider, S. K., & Connolly, T. (2017). Computer-mediated communication and social information: Status salience and status differences. *Academy of Management Journal, 38*(4), 1124–1151. https://doi.org/10.5465/256623

Zhou, W., & Shi, X. (2011). Culture in groups and teams: A review of three decades of research. *International Journal of Cross Cultural Management, 11*(1), 5–34. https://doi.org/10.1177/1470595811398799

CHAPTER 10

VIRTUAL MEETINGS

Increasing Equity, Exacerbating the Inequities, or Just 'Meh?

William H. Bommer
California State University, Fresno

James M. Schmidtke
California State University, Fresno

ABSTRACT

COVID-19 created a rapid increase in people using videoconferencing technology to interact with team members. As relatively little is known about behavioral differences between face-to-face meetings and those conducted via videoconferencing, the current study was conducted to address these issues. More specifically, we compared levels of overall activity, agentic behaviors, and communal behaviors from people in parallel face-to-face ($N = 668$) and virtual team settings ($N = 652$). Results found videoconferencing was associated with lower overall activity than occurred in face-to-face meetings. Further, the frequency of agentic and communal behaviors was reduced in videoconferences. Gender, to a much lesser degree than meeting format, was also associated with differential levels of overall activity, agentic behaviors, and counter

Managing Team Centricity in Modern Organizations, pages 293–322
Copyright © 2022 by Information Age Publishing
www.infoagepub.com
All rights of reproduction in any form reserved.

to the hypothesized relationship, communal behaviors. Meeting format and gender failed to interact to impact the behavioral outcomes. Findings showed videoconferencing cannot be considered as improving equity compared to face-to-face meetings, but it likely does not exacerbate the differences associated with face-to-face team meetings either. Recommendations are provided to alleviate potential reductions in important behaviors.

Over the past 4 decades teams have become a ubiquitous feature of organizational life. During this time, the form and functions of teams have changed, due in large part to technological advances used to facilitate team interactions. Simultaneously, and largely influenced by the availability of these technological advances, new types of teams have emerged, with virtual teams likely being the most prominent and organizationally utilized. Virtual teams are teams in which a significant amount of interaction among team members occurs via electronic media rather than face-to-face interactions (Jarvenpaa & Leidner, 1999; Maznevski & Chudoba, 2000). Due to constraints imposed by the COVID-19 pandemic, many organizational members moved to virtual settings to hold meetings and perform assigned tasks. This shift has not only affected existing organizational teams, but many new teams have been forced to launch in this novel environment.

While creating virtual teams, organizations have generally brought new members together for initial meetings to foster development. Indeed, some researchers (e.g., Marlow et al., 2017; Morrison-Smith & Ruiz, 2020; Warkentin et al., 1997) suggest that virtual teams should use traditional face-to-face meetings in the early stages of team formation to foster the development of personal relationships among team members and to improve virtual team performance. Kirkman et al. (2004), for example, found that the number of face-to-face meetings of a virtual team moderated the relation between team empowerment and team performance. As was witnessed during the pandemic, and previously in cases where team members are too geographically dispersed to make face-to-face interaction plausible, this "face-to-face first" technique may be desirable, but it may not always be possible. Further, this approach may reduce one of the potential benefits associated with using virtual teams (e.g., quickly assembling a team of people from around the world to participate) especially if teams need to be formed quickly to solve an urgent problem. Thus, an important question to ask is whether initial meetings, among team members who do not know each other, are different when those meetings occur face-to-face compared to when they are held in a virtual environment.

While meetings held via virtual settings have become increasingly common in general, their frequency skyrocketed during the global COVID of 2020. A 2020 study by Global Workplace Analytics (Kamouri & Lister, 2020) of 2865 employees found that the percentage of employees working from home on a regular basis increased from 31% pre-COVID to 88% during the pandemic. Similarly, an MIT study (Brynjolfsson et al., 2020) reported more than 50% of people were working from home in the United States. As company executives realize that excellent work can be achieved and productivity be potentially heightened, even in jobs that no one imagined could be done virtually, a growing number of companies, including Facebook and Twitter, announced that they will allow employees to work remotely on a permanent basis (Ibarra et al., 2020).

While this dramatic increase in remote work may benefit organizations by reducing the costs associated with maintaining physical office space and travel, it is not clear that employees prefer, or benefit from this arrangement. In the Global Workplace survey, only 19% of respondents indicated that they would prefer to continue working remotely in a post-COVID environment (Kamouri & Lister, 2020). Their survey results indicate that while some aspects of work are better in a remote or virtual environment, such as managing distractions or interruptions, other aspects such as working with others are perceived less favorably. When asked to compare the two contexts, 86% of respondents indicated they were satisfied with collaboration at the office pre-COVID while only 60% indicated satisfaction collaborating with others at home. This suggests that remote group interactions may create challenges to organizations in a post-COVID environment as they encourage employees to work remotely.

One reason why employees may be less satisfied with collaborations as they work from home is their level of engagement or participation in virtual meetings. Forty-three percent of managers in the Global Workplace Analytics survey thought that working from home had a negative impact on employee engagement while only 28% thought that it had a positive effect (Kamouri & Lister, 2020). An issue that might affect participation and engagement is one's membership in particular social categories and whether or not different groups of people are systematically aided or limited based upon this new way of meeting. Sex, age, and ethnicity often lead to status distinctions that are difficult to undo (Ridgeway, 1982). These status distinctions have pervasive effects on team members' participation patterns (Levine & Moreland, 1990).

At its core, employees, managers, and researchers are all left trying to catch up with the pace of the technological change that has recently taken place. There are certainly reasons for optimism, but potentially negative consequences are frequently referred to in anecdotal evidence as well as in nascent research on the topic. In this discussion of potential improvements and possible damaging consequences, the issue of gender is frequently at the front of people's minds as it is not well understood whether these changes impact men and women differently.

Many researchers in the communications and groups literature have found that gender inequities manifest themselves in meetings. For example, Cohen and Zhou (1991) found that males were given higher status in groups even after controlling for performance differences. These status differences affect how team members interact with one another. Higher status individuals tend to dominate group interactions and are more likely to engage in behaviors such as speaking, interrupting, giving commands, and criticizing others (Levine & Moreland, 1990). These status differences, however, may shift in virtual teams because social cues are less salient. For example, in a videoconference the person's name may appear on a screen rather than their physical image which can lessen the salience of their gender and subsequently reduce status differences. Conversely, some stereotypes might be reinforced in a virtual environment when working from home. For example, interruptions from children (verbal or nonverbal) may reinforce the sex-role stereotype of "mother" undercutting the perception of womens' competence (Fiske et al., 2002). It is not understood whether changing the format to virtual meetings reduces these inequities, to exacerbate them, or to largely leave them unaffected. Deborah Tannen is quoted recently as saying, "Everything that we think is going to be an equalizer turns out not to be" (Gupta, 2020, para. 28).

We are not aware of any studies that have looked at gender differences in communication behavior in the context of videoconferencing. Indeed, Dhawan et al. (2021) call for research to "shine a light on this topic" (p. 460). The current research is designed to fill this gap in the literature and in the everyday management of teams.

Meetings are a critical component in team development (Feldman, 1984; Gersick, 1988; Gersick & Hackman, 1990). Particularly important is a group's first meeting as it can lead to the development of norms (Feldman, 1984), patterns of participation (Gersick, 1988), and team habits. Supporting this argument, Gersick (1988) found that teams created interaction patterns in their first group meeting that continued through the first half of teams' existence. Similarly, Gersick and Hackman (1990) suggest that teams can form habits from their initial meeting that often remain unless conscious actions or external events cause them to break these routines. Research has also demonstrated that these early patterns can impact team performance (Zijlstra et al., 2012). Thus, examining first meetings among team members in a face-to-face setting compared to a virtual environment is critical to understanding how virtual technology affects team development. Because patterns of participation established in first meetings will likely influence future team interactions, we need to understand whether the collaboration mode influences demographic effects on communication during the team formation process.

Surveys toward virtual work arrangements have been useful, but they do have limits. For example, surveys are able to assess the degree to which people are more or less satisfied with virtual work arrangements. Surveys are also very able to assess whether these virtual meetings have been more or less productive from the perspective of both managers and their employees. What surveys are not able to accomplish, however, is to assess whether specific behaviors occur more or less often in virtual settings than they do in face-to-face settings. For this type of understanding, more control and direct observation is required. Ideally, we would be able to compare the same tasks happening in a face-to-face environment and in a virtual meeting environment. We would then be able to directly assess the frequency of behavior in each of these settings and compare them. Moreover, we would be able to determine whether or not this change in meeting format had differential impacts based on the gender of the people in these meetings. It is in the spirit of meeting these objectives that the current research is conducted.

As a result, the current study has three specific objectives related to better understanding more granular team-relevant behaviors. First, the current study will examine the modality of interaction (i.e., face-to-face and videoconference based) to determine whether it impacts the frequencies of a series of relatively common meeting behaviors. Second, by focusing on specific examples of agentic and communal behaviors, we seek to determine whether the occurrence of prototypical male (i.e., agentic behaviors) and female (i.e., communal) behaviors actually occur at different rates by gender. Third, the current study seeks to test videoconferencing's potentially differential impacts on behavior in team settings. In other words, from a team perspective, we will be reporting whether any impact on behavior is more or less positive or negative for men or women. This answers the question whether videoconferencing represents a "leveling of the playing field" for women in teams as claimed by some, or whether videoconferencing just serves to make matters even worse (as argued by others). The proposed model appears in Figure 10.1.

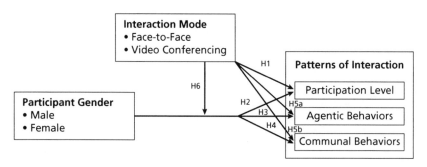

Figure 10.1 Current model.

LITERATURE REVIEW AND HYPOTHESES

Before we begin discussing our research questions and hypotheses, it is important to define a working definition of virtual meetings. Given the technologies available, virtual meetings can encompass synchronous and asynchronous interactions that can include video, chat, and voice communications or some combination of these modalities. We are primarily interested in synchronous video meetings since they most closely mirror traditional face-to-face meetings that occur in organizations. While permutations of communication modes may be important for organizations to consider in a work from home environment, videoconference meetings (i.e., via Zoom, Microsoft Teams, Google Meet, etc.) have become ubiquitous and consequently, need to be understood before moving on to more complex collaborative arrangements.

Virtual Collaboration

Differences exist in the dynamics that occur between face-to-face and virtual meetings. For example, in face-to-face communication there are few interruptions or long pauses (McGrath, 1990) and individuals can detect many individual differences, nonverbal cues, and paraverbal cues. It is the lack of these cues within a virtual environment that may lead to breakdowns in communication among team members (Rutter & Stephenson, 1977). In addition, when the ability to display emotions or attitudes through facial expressions or tone of voice is restricted, the ability to form interpersonal relationships is diminished (cf. LaPlante, 1971).

Some researchers suggest that the dynamics of virtual teams are so different from that of face-to-face teams that the research on face-to-face groups may not be relevant for studying virtual interactions (Thompson & Coovert, 2002; Warkentin et al., 1997). One reason for this claim is that much of the virtual team and collaboration literature has compared asynchronous computer mediated communication (CMC) with face-to-face meetings (see Gilson et al., 2015; Martins et al., 2004; Purvanova, 2014 for reviews). The results of this literature are equivocal. While some research finds that CMCs have more communication and information sharing problems compared to face-to-face teams (Alge et al., 2003; Daim et al., 2012), others find that asynchronous groups had more complete and detailed discussion of information (Benbunan-Fich et al., 2002). Further, some research finds that some virtual teams' communication was more task-focused than face-to-face teams (Hiltz et al., 1986) while other research finds no differences in task oriented/relationship oriented communication within virtual teams (Bordia et al., 1999).

Videoconferencing likely overcomes at least some of the limitations of asynchronous communication methods. Media richness theory (Daft & Lengel, 1986) and media synchronicity theory (Dennis et al., 2008) suggest that communication media that more closely matches the needs of a particular task in terms of richness (e.g., visual and audio cues) and timing (synchronous vs. asynchronous) are likely to lead to improved collaboration. In the case of group decision-making, face-to-face interactions are likely to lead to better outcomes as they allow individuals to share information, ask clarifying questions, provide feedback, and to identify member expertise in real time. This may be particularly important for a novel decision with information that is ambiguous. Rich communication media like videoconferencing, that more closely resembles face-to-face discussions, may be more appropriate in such cases. Consistent with this idea, Kirkman et al. (2013) found that global virtual teams that spent more time using rich communication modes performed better. However, there are limitations to videoconferencing's effectiveness. Denstadli et al. (2012) suggest that while videoconferencing may be effective for sharing information and task performance, it may be limited in its ability for team members to form relationships.

Companies have tried to improve the feel of virtual team interactions by adopting videoconferencing (Tannenbaum et al., 2012), but there is very little research that has examined how videoconferencing impacts communication among team members and whether it is a viable substitute for face-to-face communication. Mullen (2020) compared face-to-face cohorts and those utilizing videoconferencing in a master's program found no differences in learning among the two groups. Similarly, Jabotinsky and Sarel (2020) found that no differences in actual information flow between face-to-face teams and those using videoconferencing, but that the team members' perceptions were that the process was not as good. To date, we are unaware of research that has examined whether certain types of communication behaviors occur at a different rate in face-to-face interactions compared to those that occur via videoconferencing. However, given that Jabotinsky and Sarel (2020) reported that team members perceive that videoconferencing is inferior to face-to-face interaction, individuals may be less comfortable in that space and, consequently, the overall activity level will likely be lower. Stated formally:

Hypothesis 1: *Videoconferencing will be associated with fewer communication activities than face-to-face teams.*

Central to the effectiveness of collaborations, either face-to-face or virtual, is communication, but very little research has focused specifically on virtual communication (Layng, 2016). One potential benefit of virtual interactions discussed in the literature is that technology may be thought of as the "great equalizer." Many researchers suggest that CMC can result in more participation of team members who are in the minority (cf. Alvídrez et al., 2015; Curseu et al., 2008; Nunamaker et al., 1996; Swaab et al., 2016) either based upon their opinions (Curseu et al., 2008; Swaab et al., 2016) or the belonging to a demographic group that is in the minority (Alvídrez et al., 2015; Nunamaker et al., 1996). The theoretical explanation for this increased minority participation is that in a virtual environment, certain social cues may be limited and consequently, status differences among team members are reduced and these reduced status differences allow people to participate who others may be reluctant to do so. One of the most studied status differences among team members is gender. Before discussing gender differences in a virtual environment, it is important to understand gender differences in communication patterns in face-to-face interactions as they are a phenomenon with a rich research tradition.

Gender Differences in Collaborative Behavior

Two reasons why gender is considered particularly relevant is that it can determine a group member's status (Balkwell & Berger, 1996) as well affect communication styles (Leaper & Ayres, 2007; Leaper & Robnett, 2011). Because of these differences in status and communication styles, research has identified gender differences in small group participation (Bonito & Lambert, 2005). Expectation states theory (EST; Berger & Zelditch, 1977; Kalkhoff & Thye, 2006) suggests that group members often form tacit expectations of each other and the contributions they will make to the group. These expectations provide individuals with social influence in the group and may consequently affect patterns of participation.

Status characteristics theory (SCT) is a formal sub-theory of EST that describes how status characteristics drive expectations of performance (Berger et al., 1977). For a status characteristic to affect performance expectations, it needs to be both salient and it needs to be considered diagnostic of performance (Correll & Ridgeway, 2006). One reason why gender may play an important role is that it can be seen, and depending on the context, may be very salient to other members. Further, Fiske et al. (2002) suggest that gender stereotypes often contain an element of perceived competence. Thus, team members' gender may affect the patterns of participation in small groups. More specifically, women may participate less in group collaboration than their male counterparts. Research supports the idea that women tend to spend less time talking in organizations, particularly when power or status is primed (Brescoll, 2012). Further, research has also demonstrated that women participate less in mixed-sex groups than their male counterparts (see

Ridgeway & Smith-Lovin, 1999 for a review). Consistent with the research previously presented, the following hypothesis will be tested:

Hypothesis 2: *Men will exhibit more participation via an increased number of behaviors exhibited.*

In addition to the *level* of women's participation being lower than men, the *manner* they communicate may also be different. Lakoff (1973) suggested that the different roles held by men and women in society lead to differences in communication styles. According to Lakoff (1973), men tend to be more assertive while women tend to be more tentative and polite. Lakoff's (1973) observation is nearly 50 years old, there is a fair amount of more recent research that supports her hypotheses (see Leaper & Robnett, 2011 for a meta-analysis). Research also suggests that women tend to be more expressive and are better at interpreting nonverbal communications (Briton & Hall, 1995; Dennis et al., 1999; Hall & Gunnery, 2013). Further, women are also more likely to ask for others' points of view or express agreement (Eakins & Eakins, 1978) or acknowledge what another team member has said (McLaughlin et al., 1981). Women tend to communicate in ways that foster intimacy or maintain relationships (Eakins & Eakins, 1978).

The Agentic-Communal Model of Advantage and Disadvantage

In terms of specific types of communication, the agentic-communal model of advantage and disadvantage (Rucker et al., 2018) suggest that because of the hierarchical social advantage men possess, they are more likely to engage in *agentic* behaviors. Further, they suggest women, who typically occupy a disadvantaged position in the social hierarchy, are more likely to engage in *communal* behaviors and focus more on social-emotional communication. Leaper and Ayres (2007) conducted a meta-analysis of gender differences in adults use of language. They posited that men would engage in more assertive language, as it was likely to enhance their personal agency, and their results indicated that men did engage in more assertive communication compared to women. They also suggested that women would engage in more affiliative communication because it would increase others' engagement, which was also supported by their results. It is important to note that while these gender differences in patterns of communication may exist, they may be relatively unimportant. In seminal reviews of the literature on sex differences in task and social-emotional behavior, both Anderson and Blanchard (1982) and Eagly (1987) note that while there are statistically significant differences between men and women (that men tend to display more active task behaviors and women demonstrate more positive social-emotional behavior), the magnitude of these differences are quite small.

Rucker et al.'s (2018) agentic-communal model of advantage and disadvantage is designed to show how socioeconomic benefits accrue disproportionately to some people (the advantaged) relative to others (the disadvantaged). In this model, the social hierarchy categories that determine overall advantage and disadvantage are social class, race, and gender. Further, the agentic-communal model is presented as a straightforward explanation for the effects of hierarchy on individuals' thoughts, perception, and behavior. More specifically, the effects on thoughts, perceptions, and behavior are driven by inequalities in resources, opportunities, appraisals, and deference (referred to as the ROAD by the authors).

The two core propositions of the agentic-communal model of advantage and disadvantage are that (a) advantage guides people toward agency and subsequent agentic behavior and (b) disadvantage guides people toward communion and subsequent communal behavior (Rucker et al., 2018). The argument is that men typically have more advantage than women along the ROAD of inequality (in addition to potential biological or social role reasons), so men gravitate towards agency while women go toward communion. Support for this claim can be seen in men's higher likelihood to engage in unethical behavior that is self-beneficial (e.g., Dubois et al., 2015). Men also appear to engage in more utilitarian moral reasoning. A meta-analysis by Jaffee and Hyde (2000) revealed that females are more likely to demonstrate a care orientation, whereas males are more likely to demonstrate a justice orientation. Similarly, women are less likely than men to give utilitarian answers to moral dilemmas (Fumagalli et al., 2010). These are just a few examples of how a sense of advantage, regardless of its basis, tends to produce agency, whereas a sense of disadvantage tends to produce communion.

In negotiation or conflict settings, women are less likely than men to try to maximize their own interests and more likely to seek communal outcomes (Babcock & Laschever, 2003; Small et al., 2007). Increased stakes seem to further exacerbate the pattern for women to seek communion consistent with their position of relative disadvantage. Thus, when stakes are high and expectations for women's performance are held low because of gender stereotypes, women tend to underperform (e.g., Schmader, 2002).

Compared to the communication patterns shown by women, research has shown that men tend to use language to be more competitive and attempt to dominate interactions (Briton & Hall, 1995; Tannen, 1990), consistent with agency. Women, on the other hand, focus more on social-emotional communication, an element of communion (Anderson & Blanchard, 1982). Relative to their male counterparts, women also tend to pay more attention to their partners in an interaction (Ickes et al., 1986).

Consistent with the research supporting the agentic-communal model of advantage and disadvantage, the different types of behaviors exhibited by men and women will be formally assessed. More specifically:

Hypothesis 3: *Men will engage in more agentic behaviors than women.*

Hypothesis 4: *Women will engage in more communal behaviors than men.*

As stated earlier, videoconferencing may have a detrimental effect on the overall level of participation. Accordingly, it will also likely lead to lower levels of specific types of interactions. Consequently, we would expect lower levels of agentic and communal behaviors during videoconferencing compared to face-to-face interactions. Stated formally:

Hypothesis 5a: *Videoconferencing will be associated with fewer agentic behaviors than face-to-face teams.*

Hypothesis 5b: *Videoconferencing will be associated with fewer communal behaviors than face-to-face teams.*

Gender Differences in a Virtual Environment

As suggested earlier, one of the hypothesized benefits of working in a virtual environment is that the virtual setting might reduce status differences among team members and promote more equal participation (Dubrovsky et al., 1991; Siegel et al., 1986). However, it is not entirely clear how videoconferencing technology might affect the effects of status. Siegel et al. (1986) found that computer mediated groups displayed more equal participation among members, however, this research used asynchronous text-based communication. In this lean mode of communication, status differences may not be salient because members do not "see" each other, they only read messages displayed on a computer screen. In the case of gender, using text-based asynchronous communication, team members do not see gender, they focus on the message's content. The use of videoconferencing may be a double-edged sword. While it may improve understanding because of the nonverbal cues provided (e.g., tone, facial expressions, etc.), it may also make status features more salient. In addition to message content, the richer media associated with videoconferences allows team members to see status cues including gender.

The research examining gender effects on virtual communication features some of the same limitations of the research on differences between face-to-face and CMC discussed earlier. More specifically, much of this

304 • W. H. BOMMER and J. M. SCHMIDTKE

research examines gender differences in asynchronous, text-based communication. Further, the results associated with this research are equivocal. On the one hand, some research has demonstrated that gender differences in communication patterns do not change in a virtual environment (Bhappu et al., 1997; Fischer, 2011). Men tend to "talk" more (post longer messages), be more assertive and adversarial while women tend to post shorter messages and be more polite (Barrett & Lally, 1999; Herring, 1996; Savicki et al., 1996). Other research (Atai & Chahkandi, 2012; Miller & Durndell, 2004), however, finds no differences between men and women in the level of participation or the task orientation/social-emotional orientation of the messages (Geffen & Straub, 1997).

In addition to these mixed results, it is not clear whether gender differences in communication will be affected by the use of videoconferencing technology. As Dhawan et al. (2021) point out, videoconferencing may create some challenges for women. Gender stereotypes often portray men more favorably than women in terms of technology expertise, thus, technical problems with connectivity or image display may activate biases and lead to more negative evaluations of women. They further suggest that "implicit biases that have been shown to favor men over women during in-person meetings may translate to further gender gaps in leadership during virtual meetings" (p. 460). This literature suggests that women may be more disadvantaged working in a videoconferencing environment compared to face-to-face interactions. Consequently, we offer the following hypotheses:

Hypothesis 6: *An interaction effect between gender and the modality of interaction will be in the form of reducing women's behavior more than men's behavior for overall activity, agentic and communal behaviors.*

A summary of the hypotheses and proposed relationships are displayed in Figure 10.1.

METHODS

Procedures

Between September 2019 and February 2021, 1,320 completed a 150-min developmental assessment center as part of a major course requirement (i.e., the Iliad Assessment Center; Bommer & Bartels, 1996). The Iliad assessment center is a robust work simulation that allows for a wide range of behavioral observations. It has also been used in multiple previous research studies (cf. Hoover et al., 2010; Mitchell & Bommer, 2018; Rode et al., 2005; Rode et al., 2008; Walter et al., 2012).

During Fall of 2019 and Spring of 2020, the assessment was conducted entirely face-to-face, whereas in Fall of 2020 and Spring 2021, the assessment had been entirely transitioned to an online, synchronous environment utilizing Zoom as the videoconferencing platform. In neither situation were students provided monetary incentives. The results of the assessment were provided to the students in detailed feedback reports and these reports were used for a subsequent skill development assignment by each of the students. It should also be pointed out that extra credit was offered to the highest scoring students in each semester to further add to the personal stake and effort exerted by the participants.

The research design was approved through an institutional review board and deemed to be "minimal risk." Given that the research was conducted using data that provided benefit to the subjects (i.e., individual feedback was provided that was used for a developmental project), and that the participants were not required to do anything extra for the current study, ethical issues raised were minimal. All data was both confidential and anonymous as all subjects were assigned ID numbers. Further, participants were able to opt out of the task or decide that their data could not be used for research purposes.

Participants registered for an assessment center session time based upon their personal availability. Once they registered for a specific session, each participant was randomly assigned to a leaderless group. One week prior to their assessment, participants were given background material to read (e.g., company annual reports) so that they had adequate context for their activities. Once the assessment began, participants were assigned to peer-level roles of managers in a fictitious organization.

For the current study, the relevant portion of the assessment was two 25-minute leaderless team meetings. These meetings required team members to narrow a list of applicants for a senior-level position and then to reconvene and to discuss a series of customer service initiatives to aid lagging customer satisfaction scores. More specifically, they were provided with a batch of resumes in the background materials, and then were required to narrow down this initial list of candidates to three candidates who deserved further interviewing as the finalists for the position. In the second activity, the team was provided with a list of proposed improvement initiatives and were told to select the initiatives which offered the best return on investment given the company's current situation. The two sessions occurred with a 30-minute break in-between, where participants were engaged in other tasks (i.e., either responding to emails or giving a 3-minute presentation).

In both the face-to-face and the virtual settings, all of the meetings were recorded. In the face-to-face environment, a camera was placed on a tripod in the corner of a small breakout room, whereas the virtual meetings were recorded via the recording capabilities of Zoom and were saved via cloud storage.

After the assessments were completed, trained raters employed by the developers of the Iliad Assessment Center were used to complete a behavioral checklist for each individual in the meeting. The raters were blind to the identity of the students (they were in different states and had no personal connections) as well as blind to the hypothesis of the current study. All raters were trained via a frame of reference format and had been employed as raters for a minimum of 3 years. In addition, each of the raters had performed at least 500 hours of work on this task previous to this data collection, so all of the raters were extremely familiar with the procedures being utilized. The raters all had backgrounds in business or behavioral sciences, were paid for their work, and rated in pairs. Conflicts between raters are settled through reviewing the recordings and reaching agreement. Conflicts between raters were extremely uncommon with overall agreement averaging over 97%.

Participants

To be included in the study, a few conditions were necessary. First, the participants had to register and show up for the assessment. Because the focus of the current study was a specific activity (a senior-manager selection meeting), we used other checks to ensure comparable data. First, the participant had to attend the meeting, and then the participant needed to receive an affirmative rating for the specific rated behavior of "contributed to the meeting." In this way, we were able to remove people who failed to attend or who were not actively engaged (i.e., generally due to lack of preparation, lack of time management, a technical issue, or a combination of these three reasons). The final population for the study was 1,320. The numbers completing the activity in each modality were roughly equivalent (668 in face-to-face format and 652 in virtual format). In terms of gender, 55% (727) of the sample identified as male whereas 45% identified as female (593).

Measures

A series of items were on the behavioral checklist for the meeting. For purposes of the current research, nine items were classified as agentic behaviors and 12 items were classified as communal items. Both measures will be explained in more detail subsequently. Abele (2014) describes agentic content as referring to qualities relevant for goal attainment, such as assertiveness, competence or persistence, while communal content refers to qualities relevant for the establishment and maintenance of social relationships, such as being friendly, helpful, or fair. We also calculated a total activity score to provide an indication of participants' activity levels.

To select agentic and communal behaviors, we examined the definitions of each of these categories of behaviors that have been identified by previous researchers and are discussed earlier in this manuscript. Although research in this area does not designate a set of specific behaviors that are indicative of these constructs, Rucker et al. (2018) suggests that agentic communication is more "task-oriented" while communal communication is more "socioemotional" in nature. We sought to use behaviors that are either task-oriented or relationship-oriented, and common to most team meetings, and that are easily understandable regarding their face validity. These behaviors are included under their respective categories.

Agentic Behaviors

Nine specific behaviors from the assessment were identified as being agentic behaviors for the current study. These behaviors included, identifying the next appropriate step in the applicant selection process, defining the selection criteria for the personnel issue, identifying the strengths and/or weaknesses of a job candidate, providing relevant resume information for the decision process, determining the most important factors to decide the customer issue, providing both pros and cons of the specific recommendations, evaluating the consequences of the team's decision, discussing the impact on customers, and clarifying the group assignment for the customer service meeting. The Cronbach alpha reliability of these nine items was .71.

Communal Behaviors

In a similar fashion to the agentic behaviors, 12 communal behaviors were identified for the current study. These behaviors were more consistent with social facilitation and were indicative of teamwork behaviors. Six behaviors were associated with each of the activities. For the personnel selection task, arriving on time, soliciting input from other team members, checking for common understanding of issues, asking for clarification of an issue, documenting the team's decision, and monitoring the time remaining were employed. From the customer service team meeting, the list was very similar. More specifically, arriving on time, soliciting input, validating others, checking for common understanding, asking for clarification, and monitoring time remaining were used. This 12-item scale had an internal consistency as measured by Cronbach's alpha of .70.

Total Activity Level

Because the current study needed to consider whether overall participation or input varied as a function of gender, we calculated a total activity count. This measure included 32 measures that were all dichotomous to capture whether a person engaged in any action (positive or negative) or not. These behaviors included the agentic and communal behaviors previously listed, but added other behaviors relating to bringing up irrelevant information and communicating specific information that was included in the contexts for the meetings.

Analytical Procedures

Because the data was parallel in the face-to-face and virtual meeting settings, we took a series of interrelated steps to best answer the questions we set out to test in this study. More specifically, a series of ANOVAs were conducted to assess whether or not the activity level of men and women were different, and to then assess whether gender and format had significant relationships with the level of agentic and communal behaviors shown by team members. These ANOVAs also examined whether gender and format interacted to differentially impact women versus men.

RESULTS

Our first step towards answering the questions of interest was to assess whether there was a baseline difference between men and women in their overall activity level. To assess this question, we conducted an ANOVA with total activity level as the dependent measure. The means and standard deviations of the different behaviors (i.e., overall activity, agentic, communal) are displayed by format and gender in Tables 10.1 and 10.2, respectively.

Results indicated an overall significant effect for the model $F(3, 1320) = 44.49$, $p < .01$. There were significant main effects for both meeting format $F(1, 1320) = 123.21$, $p < .01$ and gender $F(1, 1320) = 8.73$, $p < .01$. As shown in Table 10.1, there was a lower overall activity level when people were in a virtual setting than in a face-to-face one. As a matter of

TABLE 10.1   Means and Standard Deviations of Behaviors by Formats

	Face-to-Face (N = 668)		Video Conferencing (N = 652)	
	M	**(SD)**	**M**	**(SD)**
Total Activity (Scale Range 0–32)	11.20	(4.21)	8.62	(4.20)
Agentic Behavior (Scale Range 0–18)	7.33	(2.30)	5.82	(2.64)
Communal Behavior (Scale Range 0–18)	7.38	(2.43)	6.05	(2.72)

TABLE 10.2   Means and Standard Deviations of Behaviors by Genders

	Men (N = 727)		Women (N = 593)	
	M	**(SD)**	**M**	**(SD)**
Total Activity (Scale Range 0–32)	10.24	(4.46)	9.54	(4.30)
Agentic Behavior (Scale Range 0–18)	6.71	(2.58)	6.42	(2.59)
Communal Behavior (Scale Range 0–18)	6.91	(2.78)	6.49	(2.51)

magnitude, of the 32 possible behaviors, the difference between face-to-face and virtual formats, the absolute difference was over two and half behaviors. As displayed in Table 10.2, this difference also varied by gender, although to a lesser degree. More specifically, men engaged in slightly more behaviors than women, representing a difference that was significantly significant and a little less than three-quarters of a behavior in absolute terms. There was no significant interaction between the format and gender. As a result, Hypothesis 1 (i.e., format's relationship with overall activity) and Hypothesis 2 (gender's relationship with overall activity) were supported, while Hypothesis 6 (the interaction between gender and format in terms of activity level) was not supported.

To address the specific issues of whether gender and format were associated with different levels of agentic and communal behaviors, we first conducted an ANOVA using the agentic behavior scale. Results indicated an overall significant effect for the model $F(3, 1320) = 44.49$, $p < .01$. Again, there were significant main effects for both meeting format $F(1, 1320) = 123.47$, $p < .01$ and gender $F(1, 1320) = 4.00$, $p < .05$. The interaction was not significant.

Tables 10.1 and 10.2 show the means for format and gender. In the face-to-face setting, the agentic behaviors were more prevalent than they were in the virtual setting. Men also showed more agentic behaviors, but the effect was much smaller than that of the meeting format effect. These results support Hypothesis 5a for videoconferencing and Hypothesis 3 for gender. The lack of significant interaction shows no support for Hypothesis 6.

To test whether there were differences associated with communal behavior, an ANOVA analysis was conducted that examined the effects of gender, format, and the interaction. Results indicated that the model was significant $F(3, 1320) = 31.99$, $p < .01$. Once again, there were significant main effects for both meeting format $F(1, 1320) = 86.39$, $p < .01$ and gender $F(1, 1320) = 8.18$, $p < .01$. The interaction between format and gender was not significant.

Much like the results associated with agentic behavior, the results in Table 10.1 show that communal behaviors were also lower in the virtual setting than in the face-to-face modality. Further, as displayed in Table 10.2

women engaged in fewer communal behaviors than men. These findings provided support for Hypothesis 5b in that videoconferencing was associated with fewer communal behaviors than face-to-face interaction. The results for gender, however, were opposite the hypothesized direction as men engaged in more communal behaviors than women, thus supporting the opposite of Hypothesis 4. We believe that this result stems from the overall higher activity level for men than women in the team meetings as was reported in Table 10.2. Additionally, the absolute effect was rather small, but the amount of statistical power was high due to the large sample size in this research. Further, Hypothesis 6 was not supported given the lack of a significant interaction between gender and format when it comes to their association with communal behaviors.

DISCUSSION

The results of the present study provide a potentially important set of research findings to a body of research that can be considered both extremely new (i.e., an examination of specific measures of agentic and communal behaviors in a videoconference setting) and extremely established (i.e., communication differences by gender). This combination has allowed for an examination based on very well-established theory, but on a topic that is relatively new and advancing in scope with what would have to be considered a breathtaking pace.

Like much research when the new and the established are brought together, our findings may offer more questions than they do answers, but we do not see that as a negative feature of the research. To the contrary, this combination seems to offer many new avenues for researchers and practitioners to make meaningful contributions to the everyday work lives of an exceptionally large number of people.

At the most fundamental level, our study indicated that the overall participation of individuals is decreased in a virtual videoconferencing setting versus a face-to-face one. While activity level is somewhat different than employee engagement, our finding does lend some credibility to the recent survey reporting that 43% of managers thought that the lack of face-to-face contact had a negative impact on employee engagement (Kamouri & Lister, 2020). This reduction in activity is also significant because previous virtual communication research has examined primarily asynchronous text-based communication and finds inconsistent results as far as the volume of communication activity; some research finds less communication among virtual compared to face-to-face teams (Bhappu et al., 1997; Hiltz et al., 1986) while other research finds no differences (Jarvenpaa et al., 1988) or even more communication (Jessup & Tansik, 1991). This decrease was significant, but the reasons for and consequences of such a decrease are still largely unknown. In general, lower behavioral activity is likely to be somewhat detrimental, but it should be remembered that our measure of activity included behaviors which could be deemed both positive and negative. Additionally, there is a difference in reporting that behavioral activity is lower versus satisfaction or performance are lower. At this point, the relationship between activity level and a number of outcomes of interest are still open questions, open questions with potentially important consequences.

For work teams, the findings regarding overall decreased activity levels should be taken as a caution sign, but one that can likely be addressed with well thought out interventions. More specifically, assuming that decreased activity is a sign of decreased engagement, then extra effort needs to be exerted to make sure that team members are actively engaged in videoconferences, and not playing undesirably passive roles. Such interventions could consist of using external facilitators to stimulate increased interactions or assigning specific roles to specific team members to stimulate increased activity among the team members. Such team roles have long been recognized in the teams literature (e.g., Stevens & Campion, 1999), but their importance in virtual settings may be even more important than in traditional face-to-face settings. It may be particularly important during teams' initial meetings as the patterns that occur can turn into habits and norms that remain with the group for long periods of time (Gersick, 1988; Gersick & Hackman, 1990).

Beyond the examination of simple activity levels, we were also able to examine the frequencies of agentic and communal behaviors in face-to-face versus videoconference settings. In terms of both agentic and communal behaviors, fewer of these behaviors were exhibited in the virtual than in the face-to-face setting. Again, the reduction in these types of behaviors would appear to have negative consequences associated with them, but it is somewhat difficult to make broad generalizations on these issues. At a minimum, it raises the issue of whether the "appropriate level" of agentic and communal behaviors are different given different modalities. In other words, it would seem that communal behaviors would be more important in virtual settings because they are not being provided via any other obvious means. In other words, if people's sole communication is virtual, it is less obvious that small talk and either relationship building or reinforcing activities would have alternative places to appear. Alternatively, it is also possible that people may value these behaviors less in a virtual setting, so the relative decrease of communal behaviors in the virtual setting is not particularly problematic. A similar argument can be constructed for agentic behaviors. While fewer were shown in the virtual setting, it may be that some of the face-to-face agentic behaviors are superfluous and do not aid performance or satisfaction. On the other hand, the decrease of agentic behaviors in a virtual setting may lead to significantly reduced outcomes for everyone involved (e.g., participant, work group, organization, etc.). These findings leave multiple potential interpretations.

For continuing work teams, the decrease in both agentic and communal behaviors may be a mixed bag. It may be somewhat difficult to determine exactly what "desirable" levels of agentic and communal behavior are for superior team functioning. Pierce and Aguinis (2013) suggest that antecedents that have a demonstrated positive linear relation to outcomes might, in fact, have a curvilinear relation when considered over a broader range such that there can be a "too-much-of-a-good-thing effect." Thus, if "too much" agentic behavior typically occurs in face-to-face settings, using virtual meeting technology may be an excellent tool to bring the agentic behavior to a more desirable level. A similar argument can be made for a team's communal behaviors. If communal levels within a team tend to be low, using more face-to-face meetings may be useful; levels of communal behavior that are too high may take time or focus away from important task-related discussions. A team member may be assigned a role to monitor how the team members are behaving during their interactions so adjustments can be made.

While the differences in modality cause relevant concern, the findings related to gender seem to suggest more of a difference than has been found in previous research. At a general level, however, these differences were still relatively small, and our tests offered much more statistical power than most previous research. This finding can be contrasted with that of Eagly (1987) and others (Anderson & Blanchard, 1982) that the differences in actual behavior between men and women are small and may be of very little practical significance. In this case, however, it is difficult to identify yet whether the differences are practically significant or not. They were clearly statistically significant for both agentic and communal behaviors. In fact, men engaged in more behaviors than women, counter to our hypothesis.

The importance of the finding that men and women performed both agentic and communal behaviors at different rates may be compounded by differences in the interpretations of these behaviors. There is a significant body of research indicating that men and women may be seen differently for engaging in the same behavior, and potentially even more harmful interpretations of behavior may exist when the degree of either type of behavior conflicts with the gender stereotype associated with the specific behavior (Heilman & Okimoto, 2007; Heilman & Wallen, 2010; Heilman et al., 2004; Moss-Racusin et al., 2010). For instance, women who act in highly agentic ways are more likely to face backlash than men who do so (Rudman & Glick, 2001; Rudman et al., 2012). Similarly, men who behave in extremely communal ways face a similar backlash effect (cf. Judge et al., 2012, Moss-Racusin et al., 2010). Given that our findings showed higher rates of communal behavior for men than women, these men may be subject to significant backlash for their behaviors.

Given these differences by gender, work teams need to use awareness as their first tool to attempt to level the playing field when it comes to team interactions. By conducting training before teams form, making both men and women aware of the gender differences, thereby giving team members a framework to better understand the role of future interventions such as team facilitators and assigning team members to predefined roles. In addition, team leaders and higher-level managers may need to play more active roles encouraging different team members to take on important roles that will help the teams interact using more equal communication patterns.

The last main area of focus in our manuscript was whether the impacts of a virtual modality apply equally to men and women. The findings associated with this issue suggested that the decrease in behaviors associated with videoconferencing were consistent for both genders. As a result, women did not suffer more of an adverse impact on videoconferencing than men did, but videoconferencing in no way played the role of "leveling the playing field" when it comes to team interactions either. Consequently, organizations should not look to videoconferencing and to virtual teams as some type of "silver bullet" to remedy workplace inequities. To the contrary, they should be aware that these new tools tend to carry the same perils and issues that their predecessors possessed.

Future Research

In the discussion of the results presented earlier, a number of potential avenues for team research were mentioned. More specifically, the link between team member behaviors and both individual and team outcomes is an obvious path for further exploration. Similarly, the potential situational requirements of "appropriate behaviors" for virtual versus face-to-face environments is one where precious little exists, but yet the implications may be exceedingly important.

An area that was not explicitly mentioned previously, however, is the use of other potentially relevant factors from status characteristics theory and the agentic-communal model of advantage and disadvantage (Rucker et al., 2018). More precisely, race or ethnicity may be seen as visible cues relating to status and may accrue a different pattern of potential benefits or consequences in a virtual setting versus face-to-face ones. Similarly, social status may be communicated via potentially different mechanisms via face-to-face and videoconferencing formats. This process may be particularly important for the use of videoconferencing where issues of lighting, camera angle, and camera quality might affect the perception or salience of these cues.

An obvious additional extension of our current work is to explore group-level factors as cues to individual behaviors. More specifically, in mixed gendered versus all one gender teams, are the cues for engaging in agentic and communal behaviors impacted in a way where the behavioral patterns change? Further, beyond homogeneous teams, does a majority or minority status of men or women impact behaviors exhibited in these relatively new virtual settings? A similar set of questions can be posed for race, age, and other potentially salient visible cues.

Finally, future research should examine whether these patterns that form during initial meetings continue over the tenure of the group. While several studies have examined the effects of initial meetings (Gersick, 1988; Gersick & Hackman, 1990; Zijlstra et al., 2012), these studies all involve face-to-face teams. It may be that in virtual teams, the patterns and norms are less stable as they lack some of the informal mechanisms to enforce them.

Limitations

This study, like all others, has limitations. Though we were able to record and observe very specific forms of behavior, the specific activity in which people were participating may have provided situational cues that we were not able to control. For instance, the task was relatively structured (narrowing down a list of candidates), so this situation could bring relatively agentic behaviors to the forefront, while simultaneously limiting the cues to engage in communal behaviors. By controlling the task and having the exact same task in both the face-to-face and virtual settings, we attempted to control for these types of differences, but it is difficult to know if the task somehow interacted with the modality in a way that we were unable to assess.

A further limitation of the current study is that we were only able to evaluate a relatively narrow range of agentic and communal behaviors and it is difficult to know how representative our findings are to the population of potential agentic and communal behaviors. We believe that the behaviors measured are relevant, but they are surely deficient in capturing anything close to the full content domain of agentic and communal behaviors.

Lastly, our population may not be fully generalizable to other situations. Most of the subjects in this study had work experience and are a little older than typical undergraduates, relatively few have what we would consider "solid professional experience." Since teleconferencing is seeing its most dramatic volume increases with white collar workers, it is not entirely clear whether the results of our study generalize to other populations. While there are some reasons to believe that our population is a reasonable one given the research questions of interest, external validity remains a legitimate issue. Further, the convenience samples presented here may reflect some type of bias. Future research should randomly assign participants to either the face-to-face or videoconferencing conditions. It is important to note that student samples have been utilized regularly in the study of teams (Mathieu et al., 2008, 2017). While field studies may create contexts that change team dynamics, Mathieu et al. (2007) suggest that studies involving student samples still can help us gain important insights into team dynamics. The use of a student sample here allows us a fair amount of control to isolate the effect of videoconferencing as teams completed a common task and faced common constraints (e.g., time, group size, etc.). Further, we examined behaviors that are typical of all teams (e.g., task clarification, arriving on time, soliciting input) regardless of context which helps the generalizability of our findings.

CONCLUSION

In a broad sense, this study set out to explore the impacts of moving from face-to-face team meetings to virtual ones. More specifically, we wanted to answer a few important questions regarding the impact of this shift in format upon the agentic and communal behaviors shown in meetings. Additionally, an important question was whether or not these impacts upon behavior (if they were present) applied equally to men and women. These questions both funnel into the overall issue raised in the title of this paper, whether virtual meetings serve to level the playing field, exacerbate differences, or do not have much of a differential effect either way.

In the introduction to this paper, we included Deborah Tannen's quote that, "Everything that we think is going to be an equalizer turns out not to be" (Gupta, 2020, para. 28). Our study leads incremental additional credence to Professor Tannen's concern. Overall, people engaged in fewer agentic and communal behaviors in virtual meetings compared to their face-to-face counterparts. Further, the women showed fewer agentic and communal behaviors than their male counterparts in both face-to-face and virtual settings. While videoconferencing did not further exacerbate these differences, it did not reduce them either. If these differences are to be reduced, videoconferences are unlikely to accomplish this task without specific interventions that are specifically intended to do so.

REFERENCES

Abele, A. E. (2014). Pursuit of communal values in an agentic manner: A way to happiness? *Frontiers in Psychology, 5.* http://doi.org/10.3389/fpsyg.2014.01320

Alge, B. J., Wiethoff, C., & Klein, H. J. (2003). When does the medium matter? Knowledge-building experiences and opportunities in decision-making teams. *Organizational Behavior and Human Decision Processes, 91*(1), 26–37. http://doi.org/10.1016/S0749-5978(02)00524-1

Alvídrez, S., Piñeiro-Naval, V., Marcos-Ramos, M., & Rojas-Solís, J. L. (2015). Intergroup contact in computer-mediated communication: The interplay of a stereotype-disconfirming behavior and a lasting group identity on reducing prejudiced perceptions. *Computers in Human Behavior, 52*, 533–540. http://doi.org/10.1016/j.chb.2014.09.006

Anderson, L. R., & Blanchard, P. N. (1982). Sex differences in task and social-emotional behavior. *Basic and Applied Social Psychology, 3*(2), 109–139. http://doi.org/10.1207/s15324834basp0302_3

Atai, M. R., & Chahkandi, F. (2012). Democracy in computer-mediated communication: Gender, communicative style, and amount of participation in professional listservs. *Computers in Human Behavior, 28*(3), 881–888. http://doi.org/10.1016/j.chb.2011.12.007

Babcock, L., & Laschever, S. (2003). *Women Don't Ask: Negotiation and the Gender Divide*. Princeton University. http://doi.org/10.1515/9781400825691

Balkwell, J. W., & Berger, J. (1996). Gender, status, and behavior in task situations. *Social Psychology Quarterly, 59*(3), 273–283. http://doi.org/10.2307/2787023

Barrett, E., & Lally, V. (1999). Gender differences in an on-line learning environment. *Journal of Computer Assisted Learning, 15*(1), 48–60. http://doi.org/10.1046/j.1365-2729.1999.151075.x

Benbunan-Fich, R. (2002). Improving education and training with IT. *Communications of the ACM, 45*(6), 94–99. http://doi.org/10.1145/508448.508454

Benbunan-Fich, R., Hiltz, S. R., & Turoff, M. (2003). A comparative content analysis of face-to-face vs. asynchronous group decision making. *Decision Support Systems, 34*(4), 457–469. https://doi.org/10.1016/s0167-9236(02)00072-6

Berger, J., Fisek, M. H., Norman, R. Z., & Zelditch Jr, M. (1977). Status characteristics and social interaction: An expectation-states approach. *Social Forces, 56*(2), 742–744 https://doi.org/10.1093/sf/56.2.742

Berger, J., & Zelditch Jr, M. (1977). Status characteristics and social interaction: The status-organizing process. In J. Berger, M. H. Fisek, R. Z. Norman, & M. Zelditch, Jr. (Eds.), *Status characteristics and social interaction: An expectation-states approach* (pp. 3–87). Elsevier.

Bhappu, A. D., Griffith, T. L., & Northcraft, G. B. (1997). Media effects and communication bias in diverse groups. *Organizational Behavior and Human Decision Processes, 70*(3), 199–205. http://doi.org/10.1006/obhd.1997.2704

Bommer, W. H., & Bartels, L. K. (1996). *The Iliad Assessment Center*. Tichen

Bonito, J. A., & Lambert, B. L. (2005). Information similarity as a moderator of the effect of gender on participation in small groups: A multilevel analysis. *Small Group Research, 36*(2), 139–165. http://doi.org/10.1177/1046496404266164

Bordia, P., DiFonzo, N., & Chang, A. (1999). Rumor as group problem solving: Development patterns in informal computer-mediated groups. *Small Group Research, 30*(1), 8–28. http://doi.org/10.1177/104649649903000102

Brescoll, V. L. (2012). Who takes the floor and why: Gender, power, and volubility in organizations. *Administrative Science Quarterly, 56*(4), 622–641. http://doi.org/10.1177/0001839212439994

Briton, N. J., & Hall, J. A. (1995). Beliefs about female and male nonverbal communication. *Sex Roles, 32*(1-2), 79–90. http://doi.org/10.1007/BF01544758

Brynjolfsson, E., Horton, J. J., Ozimek, A., Rock, D., Sharma, G., & TuYe, H. Y. (2020). *COVID-19 and remote work: An early look at US data* (No. w27344). National Bureau of Economic Research. http://doi.org/10.3386/w27344

Cohen, B. P., & Zhou, X. (1991). Status processes in enduring work groups. *American Sociological Review, 56*(2), 179–188. https://doi.org/10.2307/2095778

Correll, S. J., & Ridgeway, C. L. (2006). Expectation states theory. In J. Delamater (Ed.), *Handbook of social psychology* (pp. 29–51). Springer. http://doi.org/10.1007/0-387-36921-X_2

Curşeu, P. L., Schalk, R., & Wessel, I. (2008). How do virtual teams process information? A literature review and implications for management. *Journal of Managerial Psychology, 23*(6), 628–652. http://dx.doi.org/10.1108/02683940810894729

Daft, R. L., & Lengel, R. H. (1986). Organizational information requirements, media richness and structural design. *Management Science, 32*(5), 554–571. https://doi.org/10.1287/mnsc.32.5.554

Daim, T. U., Ha, A., Reutiman, S., Hughes, B., Pathak, U., Bynum, W., & Bhatla, A. (2012). Exploring the communication breakdown in global virtual teams. *International Journal of Project Management, 30*(2), 199–212. http://doi.org/10.1016/j.ijproman.2011.06.004

Dennis, A. R., Fuller, R. M., & Valacich, J. S. (2008). Media, tasks, and communication processes: A theory of media synchronicity. *MIS Quarterly, 32*(3), 575–600. http://doi.org/10.2307/25148857

Dennis, A. R., Kinney, S. T., & Hung, Y. T. C. (1999). Gender differences in the effects of media richness. *Small Group Research, 30*(4), 405–437. http://doi.org/10.1177/104649649903000402

Denstadli, J. M., Julsrud, T. E., & Hjorthol, R. J. (2012). Videoconferencing as a mode of communication: A comparative study of the use of videoconferencing and face-to-face meetings. *Journal of Business and Technical Communication, 26*(1), 65–91. http://doi.org/10.1177/1050651911421125

Dhawan, N., Carnes, M., Byars-Winston, A., & Duma, N. (2021). Videoconferencing Etiquette: Promoting Gender Equity During Virtual Meetings. *Journal of Women's Health, 30*(4), 460-465. https://doi.org/10.1089/jwh.2020.8881

Dubois, D., Rucker, D. D., & Galinsky, A. D. (2015). Social class, power, and selfishness: When and why upper and lower class individuals behave unethically. *Journal of Personality and Social Psychology, 108*(3), 436–449. http://doi.org/10.1037/pspi0000008

Dubrovsky, V. J., Kiesler, S., & Sethna, B. N. (1991). The equalization phenomenon: Status effects in computer-mediated and face-to-face decision-making groups. *Human-Computer Interaction, 6*(2), 119–146. http://doi.org/10.1207/s15327051hci0602_2

Eagly, A. H. (1987). Reporting sex differences. *American Psychologist, 42*(7), 756–757. https://doi.org/10.1037/0003-066X.42.7.755

Eagly, A. H. (1987). *Sex differences in social behavior: A social role interpretation.* Lawrence Erlbaum Associates. http://doi.org/10.4324/9780203781906

Eakins, B. W., & Eakins, R. G. (1978). *Sex differences in human communication.* Houghton Mifflin School.

Feldman, D. C. (1984). The development and enforcement of group norms. *Academy of Management Review, 9*(1), 47–53. https://doi.org/10.5465/amr.1984.4277934

Fischer, A. (2011). Gendered social interactions in face-to-face and computer-mediated communication. In A. Kappas & N. Krämer (Eds.), *Face-to-face communication over the Internet: Emotions in a web of culture, language, and technology.* Cambridge University Press (pp. 53–78). http://doi.org/10.1017/CBO9780511977589.005

Fiske, S. T., Cuddy, A. J. C., Glick, P., & Xu, J. (2002). A model of (often mixed) stereotype content: Competence and warmth respectively follow from perceived status and competition. *Journal of Personality and Social Psychology, 82*(6), 878–902. http://doi.org/10.1037/0022-3514.82.6.878

Fumagalli, M., Ferrucci, R., Mameli, F., Marceglia, S., Mrakic-Sposta, S., Zago, S., Lucchiari, C., Consonni, D., Nordio, F., Pravettoni, G., Cappa, S., & Priori, A. (2010). Gender-related differences in moral judgments. *Cognitive Processing, 11*, 219–226. http://doi.org/10.1007/s10339-009-0335-2

Gefen, D., & Straub, D. W. (1997). Gender differences in the perception and use of e-mail: An extension to the technology acceptance model. *MIS Quarterly, 21*(4), 389–400. http://doi.org/10.2307/249720

Gersick, C. J. G. (1988). Time and transition in work teams: Toward a new model of group development. *Academy of Management Journal, 31*(1), 9–41. https://doi.org/10.5465/256496

Gersick, C. J. G., & Hackman, J. R. (1990). Habitual routines in task-performing groups. *Organizational Behavior and Human Decision Processes, 47*(1), 65–97. https://doi.org/10.1016/0749-5978(90)90047-D

Gilson, L. L., Maynard, M. T., Jones Young, N. C., Vartiainen, M., & Hakonen, M. (2015). Virtual teams research: 10 years, 10 themes, and 10 opportunities. *Journal of Management, 41*(5), 1313–1337. http://doi.org/10.1177/0149206314559946

Gupta, A. H. (2020, April 4). It's not just you: In online meetings, many women can't get a word in. *The New York Times.* https://www.nytimes.com/2020/04/14/us/zoom-meetings-gender.html

Hall, J. A., & Gunnery, S. D. (2013). *21 Gender differences in nonverbal communication.* In J. A. Hall & M. L. Knapp (Eds.), *Nonverbal communication* (pp. 639–669). De Gruyter Mouton. https://doi.org/10.1515/9783110238150.639

Heilman, M. E., & Okimoto, T. G. (2007). Why are women penalized for success at male tasks? The implied communality deficit. *Journal of Applied Psychology, 92*(1), 81–92. http://doi.org/10.1037/0021-9010.92.1.81

Heilman, M. E., & Wallen, A. S. (2010). Wimpy and undeserving of respect: Penalties for men's gender-inconsistent success. *Journal of Experimental Social Psychology, 46*(4), 664–667. http://doi.org/10.1016/j.jesp.2010.01.008

Heilman, M. E., Wallen, A. S., Fuchs, D., & Tamkins, M. M. (2004). Penalties for success: Reactions to women who succeed at male gender-typed tasks. *Journal of Applied Psychology, 89*(3), 416–427. http://doi.org/10.1037/0021-9010.89.3.416

Herring, S. (1996). Linguistic and critical analysis of computer-mediated communication: Some ethical and scholarly considerations. *The Information Society, 12*(2), 153–168. http://doi.org/10.1080/911232343

Hiltz, S. R., Johnson, K., & Turoff, M. (1986). Experiments in group decision making: Communication process and outcome in face-to-face versus computerized conferences. *Human Communication Research, 13*(2), 225–252. http://doi.org/10.1111/j.1468-2958.1986.tb00104.x

Hoover, J. D., Giambatista, R. C., Sorenson, R. L., & Bommer, W. H. (2010). Assessing the effectiveness of whole person learning pedagogy in skill acquisition. *Academy of Management Learning & Education, 9*(2), 192–203. http://doi.org/10.5465/amle.9.2.zqr192

Ibarra, H., Gillard, J., & Chamorro-Premuzic, T. (2020, July 16). Why WFH isn't necessarily good for women. *Harvard Business Review.* https://hbr.org/2020/07/why-wfh-isnt-necessarily-good-for-women

Ickes, W., Robertson, E., Tooke, W., & Teng, G. (1986). Naturalistic social cognition: Methodology, assessment, and validation. *Journal of Personality and Social Psychology, 51*(1), 66–82. http://doi.org/10.1037/0022-3514.51.1.66

Jabotinsky, H. Y., & Sarel, R. (2020, April). Let it flow: Information exchange in video conferences versus face-to-face meetings. In *An Experimental Comparison of Video Conferences and Face-To-Face Meetings* (April 30, 2020). http://dx.doi.org/10.2139/ssrn.3589431

Jaffee, S., & Hyde, J. S. (2000). Gender differences in moral orientation: A meta-analysis. *Psychological Bulletin, 126*(5), 703–726. http://doi.org/10.1037/0033-2909.126.5.703

Jarvenpaa, S., & Leidner, D. (1999). Communication and trust in global virtual teams. *Organization Science, 10*, 791–815. https://doi.org/10.1287/orsc.10.6.791

Jarvenpaa, S. L., Rao, V. S., & Huber, G. P. (1988). Computer support for meetings of groups working on unstructured problems: A field experiment. *MIS Quarterly, 12*(4), 645–666. http://doi.org/10.2307/249137

Jessup, L. M., & Tansik, D. A. (1991). Decision making in an automated environment: The effects of anonymity and proximity with a group decision support system. *Decision Sciences, 22*(2), 266–279. http://doi.org/10.1111/j.1540-5915.1991.tb00346.x

Judge, T. A., Livingston, B. A., & Hurst, C. (2012). Do nice guys—and gals—really finish last? The joint effects of sex and agreeableness on income. *Journal of Personality and Social Psychology, 102*(2), 390–407. http://doi.org/10.1037/a0026021

Kalkhoff, W., & Thye, S. R. (2006). Expectation states theory and research: New observations from meta-analysis. *Sociological Methods & Research, 35*(2), 219–249. http://doi.org/10.1177/0049124106290311

Kamouri, A., & Lister, K. (2020). *Global work-from-home experience survey.* Iometrics & Global Workplace Analytics.

Kirkman, B. L., Cordery, J. L., Mathieu, J., Rosen, B., & Kukenberger, M. (2013). Global organizational communities of practice: The effects of nationality diversity, psychological safety, and media richness on community performance. *Human Relations, 66*(3), 333–362. http://doi.org/10.1177/0018726712464076

Kirkman, B. L., Rosen, B., Tesluk, P. E., & Gibson, C. B. (2004). The impact of team empowerment on virtual team performance: The moderating role of face-to-face interaction. *Academy of Management Journal, 47,* 175–192. https://doi.org/10.5465/20159571

Lakoff, R. (1973). Language and woman's place. *Language in Society, 2*(1), 45–79. http://doi.org/10.1017/S0047404500000051

LaPlante, D. (1971). *Communication, friendliness, trust, and the prisoner's dilemma game.* [Master's thesis, University of Windsor]. https://scholar.uwindsor.ca/etd/6636

Layng, J. M. (2016). The virtual communication aspect: A critical review of virtual studies over the last 15 years. *Journal of Literacy and Technology, 17*(3), 172–218. http://www.literacyandtechnology.org/uploads/1/3/6/8/136889/jlt_v16_3_layng.pdf

Leaper, C., & Ayres, M. M. (2007). A meta-analytic review of gender variations in adults' language use: Talkativeness, affiliative speech, and assertive speech. *Personality and Social Psychology Review, 11*(4), 328–363. http://doi.org/10.1177/1088868307302221

Leaper, C., & Robnett, R. D. (2011). Women are more likely than men to use tentative language, aren't they? A meta-analysis testing for gender differences and moderators. *Psychology of Women Quarterly, 35*(1), 129–142. http://doi.org/10.1177/0361684310392728

Levine, J. M., & Moreland, R. L. (1990). Progress in small group research. *Annual Review of Psychology, 41*(1), 585–634. https://doi.org/10.1146/annurev.ps.41.020190.003101

Marlow S. L., Lacerenza C. N., & Salas E. (2017) Communication in virtual teams: A conceptual framework and research agenda. *Human Resource Management Review, 27*(4), 575–589. http://doi.org/10.1016/j.hrmr.2016.12.005

Martins, L. L., Gilson, L. L., & Maynard, M. T. (2004). Virtual teams: What do we know and where do we go from here? *Journal of Management, 30*(6), 805–835. http://doi.org/10.1016/j.jm.2004.05.002

Mathieu, J., Maynard, M. T., Rapp, T., & Gilson, L. (2008). Team effectiveness 1997-2007: A review of recent advancements and a glimpse into the future. *Journal of Management, 34*(3), 410–476. https://doi.org/10.1177/0149206308316061

Mathieu, J. E., Wolfson, M. A., & Park, S. (2018). The evolution of work team research since Hawthorne. *American Psychologist, 73*(4), 308–321. https://doi.org/10.1037/amp0000255

Maznevski, M. L., & Chudoba, K. M. (2000). Bridging space over time: Global virtual team dynamics and effectiveness. *Organization Science, 11*(5), 473–492. https://doi.org/10.1287/orsc.11.5.473.15200

McLaughlin, M. L., Cody, M. J., Kane, M. L., & Robey, C. S. (1981). Sex differences in story receipt and story sequencing behaviors in dyadic conversations. *Human Communication Research, 7*(2), 99–116. http://doi.org/10.1111/j.1468-2958.1981.tb00563.x

McGrath, J. E. (1990). Time matters in groups. In J. Galegher, R. E. Kraut, & C. Egido (Eds.), *Intellectual teamwork: Social and technological foundations of cooperative work* (pp. 23–61). Lawrence Erlbaum. https://doi.org/10.4324/9781315807645-9

Miller, J., & Durndell, A. (2004). Gender, language and computer-mediated communication. In K. Morgan, C. A. Brebbia, J. Sanchez, & A. Voiskounsky (Eds.),

Human perspectives in the internet society: Culture, psychology and gender (pp. 235–244). WIT Press. https://doi.org/10.2495/CI040251

Mitchell, T. D., & Bommer, W. H. (2018). The interactive effects of motives and task coordination on leadership emergence. *Group Dynamics: Theory, Research, and Practice, 22*(4), 223–235. http://doi.org/10.1037/gdn0000092

Morrison-Smith, S., & Ruiz, J. (2020). Challenges and barriers in virtual teams: A literature review. *SN Applied Sciences, 2,* 1–33. http://doi.org/10.1007/s42452-020-2801-5

Moss-Racusin, C. A., Phelan, J. E., & Rudman, L. A. (2010). When men break the gender rules: Status incongruity and backlash against modest men. *Psychology of Men & Masculinity, 11*(2), 140–151. http://doi.org/10.1037/a0018093

Mullen, C. A. (2020). Does modality matter? A comparison of aspiring leaders' learning online and face-to-face. *Journal of Further and Higher Education, 44*(5), 670–688. http://doi.org/10.1080/0309877X.2019.1576859

Nunamaker Jr, J. F., Briggs, R. O., Mittleman, D. D., Vogel, D. R., & Pierre, B. A. (1996). Lessons from a dozen years of group support systems research: A discussion of lab and field findings. *Journal of Management Information Systems, 13*(3), 163–207. http://doi.org/10.1080/07421222.1996.11518138

Pierce, J. R., & Aguinis, H. (2013). The too-much-of-a-good-thing effect in management. *Journal of Management, 39*(2), 313–338. https://doi.org/10.1177/0149206311410060

Purvanova, R. K. (2014). Face-to-face versus virtual teams: What have we really learned? *The Psychologist-Manager Journal, 17*(1), 2–29. http://dx.doi.org/10.1037/mgr0000009

Ridgeway, C. L. (1982). Status in groups: The importance of motivation. *American Sociological Review, 47*(1), 76–88. https://doi.org/10.2307/2095043

Ridgeway, C. L., & Smith-Lovin, L. (1999). The gender system and interaction. *Annual Review of Sociology, 25*(1), 191–216. http://doi.org/10.1146/annurev.soc.25.1.191

Rode, J. C., Arthaud-Day, M. L., Mooney, C. H., Near, J. P., Baldwin, T. T., Bommer, W. H., & Rubin, R. S. (2005). Life satisfaction and student performance. *Academy of Management Learning & Education, 4*(4), 421–433. http://doi.org/10.5465/amle.2005.19086784

Rode, J. C., Mooney, C. H., Arthaud-Day, M. L., Near, J. P., Rubin, R. S., Baldwin, T. T., & Bommer, W. H. (2008). An examination of the structural, discriminant, nomological, and incremental predictive validity of the MSCEIT© V2. 0. *Intelligence, 36*(4), 350–366. https://doi.org/10.1002/job.429

Rucker, D. D., Galinsky, A. D., & Magee, J. C. (2018). The Agentic–Communal Model of Advantage and Disadvantage: How inequality produces similarities in the psychology of power, social class, gender, and race. *Advances in Experimental Social Psychology, 58,* 71–125. https://doi.org/10.1016/bs.aesp.2018.04.001

Rudman, L. A., & Glick, P. (2001). Prescriptive gender stereotypes and backlash toward agentic women. *Journal of Social Issues, 57*(4), 743–762. http://doi.org/10.1111/0022-4537.00239

Rudman, L. A., Moss-Racusin, C. A., Phelan, J. E., & Nauts, S. (2012). Status incongruity and backlash effects: Defending the gender hierarchy motivates prejudice against female leaders. *Journal of Experimental Social Psychology, 48*(1), 165–179. http://dx.doi.org/10.1016/j.jesp.2011.10.008

Rutter, D. R., & Stephenson, G. M. (1977). The role of visual communication in synchronising conversation. *European Journal of Social Psychology, 7*(1), 29–37. https://doi.org/10.1002/ejsp.2420070104

Savicki, V., Kelley, M., & Lingenfelter, D. (1996). Gender, group composition, and task type in small task groups using computer-mediated communication. *Computers in Human Behavior, 12*(4), 549–565. http://doi.org/10.1016/S0747 -5632(96)00024-6

Schmader, T. (2002). Gender identification moderates stereotype threat effects on women's math performance. *Journal of Experimental Social Psychology, 38*(2), 194–201. http://dx.doi.org/10.1006/jesp.2001.1500

Siegel, J., Dubrovsky, V., Kiesler, S., & McGuire, T. W. (1986). Group processes in computer-mediated communication. *Organizational Behavior and Human Decision Processes, 37*(2), 157–187. http://doi.org/10.1016/0749-5978(86)90050-6

Small, D. A., Gelfand, M., Babcock, L., & Gettman, H. (2007). Who goes to the bargaining table? The influence of gender and framing on the initiation of negotiation. *Journal of Personality and Social Psychology, 93*(4), 600–613. http://doi.org/10.1037/0022-3514.93.4.600

Stevens, M. J., & Campion, M. A. (1999). Staffing work teams: Development and validation of a selection test for teamwork settings. *Journal of Management, 25*(2), 207–228. https://doi.org/10.1016/S0149-2063(99)80010-5

Swaab, R. I., Phillips, K. W., & Schaerer, M. (2016). Secret conversation opportunities facilitate minority influence in virtual groups: The influence on majority power, information processing, and decision quality. *Organizational Behavior and Human Decision Processes, 133*, 17–32. http://doi.org/10.1016/j .obhdp.2015.07.003

Tannen, D. (1990). Gender differences in topical coherence: Creating involvement in best friends' talk. *Discourse Processes, 13*(1), 73–90. http://doi.org/ 10.1080/01638539009544747

Tannenbaum, S. I., Mathieu, J. E., Salas, E., & Cohen, D. (2012). Teams are changing: Are research and practice evolving fast enough? *Industrial and Organizational Psychology, 5*(1), 2–24. http://doi.org/10.1111/j.1754-9434.2011.01396.x

Thompson, L. F., & Coovert, M. D. (2002). Stepping up to the challenge: A critical examination of face-to-face and computer-mediated team decision making. *Group Dynamics: Theory, Research, and Practice, 6*(1), 52–64. http://doi.org/ 10.1037/1089-2699.6.1.52

Walter, F., Cole, M. S., van der Vegt, G. S., Rubin, R. S., & Bommer, W. H. (2012). Emotion recognition and emergent leadership: Unraveling mediating mechanisms and boundary conditions. *The Leadership Quarterly, 23*(5), 977–991. http://doi.org/10.1016/j.leaqua.2012.06.007

Warkentin, M. E., Sayeed, L., & Hightower, R. (1997). Virtual teams versus face-to-face teams: An exploratory study of a web-based conference system. *Decision Sciences, 28*(4), 975–996. http://doi.org/10.1111/j.1540-5915.1997.tb01338.x

Zijlstra, F. R., Waller, M. J., & Phillips, S. I. (2012). Setting the tone: Early interaction patterns in swift-starting teams as a predictor of effectiveness. *European Journal of Work and Organizational Psychology, 21*(5), 749–777. https://doi.org/10.108 0/1359432X.2012.690399

ABOUT THE CONTRIBUTORS

Enoch Kusi Asare, DBA, CPA, is an assistant professor of accounting at the Satish and Yasmin Gupta College of Business of the University of Dallas. He teaches managerial accounting, cost accounting, accounting information systems, financial statement analysis, and accounting for managers. His research is focused on behavioral accounting, organizational behavior, and small business finance. His research has been published in the *Journal of Business and Industrial Marketing* and *The International Trade Journal*. He is a co-author of *Enhancing Employee Engagement: An Evidence-Based Approach* (with J. Lee Whittington, Simone Meskelis, and Sri Beldona; Palgrave Macmillan, 2017) and "Job Engagement Levels Across the Generations at Work" (with Mark Brightenburg, J. Lee Whittington, & Simone Meskelis; IGI Global, 2020). Prior to teaching at the University of Dallas, Dr. Asare was at Texas A&M University—Texarkana, where he taught intermediate accounting, cost accounting, and advanced accounting systems. As a certified public accountant (CPA), he spent close to 10 years in the industry, where he was a specialist on a wide range of accounting issues. He currently runs an accounting and business consulting practice, where he helps small businesses prepare financial statements and advises them on a range of accounting, tax, and finance issues.

John R. Austin is the P.D. Merrill chair of business at the University of New England. He earned his PhD in organization studies from Boston College. He has worked at the intersection of scholarship and practice for over 20 years. As a researcher, he's published in leading journals including *Journal*

Managing Team Centricity in Modern Organizations, pages 323–330
Copyright © 2022 by Information Age Publishing
www.infoagepub.com

of Applied Psychology and *Organization Science.* As a consultant and executive educator, he has worked with leading companies all over the world. His research explores expertise, change leadership, and strategic foresight in organizations.

Miriam K. Baumgärtner, PhD, works as a senior researcher, project lead, and lecturer at the University of St. Gallen in Switzerland. Her research interests focus on new ways of working, leadership and mental health, diversity and inclusion, and (dis)ability. She earned her PhD in management from the University of St. Gallen and received her MSc in psychology with a focus on industrial and organizational psychology from the University of Mannheim. She worked several years for GESIS, Leibniz Institute for the Social Sciences, and gained practical experience as a consultant at Kenexa GmbH in Munich.

William (Bill) Bommer, PhD, is currently a professor of organizational behavior and leadership at California State University, Fresno. At CSU Fresno, he is also the director of the Craig International Program. He holds a PhD in organizational behavior from Indiana University and a master's degree in organizational development from Bowling Green State University. He has published over 60 research articles and three books. His research has been published in a number of leading academic journals including *Journal of Applied Psychology, Academy of Management Journal, Academy of Management Learning and Education, Journal of Organizational Behavior, Organization Science, Organizational Behavior and Human Decision Processes, Personnel Psychology, Journal of Vocational Behavior, Journal of Business Ethics, Leadership Quarterly,* and the *Journal of Management.* His current research focuses on leadership in the organizational setting with a primary focus on positive forms of leadership and leadership development. In addition to his publication record, Dr. Bommer has presented more than 75 research papers at national and international professional meetings.

Julio C. Canedo, PhD, is an associate professor at the Marilyn Davies College of Business of the University of Houston Downtown. He is certified in coaching, human resource management (HRM), and ethics. Member of academic and professional organizations like the Society for Industrial and Organizational Psychology, the Academy of Management, and the Houston Hispanic Chamber of Commerce. He has published his research in *Organizational Dynamics, Journal of Managerial Psychology, Research in Human Resource Management, AIS Transactions on Human-Computer Interaction, Journal of Business and Entrepreneurship, Oxford University Press,* and *TIP The Industrial-Organizational Psychologist.* He has presented in conferences of Academy of Management, Southern Academy of Management, Midwest Academy of Management, and Southwest Academy of Management. In addition, he has shown his work in corporate events in Latin America and provided training (pro bono) to the Houston-Galveston area members of Workforce Solutions. Julio serves as reviewer for *Human Resource Management Review, Human Resource Management, Research in Human Resource Management,* and *Journal of Managerial Psychology.* He is a member of the editorial board of *Human Resource Management Review* and *Journal of Managerial Psychology.* Finally, he serves as associate editor of *Organization Management Journal* and co-editor of *Research in Human Resource Management.*

Gabriel Dickey, DBA, CPA, is an assistant professor of accounting at the University of Northern Iowa where he is currently the Rod and Heidi Foster Accounting Fellow. He focuses his teaching and research in the areas of financial accounting and reporting, audit quality, teamwork, leadership, and agility. His research has been published in *Current Issues in Auditing, The Accounting Educators' Journal, Accountancy Business and the Public Interest,* and *The CPA Journal.* Prior to moving to the University of Northern Iowa, Gabe spent 5 years as an executive professor at the University of Northern Colorado where he also served as vice chair of the accounting program's advisory council. He was a three-time recipient of the Monfort College of Business Professor of the Year award and received the National Association of State Boards of Accountancy Student Center for the Public Trust Campus Being a Difference award. Gabe spent 17 years in the auditing profession of which 13 years were at Deloitte where he was a member of the firm's Leadership of the Profession initiative. He has significant experience with the financial reporting requirements and auditing standards for public and private companies and served as the team lead in managing a network of international teams, including training and development activities.

James H. Dulebohn, PhD, is professor of human resources and organizational behavior at Michigan State University. His research interests include leadership, virtual teams and team-centric organizations, organizational justice, eHRM, and employee compensation and benefits. His work has been published in journals including *Academy of Management Journal, Personnel Psychology, Journal of Management,* and *Journal of Applied Psychology* among others. He also has served as coeditor and author for the research volumes in the Information Age Publishing series Research in Human Resource Management including *The Only Constant in HRM Today Is Change* (2019), *The Brave New World of eHRM 2.0* (2018), *Leadership: Leaders, Followers, and Context* (2021), and *Human Resource Management Theory and Research on the New Employment Relationships* (2016). He earned his doctorate from the University of Illinois.

Sabrine El Baroudi, PhD, is an assistant professor at the Department of Management and Organization at Vrije Universiteit Amsterdam. She is also the director of the VU Center for Feedback Culture. Her research focuses on how contemporary work behaviors influence team processes and outcomes, and organizational functioning. Prior to joining academia, Sabrine worked as a consultant in the areas of HRM and marketing.

Sergey Gorbatov, PhD, writes, speaks, and teaches about the complex sciences of leadership, organizational behavior, and human resources. Outside of academia, Sergey is director, talent management at AbbVie, a Fortune 100 company. In this role, Sergey leads and supports an incredibly talented team of professionals who are responsible for the talent management portfolio across the world. Together, they establish and activate the strategies for ensuring the best talent for the business in the critically important roles. With over 15 years of experience, Sergey has delivered results in a wide spectrum of roles with deep expertise in talent management, leadership and organization effectiveness. Having performed in the HQ, regional and affiliate organizations, Sergey has first-hand knowledge of operating in multinational matrix environments at companies like AbbVie, PMI, and Shell. Sergey earned his MA in linguistics and intercultural communication at Orel State University in Russia, complemented with an MBA from IE Business School in Madrid, Spain. He obtained his PhD in management at Vrije Universiteit Amsterdam, the Netherlands. His recent book, *FairTalk: Three Steps to Powerful Feedback* (LID Publishing, 2019), enables any leader to drive results in their teams through fair, focused, and credible feedback.

James A. Grand, PhD, is an associate professor in the Department of Psychology at the University of Maryland. His research focuses on learning, decision-making, collaboration, and performance at the individual and team levels. A central theme of his work lies in exploring the emergent and dynamic processes underlying these phenomena using computational modeling and experimental techniques. His work has been recognized by both the Society for Industrial and Organizational Psychology (William A. Owens Scholarly Achievement Award) and the Academy of Management (*Organizational Research Methods* Best Paper Award). His research has been supported by grants from the Office of Naval Research, the Army Research Institute for the Behavioral and Social Sciences, the Defense Medical Research and Development Program, and the Agency for Healthcare Research and Quality. He currently serves on the editorial boards for the *Journal of Applied Psychology*, *Journal of Management*, and *Journal of Business and Psychology*. He received his BA in psychology from Auburn University, and his MA and PhD in organizational psychology from Michigan State University.

Martina Hartner-Tiefenthaler, PhD, works as a senior scientist at the TU Wien (Vienna University of Technology) in Austria. In her research, she focuses on new ways of working and is interested in the interplay of the individual, team, and organization. She has earned her PhD in social science from the University of Vienna, where she has also received her MSc in psychology with a specialization in work, organization and economic psychology. In addition to that, she has completed a BA in management, business and administration at New College Durham, UK. Complementing her experience in academia, she worked as a freelancer for various consulting firms such as Arthur D. Little.

Svetlana N. Khapova, PhD, is professor of careers and organization studies at Vrije Universiteit Amsterdam, The Netherlands. She is past division chair of the Careers Division of the Academy of Management. Her research focuses on contemporary issues related to individuals' careers and work. Her research has been published among others in *the Journal of Organizational Behavior, Journal of Vocational Behavior, International Journal of Management Reviews, Human Relations, Strategic Entrepreneurship Journal, Career Development International*. She is an author (together with M. B. Arthur & J. Richardson) of the book, *An Intelligent Career: Taking Ownership of Your Work and Your Life* (Oxford University Press, 2017).

Chenwei Liao, PhD, University of Illinois at Chicago, is an associate professor at Michigan State University's School of Human Resources and Labor Relations. His research is focused on understanding the phenomena happening in the context of leaders and followers within organizations (e.g., servant leadership, leader-member exchange, and idiosyncratic deals). Supported by awards from the National Science Foundation, the SHRM Foundation, and the Greenleaf Center for Servant Leadership, Chenwei's research has appeared in journals such as *Academy of Management Journal, Journal of Applied Psychology, Journal of Management, Leadership Quarterly, Journal of Organizational Behavior*, and *Human Resource Management Review*. He currently serves on the editorial review board of the *Journal of Management*.

Kimberly M. Lukaszewski received her PhD from the University at Albany, State University of New York. She is currently an associate professor of management at Wright State University. Her research is focused on electronic human resource management and diversity issues. Her work has been published in journals such as the *Human Resource Management Review*, the *Journal of Managerial Psychology, Journal of Business and Psychology*, the *Journal of Business Issues*, the *Journal of the Academy of Business Education, AIS Transaction in Human-Computer Interactions*, and *Communications of the Association for Information Systems*. She is on the editorial boards of *Journal of Managerial Psychology, Research in Human Resource Management, Journal of Human Resource Education*, and served as a guest editor of a special issue of *Journal Managerial Psychology* on social issues, for three special issues of *Transactions*

Human Computer Interactions on HRIS and e-HRM, and a research series in *Research in Human Resource Management.*

Akvilė Mockevičiūtė is a PhD candidate at the Department of Management and Organization, HRM group. Her research concerns feedback at the team and organizational levels. In particular, she aims to conceptualize and develop a tool to measure organizational feedback culture—A culture, where feedback flows freely, is continuously given, sought, and valued among employees. Clarifying this concept and developing a scale to measure it would enable future research into this subject and greatly serve an ultimate goal of fostering such culture across organizations. Akvilė does this by employing quantitative and qualitative methods as well as by conducting field studies with companies which aspire to strengthen their own feedback culture. Prior to starting her PhD, Akvilė has obtained her bachelor's degree in psychology at the University of Groningen and completed her research master's in educational sciences at Utrecht University, where she published an article on learning from instructional videos. Next to academia, Akvilė has been involved in projects aimed at fostering inclusivity in higher education and social innovation.

Brian Murray, PhD, is associate professor of management in the Satish and Yasmin Gupta College of Business at the University of Dallas. He was formerly the university's vice president and CFO and was board president for CARES, a multiple employer self-funded healthcare benefits association. His research includes studies of employee attitudes, retirement savings behavior, skill-based pay, leadership and performance management, and work implications for employees who are family caregivers for individuals with special needs. His work has been published in journals including the *Academy of Management Journal, Personnel Psychology, The Leadership Quarterly, Decision Sciences,* and *Human Resource Management Review* among others. He was co-editor for the *Research in Human Resource Management* volume, *Leadership: Leaders, Followers, and Context.* He earned his PhD from Cornell University.

Patrick J. Rosopa, PhD, is a professor in the Department of Psychology at Clemson University. His substantive research interests are in personality and cognitive ability, stereotypes and fairness in the workplace, and cross-cultural issues in organizational research. He also has quantitative research interests in applied statistical modeling including applications of machine learning in the behavioral sciences and the use of computer-intensive approaches to evaluate statistical procedures. Dr. Rosopa's work has been supported by more than $4.1 million in grant funding from Alcon, BMW, and the National Science Foundation. Dr. Rosopa's research has been published in various peer-reviewed journals including *Psychological Methods, Organizational Research Methods, Journal of Modern Applied Statistical Methods, Human Resource Manage-*

ment Review, Journal of Managerial Psychology, Journal of Vocational Behavior, Human Performance, and *Personality and Individual Differences.* In addition, he has co-authored a statistics textbook titled *Statistical Reasoning in the Behavioral Sciences,* published by Wiley in 2010 and 2018. Dr. Rosopa serves on the editorial board of *Group and Organization Management, Human Resource Management Review,* and *Organizational Research Methods.* He also serves as associate editor–methodology for *Journal of Managerial Psychology.*

James M. Schmidtke, PhD, University of Illinois at Urbana–Champaign, is a professor at California State University Fresno Craig School of Business and the chairperson for the Department of Management. His research focuses on sexual harassment, workplace discrimination, organizational deviance, diversity, and virtual teams. He has published in a variety of journals in human resources, management, and psychology.

Joshua A. Strauss is a graduate student in the Department of Psychology at the University of Maryland. His interests broadly concern the study of social systems and how people work together to become something greater than the sum of their parts. His main lines of research in this area focus on the interplay among team cognition, coordination, and performance. Other topics for which he is also interested are neurodiversity, creativity, and the future of work (contracting and the gig economy). He received his BA with honors in psychology, communication, and organizational sociology from the University of California–Davis.

Dianna L. Stone received her PhD from Purdue University and is now a research professor at the University of New Mexico, a visiting professor at the University at Albany, and an affiliate professor at Virginia Tech. Her research focuses on diversity and cross-cultural issues in organizations, reactions to selection techniques, privacy in organizations, and the use of electronic human resource management and artificial intelligence in human resource management. She has published over 100 articles, books, and book chapters, and results of her research have been published in the *Journal of Applied Psychology, Personnel Psychology, The Academy of Management Review, Journal of Management,* and *Human Resource Management Review.* She is the editor of *Research in Human Resource Management* (with James Dulebohn), and is a former editor of the *Journal of Managerial Psychology,* and the associate editor of *Human Resource Management Review.* She received the Scholarly Achievement Award and the Janet Chusmir Sage Service Award from the Gender and Diversity Division of the Academy of Management and received the Trailblazer Award from The PhD Project. She is also a fellow of the Society for Industrial and Organizational Psychology, the Association for Psychological Science, and the American Psychological Association.

J. Lee Whittington, PhD, is professor of management at the University of Dallas. He focuses his teaching, research, and consulting in the areas of leadership, organizational behavior, and spiritual leadership. His research has been published in *The Leadership Quarterly; Academy of Management Review; Journal of Management; Journal of Organizational Behavior; Research in the Sociology of Organizations; Journal of Management, Spirituality, and Religion; Journal of Business Strategy; Journal of Applied Social Psychology; Journal of Managerial Issues;* and the *Journal of Business Research*. He is the author of *Biblical Perspectives on Leadership and Organizations* (Palgrave Macmillan, 2015), *Enhancing Employee Engagement: An Evidence-Based Approach* (with Simone Meskelis, Enoch Asare, and Sri Beldona; Palgrave Macmillan, 2017), and *Leading the Sustainable Organization* (with Timothy J. Galpin & R. Greg Bell; Routledge, 2012). While serving as the dean, J. Lee led the effort for initial accreditation of the University of Dallas College of Business by the *Association to Advance Collegiate Schools of Business (AACSB International)*. He has received multiple awards including the *Haggerty Teaching Excellence Award, Gupta College of Business Award for Innovation,* and *Gupta College of Business Outstanding Faculty Member.* He received the King Fellow honor from the University of Dallas in 2021. The King Fellow is a professor whose life and work has made a significant contribution to the excellence of education at the University of Dallas and who exemplifies the best qualities of a teacher, colleague, and scholar at the university. He has extensive consulting, executive coaching, and leadership development experience with organizations including Life.Church, Nokia, Siemens, FedEx Kinko's, and several government and not-for-profit organizations.

Printed in the United States
by Baker & Taylor Publisher Services